Gott Strafe England is the definitive account detailing the German air attacks against Great Britain during the First World War. This method of attack was a totally new concept, taking the war away from the battlefield and into the previously safe territory of the enemy's homeland. As a result the concept of strategic bombing was born. This two-volume series will explore all the German air operations against the British Isles during 1914 to 1918, and assess the effectiveness of this new form of warfare. It will detail the routes taken by the raiders, where the bombs fell and the casualties inflicted. Alongside this are details of the responses taken by the defenders to counter the attacks. Full details about the airships, aircraft and their crews that were brought down are examined. This evidence includes contemporary accounts by those involved, in the form of intelligence summaries and personal accounts which graphically impart the full drama and horror of the events.

Gott Strafe England was conceived following the publication of the author's books on German Air Force losses over Great Britain during the Second World War, *Luftwaffe Crash Archive* (Red Kite 2013, volumes ongoing). This present work completes the overall picture by including details of those airships and aircraft that were lost on operations over Great Britain during the First World War, as there has been no previous complete reference giving details of the fate of the machines and their crews. The great amount of information available regarding the air-raids, the airships and aircraft and losses involved has been used to produce a clear overview, using many primary sources available in the National Archives, Kew and thus adding invaluable evidence to accounts written in retrospect, which rely on sometimes unreliable anecdotal evidence. 'Gott Strafe England', translated as 'God Punish England', is an expression that often appeared in the German Press and was soon picked up by the British Tommy serving over in France and Belgium, so that everything unpleasant from Jerry, to the food, mud and the Sergeant-Major was 'Gott Strafed'. The evidence given in these volumes makes it clear that this title is indeed appropriate.

Nigel J. Parker was born in Kent and initially lived in Surrey, close to the RAF Station at Biggin Hill. His interest in military aviation was nurtured at an early age – initially making model aircraft construction kits. On moving to Oxfordshire he became involved in the research and recovery of crashed aeroplanes across the country along with collecting and researching related artefacts – building up a large and unique collection. When he saw the film *Zeppelin* in 1971, his interest in airships was stimulated and he subsequently built up an extensive library on military aviation. At the age of 18 he was introduced to what was then the Public Records Office, now the National Archives, Kew – a place that has now almost become a second home. Through his interest in military aviation, he was fortunate to be the editor of the Bomber Command Association Newsletter for seven years. Having spent a career in engineering and finally running the Cryogenics Department at Oxford University for 23 years, he chose to concentrate on his writing and continue his groundbreaking research into the aviation history of the 20th century.

GOTT STRAFE ENGLAND

The German Air Assault Against Great Britain 1914–1918

Volume 1
1914–1916

Nigel J. Parker

Helion & Company

Helion & Company Limited
26 Willow Road
Solihull
West Midlands
B91 1UE
Tel. 0121 705 3393
Fax 0121 711 4075
Email: info@helion.co.uk
Website: www.helion.co.uk
Twitter: @helionbooks
Visit our blog http://blog.helion.co.uk/

Published by Helion & Company 2015
Designed and typeset by Bookcraft Ltd, Stroud, Gloucestershire
Cover designed by Paul Hewitt, Battlefield Design (www.battlefield-design.co.uk)
Printed by Lightning Source, Milton Keynes, Buckinghamshire

ISBN 978-1-909982-71-0

British Library Cataloguing-in-Publication Data.
A catalogue record for this book is available from the British Library.

For details of other military history titles published by Helion & Company Limited contact the above address, or visit our website: http://www.helion.co.uk.

We always welcome receiving book proposals from prospective authors.

Contents

List of Illustrations

Photographs

Maps

Dedication & Acknowledgements

This work is dedicated to my grandfathers, who served their country during the Great War of 1914 to 1918.

My interest in the First World War was inspired from an early age by a great-uncle, John Hall (I knew him as 'Old Uncle John'), who had served in the Army Service Corps in France – along with brief mentions of my two grandfathers (who having also served, but never lived long enough for me to meet them). I was fascinated by tales of airships that seemingly were held aloft by some invisible force – and I had a small boy's wish to be able to emulate them, and too be able to rise above the clouds. When the film *'Zeppelin'* was released in 1971 I was hooked, but my interest in German airships had to take second place while I concentrated on my research into German Air Force losses during the Second World War. While working on my first books *Luftwaffe Crash Archive* (a series which started being published in April 2013) I felt that I needed to complete the story of the German Air Force losses over Great Britain – and as I could find no single publication that gave details of all the German airships and aircraft lost on operations over Britain during the Great War, I started searching through the documents held by the National Archives, Kew. The result was such a vast haul of primary information – not only about the losses, but also the precise details about the routes the raiders took and where the bombs were dropped – I felt that I should make use of this material and make it available to a wider audience (and, especially, those like me who have been frustrated by the lack of information available through published works).

I would like to acknowledge the help and encouragement that has been given to me over the years in completing this work – notably by Simon Parry, who is responsible for nurturing my interest in military aviation and guiding me through the complexities of using the National Archives, Kew in search of those long-forgotten, elusive documents. To Guy Smith, who from an early age has been a guiding light in my interest in Zeppelins and airships. To my wife, Linda, who has had to accept my hermit-like ways and regular absence during visits to Kew – but at the same time, offers invaluable guidance and encouragement with all my research and writing (and without whom none of this would have been possible). Also, to my dog, Jack, who has been my constant companion throughout the compilation of this work.

I would also like to acknowledge the invaluable assistance given to me over the years and the work carried out by the staff of the National Archives, Kew – who are responsible and care for so many valuable documents (along with making them freely available to be consulted by members of the public). Over the years, the building has almost become a second home and refuge where one can readily lose oneself in Britain's past.

Finally, I would like to thank Duncan Rogers of Helion for having faith in my abilities in accepting my proposal for publication – and allowing me to make all this material available to a wider audience – along with his staff, including Patrick Butcher and Christian Ewen, who have worked tirelessly to bring this to print.

It should not be forgotten that the airmen on both sides of the conflict who took part in operations were incredibly brave. Aviation was still in its infancy; they all knew that the probability of death – usually by burning – was inevitable, and yet they still took to the air to challenge one another for supremacy. Therefore, those mentioned by name should be regarded as human beings – somebody's son – rather than as a friend or foe.

If you have any further details regarding events that relate to this publication, copies of photos that you wish to share, or details that you feel I may have overlooked, the author would be most pleased to hear from you.

Nigel Parker

Glossary

AA	Anti-Aircraft Artillery – usually referring to the 3 inch, 20 cwt gun or the 13 pounder, 9 cwt gun.
Beobachter	German word for 'aircraft observer'.
CC	*Deutscher Soldatenfriedhof*, Cannock Chase, Staffordshire – the last resting place of 2,143 German and Austrian servicemen who died in the Great War (and whose remains were subsequently moved to this site from cemeteries across the UK in the 1960s).
CC Mil	Commonwealth War Graves Commission Military Burial Ground, Cannock Chase, Staffordshire – the last resting place of 286 German and Austrian servicemen who died in the Great War.
Cwt	Hundredweight – the weight of a gun carriage or mounting.
Flt	Flight.
Flugzeugführer	German word for 'pilot'.
ft	Feet – giving height above sea-level that aircraft is flying.
Gotha	A biplane with twin 260 hp engines; pusher propeller configuration manufactured by Gothaer Waggonfabrik AG – carrying a crew of three.
HD	Home Defence – as in No.39 HD Squadron RFC.
HE	High-Explosive – referring to types of bombs usually designated by weight in kilograms; a streamlined thin steel walled casing – usually fitted with an impact fuse designed to give maximum blast effect (usually from 12.5 kg to 300 kg).
HMS	His Majesty's Ship.
hrs	Hours – in reference to use of the 24-hour clock.
IB	Incendiary Bomb – a steel çontainer usually weighing about 10 kg and filled with an incendiary mixture of tar and benzene, which was then wrapped in tarred rope... sometimes also containing thermite (powdered aluminium and iron oxide) to aid initial combustion.
Kaiserliche Marine	Imperial German Navy.
kg	Kilograms – metric weight. German bomb sizes were designated by their weight in kilograms (2.2 kilograms to the pound).
lb	Pounds – imperial weight. British bomb sizes were designated by their weight in pounds.

Lewis gun	A type of air-cooled machine-gun of .303 calibre often fitted on a moveable mounting on British aeroplanes – fed by a 47 or 97 round pan, top-mounted magazine. Invented by American Isaac Newton Lewis (1858-1931) and licensed to be manufactured by the Birmingham Small Arms Company (BSA).
Lieut	Lieutenant.
Maxim	A type of machine-gun – named after its inventor Hiram Maxim (1840-1916), engineer and inventor of mechanical devices including aeroplanes and engines.
MG	Machine-gun.
mph	Miles per hour.
NKG	No Known Grave.
PoW	Prisoner of War.
Pom-Pom	A type of rapid-firing gun, which fired small explosive shells one or two pounds in weight.
Pdr	Pounder – designation of an artillery piece by weight of shell as opposed to calibre, which is given in inches or millimetres.
QF	Quick-Firing – referring to a type of artillery piece.
RFC	Royal Flying Corps.
RGA	Royal Garrison Artillery.
RMLI	Royal Marines Light Infantry.
RNAS	Royal Naval Air Service.
RNVR	Royal Naval Volunteer Reserve.
Schütte-Lanz	A rigid airship design, with framework mostly made from wood. The company was formed by the partnership between Professor Johann Schütte and Dr Karl Lanz to form the Schütte-Lanz Luftschiffbau. Airships built by this company were numbered 'SL 1' to 'SL 22'.
SMS	*Seiner Majestät Schiff* – the German equivalent of the British 'His Majesty's Ship'.
SS	Steam Ship.
Staaken	Designated by the prefix 'R' and often referred to as 'Giant', this was the largest aeroplane employed during the First World War. Usually powered by four 245 hp engines and carried up to a crew of eight. Manufactured by Flugzeugwerft GmbH, Staaken, Berlin.
UX	Unexploded (as in bomb).
VAD	Voluntary Aid Detachment – supplied nursing services to the Allies.
Very Light/Veries	A flare often fired from a large calibre type of pistol; supplied with a variety of different colours. Named after its inventor Edward Wilson Very (1847-1910).

Vickers	A type of webbing belt-fed machine-gun of .303 calibre – a derivative of the Maxim and fitted to British aircraft on a fixed forward-firing mounting that could fire through the aeroplane's propeller arc when fitted with an interrupter mechanism.
Zeppelin	A rigid airship design with the rigid framework made from aluminium extrusions, which were riveted together to form the outer framework. Named after the founder of the company (Ferdinand Graf von Zeppelin) and based at Friedrichshafen, Southern Germany next to the Bodensee (Lake Constance). Zeppelin airships are identified initially by their military designation ('Z' – followed by number), but also by their production number ('LZ' – followed by number).
·303	Calibre in inches of the standard British rimmed case, rifle and machine-gun round using a cordite propellant. The Germans used the Mauser 7.92 mm calibre round.
·45	Calibre in inches of the Martini-Henry ·577 / ·450 single shot rifle that was issued to aircrew during the early stages of the war due to the large calibre round that could be filled with an incendiary mixture as an attempt to combat airships and balloons. The Martini-Henry rifle was first issued to the British Army in 1871.
"	Inches – referring to the calibre of a gun.
+	Dead.

Ranks within the German Air Force / Navy Airship Service (*Marineluftschiffabteilung*)

German	English
Admiral	Admiral
Bootsmannsmaat	Bosun's Mate
Beobachter	Observer
Deckoffizier	Warrant Officer
Fähnrich zur See	Aspirant Officer
Fahringenieur	'Pilot' Engineer
Feldwebel	Sergeant-Major
Feldwebel-Leutnant	Sergeant-Major-Lieutenant
Flieger	Aviator; Airman
Flugzeugführer	Pilot
Fregattenkapitän	Commander
Funkentelegraphistenmaat	Wireless Telegraphy Mate
Funkentelegraphistenobergast	Senior Wireless Telegraphist
Funkentelegraphistenobermaat	Wireless Telegraphy Senior Mate
Gefreiter	Lance-Corporal
Hauptgefreiter	Senior Corporal; Seaman 1st Class (nav.);
Hauptmann	Captain
Kapitänleutnant	Senior Lieutenant
Kapitänleutnant der Reserve	Lieutenant (Reserve)
Kommandeur	Commander
Korvettenkapitän	Lieutenant Commander
Kriegsmarine	Navy
Leutnant	Lieutenant
Leutnant zur See	Ensign
Luftschiffer	Aeronaut, crew of an airship

Major	Major
Maschinist	Machinist
Maschinistenmaat	Machinist's Mate
Matrose	Sailor
Oberbootmannsmaat	Master Bosun's Mate
Oberdeckoffizier	Senior Warrant Officer
Oberfeldwebel	Master Sergeant
Obergefreiter	Corporal
Oberleutnant	Senior Lieutenant
Oberleutnant zur See	Lieutenant (Junior Grade)
Oberst	Colonel
Obersteuermann	Helmsman
Obersteuermannmaat	Helmsman's Mate
Oberstleutnant	Lieutenant Colonel
Oberleutnant der Reserve	Senior Lieutenant (Reserve)
Oberleutnant	Senior Lieutenant
Obermaschinist	Master Machinist
Obermaschinistenmaat	Master Machinist's Mate
Obermaschinistanwärter	Master Machinist Candidate
Obermatrose	Apprentice Sailor
Obersegelmacher	Master Sailmaker
Obersegelmachersgast	Senior Sailmaker
Obersignalmaat	Master Signaller's Mate
Segelmachermaat	Sailmaker's Mate
Sergeant	Sergeant
Signalmaat	Signalman's Mate
Stabsfeldwebel	Master Sergeant; Regimental Sergeant Major
Steuermann	Helmsman
Steuermannmaat	Helmsman's Mate
Unterfeldwebel	Staff Sergeant
Unteroffizier	Non-commissioned Officer
Untermaschinist	Engineer (i.e. Flight Engineer)
Untersteuermann	Helmsman
Vizefeldwebel	Vice-Sergeant-Major

Other German words that are encountered in the text:

Eiserne Kreuz	Iron Cross
Friedrichshafen FF 29	
Feldflieger Abteilung 41	Reconnaissance Flight 41
Friedrichshafen FF 33b	
Hansa-Brandenburg	
See Flieger Abteilung 1	Naval Aviation Flight 1

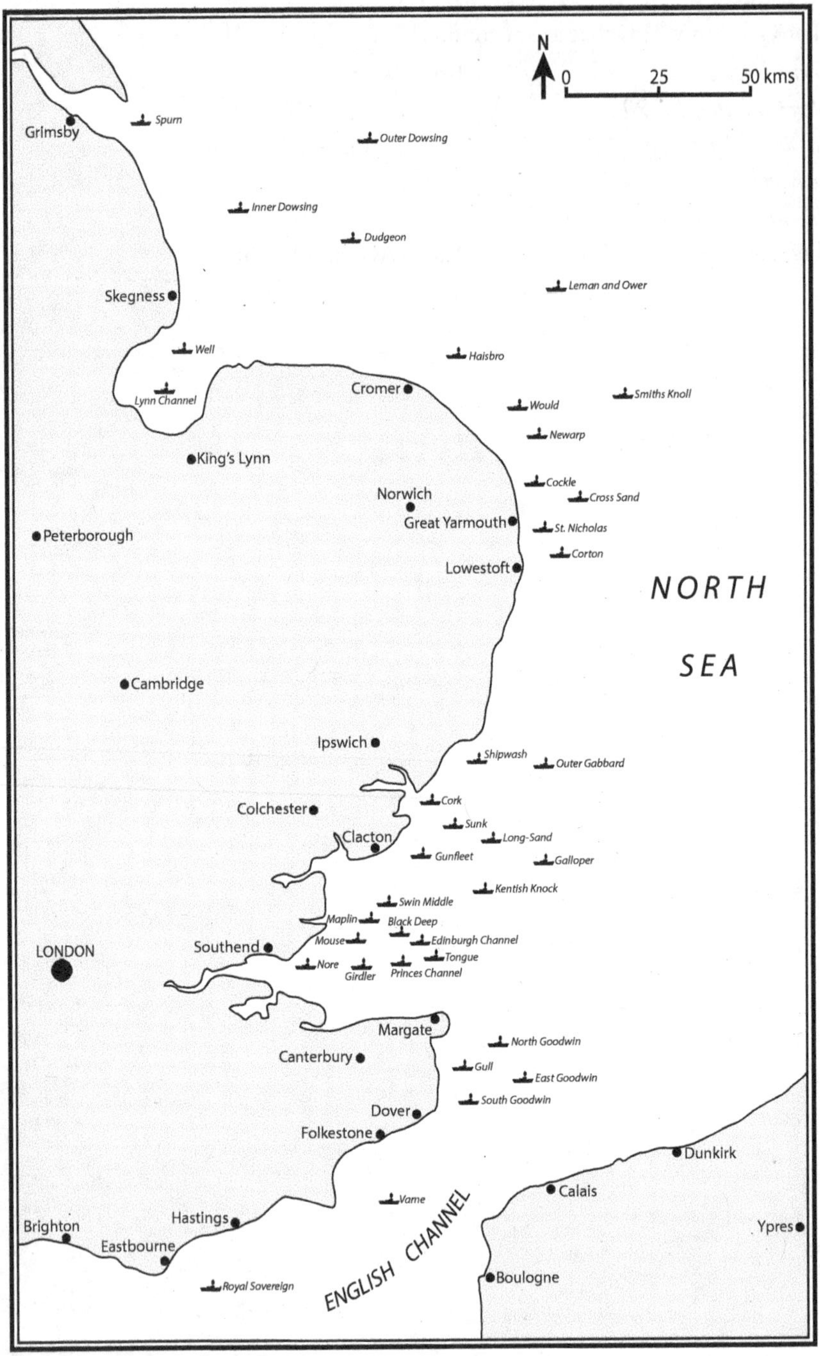

Map 1 – Location of lightships.

Introduction

The benefit of being able to see further than your enemy has always dominated the military mind – giving those who hold the highest ground the tactical advantage in any conflict. An average soldier standing on flat ground can determine the horizon at about three miles. If he were to position himself on a tower or hill of 100 feet high, his horizon will be 12 miles away – while if he were to be able to rise to 1,000 feet, the horizon then becomes 39 miles. So the challenge was to be able to rise higher and to be able to observe the activities of your enemy further behind the front line – and be forewarned of any developments of an attack – removing the element of surprise. At this point, the limitations of the human eye come into the equation – even if enhanced by suitable optical devices such as binoculars or telescope. The possibilities then became apparent of being able to cross over the enemy's lines, observe and drop bombs on his troop concentrations, supply dumps and even his homeland – which were well out of normal range and immune from the effects of your artillery – while at the same time, being out of range from his attempts to halt your own progress. The extension of this theory was from one of tactical bombing to strategic bombing, where with the right machine, one could venture with impunity over the enemy's towns and cities so as to attack his means of waging war by destroying his factories and industries that were keeping the troops at the front supplied with weapons and food (which during previous conflicts, had been immune from attack or interference).

It was in 1783 that the first hydrogen-filled balloon that was capable of lifting a man skywards was trialled by its inventor, Jacques Charles – although there was no means of forward propulsion or directional determination by the pilot, who was totally at the mercy of the prevailing winds. The first practical airship that was fitted with a means of forward propulsion – and with the ability to steer – was developed by Frenchman Henri Giffard in 1852. Already by this time, on 7 January 1785 Frenchman Pierre Blanchard and American John Jeffries had been the first people to cross the English Channel by balloon – taking off from near to Dover Castle and landing at Guines, France – their route having been determined by the prevailing wind blowing from west to east. From this point on, Great Britain could no longer assume that the threat of invasion from a continental army would solely be a seaborne invasion – and that there was a new threat from the skies. It would be another 124 years before Louis Bleriot confirmed Britain's worst fears when, on 25 July 1909, he flew his Bleriot XI monoplane from Sandgatte, near Calais, to Dover Castle.

The idea that one or more nations could utilise air power to enable the dropping of high-explosive weapons on an enemy from a balloon or airship had been a subject for considerable debate as early as 1898 when a conference was proposed by Russia between major nations to try and establish a set of rules for the conduct of future

Ferdinand Adolf Heinrich August Graf von Zeppelin (1838-1917), founder of the Zeppelin Airship Company.

wars. This was known as The Hague Convention of 1899 and included, in part 2 (regarding the respect to the laws and customs of war on land), the statement that forbade the attack or bombardment of undefended towns or habitations. A declaration, numbered 4.1, prohibited the discharge of projectiles and explosives from balloons or by new analogous methods for the following five years between the signatory nations.

Following on from the 1899 Treaty, The Hague Convention of 1907 was convened as an attempt by the major nations to expand on the points established previously. In the intervening years, airships had become an established and reliable form of transport, while Orville and Wilbur Wright had designed and built the world's first successful controlled-powered aeroplane – with Orville being the first pilot. The 1907 Convention – although it extended the previous declaration prohibiting the discharge of projectiles from the air by whatever means – was only ratified by Great Britain and the United States of America.

Count Ferdinand von Zeppelin (living in Friedrichshafen, Southern Germany) had been inspired by the idea of long-distance travel without the constraints imposed at the time by un-navigable waterways, mountains or deserts – and had started developing his own airships. On 2 July 1900 his airship the *Zeppelin LZ 1* took off from the Bodensee (Lake Constance) on its first inaugural flight. Although this venture was not an instant success, Count Zeppelin persevered with his dream – and the commercial use of the Zeppelin airship came true between 1900 and the outbreak of the First World War on 28 July 1914. During this period, the German military started to take a keen interest in the Zeppelin design, but it was the German Army who saw the initial potential of airships for use in bombing operations, while the German Navy saw them more as a means of scouting in front of the ships of the High Seas Fleet.

Another player in the development of the German airship was the Luftschiffbau Schütte-Lanz Company (based at Rheinau, near Mannheim) – the result of a partnership between Professor Johann Schütte and Dr Karl Lanz on 22 April 1909. The main difference between the airships built by the Zeppelin and the Schütte-Lanz companies was that the former used a framework of duralumin to give the airship its shape, while that of the Schütte-Lanz Company used a glued wooden framework (but this wooden structure was found to degrade through the ingress of moisture – and thus, Schütte-Lanz airships were not favoured for use by the German Navy).

The other player in German airship industry were those designed by August von Parseval and manufactured by the Luft-Fahzeug-Gesellschaft (LFG), but were of a semi (with a keel for stiffening) or non-rigid design (no internal rigid structure – relying solely on the form of the external envelope for its shape) and consisting of a fabric envelope which was filled with hydrogen – to which a gondola or basket was attached. Twenty-two airships of this type were manufactured between 1909 and 1919 – and were identified by the numbered prefix 'PL'. They were mostly used for naval observation duties – and none that were in use by the German military ventured over Great Britain during the war. Through his early work with Rudolf Hans Bartsch von Sigsfeld, Parseval developed the better-known *Drachenballoon* used by the German Army for fixed observation on its battle fronts.

The initial British involvement in airships was the construction of *The Mayfly* (or *Naval Rigid Airship Number 1*) by Vickers at Barrow-in-Furness as a means of competing with the airships then being produced in Germany, but on her maiden flight on 24 September 1911 she was caught by a gust of wind and broke her back. It was not until the outbreak of war – and the new threat from the German U-Boats – that the Admiralty started taking a renewed interest in airships (as a means of countering the threat to the fleet from submarines) as airborne-spotting platforms.

Even before the outbreak of war, it was realised that Germany was going to be making use of her airships to help offset the advantage the British Grand Fleet had over the German High Seas Fleet by using them in the long-range reconnaissance roll – and for forward artillery-spotting during naval engagements. With their long range and lifting capacity, it was very obvious that the German airships could readily reach the British mainland from Germany and drop their bombs with impunity on the undefended and helpless population. This vision of hordes of ghost-like airships hovering over the British Isles – and their crews being able to pick off individuals with their bombs at will – soon spread alarm through the population and government. At the outbreak of war, the Royal Flying Corps (under Brigadier-General Sir David Henderson) was still in its infancy and had few spare aeroplanes to contribute towards the defence of the British Isles – its five squadrons having been sent to France to support the British Expeditionary Force. Even if they had any spare aeroplanes, the poor rate of climb and speed – along with armament consisting mainly of ·45

Martini-Henry rifles firing an unreliable form of flaming bullet – precluded little hope of bringing down one of the raiders. So as to counter the airship menace, procedures were set up for the design and production of guns that were capable of a high elevation and relatively rapid fire that included the 1 pounder pom-pom. Effective means of illuminating the airships – if they were to come over at night – were also in their infancy, with few searchlights available (some which were sighted away from the electricity grid had to rely on a calcium carbide / acetylene flame for their source of illumination).

For some in government, the opinion was that the war was to be a short and limited conflict fought on the continent and to be over by Christmas – and therefore, there was little urgency and incentive to spend precious funds on air defence. On the other hand, the Royal Naval Air Service found itself somewhat superfluous to requirements – having no defined role for operating with the fleet at the time – and came under the responsibility of the Admiralty and the First Lord of the Admiralty, Mr Winston Churchill MP. The Royal Naval Air Service – with 96 aeroplanes and a number of bases and aerodromes along the coastline of Britain – were in an ideal position to be responsible for the air defence of Great Britain. In August, some units of the Royal Naval Air Service had been sent to Ostend, Belgium (under Commander C R Sampson) in support of the Marine Brigade which was stationed there, but soon after had been withdrawn to Dunkirk, France where they were to set up a more permanent base – from where throughout the rest of the war, they were to carry out effective operations against the German airships operating against Great Britain.

With their more limited range and carrying capacity (having been envisaged as operating in a tactical role over the battlefields) the German army airships tended to make use of the airfields and newly-built sheds in Belgium – hence having a shorter distance to travel to attack targets in France and England. The naval airships were initially proposed to support the German High Seas Fleet as long-range reconnaissance and with strategic bombing – their commanders having been trained in accurate navigation of the open tracts of the North Sea with few landmarks or waypoints. They usually operated from the aerodromes and sheds in Northern Germany. The problem faced by airships operating from the north of Germany was that with Holland being neutral, the airships had the option of proceeding due west over the North Sea and making landfall over the Yorkshire Coast (with the inherent risks from inclement weather and poor navigation during a long flight over the sea), or having to take a south-westerly course following the Dutch Coast, but with the dangers of advanced warning being given to the defenders.

From the outbreak of war in August 1914 the British Government were braced for the predicted onslaught from the German airship menace, but nothing happened – although as we will see later actions were taken to pre-empt this with the attacks mounted on their bases (and it was not until late December that the first bombs fell on British soil – and those were dropped by aeroplanes).

Airships, by their very nature, are large and very susceptible to the ravages of the weather. The framework needed to be light, but strong – thus both the airships produced by Zeppelin and Schütte-Lanz made use of a geodetic-type structure. The Zeppelin's framework was manufactured from numerous strips of drawn, stamped and pressed duralumin, which is a strong, lightweight alloy of aluminium that was developed by Alfred Wilm – a German metallurgist – in 1906. It was originally manufactured by Dürener Metallwerke, Düren, Germany – hence the trade name being derived from Düren and aluminium. These strips were riveted together to form open, triangular sections, which were also riveted to one another to form the outer framework and shape of the airship.

The Schütte-Lanz Company made use of glued, hollow wooden box sections to form the geodetic framework, which was then braced by wire to help maintain the shape. In both cases, onto the outside of this framework was attached all the ancillary items such as control and engine gondolas, rudders and elevators. The inside of the framework encapsulated the gas bags (usually about 18 in number) holding the hydrogen gas that gave the airship its lift – and was manufactured from goldbeater's skin, which had been reinforced with fabric to give it a little more strength. The gas bags, when inflated, occupied the majority of the space inside the framework – although there was space below them where a longitudinal walkway was situated – allowing access to all parts of the airship and gondolas (and also enabling crewmen to repair any damage to the gas bags themselves while the airship was in flight). The control wires and linkages from the control gondola also ran the full length of the ship to the rudders and elevators, along with the mechanical telegraph to the engine crews. There was also a ladder giving access to the top surface of the airship, where a platform was often situated with mountings for a machine-gun. Either side of the walkway were situated the fuel tanks, bomb load and ballast bags (water-filled sacks) – positioned so that they could be readily dropped if required through the lower part of the airship.

The outer part of the framework was covered in a thick layer of canvas – often painted with a layer of aluminium-based paint to give it greater strength and help protect the canvas from the effects of ultra-violet radiation and repel moisture. A wet airship would weigh considerably more, given that the surface area was around 10,000 square metres. Later, the airships were given a coating of matt black paint – especially around the lower portion and up the sides – to help camouflage them during night operations when illuminated by searchlights.

To the lower section of the airship were attached gondolas, which initially resembled open boat-like structures – although later becoming fully enclosed for protection of the crew against the elements. The forward gondola housed the steering and airship control mechanisms, along with the commander and his helmsmen. Often the rear section of the forward gondola housed an engine that drove a single propeller. Situated further back along the lower keel of the airship were other gondolas housing further engines. In the early Zeppelins, one gondola could house up to three engines – situated in line – two powering propellers attached by pylons attached to the sides of the airship (and connected by gears and drive shafts); the third engine driving a propeller to the rear of the gondola. The engine gondolas were large enough to allow the crew to monitor and access them so as carry out maintenance and repairs while in flight. Radiators were also fitted that could be raised and lowered in and out of the airship slipstream so as to control the amount of cooling required.

Given their vast size – averaging 160 metres in length and nine metres in diameter – airships were very susceptible to the slightest gust of wind and needed to be protected from the elements when they were not operating. To this end, the airship sheds needed to be even larger structures and were constructed at various operating bases across Europe to house the airships (sometimes capable of sheltering two or more and protect them from the elements) and allowed servicing, maintenance, refuelling and rearming to be carried out prior to operations. Often an underground pipeline was installed to the airship sheds – running directly from the hydrogen-producing plant to enable the refilling of the gas bags to be carried out with relative safety, and avoiding the need to compress the gas into high-pressure cylinders – a hazardous operation in itself. On arriving at an airfield, an airship (once down at ground level) was manoeuvred by about 200 ground crew who would attach the airship to trolleys, which in turn were attached to a rail that ran into a shed so as to avoid the airship being swung by a gust of wind as it was hauled into its housing. A number of airships were damaged or destroyed during this delicate operation of moving them in or out of their sheds.

On the 28 June 1914 Gavrilo Princip, a Bosnian-Serb, assassinated Archduke Franz Ferdinand of Austria and his wife Sophie in Sarajevo, Bosnia. His was the first action of the events that later would become to be known as the Great World War. This was to be a war that was notable for a number of firsts – especially where the armies facing one another had come to rely on a sustained industrial output of weapons, machinery and chemicals produced many miles back from the front lines. This was the culmination of the Industrial Revolution that had first swept across Europe from 1760 – drawing the civilian workforce in from the country and into the towns and cities to supply the insatiable demand for workers to run the machinery. With many of the able-bodied men who had sustained the requirements for industry now at the front, there was need for more workers – and many women came forward to fill the vacancies left by their menfolk.

Over 100 years previously, Napoleon Bonaparte famously stated that an army marches on its stomach – summarising what many commanders in the field have known before and since that if an army loses its ability to sustain itself with supplies from the rear, it will soon fail. Take out the lightly-defended and vulnerable supply lines behind an army, and its will and ability to resist will be greatly diminished. So now, Germany and her Allies had new weapons in their arsenal (the submarine) and the ability to cut Britain's supply lines with virtual impunity that she relied on from across the Atlantic and her Empire – and thus starve the essential industries of raw materials and the workers of food. In 1914 the British Navy was seen to rule the waves – and even when elements of the German High Seas Fleet managed to evade the defenders (so as to bombard a few British coastal towns), their efforts were a mere token display of aggression more inclined to stir up further anti-German sentiments than achieving anything of strategic value. The Royal Navy, though, was at a loss as to how to defeat the unseen enemy beneath the waves and protect the vital supply lines and the ships carrying troops from across the Empire who had rallied to the cause.

Germany also had other totally untried weapons in her arsenal (the airship and aeroplane) – and now she had the ability to attack Britain's factories and industrial heartlands from above as well – and whereas her navy was confined to bombarding the narrow strip of coastline, her airships (and later, her aeroplanes) could reach far inland and roam at will – spreading terror and destruction as they went. Great Britain was no longer an island – safe in the knowledge that the Royal Navy would prevail – and no one from royalty to the labourer, palace or shack, was safe from this new menace from the skies.

As Carl von Clausewitz had expounded his theories in his work *On War* (published in 1834) that war cannot be waged in a limited way, the rules of competition will force participants to use all means at their disposal to achieve victory. Now, it was Total War as not only was it the soldiers far away in France and Belgium on the front lines who were at risk, but the civilian population too – who now found themselves in the front line, but unlike the soldier, they had no weapons of their own to be able to strike back at the enemy (just to maintain the industrial output and give the soldiers far away the ability to strike back and defeat this menace on their behalf). Not only was it the families and friends of soldiers at the front who worried about their well-being – while they themselves slept soundly in their beds – the soldiers were now left wondering how their families at home were faring and would there be anything left of their homes and loved ones when they returned at the end of the fighting. So not only did the Germans and their Allies have the ability to destroy the industry that was keeping Britain and her Allies supplied with the means to wage war, but civilian workers were now seen as just part of that industrial machinery – and if they too could be damaged or destroyed, that too would have a direct impact on output. With the additional frailty of the human body and mind, a direct hit from a bomb was not required to reduce the ability of the worker to function. Even the mere perception that death or destruction lurked in the skies above them – and that it could visit them or their families at any moment, without warning, while they slept or worked, with nowhere to hide – would have the desired effect.

With their limited weight of bombs – and the inability to strike at a particular target due to the difficulties posed by navigation, target identification and an accurate bombsight – the German airships and aircraft in the first analysis may appear to have achieved little in the way of disrupting the British industrial output that was sustaining the ability to continue the war. Many bombs fell harmlessly onto the countryside. A fair number did hit the larger towns and cities, but very little damage was ever caused to industry and supply lines. It was the civilians who suffered the most from the bombing and the perceived threat from the air – physically and mentally – and although there were never any recorded reports of mass hysteria and the breakdown of law and order, the psychological effects caused by the blackout (the need to seek shelter and lack of sleep) did cause a marked drop in industrial output. By the end of 1916 the extreme vulnerability of airships was being exposed – and that in the face of determined defences, it was proved they could be defeated (even under the cover of darkness). Rather than admit that their policy was not working (as will be addressed in the next volume covering the years 1917 and 1918), Germany continued to build airships, but ones that could climb high enough and fly fast enough to avoid the defences. As they became more reliable, with longer ranges and greater load-carrying capacity, large formations of aircraft were also to feature more prominently over the next two years – being cheaper and quicker to produce than airships. With them, it was the intention that they could overwhelm the defences over a particular target – even during daylight – and destroy it, but they never were able to muster enough forces to achieve this goal. Strategic bombing alone was never going to win the war for Germany, but it laid down the future ideology as advocated by Stanley Baldwin MP in his speech to the House of Commons in 1932 that: 'The bomber will always get through'. In his speech, he expressed the opinion that in the next war, the only means of defence was offence – and that you have to kill more of the enemy's women and children more quickly than the enemy can inflict on yours.

In 1940 and 1941 Germany was again to put the theory to the test – followed by the Allied attempts from 1942 onwards – to show that if you concentrate enough bombers over one target, resistance will cease. Germany again tried with her V weapons, but it was not until the atom bombs were dropped on Hiroshima and Nagasaki that the theory was finally proved correct – and that bombing with overwhelming force can lead to peace.

On the 24 December 1914 when a German aircraft dropped its bomb on Dover, it was to herald the start of the longest and most costly experiment in the history of warfare – and was to leave hundreds of thousands dead and many more maimed (physically and mentally), with much of Europe's towns and cities reduced to ruins. One-hundred years on from the start of the experiment, the bombing of one's enemies is now seen as the desired option, with little risk to the aggressor, who has the option to travel around the globe using unmanned drones where there is no risk to the aggressor – safely ensconced in a control room far away and invisible to his enemy (and with smart bombs to reduce the risk of so-called 'collateral damage'). The psychology of bombing is complete, with the possibility of being watched by an unseen enemy who can track your every movement, strike at any moment and whose bombs can penetrate the deepest and strongest shelter. Germany initially had the right concept; they just had not developed the means of putting it into force at the time.

Author's notes

I have made use of many of the files now preserved in the National Archives, Kew (especially in the 'Air 1' series) that contain material relating to the airship and aircraft raids – and although there are many files relating to the Zeppelins involved, there appears to be very little about the losses of the Gothas during 1917 and 1918. To this extent, I have had to refer to many other publications and seek help from a number of researchers to try and piece together the fullest details possible. I have also referred to the recorded squadron histories and war diaries of those involved in combating the German raiders – although the only record that I can trace about 39 Home Defence Squadron, Royal Flying Corps (the most successful of the units in combating the Zeppelins) was a post-war one written in Norwegian by a Norwegian officer who served with the squadron – although a translation is available.

I have tried to, as far as possible, to recount the events as recorded at the time (using primary sources) to try and ensure that facts and figures are not distorted by the progress of time and poor memory – although where accounts of events are challenged by subsequent historical evidence, I have taken the revised viewpoint as fact if it can be clearly proven to be correct. The personal accounts reproduced, when available, I hope give a feel of the times – along with trying to maintain some of the terminology regularly in use.

Some of the accounts of the air raids may initially appear to go into too much detail as to times and where bombs fell, but I considered this an essential so as to encourage local historians of the future to further research their particular areas and events – and also to build up an even more detailed picture of what occurred in their locality (especially with the relentless tide of development and reconstruction).

Numbering identities of airships

It should be noted that the numbering designation for Zeppelins can be a little confusing in that the production number is given as a sequential 'LZ' – starting with 'LZ 1' and going through to 'LZ 112' for wartime production. The military designation of Zeppelins differed with the navy using the 'L' prefix, while the army initially used a 'Z' – later changed to 'LZ', which did not necessarily match the production designation.

Hence, the 27th Zeppelin produced was given the production number 'LZ 27', but being issued to the navy was given the naval tactical number 'L 4', while the 34th Zeppelin produced was given the production number 'LZ 34' – and as it was used by the army, it was also given the army tactical number 'LZ 34'. Yet the 42nd Zeppelin produced had the production number 'LZ 42', but the army tactical number 'LZ 72'.

With airships built by the Schütte-Lanz Company, the designation is always given the prefix 'SL' regardless of which service they were operated by – and run sequentially from 'SL 1' to 'SL 22'.

Throughout the text in this book, I have identified the airships by their military tactical number – hence navy is prefixed 'L' and army is prefixed 'LZ' (although where losses are recorded of airships, the production number is also subsequently given).

The British defence structure

The responsibility for air defence of Great Britain fell into various categories: the first was the Royal Flying Corps (RFC), which had initially been formed from the Air Battalion of the Royal Engineers on 1 April 1911. The second was the Royal Naval Air Service (RNAS), which was the air arm of the Royal Navy. On 1 April 1918 the two services were amalgamated to form the Royal Air Force (RAF).

Each force consisted of a number of squadrons and had their own aerodromes from which their aircraft operated from – each retaining its own particular identity and administrative routes. Thus, prior to 1 April 1918, 1 Squadron Royal Flying Corps was a different unit to 1 Squadron Royal Naval Air Service. After 1 April 1918 the amalgamated Royal Naval Air Service squadrons were often given a new identity, so that 1 Squadron Royal Naval Air Service became 201 Royal Air Force, while the Royal Flying Corps squadrons continued with the same numbering when they were amalgamated into the Royal Air Force.

The anti-aircraft guns were initially the responsibility of the Royal Garrison Artillery – although the navy were responsible for the defence of dockyards and naval facilities (although there was no precise demarcation). The searchlight batteries were the responsibility of the Royal Engineers. By 1915 the requirements for artillery and personnel in France meant that the responsibility for the defence of London was passed to the Royal Naval Volunteer Reserve. By 1917 there were also trials of using barrage balloons, with a series of curtains or nets strung between them at various points around the capital in an attempt to deter the raiders – but these proved to be relatively ineffective.

Tracking the enemy airships as they proceeded inland from the British Coast was carried out using telegrams so that if an airship or aircraft were seen or heard overhead (or a bomb fell close by) a telegram giving date, time and position was dispatched to the War Office in London – thus allowing a relatively accurate plot of the raider's progress to be recorded. Although the use of wireless technology was in its infancy during the Great War, listening stations had been set up along the British Coast – enabling the bearings to be taken of wireless transmissions from the raiding airships and often also identifying the individual raider (and they were also an aid for pre-warning of possible raids, as they tested their wireless sets prior to take-off).

Further investigation

For those who may be interested in pursuing an interest in airships further, there are a number of excellent museums that are well worth a visit:

The Zeppelin Museum, Friedrichshafen, Germany: Located on the shores of the Bodensee, the collection is housed in a purpose-built building and features numerous remains of airships and components – along with a specially-constructed section of the *LZ 129 "Hindenburg"*. The exhibits give a detailed insight into the development of the Zeppelin airship – from the earliest concept at the beginning of the 20th century, up to the present day.

For more information, see www.zeppelin-museum.de.

While in Friedrichshafen, the opportunity exists to take a trip over the town and Lake Constance in the *Zeppelin NT* airship that operates from the nearby Friedrichshafen airport.

Aeronauticum, Nordholz, Germany: The German Military Airship and Marine Aviation Museum is located adjacent to the German Naval Air Force Base at Nordholz in a specially-constructed exhibition building and tells the story of German marine aviation from the First World War up to the present day. The quality of the displays is excellent – especially concerning airship history – with some unique and personal exhibits.

For more information, see www.aeronauticum.de.

The Svalbard Airship Museum, Longyearbyen, Svalbard: Tells the story of the expeditions to the North Pole using the airships *Norsk* and *Italia*. Although perhaps one of the most inaccessible museums on earth, the quality of the displays and exhibits is of a very high standard.

For more information, see www.spitzbergenairshipmuseum.com.

If you are visiting Svalbard, a trip to the remote community of Ny-Alesund is also worthwhile so as to see the airship mooring mast used by the *Norsk* and *Italia* – one of only two that still exist in the world. For a close-up view of the mast, visitors must be accompanied by an armed guide due to the dangers of polar bears. There is also a small museum within the village housing a few airship-related items and photographs.

The Zeppelin and Garrison Museum, Tondern, Denmark: Located on the former German Airship Base near Tondern, this small museum is limited to opening at weekends during the summer months. It tells the story of the German airship operations from the base, and also details about the British raid – with some remarkable exhibits. The opportunity to be taken on a guided tour of the base is also offered, but needs to be booked at least three weeks in advance of a visit.

For further details, see www.zeppelin-museum.dk.

This is not a definitive list of airship museums, as there are many other museums that have airship exhibits; the ones mentioned are ones that the author has visited and found to be very worthwhile and informative.

Part 1: 1914

Having declared war on the Russian Empire on 1 August, German troops proceeded to march into Luxembourg on the second and Belgium on the fourth – at which point, Britain declared war on Germany. It was almost immediately that Germany started to make use of her airship force – using them for spotting the fall of the shells from the 380mm and 420mm Howitzers that were bombarding the fortifications around the city of Liège.

6 August 1914
Zeppelin Z VI / LZ 21. Type K.
Near Bonn, Germany.
Decommissioned following a rough landing in a forest, caused by shrapnel damage during a raid on Liège, Belgium. *Kommandeur: Hauptmann* Kleinschmitt.

21 August 1914
Zeppelin Z VII / LZ 22. Type L.
St Quirin, France.
Hit by French anti-aircraft fire over Alsace during a reconnaissance flight and force landed. Scrapped.
Kommandeur: Hauptmann Gaissert.

Zeppelin Z VIII / LZ 23. Type L.
Bandovilliers, France.
Hit by French anti-aircraft fire and made an emergency landing. The crew tried to set fire to the airship, but failed. Scrapped by the French Army.
Kommandeur: Hauptmann Andree.

28 August 1914
Zeppelin Z V / LZ 20. Type H.
Mlawa, Russia (now Poland).
Hit by anti-aircraft fire and made an emergency landing.
Crew taken prisoner by Russian forces:
Hauptmann Ernst Grüner +.
Leutnant Konrad Stapelfeldt.
Obermaschinist Paul Braun.
Untermaschinist Johann Glatzel.
Untermaschinist Georg Larisch.
Untersteuermann Paul Leonhardt.

Zeppelin Z VIII preparing to land at Friedrichshafen. Note the multiple elevators and rudders that were a feature of the early Zeppelins.

Untermaschinist Wilhelm Pfeufer.
Obersteuermann Wilhelm Röhling.
Unteroffizier Karl Tanneberger.
Maschinist Wilhelm Zastrow.

22 September 1914

Prior to the start of the war, it was noted in Britain that the development of airships in Germany as a potential strategic weapon in the war would inevitably lead to the bombing of the British Isles – and that, with inadequate defences in place – it was prudent to take the war to the enemy and attack the airships in their bases and destroy them before they could become an actual threat. To this extent, a Royal Naval Air Service base was established at Dunkirk, France so as to be closer to the enemy bases and also help counter any incursions over the English Channel.

In a memorandum prepared by The Director, Air Department on 1 September 1914 it was stated:

> Information has come from many different sources that the Germans are preparing a large number of airships for use against England from some bases in France and Belgium.

> Simultaneous attacks are believed to be contemplated on various places in England – and on London in particular.
>
> German airship sheds are at Metz, Cologne and Düsseldorf. The lines drawn between these places and London will give an idea of the direct line of flight. If, however, temporary bases are established, they are likely to be found somewhere near or in the area given to be searched.

Hence, four aeroplanes of the Royal Naval Air Service – flying from Antwerp, Belgium – carried out raids on the airship sheds at Düsseldorf and Cologne, although due to thick mist over the target areas, only Flight Lieutenant Charles Collet located the shed at Düsseldorf and dropped three bombs (one of which missed and the others failed to detonate).

Major C L Gerrard RMLI in his report from Antwerp of 23 September 1914 gave a graphic account of events:

> Sir, I have the honour to report that an attack was made on the airship sheds at Düsseldorf and Cologne yesterday; aeroplane nos.50 (Major Gerrard) and 906 (Lieut Collet) to Düsseldorf and nos.149 (Lieut Commander S Grey with Lieut Newton Clare) and 168 (Lieut Marix) to Cologne.
>
> The attacks were timed to be simultaneous – no.906 starting at daylight. It was clear as far as the River Roer, but a thick mist extended from that river to some miles beyond (east of) the River Rhine.
>
> Only Lieut Collet succeeded in locating his objective, and dropped his three bombs from a height of 400 feet. The first fell a little short and exploded; the others probably hit the shed, but failed to explode. The surprise was complete – and the numerous Germans in the vicinity ran in all directions.
>
> Lieut-Commander S Grey reported that a bomb accidentally dropped from his machine; he does not know where.[1]

8 October 1914

It was again planned to carry out operations against the airship sheds at Cologne and Düsseldorf, Germany by flying from Antwerp, Belgium – even though the city was under German shell fire; the population were evacuating; and all serviceable aircraft – apart from the two allocated for operations – had previously departed.

The report of operations by the squadron commander, Lieutenant Commander S D A Grey of 1 Squadron Royal Naval Air Service, regarding the attack on Düsseldorf and Cologne stated:

---

1 The National Archives (TNA) Air 1/2099/207/20/1: Reports on the air attacks on Düsseldorf and Cologne.

At about 11.30pm, Thursday 8th October 1914 the bombardment of Antwerp commenced from the south. The aeroplanes were taken out of the shed and drawn into the middle of the aerodrome to avoid damage by splinters in case the shed was hit. The aerodrome, being between the enemy and the town, shells were passing over during the entire period of the bombardment. The forenoon of 9th October, as the weather was misty and unsuitable, was spent in tuning up the machines. At 1pm, as the weather showed no signs of improvement and it was important to make the attack as early as possible, I decided to start.

Flight Lieutenant Reginald Marix in aeroplane no.168 was ordered to proceed to Düsseldorf. He left at 1.30pm – flying low over the trees in a westerly direction, circling the town and turning on an easterly course when north of it. On arriving at Düsseldorf, he dived at the shed – turning up and letting go his bombs at 600 feet. It was impossible to ascertain if one or both bombs penetrated the shed, but the destruction was complete. The roof fell in within 30 seconds and flames 500 feet high were observed – indicating that an inflated Zeppelin must have been inside. Lieutenant R Marix was under heavy rifle and shell fire during this period – and his machine suffered considerable damage. In spite of this, he managed to fly back to within 20 miles of Antwerp – at which point his petrol ran out. From here he succeeded in returning to Antwerp by a bicycle, which he borrowed from a peasant, and a car – which he got later. It was hoped to take out more petrol in an armed car at daylight and recover his machine, but the order to evacuate prevented this.

Lieutenant Commander Spencer Grey later wrote regarding his operation:

I left Antwerp at 1.20pm in aeroplane no.167 with the intention of attacking the airship sheds at Cologne. On arriving at Cologne, I found a thick mist. I had been given two different positions for the airship sheds; one to the north-west and one to the south of the town. I came down to 600 feet, but after searching

An early photograph of Lieutenant Commander S D A Grey at the controls of a motor car.

> for 10 to 12 minutes under heavy fire, I failed to locate them. I now hear they are on the south side of the Rhine, but I do not know if this is correct. Failing to locate the sheds, I considered the best point to attack would be the main station in the middle of the town, where I saw many trains drawn up, so I let fall my two bombs in this. I arrived back at Antwerp at 4.45pm and landed.
>
> At about 8.30pm the enemy commenced shelling the aerodrome itself – and in spite of the fact that the machines were constantly moved, they were eventually considerably damaged. At 11.30pm I heard from a detachment of British troops on their way to the pontoon bridge that a general evacuation had been ordered at 6pm – and as there were Germans in the woods round the aerodrome and one of my men had been fired at, it was necessary to leave – which we did in two cars, making for Ostend, which we reached at 12.30pm, the 10th October.

In a subsequent report written on 21 October 1914 Spencer Grey wrote:

> I beg to report that I have met Colonel Dobson, who has just got through from Berlin. He informs me that as a result of the last aeroplane raid on Düsseldorf and Cologne, our aviators destroyed a brand-new Zeppelin, which had just moved into the shed, and also a 'machinery hall' (probably meaning a machine or erecting shop) alongside the Zeppelin shed. He also informs me that the occurrence produced great consternation in Berlin, as they did not believe such a raid was possible for a British aviator. As a result, the Germans seized the English clerks at the American Embassy – believing that they had informed us.
> G.T.Richards. Lieutenant, RNVR.[2]

Zeppelin Z XI / LZ 25. Type M.
Düsseldorf, Germany.
Bombed in shed by Flight Lieutenant R G L Marix, Royal Naval Air Service who was piloting a Sopwith Tabloid – and which was completely burnt out and destroyed. It was impossible to ascertain if one or both bombs penetrated the shed, but the destruction was complete. The roof of the shed fell in within 30 seconds and flames 500 feet high were observed – indicating that an inflated Zeppelin must have been inside.[3]

---

2 The National Archives (TNA) Air 1/2099/207/20/1: Reports of reconnaissance and operations, September to October 1914.

3 The National Archives (TNA) Air 1/7/6/124: Report of damage done to the enemy during operations of the Royal Naval Air Service, October 1914 to June 1915.

Flight Lieutenant Reginald Matrix poses for a publicity photograph. Even though he was the first person to be credited with destroying an enemy airship, he did not receive the public acclaim that was to be bestowed upon his fellow aviators, who achieved similar feats later on in the war.

3 November 1914: 0740

During a limited naval action by the German Battle-Cruiser Squadron, commanded by *Admiral* Franz von Hipper, shells hit the beach near to Yarmouth, Norfolk – causing no damage and no civilian casualties.

21 November 1914

As the Zeppelin sheds at Düsseldorf, Germany were now out of range of British aircraft, it was decided that if use was made of the French aerodrome at Belfort, an attack on the Zeppelin production centre at Friedrichshafen – on the northern bank of Lake Constance (also known as The Bodensee) – would be possible.

Lieutenant Pemberton Billing of the Royal Naval Volunteer Reserve was entrusted with carrying out the orders regarding the operation. He reported preparations and execution of the raid:

> I have the honour to submit the attached report on the Friedrichshafen raid – carried out in accordance with your instructions – together with a report furnished by the two pilots.
>
> N Pemberton Billing Lieut RNVR.
> In accordance with instructions received on Tuesday, November 10th, I proceeded by road to Southampton. On arrival there, I got in touch with Commander E F Briggs on board *AA Manchester Importer* – on which vessel he was crossing to Havre – accompanied by Flight Commander J T Babington, 11 air mechanics, four Avro machines, one motor car and supplies. As there seemed to exist some doubt as to the arrival time of this ship, I decided to cross by the *Havre Packet*, which would enable me to complete arrangements for the acceptance

and dispatch of the consignment on arrival. At Havre, Sub-Lieutenant Brock reported that the final arrangements for the special train were now complete. Lieutenant Delanney of the French General Staff was waiting our convenience at Havre. I caused the special train to be shunted on to the quay side, and on arrival of the *Manchester Importer*, machines, cars and cases were loaded direct onto truck. Our movements were somewhat hampered by breakdown of the Havre electric power plant, which necessitated the cases being man-handled. Finally, we succeeded in getting away at 11.30pm that night. We proceeded direct to Belfort, where we arrived without incident at 9.30am, November 13th. As it was not expedient, in view of the secrecy which I had observed throughout the whole organisation – that these machines or men should be transported to the aeroplane ground in daylight – I caused the train to be shunted into a disused factory siding until nightfall. The same night, with the assistance of Roger Seyrig – Captain of Staff at Belfort – we transferred machines and men by means of motor lorries to the dirigible shed. This move was completed by 11.30pm. As the men had rested throughout the day, the work of unpacking and erecting was proceeded with at once – and carried on continuously until 3.30pm, November 14th, at which hour all machines were complete in every detail; engines had been tested, bombs shipped, release gear tested, tanks filled. I then only awaited the arrival of Commander Shepherd and Lieutenant Sippe – and suitable weather conditions – to dispatch the flight.

I confirm my telegram to you in this connection:
"Ready to start. No news Shepherd or Sippe."

To which you replied:
"Sippe, Shepherd may be in Dijon. Get in touch as soon as possible."

On receipt of this wire, I telephoned to Dijon; to Jeuvissy; and also to Havre, but failed to get in touch. Later in the evening, however, on the 14th instant, Dijon staff telephoned to say two officers had arrived by motor car – and had been given our message – and were going to Belfort at once in the car which I had requested the Dijon authorities to hold ready for this emergency. Owing to delays by sentries, through which night travelling in France is rendered exceedingly difficult, these officers did not arrive in Belfort until 10.30am Sunday, November 15th. On their arrival, Commander Shepherd reported having experienced motor trouble. The machines were ready; the weather conditions were excellent; but in view of Commander Shepherd's indisposition and want of rest, it was eventually decided not to make the attempt that day.

The following morning, the fair weather spell appeared to have broken; glass fell rapidly; wind went into east – blowing a stiff breeze; the temperature fell as low as –7° C. These conditions remained constant until the morning of Saturday, November 21st, with one exception – that of Tuesday morning

17th, when an apparent lull in the weather decided Commander Shepherd to test his machine, no.179. Unfortunately, this trial proved abortive on account of a slight accident while taxiing, which smashed the propeller and sprung the chassis; buckled the left wheel; and broke the wing tip skid. The machine was returned to the shed, where repairs were immediately effected – by which time, however, the weather conditions compelled a further postponement. The regrettable publicity occasioned by this false start rendered continued discomfiture to the officers by being confined to the shed day and night unnecessarily – and therefore, the same evening, we transferred our quarters to a hotel inside the fortifications.

In order to prevent anxiety being occasioned by the continued delay, I sent the following wire:
"Weather bound. Otherwise all correct."

Throughout the entire period – between the moment that all was ready and the start was eventually made – the practice following was adopted:

Between 7.30am and 8am each morning, the flight proceeded in the aerodrome, where they remained until 12.30pm – at which time, having regard to the fact that the duration of the flight would be at least three-and-three-quarter hours – and that after pm it became too dark to effect a landing, the attempt was in each case abandoned for that day.

The machines were kept in absolute readiness for immediate start, with the exception of the filling of castor oil in view of the exceedingly low temperatures; it was considered advisable to keep this oil at no less than 110° F. I also caused all the oil tanks to be wrapped with red and white flannel.

Every two hours, balloons were released in order to judge the velocity of wind at the varying altitudes. By the courtesy of the Meteorological Bureau – and with the assistance of telephone – we established communication with the Ballon d'Alsace and the Val Sellons (two stations over 2,000 feet altitude) and were enabled to obtain a fairly accurate idea each day as to the atmospheric conditions prevailing at different levels each side of the ridge.

During the enforced delay, Commander Shepherd's health became worse. He experienced sleepless nights; he could take no food whatever – and his condition was such as to render him, in my opinion, totally unfit to be subjected to the somewhat severe mental and physical strain likely to be occasioned by such a flight. I therefore consulted with Commander Briggs – and later, we had a long interview with Commander Shepherd, who eventually conceded to our request that unless his health materially improved, he should refrain from actively participating in the raid. It was therefore decided that the spare pilot, Sub-Lieutenant Cannon – who, Commander Shepherd informed me, had had considerable experience of 'Avro' machines at Upavon – should pilot the fourth machine.

A post-war view of Friedrichshafen Aerodrome showing the airship sheds and the very distinctive schloss, with its twin towers – that would have been a good aid for navigation – on the shore of The Bodensee. The main town and industrial area is to the right of the picture.

On Saturday, November 21st, the raid took place. On that morning, the conditions were particularly favourable. The sky was clear, glass steady, temperature about zero °C.

With ballonets before referred to, we ascertained that the wind direction at an altitude of approximately 2,000 feet was easterly, velocity varying from 25 to 30 miles per hour. Above 2,000 feet, the direction of the wind was due west, velocity 20 to 25 miles per hour.

9.30am: the four machines were brought out – and after a careful and final inspection, were lined up in position on the western side of the aviation ground and were dispatched in the following order – after a three minutes' engine test in each; also bomb release test:

9.45am: Commander Briggs' machine, 873, immediately rose to about 1,000 feet.

9.50am: Flight Commander Babington's machine, 875, left the ground and flew in the wake of Commander Briggs, who was circling the aerodrome.

9.55am: Lieutenant Sippe's machine, 874, was dispatched – circling the aerodrome in the wake of Babington. Three minutes later, Sub-Lieutenant Cannon, machine 179, was released, but failed to rise. A second attempt was made; machine again failed – and slewing round, broke its tail-skid. I then stopped Cannon leaving – my decision being guided by the following conditions: the machine was slightly damaged; the engine was about 100 revolutions short; and owing to the delay – by a determined plan – the other machines had already left (and were at that moment almost out of sight at an altitude of about 3,500 feet). I therefore ordered the machine to be returned to the shed – dismantled and unpacked.

I confirm my telegram to you as follows:

"Weather conditions perfect. Flight dispatched 9.45am. Pilots as follows: Briggs, Babington, Sippe. Fourth machine slightly damaged. Shepherd ill."

During the absence of the machines, the weather conditions remained constant.

At 1.30pm a machine was observed approaching from the NW. In landing, the offside wheel crumpled up. Pilot Lieutenant Sippe descended and reported as per attached statement. The machine had received considerable damage by rifle fire.

At 3.30am – having received no. news of the other pilots or machines – I wired you as follows:

"Raid successful. Sippe returned 1.45. Reports considerable damage to workshops. Missed Briggs and Babington during attack under shell and rifle fire. No news of them; probably landed in Switzerland. Have communicated British Minister, Berne. Wiring again later."

I also dispatched the following telegram to the British Minister at Berne:

"Reported two British aviators flying over Germany forced landing, probably Switzerland; please act."

Flight Lieutenant Sidney Vincent Sippe wearing an early form of flying helmet.

Later, Babington telephoned to say that he had landed safely at Villa Sexuel – 35 miles distant SW of Belfort. I immediately dispatched a motor car to fetch him, when he reported as per statement attached. Later, I sent motor transport with mechanics in charge of Sub-Lieutenant Cannon; had machine packed and put on rail to Versoul to await being picked up by the special train from Belfort, which was subsequently done.

I confirm my wire to you as follows:

"Babington just telephoned; forced landing near Versoul, 30 miles away. Reports further damage from this attack. Still no news Briggs."

Confirm receipt of following wire from you Sunday, 22nd:

"Congratulations; splendid work. Wire news of Briggs, and do all you can to get in touch with him. Spare no expense in search."

On the morning of Sunday, November 22nd, Belfort troops were paraded for the purpose of the Legion d'Honneur being conferred upon Flight Commander Babington and Lieutenant Sippe. At the same time, the colonel informed me that it was the intention of General Joffre to decorate Commander Briggs on the first available opportunity.

I confirm your telegram to me received Sunday:

"Party to return with machines as convenient. Briggs reported, through Dutch sources, wounded in hospital."

Also your telegram received late that evening, as follows:

"Telegraph further account of attack in detail."

To which I replied:

"Flight left Belfort 9.45, 21st November in the following order: Briggs, Babington and Sippe at three-minutes intervals. Sippe reports observing 12 shells bursting over Friedrichshafen when five miles distant; time 11.55 – presumed this fire was directed against Briggs. Sippe approaching closer encountered shell, mitrailleuses and rifle fire; crossed works at elevation of 600 feet, launched three bombs on same, fourth bomb failed to release. While effecting escape, Babington approached from the same direction at elevation of 4,000 feet, nose dive to 400 feet, release four bombs. Both pilots state positively all bombs reached objective. Considerable panic observed. Machines returned damaged by gunfire. No news of Briggs since Sippe observed him approaching Constance, except your communications. Both pilots report flying conditions bad."

Since dispatching this telegram – from information received both at Belfort, Chaumont and Havre – it may be confidently assumed that the damage caused by this raid includes the complete destruction of one Zeppelin and serious damage to the larger hangar (and also demolition of the hydrogen-producing plant, which had only been completed about seven days before the raid). Report from Romanshorn, situated 80 miles distant, states that flames of considerable magnitude were seen issuing from the Friedrichshafen factory – immediately succeeding the raid.

Monday, November 23rd. Commander Shepherd, Flight Commander Babington, left Belfort 8.30 by Wolsey car.

I confirm my wire of that morning:

"Have dispatched men, machines and officer in charge special train Havre. Proceeding by road with pilots. Am arranging transport on arrival Havre. Reporting London, Wednesday."

Later I proceeded by road to Havre – accompanied by Lieutenant Sippe and Sub-Lieutenant Brock. The condition of the roads, however, rendered travelling very difficult. In some cases, stretches of miles of surface ice were encountered. When approaching Chaumont down a somewhat steep gradient, we suddenly encountered an ice patch – on which the car turned completely round several times and eventually struck a tree off the road with considerable force. I regret to report that the car sustained serious damage – although I have pleasure in reporting, beyond minor injuries to myself, no one was hurt. I caused the car to be conveyed to Chaumont, where we joined the special train from Belfort.

I confirm my telegram from Troyes:

"Motor trouble, joined train. Report London, Thursday."

On arrival at Havre, I interviewed Captain Macgregor – Naval Transport Officer – and arranged for the immediate collection and dispatch of machines and men to Southampton, where I understand they arrived on the evening of the 26th instant. I left instructions with Lieutenant Cannon to dispatch the men to their respective stations, and cause the machines and cars to be housed at docks with man in charge – pending instructions from London.

I then proceeded at once to London, and reported to you at one o'clock. The behaviour of the air mechanics was good, while the assistance rendered by the two erectors supplied by Messrs A V Roe considerably facilitated the work in hand.

Finally, I desire to express my wholehearted appreciation of the way in which all officers worked with me to the end of promoting the success of the expedition – all service distinctions being lost in this single desire.
N. Pemberton Billing. Lieutenant, RNVR

Avros – pilots: Squadron Commander E F Briggs, RNAS; Flight Commander J T Babington, RNAS; Flight Lieutenant S V Sippe, RNAS; Friedrichshafen. From Belfort.

Raid successful; Sippe returned 1.45; reports considerable damage to workshops. Missed Briggs and Babington during attack under shell and rifle fire, no news of them; probably landed in Switzerland. Have communicated with British Minister in Berne. Wiring again later.

Babington just telephoned; forced landing near Vesoul, 30 miles away. Reports further damage from his attack. Still no news Briggs.

Telegram from Lieutenant Pemberton Billing, Belfort, 23 November 1914:

Flight left Belfort 9.45, 21st November in the following order: Briggs, Babington and Sippe at three-minutes intervals. Sippe reports observing 12 shells bursting over Friedrichshafen when five miles distant; time 11.55 – presumed this fire was directed against Briggs. Sippe approaching closer encountered shell, mitrailleuses and rifle fire; crossed works at elevation of 600 feet, launched three bombs on same, fourth bomb failed to release. While effecting escape, Babington approached from the same direction at elevation of 4,000 feet, nose dive to 400 feet, release four bombs. Both pilots state positively all bombs reached objective. Considerable panic observed. Machines returned damaged by gunfire. No news of Briggs since Sippe observed him approaching Constance, except your communications. Both pilots report flying conditions bad.

Avro 504s numbered left to right 873, 875, 874 are prepared for flight at Belfort prior to the attack on Friedrichshafen.

Sir, I have the honour to submit the attached report on flight of aeroplane no.875 (pilot, Flight Commander Babington) from Belfort, for attack on Zeppelin hangars at Friedrichshafen – together with a report on the defence armament:

Log of aeroplane no.875 (pilot, Flight Commander Babington) attack on Friedrichshafen, 21 November:

9.50am: Left Belfort. Revs 1,050.

9.52am: Shaped course for Basle astern of Squadron Commander E F Briggs in no.873.

10.10am: No.873 circling and drawing ahead to southward. No.874 on starboard quarter.

10.20am: Over Rhine at Basle, shaped course down Rhine Valley, height 4,000 to 5,000 feet.

11.30am: Over clouds between Schaffhausen and Konstanz, observed no.874 about three miles ahead entering clouds. Sighted Zeller Zee – 4,500 feet.

11.47am: Sighted Zeppelin sheds, with shrapnel bursting over them at 3,000 and 3,500 feet.

11.53am: Abreast water side shed (empty) steering down shore of lake. Observed no.874 escaping low down across lake; shrapnel bursting in rear.

11.54am: Shrapnel commenced bursting to right of machine and about 1,000 feet below. Continued course till sun in line with gun sights. Shrapnel bursting to rear. Height 4,000 feet.

11.55am: Commenced very steep descent in slight curve over sheds. Released two bombs at 950 feet. Shrapnel all passing over and bursting beyond. At 450 feet, released second two bombs – machine nearly vertical; continued dive over sheds and received shock of bomb explosion directly over shed. It is almost certain one, if not two bombs, struck the shed – and smoke was seen passing over shed to leeward from explosion of bomb only. Made detour inland and passed over lake shore at waterside shed – leaving it on starboard beam. Two machine-guns in operation near this shed. Shaped course over lake towards sun.

12.08pm: Fire ceased. Shaped course down Rhine Valley, 4,000 feet at Konstanz.

1.10pm: Over Basle. Shaped course for Belfort by sun, 4,000 feet. Passed Belfort in mist, descended at Largewalls, 2.20pm.

Observations:

Main sheds and enclosures correspond exactly with plans and information supplied by Lieutenant Pemberton Billing. Nothing unusual was to be observed, except for panic amongst workmen; the doors of the main shed were slightly open. It is believed that a complete Zeppelin was in the shed waiting for trial.

Waterside buildings: There is only one waterside shed; the doors were open and the building empty. The seaward end of the shed projects well into the water – and there are quay-ways, projecting horn-wise, from the sides of the shed. There are works under construction immediately on the leeward side of the shed; these are not very advanced and would seem to be barracks. They were not sufficiently extensive to have been hangar foundations. No men were observed at the shed quays or in the immediate vicinity – except as regards the new construction in rear.

Moral effect of raid: It was to be observed that considerable panic was prevalent amongst the workmen and others employed at the factory – and men were everywhere running in all directions – and it may be confidently expected that considerable damage was caused to the town and inhabitants by falling shell; the guns being engaged for a period of upwards of 15 to 20 minutes without ceasing.

Report on aerial defence armament: During the attack on Friedrichshafen, there were, in action, as far as could be ascertained, two automatic shrapnel throwing guns; two machine-guns of Maxim type; and a large number of rifles. As regards the defence of important places against aerial attack, I beg to submit the following remarks on the value of the types of guns encountered:

Automatic shrapnel throwing guns: With the advantage of considerable height, and operating so as to having the sun in line with the sights, I was able to observe very closely the general trend and accuracy of fire from these guns – both when directed against Lieutenant Sippe during the latter part of his escape, and against myself. Whether due to inaccuracy in the gases, or by design, consecutive shells rarely burst at the same elevation, but the difference was not much in excess of 200 feet; while at no time, except when at very close range, was the path of the projectiles within 100 feet of the machine. It seems clear that great difficulty was experienced at the guns in getting the shells correctly fused – and by descending almost vertically with the engines on, at what I judge as approximately 200 feet per second, I was enabled to keep the shrapnel bursts almost above the machine (except after a pause of some seconds in fire – after which the shells were noticeably closer, and momentarily unpleasant). It is submitted, therefore, that where automatic shrapnel-throwing guns are employed for aerial defence, the belts or feeding apparatus should be so arranged that consecutive shells are timed to burst at widely-varying ranges – as it is clear that so long as attacking aircraft are able to maintain a rapid change in elevation, there is little likelihood of their being hit. It was not possible to observe whether these shells were tracer or not.

Machine-guns and rifles: Two machine-guns and a large number of rifles were firing incessantly throughout the attack and below 300 feet. At close range, the regular discharge of Maxims and the rapid irregular fire of rifles could be distinctly heard. It is impossible, however, to give any clear account of the shooting except that for the many hundreds of rounds expended, the number of hits scored is negligible. It would seem, therefore, that no satisfactory result can be expected from Maxims or rifles against aircraft except when tracer bullets are used.

I have the honour to submit the attached report on flight of aeroplane no.874, pilot Lieutenant S V Sippe, from Belfort, for attack on Zeppelin hangars at Friedrichshafen:

Log of aeroplane no.874:

9.55am: Left Belfort. Shaped course for Basle, following nos.873 and 875.

10.23am: Arrived Basle, passed north; observed no.873 going away to south; overtook no.875. No.873 several miles to starboard. Followed Rhine at height of about 5,000 feet, keeping to north.

11am: Above clouds in Rhine Valley. No.873 passed across and took up position ahead and about a mile to port. Continued to Schaffhausen, when suddenly lost sight of no.873. No.875 about two miles astern and about same height.

11.30am: Arrived at extreme end of lake and came down to within 10 feet of water. Continued at this height over lake, passing Constance at a very low altitude, as considered less likelihood of being seen. Crossed lake and hugged north shore until five miles from objective. Started climb and reached 1,200 feet. Observed 12 or 14 shrapnels bursting slightly north of Friedrichshafen. Presumed these were directed against no.873.

11.55am: When half a mile from the sheds, put machine into dive and came down to 7,000 feet. Observed men lined up to right of shed; number estimated 300-500. Dropped one bomb in enclosure to put gunners off aim, and when in correct position, two into works and shed. The fourth bomb failed to release. During this time, very heavy fire, mitrailleuse and rifle was being kept up, and shells were being very rapidly fired. Dived and flew back north until out of range of guns, then turned back to waterside shed to try and release fourth bomb. Bomb would not release; was fired on by two machine-guns (probably mitrailleuse); dived down to surface of lake and made good my escape.

1.50pm: Arrived Belfort.

In connection with this expedition, I beg to suggest that in view of the probability of extended flights being undertaken during the forthcoming winter months, the advisability of having:

The castor oil tanks – when the rotary engines are employed – placed hard up against the engine bulkhead. In the existing machines, oil might be warmed before being used and the tanks covered with insulating jackets to prevent the radiation of heat; the petrol feeds from tanks to carburettor should be duplicated; that the base of all tanks should be armoured-plated. This protection would, probably, have obviated the accident to Commander Briggs; that the floors of the fuselage immediately beneath the pilot's knees and ankles should be armour-plated; that a much heavier type of wheel – with considerably broader hub – should be used, as on every occasion during this expedition, when a machine landed, the wheels were smashed; an increase in clearance between propeller tip and skid. The absence of clearance in this case caused the smashing of Commander Shepherd's propeller when taxiing; also reinforced tail skids.

I would further suggest that the stresses set up by chatter of tail on the ground should not be absorbed by the rudder post – as it is in the case of these machines; also, balance area of rudders should be slightly decreased.

With these few exceptions, I beg to submit that these four Avro machines, which were taken directly from the factory to and flown to Friedrichshafen without any preliminary tests whatsoever, reflect very great credit on the designers and builders concerned.

Statement made by Mr W S Churchill in the House of Commons, 23 November 1914:

On Saturday, a flight of aeroplanes under command of Squadron Commander E F Briggs, of the Royal Naval Air Service, with Flight Commander J T Babington and Flight Lieutenant S V Sippe as pilots, flew from French territory to the Zeppelin Airship Factory at Friedrichshafen. All three pilots, in succession, flew down to close range under heavy fire from guns, mitrailleuses and rifles – and launched their bombs according to instructions. Commander Briggs is reported to have been shot down, wounded and taken to hospital a prisoner. Both the other officers have returned safely to French territory – though their machines were damaged by gunfire. They report positively that all bombs reached their objectives – and that serious damage was done to the Zeppelin factory.

> This flight of 250 miles, which penetrated 10 miles into Germany across mountainous country – in difficult weather conditions – constitutes with the attack a fine feat of arms.[4]

The actual result of the raid was that one civilian was killed and two injured when a bomb hit a house in Friedrichshafen.

Commander Briggs in Avro 504 no.874 [5] was hit by small arms fire and compelled to land on the aerodrome at Friedrichshafen, where he was taken prisoner. He subsequently escaped from a prisoner of war camp.

15 December 1914

The SS *Ape* was sailing from Hull to Yarmouth and at 1610 sighted an airship travelling towards Mablethorpe – just south of the Protector Shoal buoy, north of Inner Dowsing. As the weather was misty and rainy over the North Sea, it was assumed that the airship had lost its way and had no intention of raiding England.

16 December 1914

Elements of the German High Seas Fleet, under the command of *Admiral* Franz von Hipper, carried out raids on Scarborough, Whitby and Hartlepool, Yorkshire. At 0800 the warships SMS *Derfflinger* and SMS *Von der Tann* started to shell Scarborough – hitting the Grand Hotel, three churches and various civilian properties. About 300 shells of various calibres were fired at the town – killing 17 and injuring about 100.

At 0930 the two battle cruisers moved north to Whitby, where they fired about 30 shells at the coastguard station, Whitby Abbey and other properties in the town – killing two and wounding two people.

Warships SMS *Seydlitz*, SMS *Blücher* and SMS *Molke* at 0810 started to bombard Hartlepool, with about 1,150 shells being fired at the town – hitting the steel works, gas works, railways, seven churches and 300 civilian houses (along with engaging coastal defence batteries). The light cruiser HMS *Patrol* was also seriously damaged during the engagement – and her captain was forced to ground her to prevent her from sinking.

Eighty-six civilians and seven soldiers were killed, with 424 civilians and 14 soldiers wounded.[6]

---

4 The National Archives (TNA) Air 20/412: Reports on the destruction of German airships during the Great War.

5 In accounts written at the time, Commander Briggs is recorded as flying Avro 504 no.873, although subsequent accounts give evidence that he was actually flying Avro 504 no.874. Castle, Ian. *The Zeppelin base raids, Germany 1914.* Osprey Publishing Ltd (Oxford). 2011.

6 The National Archives (TNA) Air 1/604/16/15/235: The figures given in the official account of events records that 49 men, 39 women and 39 children were killed – giving a total of 127. It is also recorded that 167 men, 178 women and 222 children were injured – totalling 567 injured – during the actions against all three towns.

Flight Commander Edward Featherstone Briggs, Royal Naval Air Service, photographed during his pre-war flying training.

An aerial view of the SMS *Seydlitz*, which was involved in the shelling of the East Coast towns on 16 December 1914.

A total of eight German sailors were killed and 12 wounded during the actions.

21 December 1914: 1300
The weather was dull, with a slight southerly wind, strength three and occasional rain.

Friedrichshafen FF.29 floatplane – no.203 of *See Flieger Abteilung 1* – dropped two HE bombs that fell into the sea about 400 yards south-west of the Admiralty Pier, Dover, Kent before heading out to sea. No damage was caused. The pilot of the aeroplane was *flugzeugführer Leutnant* Stephan von Proudzynski – and his *beobachter, Fahnrich zur See* von Frankenberg.

24 December 1914: 1055
The weather was cloudy with a slight mist; wind north-easterly, strength three.

Friedrichshafen FF.29 floatplane – no.204 of *See Flieger Abteilung 1* – dropped one HE bomb on Dover, Kent that landed in the kitchen garden of Mr Thomas A Terson (the owner of a house in Leyburne Road, near St James' Church). It left a small crater and Mr James Banks was injured when he was blown off a ladder while collecting holly for decorations at the nearby rectory. A few nearby windows were broken. The enemy aeroplane, flying at a great height, was only seen briefly from the ground through gaps in the cloud.

Once again, the crew of the aeroplane were *flugzeugführer Leutnant* Stephan von Proudzynski – and his *beobachter, Fähnrich zur See* von Frankenberg.[7]

One British aircraft took off in pursuit, but no sign of the enemy was seen.

This was the first time a bomb from an enemy aircraft was dropped on Great Britain; the first of many.

25 December 1914: 1235

Weather: The wind was very light, strength two, from the south-south-west, with the weather fine.

Friedrichshafen FF.29 floatplane – no.203 of *See Flieger Abteilung 1* – *flugzeugführer Oberleutnant zur See* Stephan Prondzynski, *beobachter Fähnrich zur See* von Frankenburg.

A German aeroplane, identified by British observers as an *Albatros*-type biplane, was spotted over the sea in the direction of Sheerness, Kent passing over the floating dock – flying from east to west at a height of about 7,000 feet. It was fired at by anti-aircraft guns situated at Sheerness, Beacon Hill and Lodge Hill at a range of about 4,000 yards, but with no apparent effect. The aeroplane then passed over Snodhurst Fort – travelling south-west up the River Medway to Chattenden – and then across the Isle of Grain at about 5,000 feet. On reaching the Thames, the aircraft turned eastwards over Gravesend and Dartford and then headed inland – passing to the north-west of Erith. By now, the German raider was being pursued by the three British aeroplanes that had taken off from the aerodromes at Eastchurch and Grain – and a Vickers FB 4 Gunbus, piloted by Second Lieutenant Montagu R Chidson, with the gunner being Corporal Martin of 7 Squadron Royal Flying Corps from Joyce Green Aerodrome. At 1320 the Gunbus no.664 overtook the enemy aeroplane at Erith – engaging it closely with machine-gun fire over Purfleet. It was then that the anti-aircraft guns fired 22 rounds – under the impression that they were all enemy machines. The result was that the two aircraft separated. Some minutes later, the German aeroplane was again spotted being pursued by a British aeroplane over Tilbury, where there was a considerable amount of fog; the movements of the two

---

7 Bavington Jones, O.G. *Dover in the European War 1914-18*. Dover Express (Snargate Street, Dover). 1919.

The plaque at the junction of Leyburne Road, Taswell Street and Taswell Close, Dover recording the events of 24 December 1914. Dover Castle is situated up the hill about a quarter of a mile to the right of the plaque.

A photograph of the junction of Leyburne Road, Taswell Street and Taswell Close, Dover.

machines appearing to be very erratic. The German aeroplane crossed the Thames at Shornmead Fort – heading north-east – and dropped two HE bombs which landed just south of Cliffe Station, but caused no damage. Soon after 1340 the German aeroplane was sighted passing over Chatham Dockyard – where again it was fired upon by anti-aircraft guns – before following the Medway as far as the Nore, which it passed at 1350 with a British aircraft pursuing it at about a mile behind. The enemy aircraft followed the coastline of Sheppy and Warden Point to Thanet before passing over Minster and out to sea in the direction of Belgium (the pursuing British aircraft abandoning the chase at Eastchurch).

The pursuing British pilot later reported that he claimed three to four hits on the enemy aircraft, but his Maxim machine-gun had jammed. His aircraft had been hit in one skid, but was unable to say whether this was due to enemy return fire, or by an anti-aircraft projectile.

Anti-aircraft guns in action and reported use of ammunition:

Location of AA battery	Calibre or type of gun used	Number / type of rounds fired
Dover, Kent		
Chatham	3”	80 shrapnel rounds
Cliffe	6 pdr	11 rounds
Thames Haven	6 pdr	11 rounds
Beacon Hill	2 × 3”	27 rounds
Lodge Hill	2 × 3”	53 rounds
Tower Hill	2 × 6 pdr	17 rounds
Detention Hill	2 × 6 pdr	30 rounds
St Mary’s Barracks	2 pdr Pom-Pom	6 rounds
Port Victoria, West	2x 6 pdr	3 rounds
Albemarle	2x 6 pdr	27 rounds
Barton Point	2x 6 pdr	11 rounds
Recreation Ground	-	6 rounds
Floating Dock (near Burntwick)	2x 6 pdr	2 rounds
Upnor	2 pdr naval gun	32 rounds
North Lock	Naval gun	12 rounds
Curtis and Harvey’s Works	6 pdr	11 rounds

It was reported that the telephones at Beacon Hill were put out of action due to the concussion from the anti-aircraft gunfire.

Dover Harbour as viewed from the air in 1914.

Friedrichshafen FF.29 float planes sit on top of railway flat wagons ready to be hoisted into the sea at Ostend, Belgium prior to operations.

The Royal Naval Air Service sent up three aeroplanes from Eastchurch and Grain aerodromes, while the Royal Flying Corps sent up one aeroplane from Joyce Green, one from Brooklands and one from Farnborough aerodromes.

A dud 13-pounder anti-aircraft shell that had been fired from the Purfleet gun fell near Dartford and was initially mistaken for a bomb.

25 December 1914

It was known that an airship shed had been built near Cuxhaven, Germany and that several reports had been received indicating that there were four Zeppelins based there.

A planned attack on the airship shed at Nordholz, near Cuxhaven, was to be undertaken by nine Royal Naval Air Service seaplanes launched from three seaplane carriers – *Engadine*, *Riviera* and *Empress* -approximately 10 miles off Helgoland, in the North Sea. The operation was to be supported by two cruisers, eight destroyers and 10 submarines. The three types of seaplane – Short Folder, Short Type 74 and Short Type 135 – were to be hoisted over the side of the carriers so as to be able to take off from the sea, but any aircraft that was not away after 15 minutes was to return to its ship and be hoisted onboard. The naval formation was then to proceed to the rendezvous point to await the return of the seaplanes – protected by the submarine force. The submarines were also to be available to rescue any ditched pilots that did not make it back to the main force. The main objective of the operation was to be the destruction of the airship sheds, but if an airship was moored outside, it too was to be attacked. In the event of a pilot being unable to reach the primary target, targets of opportunity were to be engaged, such as watercraft in the harbour at Helgoland.

In the end, seven seaplanes took off at around 0700 – each carrying three 20 lb Hales bombs. The aircraft and pilots were:

Short Type 74, no.815	Flight Commander Douglas A Oliver	HMS *Empress*
Short Type 135, no.135	Flight Commander Francis E T Hewlett	HMS *Riviera*
Short Type Folder, no.119	Flight Commander Robert P Ross	HMS *Engadine*
Short Type 135, no.136	Flight Commander Cecil F Kilner	HMS *Riviera*
Short Type Folder, no.120	Flight Lieutenant Arnold J Miley	HMS *Engasine*
Short Type 74, no.811	Flight Lieutenant Charles H K Edmonds	HMS *Riviera*
Short Type 74, no.814	Flight Sub-Lieutenant Vivian Gaskell Blackburn	HMS *Empress*

All the aeroplanes failed to find the airship shed and dropped their bombs mainly on targets of opportunity, such as warships and military installations. The ships were attacked by *Zeppelin L 6* – commanded by *Oberleutnant zur See* Treusch von Buttlar-Brandenfels – and was seen to drop nine bombs on HMS *Empress* but all missed, along with directing machine-gun fire at her before being driven off by anti-aircraft fire. *Zeppelin L 5* was also spotted during the action, but it did not come close enough to the British ships to pose a threat. Several German seaplanes also closed on the British naval formation and aimed bombs at the ships – and again all missed.

Note: Each pilot of the attacking aircraft was to supply himself with the following equipment:

Revolver and six packets of ammunition
Veries pistol and six cartridges
Perrin's lifebelt and one spare charge
Two electric torch lamps
Box of matches
Knife
Maps and charts
Provisions for 48 hours
First-aid dressing
Tools: king dicks, pliers, jet spanner, ignition wire, rubber tubing, tape, copper drift hammer, screwdriver, HH wire, special tools and spare plugs etc.[8]

A German artist's impression of the German response against the British warships.

8 The National Archives (TNA) Air 1/2099/207/23/4: Report on seaplane operations against Cuxhaven, carried out on 25 December 1914.

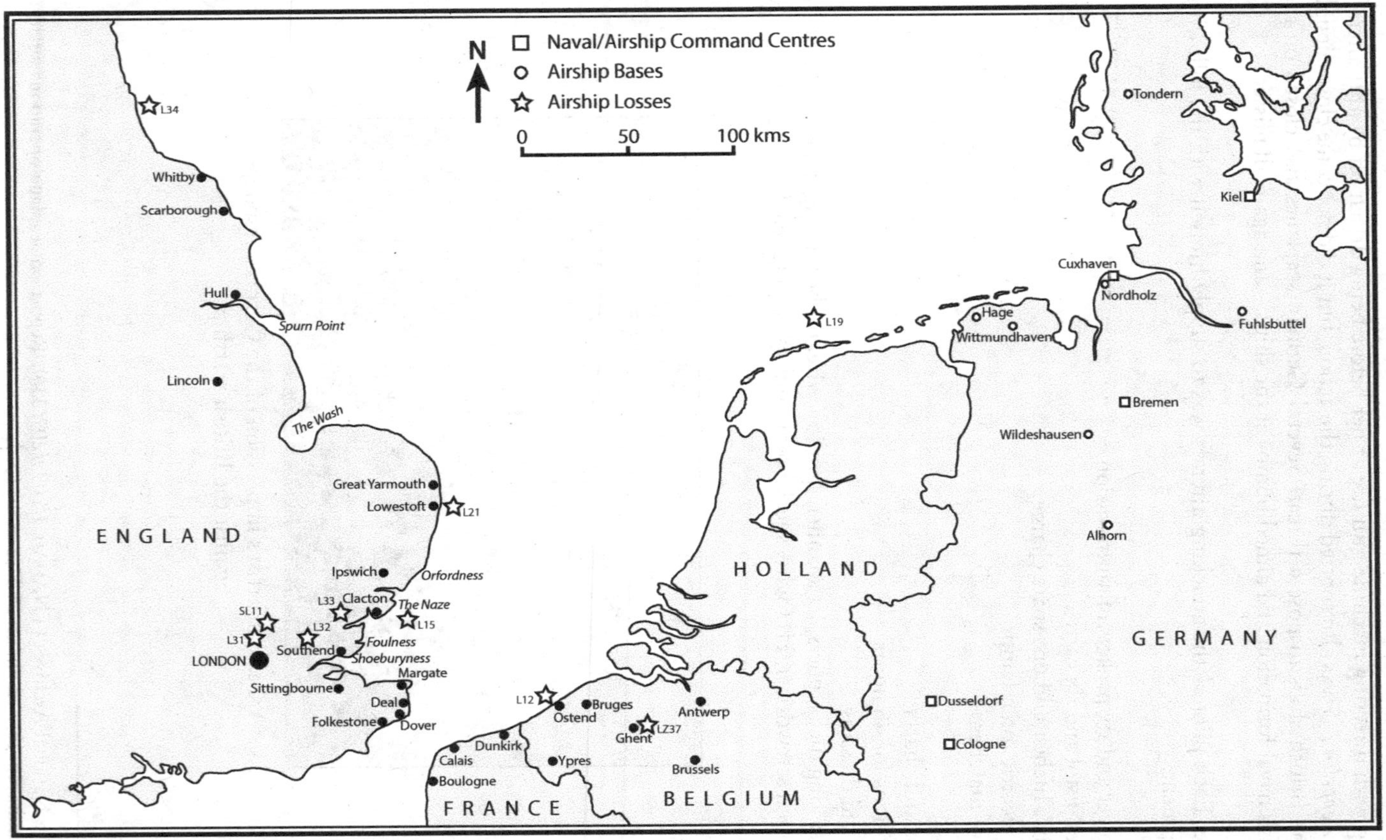

Map 2 – Airship losses / bases and the relationship of Holland to North Germany.

Part 2: 1915

At the beginning of 1915 five German naval airships were ready for expeditions against Great Britain. These were *Zeppelins L 3, L 4, L 5, L 6* and *L 7*. Initially, one or two airship reconnaissance's were pushed close to the English Coast – one of these certainly starting from the new airship sheds in Belgium, which were initially used by the German naval airship fleet due to the weakness of the army airship fleet. It was known that the new Belgian sheds were, on several occasions, occupied by the naval airships *Zeppelins L 5* and *L 8* – although the navy did not use any of the sheds for raids on the British Isles during January and April 1915 (although *Zeppelin L 8* attempted a raid starting from them in March). In the spring, new army airships of an improved design appeared, and the naval airships were then based in the North German sheds – leaving the Belgian sheds to the army airships *Zeppelins LZ 35, LZ 37, LZ 38* and *LZ 39*. The naval airship service showed, as might be expected, more appreciation than their army counterparts of the influence of meteorological conditions upon their work and never attempted to raid by moonlight (as the army airships did).

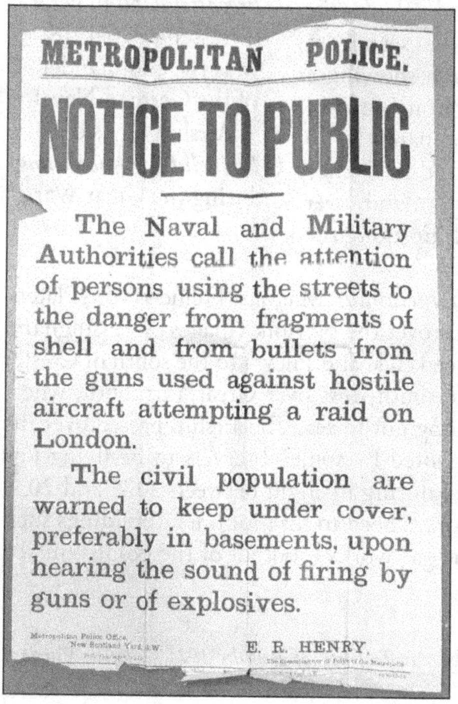

A poster issued by the Metropolitan Police on 28 December 1914 warning members of the public to take cover in the event of air raids.

10 January 1915

Two German airships left Belgium in the direction of the English Coast – probably on a reconnaissance flight – but returned without crossing the British Coast (probably due to prevailing weather conditions and strong winds over the North Sea).

19 January 1915

Weather: moderate, south-west wind, 20 miles per hour at 1,500 feet. Sky was overcast with mist and drizzling rain.

A raid was carried out on England by two German naval airships – *Zeppelins L 3* and *L 4* – although three airships were seen off the Dutch islands of Terschelling and Vlieland while returning home the next morning. It was presumed by British Intelligence that one airship – possibly *Zeppelin L 5* or *L 7* – had failed to reach the British Coast and turned back. Actually, it was *Zeppelin L 6* – commanded by *Oberleutnant zur See* Horst von Buttlar, with the head of the German Naval Airship Division, *Korvettenkapitän* Peter Strasser on board – but had to turn back due to engine trouble.[1]

Fregattenkapitän Peter Strasser (1876-1918) was the commander of the German Naval Airship Division (*Marineluftschiffabteilung*) during the Great War.

The two airships approached the British Coast in formation – making for the *Happisburgh Lightship*, which gave them their landfall. They were first seen from the British Coast at 1940 flying low – each showing a light, which was described by one observer at Ingham, Norfolk as: "Two bright stars moving, apparently 30 yards apart." Before coming in overland at 1955 they separated – one, *Zeppelin L 3*, coming inland over Happisburgh; the other, *Zeppelin L 4*, making along the coast in the direction of Bacton.

Zeppelin L 3 – commanded by *Kapitänleutnant* Magnus Freiherr von Platen-Hallermund – steered his airship south-east over the Norfolk villages of Lessingham, Ingham and Martham; then passing between Acle and Filey – to the south of Caister – and turning almost immediately to the south-west over Great Yarmouth, where the first bombs were dropped, before turning out to sea. The airship passed over the town from north-east to south, and was noted by some observers to be flying low and slowly. Nine HE bombs were dropped during its flight between 2025 and 2035 over the town, with the aim seemingly to have been to hit prominent buildings such as St Peter's Church, the drill hall and the gas works – but all of the bombs missed

1 Cole, Christopher & Cheeseman, E F. *The Air Defence of Britain 1914 – 1918.* Putnam (London). 1984.

their presumed targets. A bomb fell in Norfolk Square, two more in Crown Road and further ones in St Peter's Place, Garden Lane, Trinity House Wharf, the Fish Market, Fish Wharf and finally, one on the racecourse. The fourth bomb did the most damage, with several houses being wrecked – and most of the windows within a 40-yard radius being broken. The seventh bomb damaged some windows and roofs by concussion. The eighth fell in the river and slightly damaged a steam drifter. The fifth and ninth bombs did not explode. Two people were killed (Samuel Smith and Martha Taylor).[2]

The airship made off in a north-westerly direction and appeared to have followed the coast to Runton, where it turned out to sea at 2200.

Zeppelin L 4 – commanded by *Kapitänleutnant* Johann Fritze, which parted from *Zeppelin L 3* off Happisburgh – flew in the direction of Bacton, Norfolk; passed inland and flew along the coast to Cromer before passing out to sea. Coming back inland again, the airship circled around to the south-east between Weybourne and Sheringham at 2035. After travelling in an easterly direction over Sheringham, a flare was dropped – followed by an incendiary bomb, which hit a house in Wyndham Street – causing considerable damage, but causing no casualties. A second incendiary bomb was dropped on a building plot 300 yards further to the east. The airship was seen to go as far east as Beeston Regis and then turned north-west – and once more out to sea at 2055 (heading in a north-westerly direction off the coast towards Blakeney and Wells). The airship then again came in overland at Thornham at 2150 – an incendiary bomb being dropped in a field. From here, the raider travelled east to Brancaster Staithe, but returned to Brancaster village and dropped an incendiary bomb, which fell near the church – after which it proceeded via Holme-next-the-Sea to Hunstanton, where at 2215 an HE bomb (presumably aimed at the wireless station) fell in a field about 300 yards away. After circling over the town, which was in total darkness, the airship went out to sea twice, but returned each time and then made off along the coast to Heacham, where an incendiary bomb was dropped in a field at about 2230 close to a cottage. The airship then headed off in a south-easterly direction – dropping another incendiary bomb that landed near to a lime kiln. From here, the raider headed towards Snettisham, where an HE bomb exploded near to the church – breaking a number of windows. At this point, it was judged that the airship was so low that observers on the ground could see a light from inside the ship when the bomb doors were opened. The airship then passed over Ingoldishope, Dersingham, Wolferton, Babingley, Castle Rising, South Wootton and Gaywood before arriving over King's Lynn at 2250. The blackout in King's Lynn was deemed to be very poor – and the airship picked up the railway line at Gaywood and followed it to King's Lynn, where an HE bomb was dropped into a field next to the station. Circling out over the river, the raider returned and dropped another HE bomb on

2 Fegan, Thomas. *The Baby Killers; German Air Raids on Britain in the First World War.* Leo Cooper (Barnsley, South Yorkshire). 2002.

allotments close to the station (one HE bomb falling in Bentinck Street – demolishing two houses and damaging several more – killing a man and a woman and injuring two more civilians). A fourth HE bomb fell between East Street and Albert Street – causing considerable damage, but no one was injured. Then an incendiary bomb fell on a house in Creswell Street – causing a small fire, which was soon put out – again with nobody being hurt. A sixth bomb fell on an allotment situated at the end of Great Lewis Street, while a seventh bomb fell in the garden of a house near to the docks and an eighth HE bomb fell on the power station of the King's Lynn Docks and Railway Co – causing a considerable amount of damage to the engine room and surrounding buildings.

The airship remained hovering over King's Lynn for about 10 minutes before making off in an easterly direction and was plotted as she passed over Gayton, Westacre and Mousehole Heath – and about midnight, was seen over Acle – passing out to sea to the north of Great Yarmouth at about 0030.

No action was taken by British anti-aircraft guns or aircraft.

The three airships were sighted off the islands of Vlieland and Terscheling during the morning of 20 January. It was later reported in the German press that the crews of both raiding airships were decorated with the *Eiserne Kreuz* (Iron Cross) for their exploits.

The remains of houses in Bentinck Street in King's Lynn, which were destroyed by a single high-explosive bomb – killing two civilians and injuring two more.

Summary for 19 January 1915:

Location	Number and type of bombs dropped	Casualties	Damage
Yarmouth	9× HE	2 killed, 3 injured (including 2 soldiers)	Several houses damaged
Sheringham	2× IB		1 house damaged
Thornham	1× IB		
Brancaster	1× IB		
Hunstanton	1× HE		
Heacham	2× IB		
Snettisham	1× HE		Church damaged
Lynn	7× HE, 1× IB 2 k, 13 inj.	2 killed, 13 injured	Power station and several houses damaged; 2 houses destroyed
Total	18× HE, 7× IB	4 killed, 16 injured	

Two Royal Flying Corps aircraft from 7 Squadron were sent up to intercept the raiders, but both failed to make contact.

22 January 1915

Weather: wind light from the south-south-west and the sky overcast – clearing later during the night, with frost.

At 1710 an airship was plotted passing over Ostend, Belgium – travelling at a great speed and heading west. At 2230 the airship was sighted by a cyclist patrol at Trimingham, Norfolk – heading in the direction of Cromer. When over the cliffs, the airship appeared to stop her engines and hover for some time. Being within rifle range, she was fired at by members of the cyclist patrol. The airship then passed along the coast and was spotted at West Runton, Cromer and Sheringham before heading out to sea at about 2300.

A second airship was sighted by the admiralty ship *Louvain* over The Downs[3] off South Foreland, Kent and heading north-east at 2310 hrs – and later sighted at 2340 hrs over The Downs.

This was a reconnaissance operation by two airships that had flown from the airship sheds in Belgium. The usual practice was for airships based in Belgium and Germany

3 The Downs is an area of sea off Deal, Kent which was deemed to be a safe anchorage during storms in the English Channel and a gathering point for ships waiting to enter the Thames Estuary or the Port of Dover.

to operate on alternate nights. The identity of the airships was not established, but could have either been *Zeppelins L 3, L 4, L 5, L 6* or *L 7.*

25 January 1915
Parseval PL 19.
Damaged by anti-aircraft fire following operations against Liepaja, Latvia and compelled to land on the Baltic Sea.
Crew taken prisoner by Russian forces.[4]

17 February 1915
Zeppelin L 3 / LZ 24. Type M.
Near Farnö, Denmark.
Force landed due to a snowstorm on return from operations.
Sixteen crew interned.
Kommandeur: Kapitänleutnant Hans Fritz.

Zeppelin L 4 / LZ 27. Type M.
Blavandshuk, Denmark.
Force landed while returning from operations due to lack of fuel in a snowstorm.
Kommandeur: Kapitänleutnant Magnus Graf von Platen-Hallermund.
Obermaschinistenmaat Max Breuer +.
Obermaschinistenmaat Franz Kunze +.
Maschinistenmaat Johann Reuters +.
Maschinistenmaat Georg Gräf +.
Maschinist Ernst Eckert +.
Von Platen and 10 of his crew were interned; their names were not recorded.

21 February 1915
Weather: the day was fine, with slight local rain, the wind being very light. The moon being in its second quarter did not rise until 0215 on 22nd February.

A German aeroplane – *Friedrichshafen FF 29*, no.203 of *See Flieger Abteilung 1* – piloted by *flugzeugführer Oberleutnant zur See* Stephan Prondzynski, with *beobachter Fähnrich zur See* Heym passed over the English Coast at Clacton, Essex at 1945 and proceeded to fly west over Brightlingsea at 1905 – passing over Inworth and Kelvdon at 2020 and onto Braintree. At 2030 it dropped an incendiary bomb, which fell within 100 yards of the railway line – along which a train was travelling, but caused no damage. The enemy aircraft then turned back and dropped another incendiary bomb one mile to the east of Braintree. The bomb was said to have been picked

4 *Parseval PL 19* had originally been ordered by the Royal Navy as *Parseval no.5* but on the outbreak of war, it was taken over by the German Navy and renamed.

A *Friedrichshafen FF 29* having just returned from operations over the English Channel.

up by a soldier and thrown into the River Blackwater. The raider then flew east to Coggeshall, where at 2035 an HE bomb was dropped, but the blast only broke a few windows in the town. Finally, the aeroplane passed over Mark Tey's to Colchester – and at 2045 another HE bomb was dropped, which fell in Butt Road, near the artillery barracks. A shed and part of a house were damaged, but there were no casualties. After this, the German aircraft flew in a north-easterly direction over Bradford and Shingle Street before passing out to sea in a northerly direction at 2142.

During the duration of the raid, no aeroplanes took off to try and intercept the raider – nor did the anti-aircraft guns fire.

It was later reported that the aircraft suffered engine problems over the North Sea and had to land on the water – damaging one of its floats in the process. The two airmen were picked up by a British ship after 36 hours at sea and were landed at Lowestoft by the tug *New Boy* on 27 February.

Summary for 21 February 1915:

Location	Number and type of bombs dropped	Casualties	Damage
Braintree	2× IB		
Coggeshall	1× HE		
Colchester	1× HE		
Total	2× HE, 2× IB		

23 February 1915: 1600
Weather: wind was strength one from the south-west, with clear visibility.

HMS *Hearty* reported seven German aeroplanes passing over the *Maplin Lightship* at 1600 at a great height. The Royal Naval Air Service Station at Eastchurch sent up one aeroplane, but the crew reported no sighting of any aircraft.

It was reported that bombs were dropped near to the *Gabbard Lightship* by two *Friedrichshafen FF 29*s of *See Flieger Abteilung 1* on 22 February 1915 at 1025 – which may have been confused with the latter incident.[5]

26 February 1915: 1030
Weather: light winds from the north-west, with snow showers developing during the night.

Two *Friedrichshafen FF 29* aeroplanes of *See Flieger Abteilung 1* attempted to bomb HMS *Cordoba*, which was sailing about two miles west of the *Sunk Lightship* in the North Sea, but missed.

Two naval seaplanes took off to intercept the raiders, but failed to make contact.

4 March 1915
Zeppelin L 8 / LZ 33. Type M.
Tirlemont, France.

Having attempted a raid on England, the returning airship – having got lost in cloud – came down to ascertain her position and was hit by anti-aircraft fire off Nieuport, Belgium (five of her gas bags being punctured). She came down very low – just clearing chimney stacks at Tirlemont – crashed into trees and was wrecked.
Kommandeur: Kapitänleutnant Helmut Beelitz.

20 March 1915: 1035
Weather: there was a light breeze from the west or north-west – prevailing over the North Sea and South-East England; strength four, with weather generally fair.

Four German aeroplanes – consisting of three *Friedrichshafen FF 29*s and one *Oertz FB 3* flying boat of *See Flieger Abteilung 1* – were seen flying towards The Downs, off Kent – and at 1105 they separated with one aircraft, heading towards Ramsgate; the others heading back out to sea and the French Coast. At 1135 the lone raider dropped six bombs near a coastal steamer, which was sailing in the gateway of The Downs, but failed to secure any hits. The aeroplane was then heard heading off in a north-easterly direction.

---

5 Cole & Cheeseman – *The Air Defence Britain 1914 -1918.*

21 March 1915
Zeppelin Z X / LZ 29. Type M.
Near St Quion, France.
Stranded, due to loss of hydrogen, following enemy action following a raid on Paris.
Kommandeur: Hauptmann Alfred Horn.

13 April 1915
Zeppelin LZ 35 / LZ 35. Type M.
Near Aeltre, Belgium.
Damaged by anti-aircraft fire during a raid on Poperinghe, Belgium and crashed.
Kommandeur: Hauptmann Masius.

The airship had taken part in an air raid on Paris at the end of March, but never took part in an attack on England.

14 April 1915
Weather: practically no wind, but there was slight rain or mist over the mouth of the Tyne. North Sea was foggy; the night being very dark.

Zeppelin L 9 – commanded by *Kapitänleutnant* Heinrich Mathy – was spotted off the mouth of the Tyne and coasted as far as Blyth, where she was plotted off the harbour at 1930 (and it appeared bearings were being taken) before proceeding up the River Blyth to Cambois, where she was fired at by members of 'C' Company of the 1st Northern Cyclist Battalion, with their rifles. Over West Sleekburn, an incendiary bomb was dropped into a field before the airship headed towards Choppington, Northumberland – dropping another four incendiary bombs en route (all of which landed in fields – causing no damage). A sixth incendiary bomb was dropped in front of a house at Choppington – breaking a window in the Station Hotel at 2000. Three HE bombs landed on Glebe Farm, Choppington before the airship turned south – dropping another three bombs (two HE and one incendiary), which landed in fields west of Bedlington – and a 50 kg HE bomb landed in a field at Crowhall Farm (narrowly missing two police constables). Proceeding towards West Cramlington, the raider released another incendiary bomb – which again fell in a field – before the airship was seen hovering for a while (the crew presumably trying to establish their position). Three more incendiary bombs fell soon after in the vicinity of a railway line, but fell wide of the mark. On the way to Seaton Burn, another incendiary bomb fell – again causing no damage – along with one that fell on the village. The airship then turned west towards Dinnington Colliery, where an HE bomb fell in a field – leaving a large crater. Over Benton, another incendiary bomb fell – again into a field near to the railway station – but of six incendiary bombs that were dropped at Wallsend, three did no damage (but a fourth went through the roof of a cottage – injuring a woman and her daughter, who was having a bath). The other two bombs set fire to some railway sleepers. An HE bomb fell into the River Tyne between the electric power station and Castner and Kellner's Works; the blast from the explosion breaking windows on both sides of the river. Finally, an incendiary bomb fell at 2048 on Hebburn Quay on the south side of the river – striking a concrete floor of a dry dock and causing no damage. The airship was observed to pass out to sea at Marsden, between Sunderland and South Shields.

Two aeroplanes took off in pursuit of the raider, but failed to spot it – although it was claimed that the airship never exceeded a height of 2,000 feet.

Summary for 14 April 1915:

Location	**Number and type of bombs dropped**	**Casualties**	**Damage**
West Sleekburn	1× IB		
Barrington	4× IB		
Choppington	3× HE, 1× IB		Window broken
Bedlington	3× HE, 1× IB		
Cramlington	1× HE, 5× IB		Warehouse damaged
Seaton Burn	2× IB		
Dinnington	1× HE		
Benton	1× IB		
Wallsend	6x IB	2 injured	Cottage and railway damaged
In the River Tyne	1× HE		
Hebburn	1× IB		
Total	9× HE, 22× IB	2 injured	

15 April 1915

Weather: cloudy and misty, with a light westerly wind increasing slightly during the night to about 15 miles per hour at 1,500 feet. The sky was moonless.

Three airships raided England – *Zeppelins L 7* and *L 9* operating from Germany and *Zeppelin LZ 37* from Belgium.[6]

6 *The Official History, The War in the Air volume III* (Jones, H A. Oxford University Press, 1931, pp. 95-6) records that it was *Zeppelin L 5*, commanded by *Kapitänleutnant der Reserve* Böcker, rather than *Zeppelin L 9* – under *Kapitänleutnant* Mathy – who took part in operations on this night and carried out the raid on Southwold, Reydon and Lowestoft.

Zeppelin L 6, commanded by *Kapitänleutnant* von Buttlar, is recorded as having taken part in operations on this night rather than *LZ 37* (under *Kapitänleutnant* von Haegen). *Zeppelin L 6* is also recorded as having bombed Maldon and Leybridge. She was noted to have returned from this operation having been hit 25 times by anti-aircraft shells and ·303 bullets.

Zeppelin L 7, commanded by *Kapitänleutnant* zur See Peterson, is recorded as also carrying *Fregattenkapitän* Peter Strasser on this raid.

Zeppelin LZ 37 – commanded by *Oberleutnant zur See* Otto van der Haegen – was reported off Lydd, Kent at 2122 and reached Walton-on-the-Naze at 2330. Having coursed around over Essex, she dropped her first two HE bombs on Maldon at 0020 and another two on the village of Heybridge along with a scattering of about 30 incendiary bombs on both targets. In Maldon, a house was damaged along with a chicken coop; a girl was injured – being the only casualty. The airship was sighted over Brightlingsea, where the guard at a camp of The Royal Engineer Field Companies opened fire. At 0056 the airship was over Landguard Fort and Felixstowe, Essex where she was fired at by a Pom-Pom gun, which fired three rounds and rifle fire from Landguard, as she was estimated to be at a height of only 5,000 feet. At 0122 she was last heard passing over the Shipwash – heading out to sea.

Zeppelin L 9 – commanded by *Kapitänleutnant* Heinrich Mathy – was plotted hovering over the sea off the Suffolk Coast, near Southwold at 2140 but did not come inland until 2350 at Reydon. As she passed Bramfield, the airship was fired at by soldiers using ·303 rifles, but continued towards Halesworth and Henham Hall, where at 0025 one HE bomb and 23 incendiary bombs were dropped – falling near to the Red Cross Hospital, but caused no damage or casualties. Two minutes later, another HE and three incendiary bombs fell at Reydon – again causing no damage. Circling around to the south-east to Southwold at 0030 one incendiary bomb fell into a goods truck at the station and another on the beach close to the pier. Turning back – and once more passing over Reydon – another HE and incendiary bomb were dropped, with another two incendiaries falling at Easton Bavents, where the 6th Battalion Sussex Cyclists opened fire with their rifles; then heading off to Lowestoft, the raider stopped her engines to hover over the town – and at 0115 an HE bomb fell near the central station and harbour before she started her engines and headed off following the course of the river to Oulton Broad – dropping two HE and seven incendiaries en route. Several houses were damaged and a fire was started in a timber yard; two horses were killed and four civilians were injured at the railway station.

Zeppelin L 7 – commanded by *Oberleutnant zur See* Werner Peterson – came in overland at Brancaster, Norfolk at 0140 on 16 April and passed in a south-easterly direction – along the coast to Cromer and Happisburgh – before crossing out to sea at Gorleston at 0235 (dropping no bombs during her time while overland).

Zeppelin L 9 during a pre-operational test flight landing at Friedrichshafen Aerodrome, with the airship construction sheds in the background.

Summary for 15 April 1915:

Location	Number and type of bombs dropped	Casualties	Damage
Maldon	2× HE	1 injured	House damaged; fowl house destroyed
Heybridge	2× HE, 30× IB		
Henham Hall	1× HE, 23× IB		
Reydon	2× HE, 4× IB		Windows and roof of a cottage damaged
Southwold	2× IB		Railway station and track damaged
Easton Bavents	2× IB		
Lowestoft and Oulton Broad	3× HE, 7× IB		2 houses, stables and timber yard damaged; 6 horses killed and injured
Total	10× HE, 68× IB	1 injured	

Anti-aircraft guns in action and their reported use of ammunition:

Location of AA battery	Calibre or type of gun	Number / type of rounds fired
Landguard Fort, Harwich	–	3 rounds
Landguard Fort, Harwich	·303 rifle fire	–
Easton Bavents (6th Sussex Cyclists)	·303 rifle fire	–

The Mobile Section, Royal Naval Air Service sent out five anti-aircraft gun detachments, which failed to spot the airship.

The Royal Naval Air Service Station at Yarmouth dispatched one seaplane, but the crew failed to sight the enemy.

16 April 1915

Weather: fair, with some mist and cloud along the English Coast; wind being westerly, strength one.

At 1140 a German monoplane – an *Albatros B II* of *Feldflieger Abteilung 41* – crossed the English Coast at Kingsdown, Kent and was soon after reported over Ash – near Sandwich – making towards Herne Bay, where it turned out to sea. It then turned back again and came in overland at the mouth of the River Swale – passing Harty Ferry and appearing over Faversham at 1210. Due to an identification misunderstanding, the three-inch anti-aircraft gun at Faversham did not fire until the aeroplane was almost directly over the battery, and then fired seven rounds before the target was obscured by clouds. The enemy machine was then plotted flying westward at a height of 8,000 feet – and approaching Sittingbourne, it turned to the south-west towards Borden and dropped one HE bomb at Cryal's Farm and another near an engine house about half a mile from the church at 1220. Two more HE bombs were then dropped at Gore Court to the south of Sittingbourne; one of these fell about 300 yards from a military camp. The German aeroplane then flew off to the north-west and Kingsferry Bridge – over the River Swale – where it dropped one bomb before passing over the southern part of the Isle of Sheppey, crossed the River Swale again and at 1230 came in towards Faversham from the south-west. The Faversham Anti-Aircraft Battery resumed firing at ranges from 3,000 to 5,800 yards before the aeroplane was once again obscured by cloud, but not before 22 rounds of three-inch ammunition had been expended. In reply to this, five incendiary bombs were dropped to the south of Faversham – no damage or casualties being caused as they fell on a road and cultivated land. The aircraft carried on flying in an east-north-east direction and passed over Canterbury at 1245 – and at 1300 was plotted near Deal. It was last seen at 1350 over the sea off Deal heading in a northerly direction.

Summary for 16 April 1915:

Location	Number and type of bombs dropped	Casualties	Damage
Near Sittingbourne	4× HE		
Kingsferry Bridge	1× HE		
Faversham	5× HE		
Total	10× HE		

Anti-aircraft guns in action and their reported use of ammunition:

Location of AA battery	Calibre or type of gun	Number / type of rounds fired
Faversham	3" semi-automatic	29 rounds

Eight Royal Naval Air Service aircraft from Eastchurch – two from Manstone and three from Dover aerodromes – took off to intercept the raider, but the pilots reported as having failed to sight their quarry.

A pair of *Albatros B II* aeroplanes are prepared for operations.

18 April 1915
Weather: fine, with a very light wind from the south-east; the skies being cloudless.

An air raid was apparently attempted, with an airship being reported off the *Sunk Lightship* at 2140 but it did not cross the coast.

29 April 1915
Weather: wind moderate from east-north-east at 1,500 feet, but very light at 6,000 feet. Fog was generally on the coast, clear inland.

A raid was carried out under a full moon, but the weather was foggy on the East Coast of England, which helped conceal the raider. The raid was carried out by a single army airship – probably *Zeppelin LZ 37* commanded by *Oberleutnant zur See* Otto van der Haegen, which was first reported off the *Galloper Lightship* at 2300 as 30 miles south-east of Harwich, heading west. At 2355 the airship crossed the English Coast at Old Felixstowe and headed straight inland – reaching Ipswich at 0010 where five incendiary bombs were dropped, although one failed to ignite. One fell on a house in Brookshall Road – setting fire to it and adjoining houses – but there were no casualties and no other damage caused. Soon after, another five incendiary bombs fell at Bramford, but this time caused no damage – and at 0020 five HE and 11 incendiary bombs fell at Nettestead and Willisham, seven miles north-west of Ipswich (again causing no damage, apart to crops). Half an hour later, the airship reached Bury St Edmunds, which she circled three or four times before at 0100 dropping three HE and 40 incendiary bombs on the town, which set fire to four houses in the Butter Market. There were, however, no casualties. The raider then made off eastwards at about a height of 3,000 feet, as she could be plainly seen from Bury in the clear moonlit night. An HE bomb was dropped on Bredfield and another on Woolpit, but no damage was caused in either incident. At 0115 she reached Creeting St Mary, where an incendiary bomb was dropped, and another at Otley – followed by a further one at Bredfield at 0127 and another three minutes later at Melton (and a final one Bromswell); the results being the same. The airship passed out to sea at Orfordness at 0150 – turning north to follow the coast – passing over Aldeburgh at 0200 and was last heard at 0220 heading in the same direction. It was estimated that the airship's speed overland was between 50 to 60 miles per hour at a height of about 3,000 feet, but no action was taken by the defences as the mobile anti-aircraft guns of the Royal Naval Air Service reached Bury St Edmunds at 0145 – three-quarters of an hour after the raid – and it was deemed too foggy on the coast for aeroplanes to take off.

Summary for 29 April 1915:

Location	**Number and type of bombs dropped**	**Casualties**	**Damage**
Ipswich	5× IB		2 houses burnt out; 1 damaged
Bramford	3× IB		
Nettlestead and Willisham	5× HE, 11x IB		
Bury St Edmunds	3× HE, 40x IB		4 houses burnt out
Bredfield	1× HE		
Woolpit	1× HE		
Creeting St Mary	1× IB		
Otley	1× IB		
Bredfield	1× IB		
Melton	1× IB		
Bromswel	1× IB		
Total	10× HE, 64× IB		

The objective of the raid may have been Stowmarket, where the explosive works – established prior to the outbreak of the war – would have been well-known to the Germans. It is probable though that the airship commander missed his objective due to the fog and found himself over a lighted town which may have appeared to be Stowmarket. The great number of incendiary bombs dropped was a characteristic of army airships.

10 May 1915

Weather: a strong north-easterly wind; 40 miles per hour at 1,500 feet. Fine with little cloud and no moon.

At 0245 the army airship *Zeppelin LZ 38* – commanded by *Hauptmann* Erich Linnarz – appeared over the *SS Royal Edward* which was moored off Southend, Essex as a prisoner of war hulk and dropped an incendiary bomb, which fell close to the port side of the ship – the flames leaping up to a height of 10 to 12 feet and lasting nearly half a minute. The airship then travelled towards Southend and dropped two more bombs that fell in the water, and four HE (and a further 90 incendiary bombs) that fell on the town – two of the HE bombs failing to explode. After leaving the Southend area, she passed over Leigh and Canvey Island, where she was fired at by the anti-aircraft guns situated at Thames Haven and Curtis & Harvey's Explosive Works, Cliffe; two hits being sustained, with one shell having passed through her stern. The airship immediately did an about-turn and headed back over Southend – dropping further incendiary bombs at 0310 before passing out to sea. In Southend, one house was set alight, where a woman was killed and a man injured. A timber yard was also burnt out and a private of the 10th Border Regiment was injured.

Although a large number of fires were started in Southend, the fire brigade was commended for its energy in dealing with the fires before they could take hold and cause serious damage.

After the raid, a note was found – written in blue pencil on a piece of cardboard – and said:

> "You English. We have come and will come again soon. Kill or Cure. German."

Summary for 10 May 1915:

Location	**Number and type of bombs dropped**	**Casualties**	**Damage**
Southend	4x HE, 90x IB	2 killed, 2 injured	House and timber yard burnt out; several houses damaged by fire and concussion
Total:	4x HE, 90x IB	2 killed, 2 injured	

Anti-aircraft guns in action and their reported use of ammunition:

Location of AA battery	**Calibre or type of gun**	**Number / type of rounds fired**
Thames Haven	6 pdr	22 rounds
Thames Haven	1 pdr	49 rounds
Cliffe	3"	10 rounds
Cliffe	6 pdr	8 rounds

Eleven Royal Naval Air Service aircraft took off to intercept the raider, but none of the crews sighted the airship, which was estimated to be flying at a height of between 9,000-10,000 feet.

17 May 1915

Weather: light south-westerly wind, 20 miles per hour at 1,500 feet. Cloudy skies, dull but clear.

Flying from their bases in Belgium, three airships attempted to raid targets on the French and English Coasts. The airships involved were *Zeppelin LZ 37*, commanded by *Oberleutnant zur See* Otto van der Haegen; *Zeppelin LZ 38*, commanded by *Hauptmann* Erich Linnarz; and *Zeppelin LZ 39*, commanded by *Hauptmann* Masius.

Calais, France was bombed by *Zeppelin LZ 37* at 1145, 16 May and also at 0045, 17 May – the airship returning to Ghent, Belgium at 0200 having not joined the other two airships in proceeding across the English Channel.

At 0030 *Zeppelin LZ 38* was spotted hovering off North Foreland, Kent and dropped some bombs into the sea before approaching Ramsgate, but was fired at by anti-aircraft guns mounted on drifters, so turned north and was seen off the *Tongue Lightship* around 0100. At 0140 she came overland at Margate and flew across Thanet before dropping four HE and 16 incendiary bombs on Ramsgate – one HE bomb striking the Bull and George Hotel (penetrating to the basement and blowing out the whole front of the building). A man and a woman were seriously injured – dying three days later; another woman was slightly injured. Although a number of other buildings were slightly damaged – along with some fishing smacks – there were no further casualties. The raider then passed out to sea and followed the coast down as far as Deal and re-crossed the coast at 0210 where she hovered with propellers stopped for a while before heading towards Dover. The Dover Garrison anti-aircraft guns opened fire at 0225 and the airship was caught by searchlights, so rose to about 7,000 feet after dropping a dense cloud of water ballast and 33 incendiary bombs, which fell at Oxney. As the airship headed north, she was fired at by the guardship in The Downs – and at 0250 was sighted hovering over the North Goodwins until 0325 when she headed back towards Belgium as the day was dawning – crossing the Allied Lines near Armentières, France at 0420.

Zeppelin LZ 39 – although aiming to raid England – did not reach the British Coast, but returned to base due to some technical defect. As *Zeppelin LZ 39* passed Dunkirk, France at 0315 aircraft searching for *Zeppelin LZ 38* spotted her and went in pursuit. At 0330 she was attacked off Nieuport, Belgium by eight Allied aircraft – including one being flown by Flight Sub-Lieutenant Warneford, who was piloting a Nieuport with an observer, but found that weighed down with a Lewis gun, ammunition, hand-grenades and a ·45 inch calibre rifle he could not get his aircraft to climb sufficiently. At a height of 5,000 feet, Warneford's observer opened fire at the airship, which was 1,000 feet above them – and when the airship climbed, they could not follow. Flight Commander Bigsworth, in an Avro, climbed to 10,000 feet and overtook the airship off Ostend – and passing above from stern to bow, dropped four 20 lb bombs on the raider. Bigsworth reported noticing some heavy black pungent smoke coming out of the airship about 100 feet from the tail, but was unable to linger due to the heavy and accurate anti-aircraft gunfire that was being directed at him from Ostend. At the same time that Flight Commander Bigsworth was carrying out his bombing attack, Squadron Commander S Grey – in a Nieuport – had reached a height of 9,800 feet and was abreast of *Zeppelin LZ 39* and attacked the rear gondola with his ·303 Lewis gun from about 50 to 100 feet below, but was driven off by sustained gunfire from the two machine-guns mounted in each of the airship's gondolas. The airship was last seen proceeding at 0500 at a height of 11,000 feet in the direction of Ghent, Belgium. She safely reached her airfield at Evere, where the body of an officer and a number of wounded crew were removed.

It was later disclosed that five gas bags in *Zeppelin LZ 39* had been damaged and the starboard aft propeller had been blown off. She was finally housed at Berchem, where the damaged gas bags were repaired and the starboard propeller was replaced – along with the damaged sustained in landing (which was rectified). Due to the time taken to complete the repairs, she took no further part in operations against Great Britain – being moved to the Eastern Front, where she was severely damaged during operations against Rovno in November 1915 and decommissioned on return to base.

Summary for 17 May 1915:

Location	Number and type of bombs dropped	Casualties	Damage
Ramsgate	4× HE, 16× IB	2 killed, 1 injured	Hotel badly damaged
Oxney	33× IB		
At sea	?		
Total	4× HE, 49× IB + ?	2 killed, 1 injured	

Anti-aircraft guns in action and reported use of ammunition:

Location of AA battery	Calibre or type of gun	Number / type of rounds fired
Ramsgate	Naval guns on drifters	–
Ramsgate	Rifle fire	–
Dover	6 pdr	5 rounds
Dover	1 pdr	28 rounds
The Downs	Naval guns	–

Ten aircraft took off to intercept the airship (one from Royal Naval Air Service Aerodrome at Westgate, one from Royal Naval Air Service Aerodrome at Eastchurch and eight from Dunkirk Aerodrome, France – two aircraft making contact).

The official summary regarding the interception of the Zeppelin stated:

> At 0045 hrs a message was received from Anti-Aircraft Command that one Zeppelin had dropped bombs at Deal and, subsequently, that it had been seen over Westgate and Ramsgate proceeding south-east after changing its course towards Dover. At 0100 a message was received that an airship was over Calais and had dropped bombs there at 0045 – thus proving that there were two Zeppelins. At 0245 Flight Sub-Lieutenant Kilner, in a Voisin, left with orders to proceed up the coast as far as Zeebrugge and to endeavour to attack any airships making the Belgian Coast at dawn. At 0320 Flight Sub-Lieutenant Warneford, with passenger Leading Mechanic Meddis, left in a Nieuport with similar orders. As he left the ground, a Zeppelin was sighted at 0320 about 10 to 15 miles out to sea – opposite La Panne – proceeding slowly towards Ostend (height about 5,000 feet with its nose up in the air).
>
> The following pilots were dispatched to attack it:
> Flight Commander Bigsworth in Avro no.1009.
> Squadron Commander Spenser Grey in a Nieuport.
> Flight Lieutenant Haskins in Avro no.1004.
> Flight Sub-Lieutenant Marsden in Morane no.3240.
> Wing Commander Longmore in Maurice Farman no.1347.
>
> And from the Furnes Aerodrome:
> Flight Commander Babington in Avro no.1003.
> Flight Sub-Lieutenant Huskisson in Voisin no.555.

Flight Sub-Lieutenant Kilner reported that he proceeded as far as Zeebrugge (height about 5,000 feet). On returning, he sighted the Zeppelin at 0335 off the Belgian Coast between Ostend and Middlekerke. He estimated her height at 8,000 feet. Owing to a misfiring engine, he was unable to climb sufficiently to attack it. On sighting him, the airship turned inland towards Ostend and started to climb very steeply. He reported that the colour of the airship, with the sun on it, appeared to him to be a lightish yellow. He saw no marks on it. He estimated her speed to be 40 miles per hour – and he last saw the Zeppelin above Ostend heading approximately south-east. The armament he took with him consisted of six 10 lb bombs and a .45 inch calibre rifle with incendiary bullets.

Flight Sub-Lieutenant R A J Warneford – who left at 0320 – reported that after about five minutes in the air, he sighted the Zeppelin out to sea. He proceeded along the coast – endeavouring to climb. He had reached 5,000 feet when abreast of Ostend, and appeared to be about 1,000 feet below the airship – at which time it started climbing. His passenger opened fire with the .45 inch calibre rifle – and using flaming bullets (the first of which flamed correctly and could be followed the whole way) hit the Zeppelin somewhere in the nose without effect. The next three shots did not flame and the fifth shot flamed and hit between the gondolas. By this time, the airship had risen too high and was out of range. Warneford, therefore, proceeded towards Zeebrugge – endeavouring to gain height – but found that with the weight of a passenger, Lewis gun and ammunition, hand-grenades, a .45 rifle and incendiary bullets, he could not climb sufficiently. Whilst over Zeebrugge, he sighted a submarine, followed by a small merchant steamer, which had just left the harbour and was proceeding in a north-westerly direction. He came down 2,000 feet and attacked it with his hand-grenades, which all went off correctly. He remarked that the colour of the airship, with the sun on it, appeared to be greyish-white and that he last saw her about seven miles east-south-east of Ostend – proceeding in a south-easterly direction.

Flight Commander A W Bigsworth, in Avro no.1009, proceeded up the coast – keeping the Zeppelin in sight. When abreast of Nieuport, he was at 8,000 feet and then appeared to be abreast of – and at the same height as – the Zeppelin, which was 10 miles out. He circled and climbed to 10,000 feet and then followed the coast to Ostend – at which place, he overtook the Zeppelin and passed over her from stern to bow at about 200 feet above her. He dropped his four 20 lb bombs in a line along her back, which he could see distinctly – and afterwards, he turned starboard and passed abreast in the opposite direction. At this moment, he noticed very heavy black pungent smoke coming out of the airship at about 100 feet from her tail, which appeared to be the result of one of his bombs. The actual time of the attack was 0450 – and by this time, the Zeppelin was almost directly above Ostend – steering about east-north-east; yawing considerably above five points on either side. Very heavy and accurate anti-aircraft fire was directed on him in spite of his proximity to the airship – and the noise of the bursting of shell was so intense that he was quite unable to distinguish it from the burst of the bombs. He considered the colour of the airship to be neutral muddy-brown – as viewed from the side away from the sun. He noticed some markings in black on the side, but he did not actually locate what they were. He noticed some number on the fin. No gun, or any other object, was to be seen on top of the Zeppelin – and he did not observe any fire opened from the latter. No flag was flying. Flight Commander Bigsworth then proceeded direct out to sea to escape from the very heavy shell fire, which was extremely accurate (even at a height of 10,000 feet).

Squadron Commander Spenser Grey reached a height of about 9,800 feet when abreast of the airship, but as the airship was climbing at the time, he decided to attack the rear gondola with his Lewis gun, which he did from about 50-100 feet below it. He was subjected to very heavy machine-gun fire – and four machine-guns were sighted (two in each gondola).

He reported that:

> The gondola seemed to be about 300 feet apart – and that he judged the length of the Zeppelin to be about 450 feet. No machine-guns were mounted on the top of the fuselage. There did not appear to be any aluminium casing. The

> colour of the fabric was muddy and of a neutral tint. The propellers were only turning from 300 to 400 revolutions. He was at a height of 9,600 feet when close to her, but she very rapidly climbed about 1,500 to 2,000 feet immediately after the attack and headed for the south-east. Big markings of a blue description were visible on the envelope. No ensign was observed.

This attack was carried out about five to 10 minutes before that of Flight Commander Bigsworth, but owing to not being able to get above the airship, this officer was unable to use his hand-grenades. All the other machines, which went out, did not have time to climb to the requisite height to carry out an attack from above before the airship was lost in sight in the direction of Ghent. Mist and rain came on at 0630 which prevented further reconnaissance to ascertain her whereabouts. When last seen – at about 0500 – the airship was at a height of about 12,000 feet, with her tail down, in the region of Ghent, Belgium.

A report that a second Zeppelin had passed in the region of Armentières at approximately 0420 was received from the Royal Flying Corps.

20 May 1915
Zeppelin Z XI / LZ 30. Type M.
Posen, Germany.
Damaged while leaving its hangar; caught fire and burnt out.
Kommandeur: Hauptmann Gaissert.

21 May 1915
Zeppelin LZ 34 / LZ 34. Type M.
Insterburg, East Prussia, Germany (now Chemyakhovsk, Kaliningrad, Russia).
Gas leak due to enemy action and caught fire in emergency landing.
Kommandeur: Hauptmann Jacobi.

23 May 1915
Weather: fine, with a rising barometer, with the wind north-north-east, strength six.

A German *Albatros* floatplane dropped bombs in the vicinity of shipping off the Goodwin Sands at about 0930 – and at 0950 was spotted over Westgate, Kent before disappearing. In the early afternoon, another aeroplane was seen flying towards Dover, Kent from the direction of the English Channel – dropping bombs on shipping off the town before disappearing out to sea. Four Royal Naval Air Service aeroplanes took off from Eastchurch and Westgate aerodromes to intercept the raiders, but the pilots reported that nothing was seen. No anti-aircraft guns were brought to action.

A display of the perceived stores needed to mount an aeroplane operation against the British Isles. Whether all of this paraphernalia was carried on every operation is dubious. Of note are the large quantities of oil and lubricants that the early aeroplanes used, along with fuel. The requirement for a sea anchor seems a little superfluous.

26 May 1915

Weather: wind at 1,500 feet was 25 miles per hour from the north-east; the skies overall clear, but misty in places. The moon was in its first quarter – setting before 0200 on 27 May.

At 2118 *Zeppelin LZ 38* – commanded by *Hauptmann* Erich Linnarz – was sighted off Dunkirk, France heading west towards Britain, and was next reported at 2230 off Clacton-on-Sea, Essex. She then passed south-west via Bradwell-juxta-Mare at 2250 to Southminster – arriving at 2253. Here she was fired at by a Pom-Pom anti-aircraft gun and turned south towards Burnham-on-Crouch shortly before 2300. At 2305 she passed over Shoeburyness – under fire from a three-inch anti-aircraft gun – and turned west to Southend, where at 2313 she dropped 23 small HE bombs or grenades and 47 incendiary bombs. Two women were killed – although one was hit by shrapnel from an anti-aircraft shell and a girl was injured. The airship then went off in a north-easterly direction and was again engaged by the Shoeburyness anti-aircraft gun before passing Wakering and Burnham – where she was fired at by 'A' Company of the 2/8th Battalion Essex Regiment – then onto Bradwell and passed out to sea at the mouth of the River Blackwater at 2345.

Summary for 26 May 1915:

Location	**Number and type of bombs dropped**	**Casualties**	**Damage**
Southend	23× 5 lb grenades, 47× IB	2 killed, 1 injured	
Total	70 bombs	2 killed, 1 injured	

Anti-aircraft guns in action and reported use of ammunition:

Location of AA battery	**Calibre or type of gun**	**Number / type of rounds fired**
Shoeburyness	3"	24 rounds HE, 13 rounds shrapnel
Southminster	1 pdr	57 rounds
Burnham	Rifle fire	200 rounds Japanese ammunition

Five aircraft were sent up to intercept the raider, but nothing seen by the pilots – with two aeroplanes crashing on landing.

Hauptmann Erich Linnarz was the commander of the first Zeppelin to drop bombs on London on 31 May 1915.

31 May 1915

Weather: wind very light from north and north-west, the weather fine. The moon was in the full – rising about 2330 and not setting until after sunrise.

On this night, *Hauptmann* Erich Linnarz, in *Zeppelin LZ 38*, brought his ship to London – carrying out the first aerial attack on the Metropolis. *Zeppelin LZ 37* was also out during the night, but appeared to have got no further than Dunkirk, France. *Zeppelin LZ 38* was first reported passing Dunkirk at 2030 and Calais at 2055 before she turned out to sea across the English Channel – making for North Foreland and passing Margate, Kent where she was fired at off the Southern Mobile Royal Naval Air Service Anti-Aircraft Section at 2142. Other machine-guns of the Royal Naval Air Service Anti-Aircraft Section opened fire on her from Reculver at 2150 before *Zeppelin LZ 38* crossed over to the Essex side of the Thames Estuary during her course towards the capital, but was also fired at by anti-aircraft guns sited at Shoeburyness at 2212. Passing inland between Rochford and Rayleigh, she reached Brentwood and hesitated for a while (presumably while her commander fixed his exact position) before continuing her direct course for London. The airship passed between Woodford and Wanstead at 2315 and was spotted over London for the first time at about 400 yards south-east of Stoke Newington Station, where she commenced dropping bombs at 2320. The first bomb was an incendiary that fell on 16, Alkham Road, Stoke Newington – penetrating into two bedrooms and destroying their contents by fire. The next bomb (also an incendiary) landed on 8, Chesholm Road – falling through the roof of the back bedroom, but failed to do any more damage. This was followed by three small, 5 lb HE bombs which fell at 41, 43 and 45, Dynevor Road, Stoke Newington – blowing out doors and windows and partially demolishing the rear portions of the latter two houses. The airship now steered a course due south to about 500 yards west of the main Kingsland-Stoke Newington Road – dropping a series of bombs in quick succession. An incendiary bomb fell on 27, Neville Road, Stoke Newington – completely gutting the premises – then a 5 lb HE bomb fell in Neville Road, but failed to explode. This was followed by an incendiary which landed on a shed at the rear of 31, Neville Road, and another fell through the roof of number 47 – penetrating to the bedrooms, but caused no fire. Another incendiary bomb was dropped at 6, Allen Road, which passed through the roof of the house and into the ground floor – causing a small fire. This was followed by another bomb falling on 33, Cowper Road, which again penetrated to the ground floor – gutting two rooms and slightly injuring four children. At 69, Cowper Road an incendiary bomb fell into a small water tank, while another fell at 71, Cowper Road – causing a small fire. The next bombs were two of the small 5 lb HE bombs on 102, Shakespeare Road – one striking the coping and another on the front steps (causing considerable damage). Three more incendiary bombs landed in Arundel Grove, St Matthias Road and Barrett's Grove, but failed to cause any significant damage. Two more HE bombs fell into gardens at Woodville Grove, but failed to explode – followed by three incendiaries and an HE bomb, which fell in Midmay Road – causing slight damage. Further incendiaries were dropped on Queen Margaret's Grove and King Henry's Walk without causing any damage, but a further two caused a fire in Ball's Pond Road – killing two and injuring five civilians. Further incendiary bombs were dropped all the way down Southgate Road at close intervals – all falling into gardens and roadways (causing no damage). After crossing the Regent's Canal, the airship dropped an incendiary bomb on 6, Witham Street, which caused a small fire that was soon extinguished by the occupier. The airship now veered slightly to the south-east and dropped several incendiary bombs, which caused no damage, but two incendiaries hit 28, Hemsworth Street and 31, Ivy Street, Hoxton – gutting both premises. At 49, Ivy Lane an incendiary bomb caused severe fire damage and injured a child. The next bomb fell on Bacchus Walk, Hoxton and gutted the premises – also seriously injuring a soldier. Between here and the Shoreditch Empire, three more incendiary bombs were dropped (but failed to do any damage), but the following four incendiaries – three of which fell on the Shoreditch Empire Music Hall and one on the house next door – all failed to cause any significant damage. A 5 lb HE bomb also fell on the pavement outside the music hall. Although the audience was in the building at the time, any tendency for the audience to panic was averted by the manager addressing the audience from the stage. The next bomb to fall was an incendiary, which hit the premises of Hopkins and Figgs, Drapers at Shoreditch – again without causing any serious damage (although there were about 30 female assistants sleeping in the premises at the time). Three more incendiary bombs fell on Bishopsgate Street Goods Station, but the fires were promptly extinguished by the men on duty; then two incendiaries and an HE bomb fell into Pearl Street, Shoreditch and three incendiaries in Princelet Street – as well as an HE bomb in Fashion Street (all failed to cause any damage). Altogether, four men – including two soldiers – two women and two children were injured in Hoxton and Shoreditch. The airship then passed over Whitechapel, with incendiary bombs falling in Osborne Street and near to Whitechapel Church – and three in Commercial Road East (none doing any damage) – along with a small HE bomb that fell into a large tank of water at Johnnie Walker & Sons Whiskey Distillery. The raider then began to change course to the north-east, and at the same time dropped 11 small HE bombs – the first falling in a yard at 13a, Berners Street (injuring a horse) – followed by two in Christian Street, Whitechapel (killing two children and injuring 10 other civilians). Three more HEs failed to explode when they fell in Burslem Street, St George's, Jamaica Street and East Arbour Street. The next bomb fell in Charles Street, Stepney – and although it did explode, it only broke a few windows. The next two bombs were incendiaries and fell at Duckett Street and 16, Ben Jonson Road, Stepney – causing small fires in both instances. A distance of three miles now elapsed before the next bombs were dropped, which were two incendiaries, which fell at Wingfield Road and Colgrave Road, West Ham (but caused no damage). The next was a 5 lb HE bomb, which fell in Florence Street, Leystone followed by others in Park Grove Road, Cranleigh Drive, Dyer's Hall Road and Fillbrook Road – all of which caused very little damage. The last bomb, in Fillbrook Road, fell about 2335 with the casualties in Leystone amounting to three people slightly injured. The airship then went off towards the east – passing Brentwood, Essex at 2355 – and passed between Burnham and Southminster at 0030. *Hauptmann* Linnarz, at this point, evidently had some difficulty in fixing his position as the airship loitered over the coast for a while before passing out to sea at the mouth of the River Crouch at 0040 – although was fired upon by anti-aircraft guns at Southminster and the mobile guns of the Royal Naval Air Service at Burnham.

Summary for 31 May 1915:

Location	**Number and type of bombs dropped**	**Casualties**	**Damage**
Stoke Newington	9× 5lb HE, 24× IB	2 killed, 9 injured	One house gutted
Dalston	29× IB	2 killed, 5 injured	House burnt out
Hoxton and Shoreditch	2× 5lb HE, 23× IB	8 injured	3 houses gutted, several houses and business premises seriously damaged; Bishopsgate Station (GER) slightly damaged
Whitechapel	10× 5lb HE, 9× IB	2 killed, 10 injured	Stores slightly damaged
Stepney	4× 5lb HE, 2× IB		Glass broken and small fires
West Ham	2 IB		
Leystone	5× 5 lb	3 injured	
Total	30× 5 lb HE grenades; total weight: 150 lbs; 89× IB at 25 lbs; 2,225 lbs total weight; total weight of bombs dropped: 2,375 lbs	6 killed, 35 injured	

To commemorate the exploits of *Hauptmann* Erich Linnarz and the crew of *Zeppelin LZ 38* in dropping bombs on the capital, a special commemorative medallion was struck in Germany.

Anti-aircraft guns in action and reported use of ammunition:

Location of AA battery	Calibre or type of gun	Number / type of rounds fired
Shoeburyness	3"	12 rounds
Southminster	–	20 rounds.
Burnham (RNAS)	–	179 rounds
Reculver	·45 Maxim	–
Margate	·45 Maxim	500 rounds

Seven Royal Naval Air Service aircraft were dispatched to intercept the raider, but none saw the airship. A Royal Naval Air Service Sopwith 806 Gunbus, no.802, crashed on landing at Hendon Aerodrome – killing the pilot, Flight Lieutenant Douglas Meston Barnes[7] and injuring his observer, Flight-Sub Lieutenant B Travers.

The airship was estimated to have flown at a height of 7,500 to 11,000 feet during its flight over England – and while over London, it was not spotted or heard (hence, the anti-aircraft defences of the capital did not open fire).

It was recorded that *Zeppelin LZ 37*, commanded by *Oberleutnant* Otto van der Haegen, was attacked by aeroplanes off Dunkirk, France at 2100 – and at 2225 a battery of the Royal Naval Air Service Motor Service fired at an airship off the mouth of the River Swale, but the raider came no further west and did not drop any bombs on land.

Later, *Hauptmann* Erich Linnarz recounted his impressions of the first Zeppelin operation over London:

> On, on we sped. It was a beautiful night – a night of star-spangled skies and gentle breezes; a night hard to reconcile with a purpose as grim as ours – and then, the glimmer of water showed below and we knew we were over the sea. Tiny red specks winked at us. They were patrol boats keeping their ceaseless watch in the channel – and we were looking down their funnels into the glowing heart of their stoke-hold furnaces. England! We crossed the black ridge of the coast. Immediately from below, anti-aircraft guns spat viciously. We could hear the shells screaming past us. We increased our altitude and speed. Across the Thames Estuary we raced – wheeling inland at Shoeburyness – over Southend, which I had raided the week before, and then, following the gleaming river, we made straight for the capital. Twenty minutes later, we were over London. There, below us, its great expanse lay spread. I knew it all so well. I had spent several months there five years before. There seemed to have been little effort to dim the city. There were the landmarks – St Paul's, the Houses of Parliament and Buckingham Palace – dreaming in the light of the moon, which had now risen. I glanced at the clock. It was 10 minutes to 11. The quivering altimeter showed that

7 Flight Lieutenant D M Barnes is buried at Nunhead (All Saints) Cemetery, London.

our height was 10,000 feet. The air was keen – and we buttoned up our jackets as we prepared to deal the first blow against the heart of your great and powerful nation. Inside the gondola, it was pitch-dark – save for the glowing pointers of the dials. The sliding shutters of the electric lamps – with which each one of the crew was provided – was drawn. There was tension as I leaned out of one of the gondola portholes and surveyed the lacework of lighted streets and squares. An icy wind lashed my face. I mounted the bombing platform. My finger hovered on the button that electrically operated the bombing apparatus; then I pressed it. We waited. Minutes seemed to pass, before – above the humming song of the engines – there rose a shattering roar. Was it fantasy that there also leaped from far below the faintest cries of tortured souls? I pressed again. A cascade of orange sparks shot upwards – and a billow of incandescent smoke drifted slowly away to reveal a red gash of raging fire on the face of the wounded city. One by one, every 30 seconds, the bombs moaned and burst. Flames sprang up like serpents goaded to attack. Taking one of the biggest fires, I was able to ascertain my speed and drift. Beside me, my second-in-command carefully watched the result of every bomb and made rapid calculations at the navigation chart. Suddenly, from the depths, great swords of light stabbed the sky. One caught the gleam of the aluminium of our gondola, passed it, retraced, caught it again and then held us in its beam. Instantly, others chased across the sky – and we found ourselves moving through an endless sea of dazzling light. Inside the gondola, it was brighter than sunlight. Every detail of the car was thrown into sharp relief. The crew, at their posts, looked like a set of actors grouped in the limelight without their make-up – and so began a game of hide and seek in the sky. The helmsman and I tried every way of eluding the searchlights – practising every trick of navigation; then came the bark of the batteries. Shells shrieked past us, above us, below us. There were glowing tracer shells, which we had never seen before, but had heard all about; slim projectiles that tore a hole in the ship's fabric and then burst into flame. It was this thought that sent us home quickly. We had been over London for an hour. Soon we left the thrusting searchlights behind. We could see ahead of us the sea – through which the moon had laid a silver path to guide us home. As we crossed the black ridge of the shore, we were met with a further attack from the anti-aircraft guns at Burnham and Southminster. I think our gondola light, now alight and casting a feeble glow over the cabin, perhaps had betrayed us. I put it out. Shell after shell whizzed past – some of them were the dreaded incendiary type. Some burst dangerously near. On, on we flew – and at last, we were out of range and the firing died down. Now, a new menace threatened us: aeroplanes. We went in dread of these, since your pilots failed to reach us with machine-gun fire, they were to climb above us and ram our gas bags with their machines. Evidently, the supreme sacrifice meant nothing to these brave men.[8] One by one

8 No record of such orders can be found in any documents or any account from Allied airmen.

they came from the airfields that had been established round the coast to intercept returning raiders. My look-out thought he spotted one flying towards me, Higher we rose – out of reach. The British aeroplanes were faster than we were, but they couldn't reach our height limit. Presently, in the fading moonlight, we could see the waves beating against the Belgian Coastline far below. We were feeling cold and hungry; exhausted and spent from the high-pitched hours of that night – rather like the remorseful reveller returning in the hour before the dawn. It was almost dawn. The first vague light was edging the horizon as we flew over invaded Belgium. We had been away 10 hours. The first attack on London had been accomplished. Our bomb rack was empty. Behind us, we could make out the red glow of fire on the sky's rim. It was ravaged London – and as we sank to earth and the gondola bumped across the landing ground at Brussels-Evere, the sun rising in front of the Zeppelin sheds smeared the sky with crimson streaks – as though fingers dipped in blood had been drawn across the horizon.

4 June 1915

Weather: wind light from the west, 10 miles per hour at 1,500 feet. Weather fair, with local mist on the coast. Moon was waning and rose at 0025 on 5th June.

During the night, two naval airships – *Zeppelins L 9* and *L 10* – attacked the English Coast, with *Zeppelin L 9* (being commanded by *Kapitänleutnant* Mathy) being reported 85 miles east of the Humber at 1930. She came towards England very slowly – lying off the coast of Yorkshire until dark – and it was not until 2255 that the airship was spotted off the coast at Ulrome, heading north towards Fraisthorpe – after which she returned southwards to Ulrome at 2320. At 2345 she went out to sea again – her commander apparently not being sure of his position – and slowly followed the coast northward till she reached Flamborough Head at 0030, 5 June (and when one mile north of the Head, ventured inland again – heading towards the south-west and dropped an incendiary bomb between the villages of Kilham and Langtoft, doing no damage). When the airship reached Driffield, she appeared to hover for some time – and at 0105 dropped two HE bombs (one falling in a field; the other in a garden). She then turned south towards Hull, but probably owing to ground mist rendering visibility difficult, her commander gave up the attempt to reach Hull and turned back – passing Fraisthorpe and over Bridlington at 0115. Ten minutes later, the airship was seen over Flamborough Head – under fire from the Coastguard. The airship flew very low and was clearly seen – estimated to be only 1,000 feet up.

Zeppelin L 10 was first sighted at 2135, 4 June south of the *Sunk Lightship* by four armed trawlers (*Resono, Lord Roberts*, *Cygne* and *Zephyr* – the latter opening fire with her deck gun). At 2245 the airship was spotted between the Gunfleet and Foulness – going south-west towards Shoeburyness – and at 2300 she passed over Sheerness, Kent and turned south-east over Sheppey to Whitstable, where she turned again north-west – circling in the direction of Faversham, which she passed over five minutes later. Between 2320 and 2330 she was over Sittingbourne which she circled twice – dropping three HE and eight incendiary bombs. One house was burnt out and a man and woman injured. The airship then went off towards the south-west and Maidstone – eventually turning towards Chatham, where she was reported as being overhead at 2345 – and anti-aircraft fire was opened up (one ineffectual HE bomb being dropped at Rainham). The airship then went on towards Tilbury, where she was again fired upon by anti-aircraft guns at 2357 – although the airship hovered here for half an hour – and at 0025, 5 June dropped five HE and three incendiary bombs on Gravesend. The yacht club (that was being used as a military hospital for wounded soldiers) was set alight – although all the patients were removed safely to Chatham. Other considerable damage was done to property, with two houses destroyed and one badly damaged; a stable with four horses in it was also destroyed. Two men, three women and a child were injured. The airship then passed off towards the north-east – following a course of Laindon, Manningtree, Holbrook, Wherstead, Ipswich, Woodbridge, north of Orford, Aldeburgh, Leiston and passed out to sea near Dunwich at 0135 (being last heard off Southwold). She had flown low over the Suffolk countryside – being clearly seen and heard as if her captain was trying to get his bearings.

Summary for 4 June 1915:

Location	Number and type of bombs dropped	Casualties	Damage
Yorkshire, East Riding			
Kilham	1× IB		
Driffield	2× HE		
Kent			
Sittingbourne	3× HE, 8× IB	2 injured	Several fires; house burnt out
Rainham	1× HE		
Gravesend	3× HE, 3× IB	6 injured	2 houses demolished (1 badly) and several others slightly damaged. Yacht Club Hostel burnt; stable burnt (4 horses killed)
Total	9× HE, 12× IB	8 injured	

Anti-aircraft guns in action and reported use of ammunition:

Location of AA battery	Calibre or type of gun	Number / type of rounds fired
Kingsnorth	1 pdr Pom-Pom	1 round
Sheerness (Burntwick)	–	–
Chatham	–	–
Tilbury	–	–
Aldeburgh	RNAS	–
Flamborough Station	Rifle fire from Coastguard	
Sittingbourne	Rifle and Maxim fire	

Eight aircraft of the Royal Flying Corps and Royal Naval Air Service took off, but none of the airmen saw the airship.

7 June 1915

Weather: Light variable winds prevailed over the North Sea, with a dead calm in the Humber District. Fog and mist were reported locally on the East and North-East Coasts, but generally fair. The waning moon rose about 0100.

On the afternoon of 6 June two naval airships – *Zeppelin L 9* (commanded by *Kapitänleutnant* Heinrich Mathy) and *Zeppelin L 10* (commanded by *Kapitänleutnant* Klaus Hirsch) – left their sheds in Germany to raid England. The military airships *Zeppelin LZ 37*, commanded by *Oberleutnant* Otto van der Haegen; *Zeppelin LZ 38*, commanded by *Hauptmann* Erich Linnarz; and *Zeppelin LZ 39*, commanded by *Hauptmann* Masius, rose from their sheds in Belgium (also with purpose of raiding England), but *Zeppelin LZ 38* descended almost immediately due to technical problems.

Kapitänleutnant Heinrich Mathy (1883-1916) was considered one of the most skilled and audacious commanders in the German Airship Service.

Zeppelin L 9 and *Zeppelin L 10* both reached the Norfolk Coast at about 1930 but *Zeppelin L 10* then turned back (probably due to engine trouble) – leaving *Zeppelin L 9*, which was clearly seen 12 miles north-east of Mundesley at 2015. At 2040 she was reported from Cromer as going north, out to sea – and five minutes later, was steering south-west, two miles out to sea. A quarter of an hour later, she went off in a north-westerly direction – flying very low – and at 2140 was two miles from the Lincolnshire Coast off Sutton-on-Sea (still steering north-west). At 2150 *Zeppelin L 9* crossed the Lincolnshire Coast at Theddlethorpe – flying west – and at 2210 was reported by HMS *Thrasher* as being off the Spurn. At 2240 a flare was dropped at Withernsea (presumably due to the amount of fog off the mouth of the River Humber) and *Kapitänleutnant* Mathy was unwilling to approach Hull by way of the river. Another flare was dropped at Bridlington before the airship came straight down on Hull – passing south-west of Hornsea and dropping two incendiary bombs at Wyton Bar before reaching the neighbourhood of Hull and Sutton at 2335. Although Hull was shrouded in fog, it cleared over the city for a while – and at 2348 one HE and one incendiary bomb fell in the Alexandra Dock. A second incendiary fell on the stern of the Swedish steam ship *Igor*, which was lying in the Victoria Dock basin – causing slight damage. A third incendiary fell through the roof of a timber shed on the quay at the basin – causing a small fire. An HE bomb then followed – hitting the railway lines close by and making a crater, which destroyed about 12 feet of track. An incendiary bomb followed, which was promptly extinguished in Alexander Terrace, Delapole Street. An HE bomb then exploded in St Paul's Avenue, Church Street – partially destroying three houses and injuring several people. An incendiary bomb then fell in Feather Lane on the footpath (causing no damage) but an HE bomb in East Street demolished two houses – killing a man, woman and child. Two incendiaries in Church Street and Clarence Street did no damage – and a third fell in a grain warehouse in High Street, but was smothered in loose grain and extinguished. Two more incendiaries and an HE bomb also fell in High Street – injuring five people and damaging property to a radius of 500 yards. Three incendiary bombs then set fire to a large draper's establishment in the Market Place, which was completely burnt out, and also to a public house at the Old Corn Exchange – causing a small fire. An incendiary bomb in Mytongate did no damage, but another dropped through the roof of the Golden Gallon Inn did considerable damage before it was extinguished. Two incendiaries which fell in Blanket Row killed a man and two boys and injured another boy. Three HE bombs then fell together into the Humber Dock; the concussion from the exploding bombs broke a number of windows in the surrounding buildings. Two incendiaries then caused a fire at Myton Place, to the north-west of the dock. The airship continued on her course, following the quays (presumably with the warehouses as a main target) before turning west to attack the western part of the city and the north-east railway line. One HE bomb fell in-between Gowin's Place and Porter Street – demolishing several small houses and killing three people. In Sarah Ann Place, close by, an incendiary bomb killed one person. Between Albert

Terrace and Pease Street, an HE bomb smashed several windows and caused minor damage. In the streets of Great Thornton, Walker, Goodwin and Campbell, five incendiary bombs caused slight damage to houses; set a hay loft alight; and injured two people. In St Thomas' Terrace, an HE bomb totally demolished two houses and shattered the roof of nearby St Thomas' Church – killing two women and a man – and injuring a further two women. In the streets of South Parade, Regent, Coltman, Gee, Chomley and Constable, seven incendiary bombs killed two girls and burnt two motor cars, but caused no damage to surrounding buildings. The last bomb to fall on this part of the city during this raid was an incendiary, which fell through the roof of a house in Selby Street, but caused no serious damage. The airship then made off eastwards – in the direction she had come – and dropped no more bombs until she was north of Victoria Dock, where two incendiaries were dropped in Danson Lane (one fell in the playground of a school – breaking all the windows in the school building; the other bomb set fire to a furniture warehouse). A third incendiary and an HE bomb fell together on a large sawmill also in Danson Lane – destroying it – although the fire was extinguished by North Eastern Railway firemen. An incendiary bomb then set fire to a house in Bright Street, which was burnt out. Another fell on railway lines near to Waller Street – slightly damaging the track and breaking windows at Southcoates Station – and was followed by an HE bomb in the same street, which entirely destroyed three houses and damaged others – killing a man, three women and a child. An incendiary bomb was then dropped on the Rovers Football Ground – followed by another in Woodhouse Street (causing no damage).

The airship had approached Hull at about 8,000 feet, but as soon as the commander had realised that there was no anti-aircraft guns defending the city, he had come down to 5,000 feet to carry out his bombing. There were no anti-aircraft guns mounted at Hull – and the only defence that could be mustered were the guns of HMS *Adventure*, which was being repaired in Earle's Yard.

Departing Hull, the airship followed the line of the Humber towards the sea – passing over Paul at about 1210, 8 June – and Sunk Island 10 minutes later, where the Maxim machine-guns and those at Stallingborough opened fire (supplemented by rifle fire from the latter). A minute later, the Pom-Pom situated at Immingham and a Maxim on the SS *Kale* also opened fire on the airship. The airship veered off eastwards and then went on – flying high towards Grimsby, which she reached at 1225 and stopped her propellers – hovering for a short time over the town and docks. Seven incendiary bombs were dropped on the docks – one of which did not ignite and damaged three railway trucks. Rifle fire was opened at her from New Clee as she left in a south-easterly direction – and was also met by Pom-Pom fire from Waltham (whereupon the airship altered course to the east and passed out to sea at Teney Haven at 1235 – and was last spotted from Donna Nook at 1240 heading south-east). It was noted that rioting broke out in Hull at 0230 with German (and perceived German) shops being sacked before troops were able to restore order.

The damage caused by the raid on Hull were extensively photographed. The results of a high-explosive bomb that fell at numbers 11 and 12, Earls Street are graphically illustrated. Edward Jordan was killed at number 11, with Mr and Mrs Jordan being seriously injured. Mr and Mrs Hill of number 12 were killed.

The result of an incendiary bomb falling at number 9, Blanket Row, Hull. The bomb set fire to the room in which three boys were sleeping – killing Norman, aged 10. George, aged 15, was dragged out and ran all the way to Monument Bridge, where he collapsed and was carried to the infirmary, where he died. Horace, aged seven, was seriously injured and taken to the infirmary. The fire was extinguished by the father.

Hull. The result of the great fire at Davis' Display Store and The Fleece Inn – which stood in the far corner on the left – caused by an incendiary bomb. At first, it was thought that no one was killed, but 10 days after the incident, a woman's body was found under the rubble. She was unidentified and was not reported missing.

Summary for 7 June 1915:

Location	Number and type of bombs dropped	Casualties	Damage
Yorkshire, East Riding			
Wyton Bar	2× IB		
Hull	13× HE, 39× IB	24 killed, 40 injured	Serious damage to city (almost 40 houses demolished or wrecked and many damaged); school damaged; sawmill burnt out
Lincolnshire			
Grimsby	7× IB		3 railway trucks damaged
Total	13× HE, 48× IB	24 killed, 40 injured	

Anti-aircraft guns in action and reported use of ammunition:

Location of AA battery	**Calibre or type of gun**	**Number / type of rounds fired**
Sunk Island	·303 Maxim	152 rounds
Stallingborough	·303 rifle	40 rounds
Stallingborough	·303 Maxim	49 rounds
Immingham	1 pdr Pom-Pom	6 rounds
Waltham	1 pdr Pom-Pom	12 rounds
New Clee	·303 rifle	145 rounds
HMS *Adventurer*	–	–
SS *Kale*, Immingham	–	–

Zeppelin LZ 37 / LZ 37. Type M. 0225.

Convent, Mont St Amand, Ghent, Belgium.

Zeppelin LZ 37 – along with *Zeppelin LZ 38* and *Zeppelin LZ 39* – took off from their bases in Belgium, but *Zeppelin LZ 38* descended almost immediately – leaving *Zeppelins LZ 37* and *LZ 39* to continue towards the English Coast, but due to fog, they were unable pinpoint their position and returned to Belgium. On her return, *Zeppelin LZ 37* was sighted and bombed (by Flight Sub-Lieutenant Reginald A J Warneford in a Morane-Saulnier Parasol 3253 of 1 Royal Naval Air Service Squadron) and crashed in flames. The burning wreckage fell into the grounds of a convent – killing two nuns and a child.

Steuermann Alfred Mühler fell one-and-a-half miles in the forward gondola, onto the roof of the convent and was precipitated into the building and onto a bed. He survived, but was badly burnt.

Oberleutnant Otto van der Haegen +.
Oberleutnant Kurt Ackermann +.
Maschinist Karl Clauss +.
Unteroffizier Hermann Kirchner +.
Fahringenieur Karl Mahr +.
Unteroffizier Wilhelm Müller +.
Maschinistenmaat Gustav Ruske +.
Untersteuermann Otto Schwarz +.[9]

The report submitted regarding the action by Rex Warneford is as follows:

9 Some publications mention that 20 airmen were in the airship when it crashed, but the names of those mentioned in this publication are those recorded in German records.

The Morane-Saulnier Parasol, with which Rex Warneford managed to climb above and drop bombs onto *Zeppelin LZ 37* – thus destroying the airship.

No.1 Naval Aeroplane Squadron:
I left Furnes at 1am on June the 7th on Morane-Saulnier Parasol no.3253 – under orders to proceed to look for Zeppelins and attack the Berchem St Agathe Airship Shed with six 20 lb bombs. On arriving at Dixmunde at 1.05am I observed a Zeppelin – apparently over Ostend – and proceeded in chase of the same. I arrived at close quarters a few miles past Bruges at 1.50am – and the airship opened heavy Maxim fire, so I retreated to gain height – and the airship turned and followed me. At 2.15am he seemed to stop firing – and at 2.25am I came behind, but well above the Zeppelin (height then 11,000 feet) and switched off my engine to descend on top of him. When close above him, at 7,000 feet, I dropped my bombs – and, whilst releasing the last, there was an explosion, which lifted my machine and turned it over. The aeroplane was out of control for a short period, but went into a nosedive – and the control was regained. I then saw that the Zeppelin was on the ground in flames – and also that there were pieces of something burning in the air all the way down. The joint on my petrol pipe and pump from the back tank was broken, and about 2.40am I was forced to land and repair my pump. I landed at the back of a forest, close to a farm house. The district is unknown on account of the fog and the continuous changing of course. I made preparations to set the machine on fire, but apparently was not observed, so was enabled to effect a repair and continued at 3.15am in a south-westerly direction after considerable difficulty in starting my engine single-handed. I tried several times to find my whereabouts

Flight Sub-Lieutenant Rex Warneford, VC (1891-1915).

> by descending through the clouds, but was unable to do so – so eventually, I landed and found out that it was Cap Gris Nez, and took in some petrol. When the weather cleared, I was able to proceed and arrived at the aerodrome about 10.30am. As far as could be seen, the colour of the airship was green on top and yellow below – and there was no machine-gun platform on top.
> I have the honour to be, Sir,
> Your obedient servant,
> R A J Warneford. Flt Sub-Lieutenant.

Flight Sub-Lieutenant Reginald Alexander John Warneford was awarded the Victoria Cross for his actions against *Zeppelin LZ 37*, but was killed in a flying accident at Buc Aerodrome, Paris on 17 June 1915 when he and his passenger fell from their inverted aircraft while carrying out a flying display.

Zeppelin LZ 38 / LZ 38. Type P. 0230.

Evere Airship Sheds, Brussels, Belgium.

On return from her unsuccessful attempt to bomb Britain, this airship was bombed in her shed by Flight Lieutenant J P Wilson, Royal Naval Air Service; and Flight Sub-Lieutenant J S Mills, Royal Naval Air Service – flying from Dunkirk, France – and was totally destroyed.

Bombs were dropped on the shed, which was observed to be in flames. It was almost certain that a Zeppelin was inside, as the flames reached a great height – coming out from both sides of the shed.

Both a Zeppelin and a Parseval were destroyed, a correspondent of the *New York Tribune* reported.

The plaque on the wall of the Mont St Amand Technical School, Ghent recording Rex Warneford's victory over *Zeppelin LZ 37*.

A photograph of the exterior of the Mont St Amand Technical School, Ghent.

Evere Airship Shed, taken on 13 August 1915 from the roof of a house on the Evere-Saventhem Road. The sliding doors at the end of the shed were erected following the air raid of 7 June. The portion of the shed that was destroyed – and subsequently repaired – was at the same end of the shed.

Also, five Taubes in the shed were burnt and 19 German soldiers were killed (report in the publication *Temps* by an eyewitness of the exploit).

Extract from an intercepted letter, London, 26 June 1915:

> … The recent air attack on the Zeppelin sheds at Evere and Berchem St Agathe near Brussels has caused a terrible state of confusion among the German Garrison at Brussels. When the first bombs dropped on the Evere Shed, where two new Zeppelins were destroyed, two motor-guns were dispatched into the country to try and shoot the Allied aviators down. The first motor ran across a railway barrier, which happened to be closed and was smashed; the second ran over a peasant and plunged into a ditch, where it broke down. The loss of two motor-guns is very serious, as the Germans only possess three more of them in Brussels – all the others having been sent to the front in Flanders …[10]

10 The National Archives – (TNA) Air 1/2099/207/20/9: report of damage to enemy during operations.

Report submitted regarding his actions, by J Mills:

> Sir, I have the honour to report the following:
> Acting under instructions, I left the aerodrome on my machine – a Henri Farman – at about 12.45am. Just before turning to head for my destination, I noticed a thick bank of cloud coming up from the west. I soon picked up my course – flying over various Belgian towns under German occupation; all of which were brilliantly illuminated, though with shaded lights. I easily recognised Ghent – passing over the southern portion of it, where two large lamps were to be noticed. The most westerly, on my approach, kept signalling – and it continued until I had left it behind. I arrived at Brussels about 2.15am – going straight for the Zeppelin sheds. As I passed over, a light was flashing out a signal in the same manner as at Ghent, but using a different sign. I easily picked up the vicinity of the aerodrome by the cemetery, but could not sight the sheds. As the light was still very dim, I continued to circle around – dropping from about 5,500 feet to about 4,000. After flying about in this way for about 15 minutes, I suddenly saw my target, but by this time, I had been seen – and a searchlight was used, with no effect, and fire had been opened on me from a very great number of guns (about five or 10 minutes after my arrival on the aerodrome). The guns on or near the shed were not fired until I got close to my object, when they then opened a terrific bombardment – causing me to steer off. I then got on a line heading north – going diagonally over the shed – but the fire was so intense that I had to alter my intention. I then decided to get more height – and, reaching 5,000 feet, I got on a line heading about NW – and going straight for the shed, dropped all my bombs (12 in number, one after the other) when I thought I was in position, which was about 2.40am. On looking back, some seconds afterwards, I saw the shed burning furiously; flames coming from almost every part – reaching to a considerable height and with much black smoke pouring out of the top of the shed. The firing near the aerodrome seemed to stop after the shed had caught fire, but I was fired on from the western side of the city several times. Just as I thought I was clear, a large illuminating ball of flame came up to me just behind my machine. It continued to give a very red glow for a considerable time – probably 30 seconds – and it gave me the impression that my machine was on fire. I was fired at once or twice on my way back – once in particular when flying over a *Drachenballoon*, which I had not observed. I left Brussels at about 2.45am – and did not recognise a single place on my return journey – and steered the whole way back by compass, going almost due west. After flying for close to two hours after leaving Brussels, I considered I must be well over the lines, but as I had been flying for the last hour over thick fog, I had no idea as to where I was. I descended from 7,000 feet to 1,200 feet – looking for a thin patch, but finding none. I finally dived through the clouds – pulling up 10 feet from the

sea. Turning south, I picked up the beach and landed – finding myself at a place called Le Clipon, about one third of the way to Calais from Dunkirk; the time then being about 4.45am. I then telephoned the camp – informing the CO of my descent.
I have the honour to be, Sir,
Your obedient servant,
J S Mills. Flt Sub-Lieutenant.

Transcript of the report submitted by J Wilson:

Sir, I have the honour to submit the following report of my attack on the airship shed at Evere, north-east of Brussels on the 7th June:

At 12.40am left aerodrome in Henri Farman no.3999 carrying three 65 lb bombs set for contact, as a fuel supply of five and three-quarter hours. The night was bright, but there was no moon. I proceeded on a course 113° – passing Thielt on the right. I approached Brussels – steering towards the north of it. No lights were observed at Berchem St Agathe at 2.05am. The locality was well-marked by a searchlight, which was signalling at regular intervals of half to three-quarters of a minute – in a north-north-westerly direction – four long flashes. It was not yet light enough to distinguish the shed, so I waited for 15 minutes. During this time, the signalling from the searchlight continued, but no fire was opened on me at all – and I answered the signals with a pocket flash lamp with a succession of four 'shorts', which appeared to satisfy them. At 2.20am the shed was just visible. I proceeded to attack it at 2,000 feet from the south-east. The first bomb which dropped fell just outside the south-east corner of the shed. I then turned round and approached again from the same direction and dropped a second bomb – and though I did not actually see the explosion, the flash appeared to come from the centre or side of the shed, and the third pitched outside the north-west corner. The explosion shook the machine considerably – and the second explosion was extremely bright. I then steered away to the north-westward – circling round Brussels – and afterwards, steering a south-westerly course. On looking at the shed, it appeared that a large column of black smoke was above the shed, but no flames were observed. On reaching Itterveek, or thereabouts, to the south-west of Brussels, I was at a height of 7,000 feet when a very bright star shell, or rocket, came up quite close to me and remained in the air for 10 to 15 seconds and then died out. At the time, I did not realise what this was and thought that it might be an attacking aeroplane, until the light went out. After this, I steered a westerly course – and when in the region of Tournai, a very thick mist was encountered and I was completely lost. At 5.15am I sighted a patch of ground and immediately made for it – and effected a successful landing in a field. This turned out to be in the vicinity of Montreuil.

The following points are of interest:

It was noticed on the way out that the towns of Thoutout, Roulers, Thielt and Alost were all lit up and were very visible, but that Ghent and Brussels both appeared to have shaded lights.

The searchlight at Evere was easily picked up and appeared to have a ring of red lights in the shape of an oval close to it. When the first bomb was dropped, all lights were immediately extinguished.

The searchlight at Ritterbeck, to the SSE of Brussels, was very plain. It was signalling some group, which I did not actually take in, as it was facing the other way. One of the most noticeable features in locating the Evere Shed was the very large double-oval ring on the ground to the south-east of the shed.

During the whole attack, as far as could be ascertained, no gunfire was opened at all, but the presence of the star shell previously mentioned was extremely unexpected and disconcerting.

The map supplied to me – and the information given previous to my starting – were very accurate and of the greatest of value.

I have the honour to be, Sir,
Your obedient servant,
J P Wilson. Flight Lieutenant.

15 June 1915

Weather: on the North-Eastern Coast, the weather was fine, with winds of 20 to 25 miles per hour at 1,500 feet and 11 miles per hour at 6,000 feet. A clear, cloudless sky. No moon.

A raid was carried out on England – probably by *Zeppelin L 10*, commanded by *Kapitänleutnant* Klaus Hirsch – and crossed the coast of Northumberland between Newbiggin and Blyth at 2325 – proceeding in a south-westerly direction at a height of 6,000 feet. It was assumed that the purpose of the raid was to bomb the shipbuilding and engineering works situated on the Tyne. The course taken meant that the airship passed over Newsham, Gosforth and Benton so as to avoid the anti-aircraft batteries based at the mouth of the river. No bombs were wasted, as they were on the previous raid – being dropped into open country north of the river, with the first being dropped at Wallsend. The initial course steered would have taken the airship direct to Newcastle, but when north-west of Wallsend, she altered course and bore down upon Palmer's Works, Jarrow. Wallsend was reached at 2340 – the airship travelling at a speed of 60 miles per hour. Owing to the sudden appearance of the airship (and the fact that telephone arrangements were not yet fully developed to deal with such emergencies), many of the Tyneside industrial establishments did not receive the order to extinguish lights until the airship was upon them – and consequently, showed a full blaze of light. Siren blasts sounded by HMS *Patrol* as a warning were not understood – and Palmer's Works presented a perfect target to the raider. At Wallsend, one incendiary and two

HE bombs were dropped south of the Infectious Diseases Hospital; one fell near Holy Cross Church and another at Burn Close – none of them causing any significant damage. Two incendiaries fell near the secondary schools at Church Bank – followed by six HE and three incendiary bombs on the North Eastern Marine Engineering Company Works – setting fire to a stack of timber and a large quantity of patterns; wrecking the roof of the foundry; and narrowly missing the large tower crane and two sets of 15 inch gun mountings awaiting shipment in monitors. Damage was caused to houses in Wallsend – and though there were no fires, the engineering works suffered heavily, with machinery being displaced and damaged to the value of £30,000. There were, however, no casualties. Slight damage was also done to Wallsend Colliery. The airship then passed over the Tyne to Hebburn, where one incendiary and one HE bomb fell on Hebburn Colliery – causing slight damage. These were followed by one HE and three incendiary bombs on the Ordnance Works Football Field, Jarrow which broke windows in a large number of houses in the neighbourhood. One HE and two incendiary bombs followed in Blackett Street – breaking more windows. The airship then turned north-east and went over Palmer's Jarrow Works – dropping seven HE and five incendiary bombs, which caused considerable damage to the engine construction department – killing 17 workmen and injuring 72. Much damage was caused to stacks of steel plate in the yard; the yard clock stopped at 1140. One incendiary bomb fell at the back of Berkley Street and another in Curlew Road, Jarrow – causing minor damage. The airship then re-crossed the Tyne to the north bank and dropped bombs on Wilington Quay and East Howden. Two incendiaries and one HE bomb fell inside Cookson's Antimony Works – destroying a shed, crane and weighing machine. These were followed by an incendiary bomb in Pochin's Chemical Works, two incendiaries in Stephenson Street and one HE bomb in Coach Open (the latter bomb killing Police Constable Telford). An incendiary bomb then fell in the Tyne Commissioners' Yard, another in Dock Street and two in Tyne View Terrace. A considerable amount of damage was done to small house property by these bombs.

The airship then pursued a straight east-north-east course to the sea – crossing the river again between the Albert Edward Dock and Haxton Colliery at Aithes, where two HE bombs were dropped (one falling in the river; the other on a fairground adjoining the Staithes – the explosion setting fire to a scenic railway and breaking a number of windows in surrounding houses). The airship passed straight over South Shields and dropped another HE bomb between the Tynemouth Battery and Frenchman's Point on the Bents Ground, just outside the area of the South Marine Parks. Slight damage was done to the park railings and to windows in the neighbourhood at South Shields. Finally, an incendiary bomb fell on the sands. The airship went out to sea at 2352 following an east-north-east course at a height of about 6,000 feet. The anti-aircraft gun, located at Low Walker, opened fire at a range of 3,000 feet and increased the range to 3,500 feet for the second shot, which the gunners claimed was a very near-miss. The guns at Carville and Pelaw opened fire at 4,000 feet range – and the Pom-Pom at South Shields at 5,000 feet. In addition to these guns, a 4.7 inch gun of the Heavy Battery Durham Royal Garrison Artillery – stationed at Cleadon

– fired five rounds of shrapnel at the airship. Rifle fire was also opened on her at East Boldon and by men of No.3 Supernumerary Company, Durham Royal Garrison Artillery at Jarrow. One house was damaged by an anti-aircraft shell at Wallsend.

Summary for 15 June 1915:

Location	Number and type of bombs dropped	Casualties	Damage
Northumberland			
Wallsend	10× HE, 6× IB		Serious damage to North East Marine Engineering Works; slight damage to colliery; several houses slightly damaged
Willington Quay and East Howdon	2× HE, 8× IB	1 killed	Antimony Works damaged; several houses seriously damaged
Durham			
Hebburn	1× HE, 1× IB		Slight damage to colliery property
Jarrow	9 HE, 12 IB	17 killed, 72 injured	Plant at Palmer's Works seriously damaged; glass and roofs of a large number of houses damaged
Blyth	3× HE, 1× IB		Fairground and a large number of houses damaged
Total	25× HE, 28× IB	18 killed, 72 injured	

Anti-aircraft guns in action and reported use of ammunition:

Location of AA battery	Calibre or type of gun	Number / type of rounds fired
Carville	3"	3 rounds
Pelaw	13 pdr	3 rounds
Low Walker	6 pdr	6 rounds
South Shields	1 pdr	25 rounds
Cleadon	4.7"	5 rounds
East Boldon	Rifle fire	–
Jarrow	Rifle fire	–

A selection of ordnance – as used by the Germans against Great Britain – is displayed. From left to right are an incendiary bomb; 50 kg, 12 kg, 20 kg high-explosive bombs; a sea flare (for determining an airship's drift while over the sea at night); a 250 kg high-explosive bomb; and another incendiary bomb.

Two naval aeroplanes went up from Whitley Bay – one at 2340 and the other at 2350 – but the airmen did not see any target and landed safely.

Great consternation was expressed by the local authorities following this raid that there was not ample air raid warning given – even though the Zeppelin had been first sighted at about 1828 in the neighbourhood of Flamborough Head and that a warning siren had been sounded just before the first bombs fell (but those working in the foundry and shipyards had not heard it). It was also noted that workmen were reluctant to continue working at night unless there was a system installed that they could rely on to give them ample warning of danger.

For further details, see appendix V.

3 July 1915

Weather was fair to overcast, with local mist or fog. The wind was from the west, strength two.

At 1120 two enemy aircraft – one an *Albatros* floatplane and the other a *Gotha WD2*, no.257 of *See Flieger Abteilung 1* – came in from the North Sea near to the *Inner Gabbard Lightship* off Essex, and at 1128 were engaged by HMS *Lord Roberts* five miles north-west of Longsands. They then made off to the west-north-west – and at 1143 were seen off the coast near Felixstowe, where some Royal Navy destroyers (which were just putting to sea off Harwich) fired about nine rounds at them, but with no effect. In reply, four bombs were dropped into the sea in front of the signal station at Landguard. After leaving the Harwich area, the two machines separated (with one flying north and the other south). The seven Royal Naval Air Service and two Royal Flying Corps aeroplanes sent up to intercept them failed to find either. Land-based anti-aircraft guns were not brought to action due to the height of the enemy aircraft.

25 July 1915

At 1015 to 2220 enemy aircraft were reported dropping bombs to the south-east of the *Kentish Knock* and the *Galloper Lightships* – evidently aimed at shipping.

27 July 1915

At 1007 two German aeroplanes were seen approaching the *Galloper Lightship* from an easterly direction, but at about three miles off, they made off towards the east.

2 August 1915

Operations against hostile aircraft:

1840 hrs: Flight Sub-Lieutenant Bittles, Royal Naval Air Service in Sopwith Schneider no.8149 (Clerget 110 HP) left HMS *Brocklesby* on sighting a Zeppelin one mile to the north-west and was heading in a north-westerly direction. He reported:

> After leaving the water, I steered a course approximately W by N, which brought me about five miles due south of the Zeppelin. I then steered right for him (being 3,500 ft high) – and as far as I could judge, about 200 feet higher than the Zeppelin, I was rapidly overhauling him on his port quarter – and should think I was within two miles of being right over him – when he evidently sighted me or Flight Lieut Smith below him, for he climbed steeply and disappeared into cloud. I then climbed above the cloud to a height of 6,500 ft – and after circling round, being unable to sight him again, I steered a course for Yarmouth. Weather conditions were very poor; from a height of 2,000 feet, it was impossible to see the water or anything below me.

1845 hrs: Flight Sub-Lieutenant Smith in Sopwith Schneider no.3736 (100 HP Monosoupape) left HMS *Brocklesby* to attack the same Zeppelin. He recorded:

> Observed Zeppelin, flying slowly about 3,000 ft approximately 10 to 12 miles north. On getting off the water, the engine started missing. I steered a course to the westward of the Zeppelin to intercept it, as it was proceeding towards the coast. I climbed up to 2,500 feet – and being unable to climb higher, I turned towards it. As I got underneath her, she saw me and started to rise. I manoeuvred for a position to fire at her with my machine-gun, but she got out of range before I was able to do so. I then circled round two or three times and observed

> her number on her bows (*L 33*). She then turned and steered a course east by a trifle south. I then returned to Yarmouth.
>
> **Note:** It was considered that the reason this engine kept missing was due to the pilot not properly adjusting his petrol supply (having had little experience with this type of machine).

At approximately 2215 Zeppelins were reported approaching the vicinity of Yarmouth and Lowestoft. Flares were lit at Burgh Castle Night Landing Ground and Flight Lieutenant Pulling left in BE2c, Royal Flying Corps aeroplane no.8418, ascended to a height of 7,000 feet and proceeded to cruise round this lighted area. At approximately 2330 a Zeppelin approached Burgh Castle at a height of about 8,000 feet and was sighted by Flight Lieutenant Pulling, who attacked it with machine-gun fire. His report stated:

> Sight hostile airship steering NW at about 8,000 ft. Proceeded underneath and attack with Lewis gun. Jamb after first few rounds; unable at first to move cocking piece or tray, so attempt to climb above Zeppelin. Find it impossible to keep up with Zeppelin at climbing speed so turn attention to gun; succeeded in removing tray and clearing jamb; again attack, tray blowing off, place new tray on gun and fire complete charge into Zeppelin – several bullets exploding on contact with the airship. Course meanwhile, due west. Lose Zeppelin while placing third tray on gun and unable to pick up again. Steer east and sight flares; landing down wind and wrecking machine against hedge at 0015 hrs. Difficulty experienced in placing trays in darkness. Speed of airship about 55 knots.[11]

6 August 1915
Zeppelin L 5 / LZ 28. Type M.
Plungiany, near Mitau, Lithuania.
Damaged by Russian forces and force landed.
Kommandeur: Kapitänleutnant der Reserve Franz Georg Ehrlich.

9 August 1915
Weather: wind was calm to light and variable, mainly from the south; the weather cloudy and dull, with some rain and mist; the air being very humid.

Five naval airships, coming from the North German sheds, raided England: *Zeppelins L 9, L 10, L 11, L 12* and *L 13* (the last four ships being the new 1915 standardised class). *Zeppelin L 9* directed her attack against Hull, but was confused by an aeroplane

11 The National Archives – (TNA) Air 1/632/17/122/59: Lowestoft Naval Base; operations against hostile aircraft.

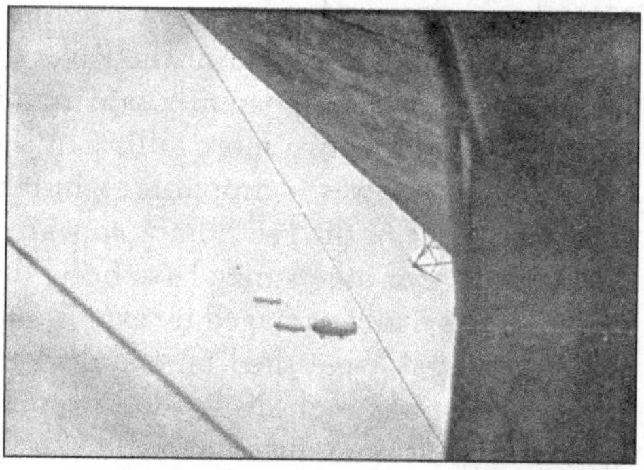

Zeppelins L 9, *L 10*, *L 11* and *L 12* head out across the North Sea towards England for another raid.

attack, lost her way and bombed Goole instead. *Zeppelin L 10* passed over Suffolk and Essex to attack the Thames Estuary and bombed Eastchurch. *Zeppelin L 11* attacked Lowestoft in mistake for Harwich. *Zeppelin L 12* attempted to bomb Dover, was hit by guns of the fortress and finally fell into the sea off Ostend, Belgium where she was destroyed by our aeroplanes. *Zeppelin L 13* – on her maiden voyage – entered the Thames, but went away without coming overland.

Zeppelin L 9 was commanded by *Hauptmann* August Stelling[12] – an army officer – and was first sighted off Ulrome, on the Yorkshire Coast, at 2015. Five minutes later, she passed over the Naval Air Station at Atwick – going south at a height of about 3,000 feet. She was fired at with rifles from Skipsea. Two aircraft rose at 2025 from the aerodrome in pursuit, but the airship (which was then over Hornsea) immediately rose to 10,000 feet, stopped her engines and drifted – evidently listening for the aeroplanes. On their approaching her, she steered eastwards and out to sea – and was lost in the fog. Ten minutes later, she reappeared to the north of Fraisthorpe (six miles south of Bridlington), but again went out to sea – and was next seen off Hornsea (and again at 2110 heading north). Another naval aeroplane took off from Atwick, and the airship promptly headed out to sea again – followed by the aeroplane for 35 minutes. The airship now kept out to sea for an hour – finally coming in at Aldborough at 2205 (passing over Atwick at 2215 on a heading west-north-west). Ten minutes later, she struck the railway at Hulton-Cranswick and turned south along it – evidently making for Hull. Before he had got far, the airship commander evidently became unsure of his position – and between 2230 and 2250 circled twice over the neighbourhood of Leconfield. Finally, he went off north-west of Beverly in a south-westerly direction – and at 2303 passed South Cave. At 2310 the airship reached the Humber and followed it westward towards Goole, which was showing lights and was severely bombed at

12 A well-known pre-war pilot of the Parseval Airship Company. Shortly before the war, he had piloted the *Parseval no.4* airship to England for the British Government, which had acquired it for the Royal Navy, and flew it over London.

2315. An empty goods train was travelling along the line from Hull to Goole and reached the Hook Bridge (over the River Ouse at Goole) at 2315 at the same time as the airship, which apparently saw it and dropped three incendiary bombs just east of the bridge – two more falling in the river. *Zeppelin L 9* then flew over the town from east to west – dropping eight HE and 13 incendiary bombs on the town and docks. One of the HE bombs appeared to have been the large type (weighing 200 kg) and two others may have been 100 kg. Ten houses were demolished and several others badly damaged by explosion and fire; a dozen civilians being buried in the debris. A large shed on the dock-side was badly damaged – and in Aire Street, which was exclusively shop property (although no building was actually struck), a great amount of damage was done by the concussion of a large HE bomb which fell on the dock wharf opposite. Almost every window in the street was destroyed – and the doors were torn from their hinges. An incendiary bomb went through the roof of the Exchange, but did no damage. The total amount of the damage in the town was estimated to be £7,000. The fires were speedily got under control. One man, nine women and six children were killed; two more women were seriously injured and two men, two women and five children were slightly injured. All were persons in poor circumstances – and all the men were civilians. The airship then went off westwards – dropping 16 incendiary bombs as she went, which fell between the Lancashire and Yorkshire railway goods sidings and the North-Eastern Loop Line between the docks and the Dutch River Bridge. No damage was done. She passed Snaith at 2325 and then went north to Selby – where she passed over the Olympia Company's oil tanks – and turned eastwards at 2330. A quarter of an hour later, she dropped three incendiary bombs (one of which failed to ignite) in an open field at Hotham, seven miles south of Market Weighton; no damage being caused. She passed north of Beverly (again about midnight), went south and then east; was seen at Sigglesthorne just before 0010, 10 August and passed out to sea at Hornsea at 0012. There was a heavy ground mist the whole time the airship was over East Riding, which was probably the chief cause of her inability to find Hull – after which she had been confused as to her exact landfall by the action of the aeroplanes at Atwick.

Zeppelin L 11: This airship was commanded by *Oberleutnant zur See* Freiherr Horst von Buttlar and was first reported by HMS *Cynthia* six miles off the *Shipwash Lightship* at 2150 (appearing to have been in company with *Zeppelin L 10*). She struck the coast at Dunwich, Suffolk at 2200 and swung north – passing over Wrentham at 2210 and then over Pakefield, where an HE bomb was dropped on a farm (doing slight damage to fences and windows) and made Lowestoft from the south-west. At 2218 she began bombing the town. An HE bomb first demolished a wall and two greenhouses between The Avenue and London Road. The airship then went out to sea near the Claremont Pier and circled to the south – dropping four water flares, which fell in the sea and ignited. Having thus obtained the exact position of the town, she came in again near the Grand Hotel – and circling northward, dropped six more HE bombs. The first wrecked two small houses and a shop in Lovwell Road – killing a woman and burying another woman and two children (who were rescued from the debris unhurt). The second dropped in a back garden in Lorne Park Road – damaging walls and outbuildings. The third also fell in a back garden in Wellington Esplanade – doing similar damage. The fourth did some damage to a house in Wellington Esplanade. The fifth destroyed the roof and two or three rooms of a house in the same street – injuring a woman and three men of the 2/4th Battalion, Norfolk Regiment billeted in the house. The sixth fell on the pavement in Wellington Road – doing only slight damage. The total damage was estimated at £4,971. One woman was killed and three soldiers, two women and two children injured. Naval 6 pounder anti-aircraft guns went into action against the airship – firing 12 rounds – without visible effect. She went out to sea in a north-easterly direction at about 2225.

Zeppelin L 10: The airship was commanded by *Kapitänleutnant* Klaus Hirsch – an officer who had proved himself to be a good navigator and a resolute commander. The airship approached the coast in company with *Zeppelin L 11* and was sighted off Aldeburgh, Suffolk at 2140 and 10 minutes later came in overland – passing over Leiston at 2200 and reaching Dennington at 2210. At this point, she turned south-west – passing Framlingham, Otley – and on reaching Tuddenham, turned west. At 2235 she turned onto a south-westerly course when over Bramford – and was next heard at 2315 when she appeared over Coggeshall, heading south – passing over Kelvedon, Witham, Wickham Bishops and Maldon. At 2345 a flare was dropped at Little Stambridge (presumably to pinpoint her position) and at 2357 passed over Shoeburyness out into the Thames Estuary – dropping her first bombs (aimed at vessels on the river in the area of the Nore); five or six explosions were heard. The airship was next sighted off Sheppey and passed over Eastchurch village at 0009, 10 August and dropped six HE and six incendiary bombs on the aerodrome, but caused little damage. One of the HE bombs was later estimated to be of a 100 kg type – the first time one of these had been encountered. At 0008 two aircraft had taken off from the aerodrome to try and intercept the raider, but were unable to sight the airship in the fog and darkness. The raider passed on southwards – dropping two more HE bombs at Pumphill (half a mile south of Eastchurch) at 0015 – and at 0025 passed over Teynham and turned eastwards along the Swale – passing Leysdown and Faversham. The raider then passed out to sea near Whitstable at about 0030 – last being reported passing the Galloper at 0125.

Zeppelin L 12 was commanded by *Oberleutnant zur See* Werner Peterson, with *Leutnant* Brodrück being the second-in-command. The airship was first reported in company of *Zeppelin L 13* as approaching the *Edinburgh Lightship* from the east at 2215 (with both airships flying parallel courses) and were off the coast of Reculver, Kent between 2230 and 2240. The airships then parted company with *Zeppelin L 13* – following the estuary – and *Zeppelin L 12* turning eastwards to appear over Westgate at 2248. A Royal Naval Air Service aeroplane took off from Westgate to try and intercept, but failed to find either of the raiders and crashed on landing – killing the pilot, Flight Sub-Lieutenant Reginald Lord.[13] The airship then followed the coast along to North Foreland before turning west over Ramsgate and then proceeded to hover over The Downs for over an hour – being sighted over Kingsdown at 0005, 10 August – drifting towards the sea. At 0028 she approached Dover from the south – passing over the harbour at a height of about 5,000 feet and dropping about 12 bombs (all of which fell in the harbour, except for three incendiaries which fell on the Admiralty Pier). Two hit the parapet and burnt themselves out and the other fell through a corrugated iron roof near the transport office – setting fire to the platform. An HE bomb burst under the bows of the admiralty trawler *Equinox* – wounding three men (one seriously, who later died of his wounds). The ship was riddled with shrapnel, along with the admiralty trawler *Cleon*, which was moored alongside. The anti-aircraft guns in the harbour opened accurate fire on the airship (which appeared unexpected to the crew) – and the second or third round from a 3 inch gun was observed to hit her, as she was seen to reel and lifted her bows slightly. She then dropped all her water ballast, rose swiftly and at 0035 disappeared in a south-easterly direction. She was pursued by a naval and military aeroplane, but owing to her rapidly banking to a great height, they were unable to engage her and soon lost sight of her in fog.

13 Flight Lieutenant Reginald Lord – aged 23 from Newcastle – is buried in Margate Cemetery, Kent.

These pieces of Zeppelin bomb were removed from the woodwork of His Majesty's Armed Trawlers *Equinox* and *Cleon* following the raid on the Port of Dover, Kent by *Zeppelin L 12*. They are now conserved in the National Archives.

Zeppelin L 13 was commanded by *Kapitänleutnant* Heinrich Mathy, who had taken her over with his old crew from *Zeppelin L 9*. She was on her maiden voyage to England and was the latest production of the Zeppelin factory at Friedrichshafen, Germany. She was seen in company with *Zeppelin L 12* off the *Edinburgh Lightship* at 2215 and appeared off Reculver, Kent with her half an hour later – where they separated – and *Zeppelin L 13* proceeded up the River Thames (being reported from Wakering Haven and off Shoeburyness at 2310). She then returned to the mouth of the Thames and at 2355 was off Foreness. Here she stopped her engines and drifted for an hour – probably owing to some defect. At 0048 she was sighted off the North Foreland – heading south – and at 1259 she began dropping bombs in Sandwich Bay. She then headed off to the east towards Belgium, where a radiator burst.

Four airships were sighted off Ameland, Holland returning to Germany (consisting of *Zeppelins L 9, L 10, L 11* and either *L 6* or *L 7*), which had not taken part in the raid.

Summary for 9 August 1915:

Location	Number and type of bombs dropped	Casualties	Damage
Yorkshire, East Riding			
Hotham	3× IB		
Yorkshire, West Riding			
Goole	8× HE, 34× IB	16 killed, 11 injured	10 cottages and 2 warehouses in docks damaged
Suffolk			
Lowestoft	7× HE, 4× IB	1 killed, 7 injured	2 houses completely wrecked; several others seriously damaged
Pakefield	1× HE		
Kent			
Nore (in sea)	6× HE		
Eastchurch	8× HE, 6× IB		Near to aerodrome, windows broken
Dover	9× HE	3 injured	Slight damage to trawler and Admiralty Pier
Total	39× HE, 50× IB	17 killed, 21 injured	

Anti-aircraft guns in action and reported use of ammunition:

Location of AA battery	Calibre or type of gun	Number / type of rounds fired
Lowestoft	2× 6 pdr (naval)	
Dover		12 rounds
Langdon Fort	3"	10 rounds (airship hit by 2nd or 3rd round)
Drop Redoubt	2× 6 pdr	52 rounds
Castle	3× 1 pdr	–
Langdon Fort	2× 1 pdr	379 rounds
Capel	2× 6 pdr Hotchkiss	3 rounds
Skipsea	Rifle fire	2 rounds

Eighteen Royal Naval Air Service aircraft were sent up in pursuit of the raiders. Two aeroplanes crashed on landing, with Flight Sub-Lieutenant Reginald Lord being killed when his Sopwith Tabloid no.1212 crashed at Westgate Aerodrome, Kent[14].

Of the six bombs dropped on the Royal Naval Air Station, Redcar no serious damage was done – with one electric cable being cut and one window of Low Farm Cottage broken. A few of the ratings who were in charge of flare lights were hit by small pieces of bomb; no serious injury. A mole was killed. Holes were made in the ground five feet deep and 12 feet in diameter.

Eleven aircraft from Dunkirk were sent up to try and intercept the raiders on their return. Their results are detailed below:

Zeppelin L 12 clearly showing the tactical identification number. Also of note is the enclosed forward gondola and the precarious defensive machine-gun position on the top of the envelope.

14 Flight Sub-Lieutenant Reginald Lord is buried at Margate Cemetery, Kent.

10 August 1915
Zeppelin L 12 / LZ 43. Type P.
Sea: English Channel.
Hit by a shell fired by a 3 inch anti-aircraft gun, Langdon Fort, Dover.

The airship *Kommandeur* recounted in his report the events:

> Seriously damaged the airship; gradually descended until landed on the sea a few miles off Ostend and was taken in tow by German torpedo boats that had been summoned to her assistance. She was located by British naval aircraft flying from Dunkirk, Belgium at 0900 hours flying just above the water under escort by four torpedo boats. The British aircraft bombed her from 150 metres and was then followed by two more British aircraft, which also carried out bombing attacks. The airship was then towed through the water – reaching Ostend harbour about 1200 hours – and was moored alongside the quay, with workmen endeavouring to haul her out of the water. At about 1400 hours the airship broke her back and the rear half slipped back into the water.
>
> The airship was subsequently scrapped on site; the materials being taken to Germany by rail.
>
> Signed *Oberleutnant zur See* Werner Peterson.

Report by Wing Commander Gerrard, Royal Naval Air Service regarding the action of no.2 Aeroplane Wing, Royal Naval Air Service against a Zeppelin on 10 August 1915 as submitted to The Director of the Air Department, Admiralty, Whitehall, London, SW:

Having landed on the sea – and with her rear gas bags punctured – *Zeppelin L 12* broke her back before being taken under tow by ships of the *Kriegsmarine* and Belgian tugs.

At 0815 hrs on 10th August 1915 a signal was received by no.2 Wing RNAS Dunkirk that a damaged Zeppelin was in tow going towards Ostend. Following proceeded to attack Zeppelin. Weather conditions very bad; there being thick mist along the coast. At 0825 hrs Flight Commander Smyth-Pigott in a BE2c proceeded seaward to Ostend – reaching 2,000 feet in thick clouds. Three miles seaward he observed a Zeppelin apparently about his own level, so turned away to gain more height. He lost sight of it and after a few minutes, came lower again when he sighted it above the water – and apparently in the process of being hauled down. He glided to 500 feet and dropped two 20 lb bombs; then retreated into clouds and prepared for a second attack. Turning and coming down to 500 ft again, he observed the rear compartment but one to be broken – apparently not due to a direct hit, but from concussion of one of the 20 lb bombs (the mark of which was observed on the water alongside). The Zeppelin was surrounded by four TEDs, which opened heavy machine-gun fire – as well as anti-aircraft batteries from the shore. The pilot then dropped six grenades – apparently without further result. Next observations, however, showed the Zeppelin's back was broken. Machine was hit twice; one in the propeller and one in the fuselage. Returned 0930 hrs.

0935 hrs: Flight Lieutenant D K Johnson, on a Henry Farman, proceeded to Ostend for the purpose of continuing the bombardment, but did not return. The weather was still very thick.

At 09.45 hrs Flt Sub-Lt Besson left on a Bristol Scout. Fog was lifting at this time, but clouds were heavy and low. He approached Ostend at 1,000 ft and observed Zeppelin being towed between harbour piers. From a height of 1,500 ft he attacked with four 20 lb bombs and observed the first bomb to fall about 30 yards on the west side of the objective, which he straddled with the remainder, but was unable to see the result. Turning out to sea for a second attack, he climbed to 2,000 ft and dropped 12 grenades, but was unable to see the effect. The Zeppelin appeared to be badly crushed in the rear half. Machine was subjected to extremely heavy fire from anti-aircraft batteries all the time. Returned at 1045 hrs.

At 0955 hrs Flight Lieut Bettington, on a Bristol Scout, approached Ostend at 2,000 ft in clouds and came out nearly over the Zeppelin – and saw kites at about his level (apparently intended to foul him). He dropped six grenades, two 20 lb bombs and then six more grenades – apparently straddling the target – though on turning away, the Zeppelin appeared in the same condition and position as before. Also under heavy fire all the time. Returning late owing to engine trouble.

At 1120 hrs the weather was clearing rapidly. Flt Sub-Lt Bush, on a BE2c, reached a height of 6,000 feet and glided over the Zeppelin at 1,800 ft; dropped 12 grenades in couples at the object. Result unobserved owing to extremely heavy fire. Zeppelin was observed to be alongside the quay adjoining the railway station, with the rear half completely crumpled up. It appeared that the front half was being dragged up on to the quay. Returned 1240 hrs.

At 1320 hrs Flt Sub-Lt Leslie, in a Henry Farman, approached Ostend at a height of 9,000 feet; good view of Zeppelin, which was half on quay and half in water; dropped seven 20 lb bombs at a height of 8,000 ft – and when last seen Zeppelin, was in the same position, but a crowd of workmen easily noticeable at first had entirely disappeared. Owing to the extreme fierceness and accuracy of the fire – and the thickness of the black smoke from HE shells – observation was carried out with great difficulty. Visibility clear. Returned 1500 hrs. Shrapnel bullets through wings and one through the nacelle.

At 1330 hrs Flight Lieut Buss, on an Avro, approached the Zeppelin from seaward at 9,000 ft. The Zeppelin was observed to be hauled up on the quay. Her back was broken. Rear half appeared to be pointing into the air. Groups of workmen were on the quay by the side of the airship. When over the target, four bombs were dropped – and when next observed, the Zeppelin was partly in the water again. The workmen had all disappeared. Visibility clear. Returned 1505 hrs. One interplane strut was struck by shrapnel.

At 1340 hrs Flight Commdr Robinson, on Nieuport (fighting class), accompanied Sub-Lieut Leslie as protection against hostile aircraft, while dropping bombs from Henry Farman on Zeppelin moored at quay at Ostend. Being fired at heavily, he remained in the offing to seaward of Ostend until Sub-Lieut Leslie was well away. He observed no result after the bomb dropping, but the Zeppelin's position and attitude was the same as previously reported. Three German TEDs were steaming about three miles seaward of Ostend, which on being flown over, turned and steamed easterly.

Having being towed back to the land, *Zeppelin L 12* was partially hauled up onto Ostend Quay.

Following all the efforts to salvage her, *Zeppelin L 12* caught fire and was destroyed – leaving only her scorched framework to be salvaged for the valuable aluminium.

At 1835 hrs Flt Sub-Lieut Besson, on a Nieuport, approached Ostend from a height of 12,000 ft. Zeppelin was observed to have the rear half in the water and the remainder was covered by the smoke of a big oil flare burning alongside. When over the target, he dropped four 10 lb bombs, but could not see the effect. Proceeding to Zeebrugge, he dropped from a similar height two 10 lb bombs on the anti-aircraft guns on the west side of the town. The *Wieligen Lightship* was showing a light and was in the same position as previously reported. Seaplane vessel previously reported near the mole had left. Machine arrived back at 1735 hrs.

It was observed that the bombardment was discontinued after 0100 hrs – with the exception of the evening reconnaissance – as the sky was so clear that inaccurate attacks from a great height were possible (and in view of the fact that the French authorities were to carry out a night attack with seven machines and requested that these operations should be left entirely to them so as to avoid confusion).[15]

12 August 1915

Weather: fine over the North Sea; wind clam to very light from the west and south-west.

On the night of 12 August three naval airships – *Zeppelins L 9*, *L 10* and *L 11* – were reported approaching the English Coast, but only *Zeppelin L 10*, commanded by *Kapitänleutnant* Klaus Hirsch, actually crossed the coast and attacked Woodbridge and Harwich, Essex. One of the other airships reconnoitred the mouth of the Thames and possibly came overland, but dropped no bombs. *Zeppelin L 10* crossed the coast at Pakefield, Suffolk at 2125 and flew south-westward – passing between

15 The National Archives – (TNA) 1/629/17/122/15: report of 2 Wing Royal Naval Air Service operations against Zeppelins and sheds.

Kessingland and Carlton Colville at 2130 – and was fired at by Maxims of the Shropshire Yeomanry while over Benacre. She passed over Covehithe at 2135 and Bassingham at 2205 where she dropped a couple of fuel tanks. Turning south, she passed between Great Glenham and Framlingham – and from 2215 hovered over Wickham Market for five minutes, where she dropped two flares. Then heading southwards to the railway at Pettistree, she dropped an incendiary bomb (which did no damage). The airship then turned and followed the railway line to Woodbridge – and just outside the town, was fired upon by machine-guns and rifle fire from the troops of the 2/3rd Battalion, London Infantry Brigade. This drew return fire from the airship, which dropped four HE and 20 incendiary bombs on the town. Five cottages were destroyed and one partly wrecked. Sixty-four other buildings and a church were damaged. Six people were killed and seven injured. One of the incendiary bombs that was dropped was found to have a ·303 bullet embedded in it – either having hit the bomb while it was in the airship, or during its descent. Leaving Woodbridge at about 2230 the airship headed towards Ipswich, where it dropped three incendiary bombs at Kesgrave (which caused no damage). At 2240 while over Rushmere Heath, anti-aircraft motor machine-guns of the Royal Naval Air Service opened fire and received two HE bombs in reply, which although exploding near the guns, did no damage. *Zeppelin L 10* then turned away from Ipswich and headed towards the River Orwell – crossing it at 2255 near Pinmill. The airship then passed westwards for a short while and was spotted over Woolverstone at 2300. She then turned south – passing Holbrook at 2305 – and slowly veered round towards Harwich. At 2310 she dropped one HE bomb on Shotley Marshes and then crossed the River Stour. Shortly before 2315 eight HE and four incendiary bombs fell at Parkestone. Two of the HE and two of the incendiaries fell in the river and one HE in the mud. Of the others, two houses were wrecked and windows broken in a number of properties. Seventeen people were injured. It was presumed that the airship was attracted to Harwich by lights that were showing at the time in the harbour, as a squadron of destroyers had just entered and were in the process of mooring. After bombing Parkestone, *Zeppelin L 10* went off over Fagbury Point and Trimley and out to sea at 2325 after being fired at by armoured cars of the Royal Naval Air Service, situated at Shingle Street. She then followed the coast along – and in again over Orford – before finally passing out to sea over Orfordness at 2336.

Zeppelin L 11, commanded by *Freiherr* Horst von Buttlar, was sighted off the Kent Coast at 2100 – and after hovering over the sea off various East Kent towns until 0048 she then headed off towards Germany without dropping any bombs. *Hauptmann* Stelling, commanding *Zeppelin L 9*, followed *Zeppelin L 10* until reaching Lowestoft and hovered in the vicinity before heading out to sea.

Summary for 12 August 1915:

Location	Number and type of bombs dropped	Casualties	Damage
Suffolk			
Pettistree	1× IB		
Melton	1× IB		
Woodbridge	4× HE, 20× IB	7 killed, 6 injured	5 houses destroyed, 1 wrecked; many damaged
Kesgrave	3× HE, 3× IB		
Rushmere	2× HE		
Shotley	1× HE		
Essex:			
Parkestone	8× HE, 4× IB	17 injured	2 houses wrecked, others damaged; telephone wires broken
Total	18× HE, 29× IB	7 killed, 28 injured	

Anti-aircraft guns in action and reported use of ammunition:

Location of AA battery	Calibre or type of gun	Number / type of rounds fired
Benacre	Maxims, Shropshire Yeomanry	–
Woodbridge	·303 Maxims and rifle fire; 2/3rd Bn, London Infantry Brigade	–
Rushmere	.45 Maxim gun cars; RNAS machine-gun and rifle fire with .45 incendiary ammunition	–
Harwich		
Ray Hill	6 pdr	1 tracer round
Beacon Hill	Pom-Pom	2 rounds
Shingle Street	.45 Maxim gun cars; RNAS	–

Four aircraft were sent up from Yarmouth to intercept the raider without results.

Being able to drop one's bombs on the desired target was a problem that has haunted aviators for many years, as there are many factors that have to be taken into consideration when determining the sighting of a target – from a moving object operating in three dimensions and the fall of the bomb, which has various forces acting upon it that will shift it from its intended course. Airships, at times, had the ability to hover relatively stationary over a target – thus eliminating the factor of determining their ground velocity from the equation, but wind speed and drift were much more difficult to determine (along with whether the airship was completely level). The other factors that came into play were the effects of wind and the aerodynamic shape of the bomb – along with actually being able to identify your intended target (let alone being over the correct town or city). The Germans were quick to identify the need for an efficient and accurate bombsight – and they soon turned to Carl Zeiss of Jena (who were well-known for their manufacture of high-resolution optics and precision instrumentation) to come up with a solution.

17 August 1915

Weather: wind from the north but very light; 10 miles per hour at 1,500 feet. Fine but cloudy, with thunderstorms in East Anglia during the afternoon of 17 August.

Three airships – *Zeppelins L 10, L 11* and *L 14* – crossed the North Sea, with *Zeppelin L 10* reaching London and *Zeppelin L 11* dropping bombs in Kent. *Zeppelin L 14* was on her maiden voyage and merely approached the Norfolk Coast and then went away after dropping her bombs in the sea.

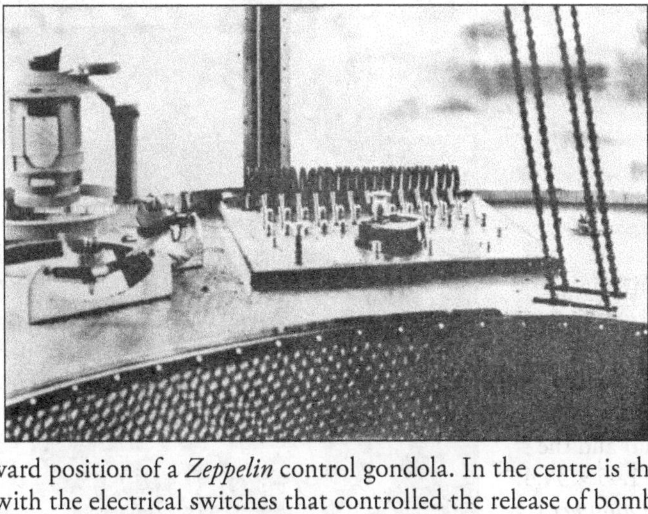

The forward position of a *Zeppelin* control gondola. In the centre is the control panel, with the electrical switches that controlled the release of bombs either individually or in a salvo. To the left is the bombsight – clearly showing the eye piece that the commander would determine his intended target through – before operating the bomb release switches with his right hand. The chain linkages to the right of the photograph controlled the airship's rudder and elevator.

A close-up of the Carl Zeiss-manufactured bombsight that was recovered from the wreckage of *Zeppelin LZ 85* at Salonika, Greece.

The airship *Kommandeur's* view of the bombsight – giving the manufacturer's logo (encompassing Carl Zeiss-Jena) and the calibration 1.45 × 34.4. The *werke nummer* is *nr54*. Note the nice addition of a bracket holding the stopwatch next to the eye piece.

Zeppelin L 14, commanded by *Kapitänleutnant der Reserve* Alois Böcker,[16] was first reported off the *Would Lightship* at 2020. At 2145 she passed the *Haisbro Lightship* going north, and then turned and passed the lightship at 2200 following the coast. At 2240 she passed the *Cross Sand Lightship* heading north-north-west – and at 2250 returned at a height of only 200 feet and dropped an incendiary bomb aimed at the lightship, but missed. She was next spotted near Yarmouth, Norfolk at 1110 and off Caister at 2325 heading out to sea. The airship was next reported at 2340 over the *Cross Sand Lightship* – south of which she dropped about 15 bombs into the sea and fired at a steamer with machine-guns – before heading off across the North Sea.

Zeppelin L 10, commanded by *Kapitänleutnant* Klaus Hirsch, made the English Coast at 2225 at Sizewell Gap and then rounded Orfordness into Hollesley Bay, Suffolk at 2250. At 2256 she came overland at Shingle Street, where she was fired at by two armoured cars of the Royal Naval Air Service. Her commander was presumed to be feeling her way cautiously – no doubt in order to be certain of his position and avoid the anti-aircraft guns at Harwich. The airship passed Holbrook and at 2125 reached Manningtree – there meeting the railway line, which she followed for the greater part of her journey to London. At 2132 she turned south of Stratford St Mary and at 2140 passed Colchester. At 2208 she went over Writtle and at 2217 was at Ongar, where she dropped a fuel tank. From there, she followed the railway to Epping – heading onto Waltham Abbey, where a 1 pdr anti-aircraft gun opened fire at her. Then turning south-west to Chingford, where she was at for 2230, at about 2234 she dropped her first bombs at Walthamstow. The first incendiary fell in Lloyd's Park (doing no damage) and a second incendiary fell in Hoe Street, near Orford Road (also causing no damage). A third fell close by on the Stratford Co-operative Store buildings in Hoe Street – penetrating the roof and floor of a shop, but was quickly extinguished by a watchman. The airship now picked up the Midland Railway Line from Tottenham to Forest Gate and followed it more or less throughout her course to London.

The first HE bomb now fell on Baker's Avenue, Leyton – demolishing four flats and shattering all the windows in the street. Four men, two women and two children were injured. Three more HE bombs then fell close by in the grounds of the Baker's

16 *Kapitänleutnant der Reserve* Alois Böcker was originally an officer of the Mercantile Marine. In the war, he had previously commanded the airship *Zeppelin L 5*, which was destroyed over the Baltic in July 1915. When in command of *Zeppelin L 14*, he distinguished himself during two raids: on Hull on 5 March 1916 and one on Edinburgh on 2 April 1916. In a raid on 31 January 1916 he took his airship further west than any airship had been over England: to the neighbourhood of Shrewsbury. In the autumn of 1916 he commanded *Zeppelin L 33* and was brought down in her after a raid on London on 26 September. His second-in-command on *L 14*, *Oberleutnant zur See* Frankenberg (who was also on *Zeppelin L 33* in the same capacity), was not on board the airship when it was brought down and the crew captured. Later, he commanded *Zeppelin L 21* and was killed when the airship was brought down in flames off Lowestoft on 28 November 1916.

Almshouses, Lea Bridge Road – shaking the buildings, breaking the windows and seriously injuring one woman. An HE bomb followed in the roadway of the Lew Bridge Road – destroying the tram lines and pavements. One HE and three incendiary bombs next fell in Lea Bridge Road – badly damaging the buildings of the tramway depot; caused a slight fire; and broke windows in seven shops. One man was slightly injured. The airship then dropped an HE bomb in Dunton Road – badly damaging a house and breaking the windows of many others. This was followed by an HE bomb in Parmer Road – south of the railway – which also damaged a house. The raider then dropped four HE bombs on and around the railway station at Leyton – wrecking the station booking office and billiard saloon – and seriously damaging a house (and breaking windows in a large number of others) and a Wesleyan chapel. A steamroller was also badly damaged and three men and a woman were killed – with seven men, four women and three children being injured. Two incendiary bombs then dropped in Grosvenor Road – doing very little damage. A single HE then fell in Claude Road – wrecking a house and breaking glass of 175 others in the neighbourhood. A man, woman and child were killed; while the incendiary bomb that followed in Murchison Road scarcely did any damage. One HE and two incendiary bombs then fell in Albert Road – the HE badly damaging one house – and the incendiaries each caused a small fire. A woman and child were slightly hurt. Another incendiary in Twickenham Road also caused a small fire, but no casualties. This was followed by two HE in Oakdale and Ashville roads – causing a great deal of damage; badly damaging 30 houses and breaking the windows of 123 besides killing two men and injuring four men, 11 women and six children. The Zeppelin was now a quarter of a mile south of the railway, which she had been following, and bore eastwards in order to regain it. Crossing the Great Eastern Railway Line to Chingford between Grove Green and Norman roads, she dropped an incendiary bomb on the railway line, which caused no damage. Serious damage was now done by a couple of incendiary bombs which fell on St Augustine's Church, Lincoln Street, Leytonstone – the resultant fire gutting the building. Another incendiary bomb in Mayville Road caused a fire in a kitchen and an HE bomb in Southwell Grove Road demolished the backs of two houses and broke the windows of 132 houses nearby – one man being killed. Another HE and two incendiary bombs that fell on Wanstead Flats (just north of the Midland Railway and east of Montague Road) broke the windows of 73 houses. The last HE bomb to be dropped on London fell near the model yachting lake in Wanstead Flats. The concussion broke windows in 75 private houses in the neighbourhood, but did no other damage. Four incendiaries followed on the Flats: one near the Woodford Road, two close to the bandstand and one at the head of Tylney Road – causing no damage. These bombs – which fell at about 2245 – were the last dropped by the airship in the London District. The airship now went off parallel to and on the north side of the Great Eastern Main Line – passing between Ongar and Brentwood at 2300 and reaching Chelmsford at 2315 – and dropped two HE bombs (one exploding in a field to the west of the town and the other passing through a house in Glebe Road – embedding itself in the earth beneath the basement without exploding). The airship, having passed north of Chelmsford, now crossed to the south of the railway – and after passing north of Mersea Island, reached Wivenhoe, where she turned northward, passed to the east of Colchester and dropped a flare (Blendbombe), which lit up the whole of the surrounding countryside with an intense glare. At 2350 she turned north-east near Stratford St Mary and followed a route past Holbrook and reached the River Orwell at Wherstead – turning down-river towards Harwich – but at the Trimley Bend, turned south-east to Felixstowe, crossed the mouth of the Deben and went out to sea at 0020 at Shingle Street (being the same spot where she crossed on her inward journey) and once again came under fire from the armoured cars of the Royal Naval Air Service. On her return to Germany, *Zeppelin L 10* passed over the Dutch island of Vlieland, where she was fired upon by the Dutch defences.

Zeppelin L 11, commanded by *Oberleutnant zur See* Horst von Buttlar, passed the *Gunfleet Lightship* shortly before 2100 and crossed the coast at Herne Bay, Kent at 2130. She came in low over the pier from the sea, but rose to 7,000 feet immediately upon being fired at by rifles of the men of the 42nd Provisional Battalion. She went directly south over Herne to Canterbury and at 2135 crossed the city from east to west at a height estimated to be 8,000 feet – afterwards going south-east towards Chartham (following the railway to Ashford). At Chartham, she diverged from the line southward – following the straight line of the Roman Road, Stone Street, which was mistaken for a railway line. She passed over Hastingleigh about 2145 and at Smeeth turned west along the railway. On approaching Ashford at 2155 she made a half-circle round the town to the north and then went off towards Great Chart – afterwards returning to the south of the town and passing directly overhead until she reached the Canterbury Road, where she turned north-west; dropping bombs as she went. Eight incendiary bombs fell in gardens on the east side of the road and in a monastery close by. No damage resulted beyond the killing of a couple of chickens. These were followed by 10 incendiary and two HE bombs which fell in fields near the sanatorium on the Maidstone Road; the only casualty being a sheep. The airship then headed off in the direction of Faversham, turned north and at about 2230 was plotted three miles east of Faversham. She then turned south and retraced the course as far as Molash. Here she circled – presumably seeking a target – and finally (at about 2300) dropped 16 HE and 25 incendiary bombs in open country in the parishes of Badlesmere and Sheldwick near the Lees Park VAD Hospital.

The anti-aircraft gun at Faversham was unable to come to action owing to the current for the searchlight having been cut off from the powder works as the managing director considered that the light was too near the works and betrayed their position. At about 2315 the airship went away in a north-easterly direction, passed over Hernhill and out over the River Swale at Graveny. She was heard over the Swale from the Isle of Sheppey at 2330 and then passed in over the coast again and south of Whitstable (over Blean Woods and north-west of Herne), where she was again subjected to rifle fire at about 2340 from the 57th (West Lancashire) Division Bicycle Company. On being fired upon, she veered away to the north and finally passed out to sea at 2345 at Herne Bay – being last heard off Shellness in the direction of the Thames Estuary.

Summary for 17 August 1915:

Location	**Number and type of bombs dropped**	**Casualties**	**Damage**
Walthamstow	3× IB		Slight damage to shop
Leyton	16× HE, 10× IB	9 killed, 38 injured	Large number of houses damaged; railway station partly wrecked; tramway depot damaged; several small fires
Leystone	1× HE, 3× IB	1 killed	Church destroyed by fire; 2 houses partially destroyed
Wanstead Flats	2× HE, 8× IB		Many houses damaged
Chelmsford	2× HE		Houses damaged
Ashford	2× HE, 19× IB		Sheep and 2 fowls killed
Badlesmere and Sheldwick	16× HE, 25× IB		Church windows broken
In sea	15-20× HE		
Total	60× HE, 68× IB	10 killed, 38 injured	

Anti-aircraft guns in action and reported use of ammunition:

Location of AA battery	**Calibre or type of gun**	**Number / type of rounds fired**
Shingle Street	4x Maxims (RNAS)	Twice in action
Waltham Abbey	1 pdr QF	2 rounds
Herne Bay	Rifle fire	–
Herne	Rifle fire	429 rounds Japanese small arms ammunition

Six aircraft were dispatched to intercept the raiders, but only one caught sight of one of them in the distance and was blown up on landing when its bombs exploded; the two crew being injured.

3 September 1915
Zeppelin L 10 / LZ 40. Type P.
Neuwerk Island, Germany.
Caught fire after being struck by lightning.

Kapitänleutnant Klaus Hirsch +.
Oberleutnant zur See Josef Sticker +.
Obermaschinistenmaat Gustav Lieder +.
Bootsmannsmaat Heinrich Paradies +.
Maschinistenmaat Alfred Beyer +.
Maschinistenmaat Hans Popp +.
Maschinistenmaat Friedrich Bormann +.
Matrose Albrecht Schoberth +.
Signalmaat Karl Felsch +.
Maschinistenmaat Adolf Schöpfin +.
Steuermann Albert Gantz +.
Signalmaat Max Schwarzer +.
Funkentelegraphistenobermaat Georg Helgemayer +.
Funkentelegraphistenobergast Gottlieb Weiss +.
Obermaschinistenmaat Artur Höfer +.
Maschinistenmaat Karl Wichmann +.
Segelmachermaat Otto Jahn +.
Maschinist Artur Wolgien +.
Obermaschinistenmaat Otto Lehmer +.

7 September 1915

Weather: very quiet conditions over the North Sea; the winds being calm to light and variable; the sky cloudless to overcast and the lower atmosphere a little misty locally up the East Coast. A dark period for the moon, which rose at 0400 on 7 September and set at 1952 on 14 September.

Zeppelins LZ 77, *LZ 74* and *Schütte-Lanz SL 2* were involved in the night's raid, which came as a shock to the defenders as there was no indication of an impending raid (and neither were the airships sighted prior to their crossing the coast).

Zeppelin LZ 77, commanded by *Hauptmann* Alfred Horn, was first seen from the *Kentish Knock Lightship* travelling west at 2205 and next sighted over Clacton-on-Sea, Essex at 2240 still travelling west. The coast watching troops at Clacton fired a few rounds of small arms ammunition as she passed. She was sighted over Brightlingsea at 2250 and, changing course slightly to the north-west, passed south of Wivenhoe at 2255 to Coggeshall at 2310. She then turned south and was sighted west of Kelvedon and Witham. Thence, she went west to Great Waltham – and following the River Chelmer, passed north-west of Felstead and then turned south-west again to Leaden Roding, where she was at 2357. At about 0015, 8 September she was over Hatfield Broad Oak – the most westerly point to which she penetrated inland. The airship seemed to be wandering slowly – perhaps searching for a suitable target, or in a quest for navigational pinpoints. It was improbable that her objective was London, as the glare from the capital must have been clearly visible to the crew. The airship then turned sharply to east-north-east and passed at moderate speed over Dunmow at

0025 to Bocking, where she turned north-east – passing between Cavendish and Sudbury, and then between Bury St Edmunds and Stowmarket. She arrived in the neighbourhood of Walsham-le-Willows at 0105. Once more altering course to the south and east, the first bomb was dropped at Monk Soham at 0130; the incendiary bomb failing to ignite. Following the same course, the first HE bomb fell on Framlingham and also failed to detonate. The next attempt was at Great Glenham, where two incendiary bombs were dropped amongst some farm buildings, where a reaper and self-binder were destroyed. Passing Benhall at 0142 three incendiary bombs were dropped – one failing to ignite, but all failed to cause damage. The ship was sighted over Benhall as being stationary – and presumably, the commander was unsure of his position, for the airship suddenly turned north-west and circled Saxmundham for five minutes before following the railway line in the direction of Leiston, and then turned again north-north-east and passed over Theberton at 0153. At 0205 the airship was sighted to the south of Southwold and north of Dunwich – whereupon finding the coast, followed it as far as Lowestoft and at 0220 passed out to sea in a north-easterly direction. At 0405 three explosions were heard out to sea in the direction which the airship had taken – and were no doubt bombs dropped in the sea (possibly being aimed at shipping).

Schütte-Lanz SL 2, commanded by *Hauptmann* von Wobeser, was first picked up at 2215 north of the *Tongue Lightship* proceeding due west. At 2250 she crossed the coast at the mouth of the Crouch – flying very low – and was fired at with rifles by the look-out post at Holliwell Point, Essex. She immediately rose and went on westward – following the river to Burnham. Heading south-west, she reached Rochford soon after 2300 and headed to London – following the railway line most of the way and passing Wickford, Billericay, Brentwood, Harold Wood, Romford and Leytonstone. Here she turned south – following the left bank of the River Lea and making straight

Army Zeppelin LZ 77 manoeuvring close to the ground. Note the anchoring guide rails used anchoring the airship once it is on the ground and guiding into its hangar.

for the Isle of Dogs. Here she dropped seven incendiary bombs and one HE bomb at 2345 in a line between Havannah Street and Gaverick Street, Millwall. The first IB failed to ignite, but 11 people were injured by the HE bomb which fell in Gaverick Street – demolishing three houses and severely damaging two others. An incendiary bomb was then dropped on a barge in the river off Snowden's Wharf – damaging it and severely burning two men. This was followed by an HE bomb which fell in the Thames mud above the low-water mark on the Millwall side and three incendiary bombs at Deptford at 2350. The first fell in the Royal Victualling Yard – destroying barrels of wire; the second fell in the Supply Reserve Depot, Army Service Corps – breaking the glass roof; while the third fell in Hughes' Field – setting fire to a small dwelling house and killing the five occupants. The airship now followed the Thames in the direction of Woolwich – crossing Deptford Creek. She dropped two incendiary bombs in Norman Road (one doing slight damage) and one in Greenwich Road (causing no damage). Three more incendiaries were dropped – one falling in South Street and one in Brand Street (neither of which ignited) and one on Royal Hill, which did no damage. Another followed in Greenwich Park, close to the Observatory, and another three in the park – one of which did not ignite; then a blind HE bomb fell in the garden of Mr Justice Scrutton's residence in Mycenae Road, followed by an incendiary in Glenluce Road along with an incendiary and HE bomb in fields near Victoria Road. An incendiary then fell in Charlton Lane near the Horse and Groom public house – doing slight damage – and was followed by another in Pett Street, Woolwich, which broke a number of windows and injured three people. From Woolwich, the *Schütte-Lanz* crossed the river and was engaged by a 6 pounder gun in the Arsenal, with three rounds, without effect; the airship being reported flying at about 8,000 feet and travelling very fast. When across the river, she turned west again – appearing over Southwark at 0005 where she dropped two HE bombs in Keetons Road, which damaged two houses and wrecked a greenhouse, followed by one HE bomb in Ilderton Road, where a house was wrecked and six people killed. Crossing the Surrey Canal, the airship dropped her next bomb – an HE in Sharratt Street – where a house was badly damaged and five people seriously injured. Another HE bomb then fell in Hunsdon Road, New Cross – doing slight damage and injuring a policeman – followed immediately by another HE in Monson Road, which damaged a school. Two HE bombs then fell on sidings of the London, Brighton and South Coast Railway at New Cross (doing slight damage to the track and rolling stock), followed by two HE bombs which destroyed one house and severely damaged two others in Childeric Road – killing three and injuring six people. These were followed by two more HE bombs which fell on Clifton Hill – demolishing one house and damaging two others – and a school besides Angus Street; two people being killed and three injured. The last bomb also fell in Edward Street – damaging 100 houses, but caused no casualties. The airship then passed on between Brockley and Lewisham at 0027 – apparently following the railway line to Chislehurst, where two airships were seen at 0033. The other airship was presumably *Zeppelin LZ 74*, which was closely following *Schütte-Lanz SL 2*, which passed over Bexley Heath and reached

Erith at 0040. Having found the Thames again, she appeared to follow it to Purfleet, where she crossed to Essex at 0045 and steered a steady north-easterly course for the coast via Pitsea, Rayleigh and Mundon to Maldon – from where she followed the River Blackwater past Tollesbury to the sea. She then passed inland between Wivenhoe and Brightlingsea at about 0145 – past Thorrington and Walton-on-the-Naze and Harwich. Here she was fired at by a Pom-Pom on Beacon Hill and by another at Landguard without result. At 0215 she passed Felixstowe and was seen flying out to sea at an estimated height of 5-6,000 feet and at a speed of 40 to 50 miles per hour. The searchlights at Harwich could not be used, as a naval aeroplane (with Commander Hope Vere as the pilot) went up in pursuit from Felixstowe and it was considered that the light may have dazzled him. The machine, subsequently, crash-landed at Trimley and was wrecked; the pilot escaping unhurt.

Schütte-Lanz SL 2 came to grief on her return to Belgium. She apparently crossed the Dutch Coast very early in the morning at Zandvoort (near Haarlem) and was seen at Amsterdam and Hilversum flying at about 9,000 feet, went south, passed 's-Hertogenbosch and was over Breda about 0700. She was seen with only one engine working – perhaps owing to shortage of fuel. She there attempted to land – and when descending, the commander lost control and fell (hitting a house) and was severely damaged.

It was supposed at the time that the airship had been damaged by anti-aircraft fire, as a large hole was observed in one of the gondolas, but it was most probably due to her accident, as nothing appeared to be wrong with her until she reached Belgium. She remained – undergoing temporary repairs at Berchem until 17 October 1915 – when she proceeded east and was partially rebuilt at Mannheim. *SL 2* took part in no further raids over England – and was presumably scrapped. Her commander was last heard of as being posted missing in *Schütte-Lanz SL 10* (over the Black Sea).

Zeppelin LZ 74, commanded by *Hauptmann* George, came in over Bradwell-Juxta-Mare, Norfolk at 2255 and followed the course of the River Blackwater to Maldon and then Danbury, Great Baddow before being sighted near Chelmsford. She then set course for the valley of the Lea – via Ongar and North Weald Bassett – to Broxbourne. There she turned south along the river and railway – reaching Cheshunt, Hertfordshire at about midnight and flying at a height of about 9,000 feet. Here 18 HE bombs were dropped – one of which failed to explode – along with 27 incendiaries which fell between Windmill Lane and Turkey Street. Minor damage to property resulted in Windmill Lane, where the first HE bomb fell – seriously damaging six houses. At the rear of Turner's Hill, nine of the HE and five of the incendiary bombs fell – seriously damaging a coach house and garage and breaking a large number of windows. Two more of the HE bombs landed on the Great Eastern Railway, Cheshunt and Edmonton Branch – damaging the line. Then the next six HE bombs and 21 incendiaries damaged nurseries in Park Lane and Bullsmoor Lane – shattering glass in greenhouses and starting three small fires. No damage was caused by the last bomb – an incendiary that fell in a field near Turkey Street on the north side of the New River. The airship was now engaged by anti-aircraft guns at Waltham Abbey, which fired one round from a 3 inch gun and two rounds from a 6 pounder without result. The airship then followed the right bank of the River Lea towards London, passing Edmonton and Finsbury Park, and arrived over the city of London at 0020 – dropping an incendiary bomb on 10, Coopers Row near Fenchurch Street. A store was set alight, but the fire was soon extinguished and little damaged caused. She now crossed the Thames, travelled slowly on a south-easterly course and was next reported over Peckham Rye; then Honor Oak Park; and then Bromley. She now turned north-east – in company with *Schütte-Lanz SL 2* – at about 0035 and was near Chislehurst with her, but at considerably greater height. Here the airships set course to the north-east – past Bexley Heath and crossed the river to Purfleet, where she was engaged by a 3 inch gun (which fired two rounds) and a Pom-Pom (which fired nine rounds). The raider was now flying at a height of about 10,000 feet and at a speed of 40 miles per hour. No hits were observed and the ship went on via Laindon to Chelmsford before being seen at Broomfield – at the same time turning from north to north-east to follow the railway. She went on parallel with the line about a mile south – passing Witham, Tiptree, Colchester and Mistley – from where she followed the railway and the River Colne to Harwich at 0212. She passed out to sea over the *Cork Lightship* and returned to Belgium by passing over part of Holland.

Summary for 7 September 1915:

Location	Number and type of bombs dropped	Casualties	Damage
Suffolk			
Monk Soham	1× IB		
Framlingham	1× HE (ux)		
Great Glenham	2× IB		Agricultural machine destroyed
Benhall	3× IB		
London			
Millwall	1× HE, 7× IB	11 injured	3 houses destroyed, others damaged
On a barge near Snowden's Wharf	1× IB	2 injured	Barge damaged by fire
River Thames	1× IB		
Deptford:			
Royal Victualling Yard	1× IB		Slight damage
ASC Depot	1× IB		Slight damage
Hughes' Field	1× IB	5 killed, 2 injured	House damage by fire

Location	Number and type of bombs dropped	Casualties	Damage
Childeric Road	2× HE	3 killed, 3 injured	Tenement house destroyed, 3 damaged; road torn up; gas and water mains damaged
Clifton Hill	2× HE	2 killed, 6 injured	House destroyed; school and 3 houses damaged
Edward Street	1× HE		2 houses damaged
Southwark			
Keetons Road	2× HE		2 houses and greenhouses damaged
Ilderton Road	1× HE	6 killed, 6 injured	House wrecked; windows of school and baths broken
New Cross:			
Sharratt Street	1× HE	1 injured	House badly damaged
Hunsdon Road	1× HE	Policeman injured	Slight damage to garden and fence
Monson Road	1× HE		School playground damaged; windows broken
London, Brighton and South Coast Railway Sidings	2× HE		Damage to line and rolling stock
Greenwich			
Norman Road	2× IB		Wooden building damaged by fire
Greenwich Road	1× IB		
South Street	1× IB		
Brand Street	1× IB		
Royal Hill	1× IB		
Greenwich Park	4× IB		
Charlton			
Beaconsfield Road	1× IB		
Mycenae Road	1× HE (ux)		
Glenluce Road	1× IB		
Victoria Road	1× HE		Windows broken
Charlton Lane	1× IB		Fence and roadway damaged

Location	Number and type of bombs dropped	Casualties	Damage
Woolwich			
Pett Street	1× IB		
Kingsman Street	1× HE	3 injured	Roadway damaged; gas and water mains broken; windows broken
City of London:			
Crutched Friars	1× IB		Bonded store slightly damaged by fire
Middlesex			
Cheshunt	18× HE, 27× IB		Large number of cottages, greenhouses and small buildings damaged
Total	37× HE, 60× IB	18 killed, 38 injured	

Anti-aircraft guns in action and reported use of ammunition:

Location of AA battery	Calibre or type of gun	Number / type of rounds fired
Woolwich No.4	6 pdr QF	3 rounds
Woolwich No.11 (Royal Albert Docks)	13 pdr	1 round
Cheshunt	6 pdr	2 rounds
Enfield Lock	3" QF	1 round
Waltham Abbey	3"	1 round
Waltham Abbey	6 pdr	2 rounds
Purfleet	3"	2 rounds
Purfleet	Pom-Pom	9 rounds
Landguard	Pom-Pom	6 rounds
Beacon Hill	Pom-Pom	3 rounds
Holliwell Point	Rifle fire	–

Two Royal Naval Air Service aircraft took off to intercept; neither engaged; one crashed on landing.

8 September 1915

Weather was fine, with local mist, with very light winds.

During the afternoon, three Naval airships (*Zeppelins L 9, L 13* and *L 14*) left the North German sheds – and in the evening, army airship *Zeppelin LZ 77* left its Belgian shed bound for England.

Zeppelin L 9, commanded by *Hauptmann* August Stelling, came in over the Yorkshire Coast at about 2115 at Port Mulgrave between Whitby and Kettleness. She went westwards to near Mickleby and then north over Hinderwell to Staithes (where she circled) and then went westwards to Ings House, where at about 2130 she dropped an incendiary bomb (which caused no damage) and a fuel tank. A short while later, an HE bomb landed at West Loftus (again without result), whereupon the airship turned northwards – dropping four incendiary bombs near Carlin How. Two fell in Scarfe's Field and two in Watson's Garden – none of which did any damage. At 2135 – over Skinningrove – nine HE and 12 incendiaries were dropped; aimed at the iron works. The water main and electric light cables were severed; two railway trucks burnt; a concrete step way at the jetty damaged; and other minor damage caused. An incendiary bomb which hit the top of the benzol house (which was composed of concrete) did not penetrate, while an HE bomb fell within 10 feet. Another HE bomb narrowly missed the TNT stores. There were no casualties, as the workers had taken refuge in the neighbouring mines and elsewhere upon hearing the first alarm. After circling the works, the airship made off in the direction of Hinderwell – and on passing Kettleness, turned south and finally went out to sea at 2145 near Sandsend.

Three Royal Naval Air Service aeroplanes took off in pursuit, but all failed to see the airship.

It was noted that the Skinningrove Iron Works had been largely erected by German contractors and German workmen, so full information of the layout of the plant must have been possessed by the German airmen.

Zeppelin L 13, commanded by *Kapitänleutnant* Heinrich Mathy, was first heard off the Norfolk Coast north of Holkham at 1935 – and some armed trawlers opened fire at her off Barrow Gap. Her commander was feeling his way towards the mouth of The Wash, which he reached at 2025, and then turned and followed the coast – passing over Hunstanton – and was seen off Dressingham by a fishing boat before being seen by the SS *Annandale* at the mouth of the Lynn Cut going slowly up the river. For four minutes she stopped and hovered at about 1,500 feet (evidently pinpointing her position) before proceeding between Lynn and Terrington St Clement – picking up the River Ouse near Wiggenhall St Germans and setting course for London. *Kapitänleutnant* Mathy followed the river and railway to Downham Market and then followed the Bedford Level (probably making for the railway that went south) until he reached Mepal, where an error was suspected as a flare was dropped over Sutton, and so left the line of the level – heading south. The airship continued past Haddenham, Histon, north-west Cambridge, Royston, Buntingford and Ware – turning south-south-west – intending to attack London from the north-west. At 2228 Potters Bar was passed; then High Barnet, where an inscribed ham bone – attached to a small parachute – was dropped. On it was written: 'Edwart [sic] Grey – What shall I, poor devil do'; and on the reverse: 'A memento from starved-out Germany'.

Turning south-south-east and proceeding slowly, the first bombs were dropped on the residential suburb of Golders Green at 2240 (probably being aimed at the aviation ground at Hendon). Five incendiary bombs were initially dropped – all landing in a field adjoining the Decoy Farm – followed by an HE bomb in a field close by, which was owned by the Express Dairy Company (indicating a near-miss to the company which, presumably, was the target). An incendiary bomb fell on waste ground at the corner of Leeside Crescent and Prince's Park Avenue and two fell in a wood adjoining Leeside Crescent (about 70 yards from Alba and Russel Gardens). These were followed by an incendiary bomb through the roof of an empty house in Highfield Road and one in the garden at the rear of 19, Alba Gardens. The last bomb dropped here was an HE that fell in a garden between Alba Gardens and Russel Gardens and blew out the windows of a large number of houses. The airship then continued her course over north-west London at a slow speed – passing over Child's Hill, Frognal, Belsize Park, Primrose Hill and the north-east corner of Regent's Park to the vicinity of Euston

An unusual early form of propaganda leaflet. Sir Edward Grey was the British Foreign Secretary from 1905 to 1916.

Station. At 2245 three incendiary bombs were dropped – two of which fell between Woburn Place and Upper Bedford Place; the third in Russel Square at the junction of Woburn Place and Southampton Row. A hotel in Bedford Place was damaged by fire. An HE bomb was then dropped in the centre of Queen's Square and broke many windows, but caused no serious damage to the several hospitals situated there. Five incendiary bombs then fell in Osmond Yard – followed by others in East Street, Emerald Street, Theobald's Road and Lamb's Conduit Passage, where at 2249 an HE bomb also fell. A great deal of damage was caused by the resulting fires before they could be extinguished, while the HE bomb wrecked a public house in Red Lion Street and the premises of the National Penny Bank (situated at the corner with Theobald's Road) along with damaging several houses. One man was killed and 16 people injured in Lamb's Conduit Passage. The airship then dropped one HE and one incendiary bomb between Bedford Row and Jockey's Fields, which did no damage in the former, but destroyed a house in the latter (which was used as a cycle club) and injured four women. At 2251 seven incendiaries fell; two on Raymond Buildings and Grays's Inn; one in Gray's Inn Road; and four between Clerkenwell Road and Portpool Lane – followed by one HE bomb off Leather Lane. The incendiary bombs caused several more or less serious fires, and the HE bomb killed four children and injured six adults and a child in Laney's Buildings, Portpool Lane (besides damaging several buildings). Two incendiaries then fell in Cross Street, Kirby Street, Hatton Garden (doing a certain amount of damage) followed by an HE bomb, which burst in Farringdon Road (greatly damaging business premises) and in Great Saffron Hill. The headquarters of the 6th Battalion, London Regiment were also damaged. After crossing the boundary of the city, the airship passed over Smithfield Market, where three incendiary bombs fell in the roadway south of Central Avenue, and dropped one HE and three incendiary bombs in Bartholomew Close – killing two men and a boy and injuring two women. Ten incendiary bombs and two of the Zeppelin's fuel tanks then fell between Noble Street and Aldermanbury and set fire to several blocks of business premises in Silver Street, Wood Street, Addle Street and Aldermanbury – many being totally destroyed. An HE and incendiary bomb then fell between Aldermanbury and the Guildhall – damaging a block of offices; then a further two incendiary bombs fell in Basinghall Street – causing slight damage through fire. An incendiary bomb then fell in Coleman Street, followed by two HE bombs in Moorgate Street – one of which failed to explode, but the other injured six women and damaged office buildings. The airship then headed off in a north-easterly direction towards Liverpool Street Station – dropping three incendiary bombs on the searchlight situated on the top of Salisbury House, but were immediately extinguished. These were followed by an HE bomb on London Wall Buildings, Bloomfield Street (which wrecked the London Territorial Force Record Offices) and another HE landed on an omnibus at the corner of the street with Liverpool Street – killing three and injuring many others. An HE bomb then fell in Sun Street Passage (situated between Broad Street and Liverpool Street Stations) – blowing a hole in the pavement and injuring one. The next HE bomb to be dropped fell on the Great Eastern Railway (north of Liverpool Street Station) – damaging the railway line. The last HE bomb fell in Norton Folgate and destroyed another omnibus – killing nine and injuring 10 – along with damaging buildings in Shoreditch High Street. The airship was finally seen over Edmonton, where she suddenly rose from about 8,500 feet to over 10,000 feet in response to a shell that burst quite close to her (having been fired at from the anti-aircraft battery situated on Parliament Hill). It appeared that the airship was fired at by every anti-aircraft gun of the London defences that were in range, but shooting (in most cases) was somewhat wild. A certain amount of damage was caused to the capital by anti-aircraft shells in such areas as Hoxton, Bethnal Green, Mile End Road, East and West Ham, Canning Town, Poplar, Lambeth, Kentish Town, Highgate, Holloway and Highbury – with four civilians being injured by shrapnel.

At about 2340 a small balloon with a battery attached was dropped at Elmdon – presumably from *Zeppelin L 13*, which was heard shortly after circling Saffron Walden before heading off towards Bury St Edmunds and passed out to sea just before 0200 between Caister and Yarmouth.

Zeppelin L 14, commanded by *Kapitänleutnant der Reserve* Alois Böcker, was first sighted off the *Haisbro Lightship* – situated off the Norfolk Coast – at 1920 and followed the coast westward as far as Blakeney, where at 2010 she turned overland – heading west – before turning south-east near Walshingham. At 2045 she dropped her first bombs – one HE and 14 incendiaries – on Bylaugh Park, where there was a yeomanry camp, which had failed to extinguish its lights, but caused no casualties (apart from a cow). At 2055 the airship appeared over the town of East Dereham, where 24 HE and 16 incendiary bombs fell. Nine of the HE bombs fell in the parish of Scarning – causing no damage, but the remainder destroyed three houses and started fires in the town. Two soldiers and two civilians were killed, along with seven injured. A German officer's cap and a parachute were found in a meadow at Scarning – containing copies of German newspapers and a leave pass dated 7 September 1915, Nordholz and signed by *Oberleutnant zur See* Frankenberg, *Zeppelin L 14*. The airship then headed off in a north-easterly direction and crossed the coast out to sea at about 2130 near Holt.

Zeppelin LZ 77, commanded by *Hauptmann* Alfred Horn, was sighted off Dunwich at 2040 heading south – and at about 2130 dropped eight HE bombs near the *Galloper Lightship* before heading towards the Straits of Dover. The airship was last seen heading east off Walmer at 2240.

The premises of Messrs Glen in Addle Street, London were destroyed by fire, while an ornate fountain in nearby Bartholomew Close was smashed and the windows of nearby buildings shattered.

Summary for 8 September 1915:

Location	Number and type of bombs dropped	Casualties	Damage
Middlesex			
Golders Green	2× HE, 10× IB		Minor damage to suburban residences
County of London	6× HE, 22× IB	16 killed, 51 injured	National Penny Bank premises and others in Bloomsbury wrecked; workmen's dwellings off Gray's Inn Road badly damaged; houses in Farringdon Road, Norton Folgate and Shoreditch High Street damaged; omnibus destroyed in Norton Folgate; railway damaged north of Liverpool Street Station
City of London	7× HE, 23× IB	6 killed, 26 injured	Heavy damage by fire to business premises in Wood Street and Addle Street; Bartholomew Close wrecked; severe damage in Little Britain, London Wall, Basinghall Street, Aldermanbury and Moorgate Street; railway damaged between Broad Street and Liverpool Street Stations; omnibus destroyed in Liverpool Street
Norfolk:			
Bylaugh	1× HE, 14× IB		Cow killed
East Dereham	15× HE, 16× IB	4 killed, 7 injured	
Scarning	9× HE		
Yorkshire, North Riding			
Ings House	1× IB		
West Loftus	2× HE		
Carlin How	4× IB.		
Skinningrove	9× HE, 12× IB		Some damage to iron works
Total	50× HE, 102× IB	26 killed, 94 injured	

Anti-aircraft guns in action and reported use of ammunition:

Location of AA battery	Calibre or type of gun	Number / type of rounds fired
Plumstead Marshes	1 pdr QF	45 rounds
Plumstead Marshes	3" QF	6 rounds
Royal Arsenal	6 pdr QF	12 rounds
Erith	6 pdr QF	10 rounds
Abbey Wood	6 pdr QF	11 rounds
Plumstead Common	13 pdr	9 rounds
Royal Albert Docks	13 pdr	20 rounds
Nine Elms	6 pdr QF	7 rounds
Blackheath	3" 20-cwt	11 rounds
Clapton	3" 20-cwt	14 rounds
Gresham Street	1 pdr	11 rounds
Green Park	3" 20-cwt	11 rounds
Waterloo	1½ pdr	4 rounds
Temple	6 pdr	5 rounds
York Road	6 pdr	3 rounds
Finsbury Park	3"	8 rounds
West Ham	3" 20-cwt	6 rounds
St Helens	1 pdr	15 rounds
Honour Oak	3" 20-cwt	13 rounds
Parliament Hill	3" 20-cwt	12 rounds
Foreign Office	6 pdr	7 rounds
Crown Agents	1 pdr	32 rounds
Tower	3" 20-cwt	16 rounds
Cannon Street	1 pdr	11 rounds

The airships were also engaged by rifle fire and five rounds of incendiary were fired from a ·45 Martini Henry rifle at Waterloo.

Six aircraft of the Royal Naval Air Service took to the air (but all failed to find any of the raiders) and one aircraft crashed on landing at Bacton and the bombs it was carrying exploded – killing the pilot, Flight Lieutenant G W Hilliard.[17]

17 Flight Sub-Lieutenant G W Hilliard, Royal Naval Air Service – aged 30 – is buried at Caister-on-Sea (Great Yarmouth) Cemetery, Norfolk.

11 September 1915

Weather: clear sky, with a slight haze; wind at 1,500 feet was from the east at 20 miles per hour.

Zeppelin LZ 77, commanded by *Hauptmann* Alfred Horn, was sighted passing the *Kentish Knock Lightship* at 2035 – travelling north-west towards the coast – and crossed the Essex Coast at 2310 at 3,500 feet three-quarters of a mile south of Tillingham Coast Guard Station, where she was fired upon by rifle fire by the posts at Tillingham and Holliwell Point (whereupon she rose to 5,000 feet and turned slightly south). Heading westwards, she passed by Southminster, where a 1 pounder Pom-Pom fired eight rounds with no apparent effect. Passing Latchingdon, she dropped a fuel tank before veering south-west towards Maldon and onto North Weald Bassett, where she circled at 2350 before dropping 52 incendiary bombs (five of which failed to ignite) and eight HE bombs (all of which failed to explode on account of the safety pins not being withdrawn) on the Royal Field Artillery Camp, situated between Wintry Park and Hayles Farms. After steering what appeared to be a random course, the airship was reported by the Caistor Coast Guard Station as to be heading out to sea at 0205.

Summary for 11 September 1915:

Location	Number and type of bombs dropped	Casualties	Damage
North Weald Bassett	8 HE, 52 IB		

Anti-aircraft guns in action and reported use of ammunition:

Location of AA battery	Calibre or type of gun	Number / type of rounds fired
Southminster	1 pdr QF	8 rounds

12 September 1915

Weather: considerable amounts of ground fog near the coast; wind at 1,500 feet was 15 miles per hour from the south.

Zeppelin LZ 74, commanded by *Hauptmann* George, was reported as having been sighted out to sea off Nieuport, Belgium at 1950 and passed the *Kentish Knock Lightship* – flying very high at 2227 steering north-west. At 2245 she crossed the coast near Walton-on-the-Naze, Essex and followed the railway line past Thorpe-le-Soken, Little Clacton, Weeley, Great Bentley, Wivenhoe and Colchester to Wormingford, where she dropped two HE bombs in a field; then onto Mount Bures, where a third HE bomb fell – again without causing damage. At 2330 11 HE and five incendiary bombs were dropped at Hills Farm, Stratford St Mary; where four of the HE bombs exploded – causing slight damage to houses. At this point, an Armoured Car

Company of the Royal Naval Air Service opened fire on the airship with their Maxim gun, but the raider turned as if searching for its adversary. Heading east, the airship then dropped four HE and four incendiary bombs on East Bergholt before turning north-east past Ipswich (and again was engaged by the Royal Naval Air Service armoured car – with the result that she dropped four HE bombs at Rushmere; one of which failed to explode). The Zeppelin zigzagged away in a north-easterly direction – flying very low – and on passing Woodbridge, was fired at by another Royal Naval Air Service armoured car (and again at 0005 as she passed Aldeburgh). She drifted northward along the coast with her engines switched off – presumably so as not to attract further attention – finally passing out to sea near Southwold.

Summary for 12 September 1915:

Location	**Number and type of bombs dropped**	**Casualties**	**Damage**
Wormingford	2× HE		
Mount Bures	1× HE		
Stratford St Mary	11× HE, 5× IB		
East Bergholt	4× HE		
Rushmere	4× HE		
Total	22× HE, 9× IB		

Anti-aircraft guns in action and reported use of ammunition:

Location of AA battery	**Calibre or type of gun**	**Number / type of rounds fired**
Stratford St Mary	·45 Maxim on armoured car	2 belts
Rushmere	·45 Maxim on armoured car	2 belts
Woodbridge	·45 Maxim on armoured car	A few rounds
Aldeburgh	·45 Maxim on armoured car	1 belt

13 September 1915

Weather: the sky was recorded as being cloudy, with light to moderate westerly breezes and some rain; wind was from the south-west, strength four.

At 1740 a seaplane was observed approaching Margate, Kent from the east. When it was over Cliftonville (one-and-a-half miles west of Margate Railway Station), it dropped 10 HE bombs – six of which fell in the streets and gardens to the eastern part of the town; the remainder fell on the foreshore. Two women were killed, with two men and four women being injured. Very little damage was done – and nothing of military importance.

Two Royal Naval Air Service BE2c aeroplanes took off from Maidstone and pursued the enemy raider out to sea, but were unable to get close enough to engage. Anti-aircraft guns did not go to action.

Four naval airships – *Zeppelins L 11, L 13, L 14* and *L 15* – were reported as making their way towards England (across the North Sea) towards evening. *Zeppelin L 14* approached the Norfolk Coast, but turned back, while *Zeppelin L 13* took a more northerly course (in the direction of the Humber), but also turned back.

Zeppelin L 11, commanded by *Oberleutnant zur See* Freiherr Horst von Buttlar, was considerably impeded by fog and clouds – and was first reported off Thorpeness at 2305. At 2337 – when off Felixstowe and the *Sunk Lightship* – she was fired on by the 6 pdr guns at Felixstowe and immediately turned back northwards along the coast to Woodbridge Haven; and then came inland over Bawdsey Marshes – passing over Harwich Harbour, Essex (which was not attacked – presumably due to clouds). Following the Orwell as far as Pinmill, she turned north-east and was fired at by a Royal Naval Air Service Maxim gun mounted on a motor car at Levington Heath – and in response, dropped five HE and two incendiary bombs in fields near Bucklesham. The airship then dropped two HE and three incendiary bombs in a field near Newbourne; and then eight HE and four incendiary bombs in a mangold-wurzel field near Hemley – blowing out a window at Hemley Hall. Finally, having crossed the River Deben, two HE and 20 incendiaries were dropped on the marshes at Wood Hale Farm, Sutton. The airship then passed straight out to sea near Orfordness at 0025. Of the HE bombs, one at Bucklesham, one at Newbourne and two at Hemley were of 100 kg in weight; the rest of the HEs being the normal 50 kg bombs.

Zeppelin L 15, commanded by *Kapitänleutnant* Joachim Breithaupt, carried out her first overseas voyage with a reconnaissance of the Thames Estuary. She was sighted off Shoeburyness at 2348 and then turned east to Margate, Kent where she dropped three bombs (aimed at a steamer). She then turned north and was sighted 25 miles east of Dunwich at 0315 before heading home across the North Sea to Germany.

Summary for 13 September 1915:

Location	Number and type of bombs dropped	Casualties	Damage
Suffolk			
Bucklesham	5× HE, 9× IB		Slight damage to cottage
Newbourne	2× HE, 3× IB		
Hemley	8× HE, 4× IB		Slight damage to house and crops
Sutton	2× HE, 20× IB		
Sea, Kent			
Off Margate	3× HE		
Total	20× HE, 29× IB		

Anti-aircraft guns in action and reported use of ammunition:

Location of AA battery	Calibre or type of gun	Number / type of rounds fired
Felixstowe	6 pdr	12 rounds
Levington Heath	·45 Maxim (RNAS Mobile Section)	120 rounds

14 September 1915
Weather was recorded as breezy, with wind from the west, strength two.

At 1012 an enemy seaplane was seen approaching the coast near Westgate, Kent but turned out to sea without crossing the coast.

8 October 1915
Zeppelin Viktoria Luise / LZ 11. Type G.
Liegnitz, Germany (Legnica, Poland).

Destroyed while entering hangar.

8 October 1915
Zeppelin LZ 74 / LZ 44. Type P.
Near Orthe, Schnee Eifel, Germany.

Stranded after colliding with a mountain; her gondolas being torn off and most of the crew being deposited in a wood. The barrel of the airship finally came down, with two crew on board – having taken refuge in the central gangway near to the German General Headquarters at Mézières. Scrapped.
Kommandeur: Hauptmann George.

13 October 1915
Weather: the wind was very light over the North Sea – being mainly southerly in direction, with westerly currents round the East Coast. There was mist on the East Coast, but elsewhere the sky was clear with a few light clouds.

Five *Zeppelins* – *L 11*, *L 13*, *L 14*, *L 15* and *L 16* – left the German sheds in the morning and made their way across the North Sea.

Zeppelin L 13 was commanded by *Kapitänleutnant* Heinrich Mathy. Having hovered near the *Haisbro Lightship* for nearly an hour, she ventured overland at 1815 – travelling due west from Happisburgh until reaching Aylsham, Norfolk, where she turned south-west to follow the Midland and Great Northern Joint Railway and followed a train which was heading for Norwich until the driver spotted her and stopped at Drayton.

Having hovered for some time so as to pinpoint her position, she headed off to the west towards Dereham and then followed a course over Griston, Brandon, Soham, Exning, Newmarket, Saffron Walden and to the north of Harlow. Once more turning westward to Ware, Hertford the airship was sighted and fired at by a 13 pounder anti-aircraft battery sited at Birchwood Farm (one mile north-west of Hatfield). On being fired at, the airship dropped four HE bombs – one failing to explode, but all failed to cause any damage beyond a few broken windows. At this point in time, the airship was drifting with her engines off. Altering course, she then followed the River Colne past Uxbridge and Staines and crossed the Thames at Weybridge at about 2150. The Zeppelin was observed to be travelling slowly – apparently unsure of her position, as a flare was dropped at Clandon before hovering for a while over Guildford; before heading up the valley eastwards towards Chilworth and dropping a second flare. The 1 pounder gun at the powder works opened fire on her – causing her to veer off west-wards – before returning a few minutes later to Guildford and then off westwards towards St Catherine's, where a flare was dropped, followed by 12 HE bombs. There were no casualties, but damage was caused to houses and the up-line of the London and South-Western Railway. Two bombs fell in the River Wey and killed a swan. The airship then went off over Chilworth – being fired at by the anti-aircraft gun – without result. About 2305 she passed over Tandridge Camp, near Oxted before turning north (having sighted *Zeppelin L 14* – and went to join her). When west of Hayes, *Zeppelin L 13* hovered for a while waiting for *Zeppelin L 14* before both airships proceeded towards Bromley. Over Bickley, they separated – with *Zeppelin L 13* turning north; the airships apparently having nearly collided. *Zeppelin L 13* proceeded over Sidcup and turned over Bexley Heath towards Woolwich – passing to the south – turned and approached from the south-west. She was picked by the Blackheath searchlight and the anti-aircraft gun fired 17 rounds at her; the Honor Oak gun firing nine rounds. She sailed over the whole length of the barracks and arsenal. On the former, she dropped three HE and 14 incendiary bombs; on the latter, two HE and five incendiary bombs. The first HE bomb to fall landed in the middle of the parade ground of the barracks – breaking windows in the Royal Artillery Mess; the second on the barrack dining room in the East Square – completely destroying it – and the stables below (killing a horse and injuring nine others – along with four soldiers). The incendiaries which fell in the East Square and Depot Barracks did practically no damage, apart from a few small fires (which were quickly extinguished). Another incendiary bomb fell in St John's Churchyard and eight others in streets and gardens close by – damaging St John's Church School, a house in Wellington Street and shops in Cross Street, Beresford Square and Thomas Street (where a shop was burnt out). Three incendiaries fell near the surgery at the Arsenal; another in a machine shop in Avenue G – along with one in 5th Street. One HE bomb fell in the main machine carriage shop – wrecking a crane and a machine. Nine men were injured – of whom one later died of his injuries. The last HE bomb fell in the magazine area on Plumstead Marshes, but did no damage; the airship then heading off to the north-east. The Woolwich anti-aircraft guns had opened fire at 2354 but their aim was poor; the West Ham gun having fired 14 rounds and the Clapton gun was also in action. *Zeppelin L 13* crossed the river at Barking Reach and was engaged by the anti-aircraft gun sited at Sutton's Farm, which fired 10 rounds. The fifth round burst close to the airship – causing her to turn sharply before being engaged by the gun at Beacontree Heath, which also fired 10 rounds. Passing towards Romford, the airship was fired on by Erith and Purfleet guns – although far out of range at this point. She may have been damaged, as it was claimed that she dropped smoke balls and that a light was seen in her aft gondola (possibly connected with repairs, as she was seen to be very low near Ingelestone – and it appeared a propeller was damaged). Obviously unsure of her position, the airship gradually made her way northwards – making no attempt to pass out to sea – even though she was fired at by a Maxim gun situated near Mark's Tey and a Pom-Pom near Colchester. Finally, she passed out to sea at Dunwich at 0200.

Zeppelin L 14, commanded by *Kapitänleutnant* Alois Böcker, crossed the coast at Bacton, Norfolk at 1830 and was immediately fired at by the Cyclist's Maxim Detachment; then, as she passed North Walsham, she was again fired at. Passing Thetford, the Zeppelin turned due south and followed this course for a considerable distance – crossing the mouth of the Thames and the Isle of Sheppey unhindered. At 2115 she was over Otterpool Camp, Shorncliffe, Folkestone where she dropped four HE bombs on the camp of the 8th Howitzer Brigade and the 5th Brigade Canadian Field Artillery – killing 15 soldiers, wounding 11 and also killing 11 horses; no damage being done to guns or equipment. The airship then turned north-east towards Westenhanger Camp – dropping two more HE bombs on the racecourse. Here she passed out to sea. Her commander – then realising that he was over the south coast – turned inland again and followed the coast nearly to Hastings before heading north-west towards South London. Passing over Frant, she dropped seven incendiary bombs – one failing to ignite, but causing no damage; then onto Tunbridge Wells, where at 2240 three HE bombs were dropped, but only broke a few windows. By now the mist was so thick that the airship could not be seen from the ground; only her engines being audible. At 2340 she reached Croydon, where she dropped 17 HE bombs which fell in a line from Eldridge Road, over the railway and across Addiscombe Road to the corner of Exeter Street and Stretton Road. Finally, a dud incendiary bomb fell in South Norwood. A number of residences were hit and destroyed or damaged – killing nine civilians and injuring 15. The airship then passed to the east of Crystal Palace and was sighted in company with *Zeppelin L 13* before turning north-east at a height of 10,000 feet – crossing the river between Erith and Purfleet, where she was fired at by guns situated at both places. Continuing on a north-easterly track, she passed Samundham before turning south-east to cross out to sea near Aldeburgh at about 0145.

Zeppelin L 15, commanded by *Kapitänleutnant* Joachim Breithaupt, crossed the coast at Bacton, Norfolk at 1825 and was fired upon by the Maxim battery of the Royal Naval Air Service. Following a south-westerly course, she dropped a flare at Elvdon and turned south – passing over Bury St Edmunds until she reached Braintree, where she turned west and dropped a fuel tank at Matchling and was also seen light

A number of terraced houses in Oval Road, Croydon were on the receiving end of some of the 17 high-explosive bombs dropped on the town by *Zeppelin L 14*.

signalling to *Zeppelin L 13* that was coming up behind her. She went on following the line of the river and railway past Roydon and Hoddesdon to Broxbourne, where she was fired at by a 13 pounder anti-aircraft gun battery with eight rounds. The airship replied with four HE bombs – three of which fell within 100 yards of the gun emplacement, but causing no casualties (but a 30-cwt lorry belonging to No.50 Company, Royal Engineers and the motor car attached to the gun battery were destroyed). The Zeppelin then proceeded south-west away from London before turning back onto a south-easterly course – drifting towards the capital with her engines shut off to avoid detection. The first bomb that fell on the city landed at 2125 at Exeter Street, The Strand followed by a second in Wellington Street, which landed between the Lyceum Theatre and the *Morning Post* office. The third landed in Catherine Street; the fourth and fifth in Aldwych; the sixth and seventh landing between Aldwych and New Inn. Two incendiaries fell on the Royal Courts of Justice and the eighth and ninth HE bombs in Carey Street. The tenth fell on the roof of a house in New Square, Lincoln's Inn followed by an eleventh on Old Square and the twelfth in the roadway of Chancery Lane. Three more incendiaries fell north of Holborn in South Square, Gray's Inn followed by a thirteenth HE bomb on the north-eastern corner of Gray's Inn Square. Four more incendiaries fell on or near to Hatton Garden – and a further one in Farringdon Road. The resulting devastation caused by this bombing was considerable, with houses in Exeter Street damaged; one person being killed, two injured. In front of the Lyceum Theatre, 17 people were killed and 21 injured. In the Catherine Street incident, nine were injured, while in Aldwych – The Strand Theatre being only slightly damaged – four were killed and 15 injured when a bomb landed in the road. The wooden sheds of the Belgian Refugee Committee clearing house were badly damaged – and part of the Law Courts were slightly damaged by fire caused by an incendiary bomb. The upper storeys of two old houses in New Square, Lincoln's Inn (dating from the year 1697) were wrecked, but the solidly-built lower portion remained intact. The bomb that landed in Chancery Lane smashed water and gas mains, wrecked the fronts of buildings on the east side and broke all the windows of Stone Buildings, Lincoln's Inn on the west side. In Gray's Inn, the hall and houses were wrecked – and in Hatton Garden and Farringdon Road, buildings were also badly damaged by fire caused by the incendiary bombs. The next bomb to be dropped fell in the road at Finsbury Pavement and another two HE bombs damaged several buildings – killing four and injuring 10. Another HE fell on a small hotel in the Minories (partly demolishing it) and damaging a number of nearby properties in the Minories, Aldgate and Houndsditch – killing one and injuring eight people and killing a horse. The following two HE bombs dropped fell on either side of the London, Tilbury and Southend (Midland) Railway between Great Prescot and Royal Mint streets – damaging a number of houses and injuring six people. Leman Street Station was also damaged. The last bomb (an HE) fell between Wellclose and Prince's Squares – destroying a tarpaulin factory and damaging a number of other buildings; only a horse being killed. The Zeppelin then went off over the London and West India Docks to Limehouse before turning northwards when fired at by the Woolwich anti-aircraft guns. The anti-aircraft guns had been in continuous action, but appeared unable to reach the Zeppelin's height of 8,000 to 9,000 feet – though considerable damage was caused to property due to falling shrapnel. Proceeding in a north-easterly direction – and being fired at by various gun batteries – her engines were noted as being particularly noisy and flying very slowly. On reaching Ipswich, she was fired at by a Royal Naval Air Service Pom-Pom detachment – and in reply dropped four HE bombs at Rushmere, but caused no damage. Continuing on her course, she passed out to sea near Aldeburgh at 2355.

Zeppelin L 16, commanded by *Oberleutnant zur See* Werner Peterson, also came in over the coast at Bacton, Norfolk at 1840 and was almost immediately fired upon by

Buildings at the back of Gray's Inn Square, London were completely wrecked by a high-explosive bomb dropped from *Zeppelin L 15*.

the cyclist Maxim detachment operating in the area. Proceeding west-south-west, the airship dropped an HE bomb which fell at Banningham – causing no damage. After following a zigzag course, a fuel tank was dropped at Attleborough – and soon after, another fell at Eccles. Heading in a southerly direction, her commander must have been unsure of his position as he brought his airship down to about 4,000 feet over Chelmsford, but was fired at by a Maxim machine-gun (and later by a Pom-Pom) at Kelvdon Hatch. Having turned north-west before reaching the outskirts of London, the Zeppelin headed towards Hertford, which at the time was not blacked out. On arriving over the junction of the Rivers Lea and Beane (near to the gas works), seven incendiary bombs fell close to the swimming baths, but caused no damage; then an HE bomb fell on the allotments at Folly – followed by another at Priory Road Farm (both on the banks of the River Lea) – a house in Frampton Street being demolished. The third HE bomb fell in the Bull Plain – demolishing one house and seriously damaging five (including the Conservative Club). Six people were killed and another eight injured. The next two HE bombs to be dropped fell at the junction of Maidenhead Yard, Mill Bridge and The Wash – wrecking a flour mill and some stables (along with a wine store and seven shops being damaged to a lesser extent); three civilians and two soldiers being injured. Soon after, 12 incendiary bombs fell on Old Cross (round the Municipal Library and the School of Art). As the raider passed over St Andrew's Church, two more HE bombs were dropped – landing in North Road and a garden – also soon followed by seven incendiaries. One soldier was killed and a civilian injured – while a house, a motor works and an inn were seriously damaged (with 29 houses in North Road, 16 in St Andrew's Street and two in Hertingfordbury Road slightly damaged). The airship then followed the line of the North Road and the River Beane – dropping an eighth HE bomb (that failed to explode) and three incendiary bombs which landed in gardens. A ninth HE bomb exploded in the road near the hospital gate – killing a soldier and two civilians. Finally, five more HE and an incendiary bomb landed in fields west of the hospital – causing no further damage or injuries. The airship then headed off in a north-easterly direction and passed out to sea at Mundesley at 0005 – close to where she had come inland a few hours earlier.

Zeppelin L 11, commanded by *Oberleutnant zur See* von Buttlar, was sighted between the *Cockle* and *Newarp Lightships* at about 1930 heading north before passing over the *Haisbro Lightship* and crossing the English Coast at Bacton, Norfolk (where she was fired at by a Royal Naval Air Service Maxim Machine-Gun Section) before turning inland and circling over Horstead, Coltishall and Great Hautbois (where she dropped her bomb load). Four HE and three incendiary bombs fell around Horstead – landing in open fields; then on Coltishall and Great Hautbois, nine HE fell – two failing to explode. They all fell in fields near to the Great Eastern Railway Station at Coltishall (along with a further seven incendiary bombs), but apart from a few broken panes of glass, no damage was recorded. The airship then headed towards Norwich, where she was fired at by a Territorial Royal Horse Artillery gun sited at Mousehole Heath – at which point she turned east and passed out to sea just north of Great Yarmouth.

Summary for 13 October 1915:

Location	Number and type of bombs dropped	Casualties	Damage
Norfolk:			
Banningham	1× HE		
Horstead	4× HE, 3× IB		
Coltishall and Great Hautbois	9× HE, 7× IB		
Suffolk:			
Rushmere	4× HE		
Hertfordshire:			
Hatfield	4× HE		
Hertford	14× HE, 30× IB	9 killed, 15 injured	10 buildings wrecked or demolished; 141 buildings slightly damaged
Broxbourne	4× HE		2 military vehicles destroyed
London:			
West Central	13× HE, 6× IB		Large number of houses and buildings damaged (including Lincoln's Inn Chapel and Gray's Inn Hall)
East Central and City	2× HE, 5× IB		Several large business premises destroyed
East	4× HE		Small hotel demolished; small railway station and large number of tenement houses damaged
Woolwich Barracks	3× HE, 14× IB		Barracks and Royal Artillery Mess damaged
Town	9× IB		House and shop burnt out
Arsenal	1× HE, 5× IB		Crane wrecked
Plumstead Marsh	1× HE		
London (Total):	25× HE, 39× IB	38 killed, 94 injured	

Location	Number and type of bombs dropped	Casualties	Damage
Surrey:			
Croydon	17× HE	9 killed, 15 injured	3 villa residences destroyed
South Norwood	1× IB		
Shalford	12× HE		
Kent:			
Otterpool Camp	4× HE	15 killed, 11 injured	
Westenhanger	2× HE		
Tunbridge Wells	3× HE		
Sussex			
Frant	7× IB		
Total	102× HE, 87× IB	71 killed, 128 injured	

Anti-aircraft guns in action and reported use of ammunition:

Location of AA battery	Calibre or type of gun	Number / type of rounds fired
Mobile Section, East Royal Naval Anti-Aircraft Corps		
Bacton	·45 Maxim	200 rounds
Rushmere Heath	Pom-Pom	150 rounds
Rushmere Heath		25 tracer rounds
Woodbridge	·45 Maxim	80 rounds
Melton (NE Woodbridge)	·45 Maxim	80 rounds
Marks Tey	·45 Maxim	150 rounds
Chelmsford	·45 Maxim	50 rounds
Colchester	Pom-Pom	42 rounds
Colchester	·45 Martini Henry rifle	28 tracer rounds
Newmarket	·45 Maxim	70 rounds
Norfolk		
Mousehold Heath, 1/1st Leicestershire RHA	15 pdr (BLC field mounting)	2 rounds

Location of AA battery	Calibre or type of gun	Number / type of rounds fired
North Walsham, 1/6th Norfolk Cyclists	·303 machine-gun	600 rounds
Essex		
Wrabness, 3rd Bn, Essex Regt	2 Maxims	200 rounds
Thames and Medway Garrison		
Eastchurch	1 Pom-Pom	23 rounds
Waltham and Enfield defences		
Monkhams Hill	6 pdr	7 rounds
Grange Camp	Pom-Pom	40 rounds
Kelvedon Hatch	Pom-Pom	7 rounds
Woolwich Arsenal defences		
Plumstead	4x Pom-Pom	138 rounds
Plumstead	3x 13 pdr (mobile)	67 rounds
Plumstead	3" 20-cwt	24 rounds
Albert Dock	13 pdr (mobile)	8 rounds
Arsenal	2x 6 pdr	61 rounds
Abbey Wood	6 pdr	3 rounds
Erith	2x 6 pdr	35 rounds
Purfleet	3" 20-cwt	22 rounds
Purfleet	2x Pom-Pom	67 rounds
London anti-aircraft defences		
Broxbourne	13 pdr 6-cwt (mobile)	10 rounds
Loughton	13 pdr 6-cwt (mobile)	4 rounds
Hatfield	13 pdr 6-cwt (mobile)	3 rounds
Beacontree Heath	12 pdr 6-cwt (mobile)	9 rounds
Hainault	13 pdr 6-cwt (mobile)	6 rounds
Suttons Farm	13 pdr 6-cwt (mobile)	8 rounds
Clapton Orient	3" 20-cwt	2 rounds
West Ham	3" 20-cwt	31 rounds
Finsbury	3" 20-cwt	6 rounds
Parliament Hill	3" 20-cwt	6 rounds
King's Cross	3" 20-cwt	6 rounds
Tower	3" 20-cwt	8 rounds
Green Park	3" 20-cwt	5 rounds

Location of AA battery	Calibre or type of gun	Number / type of rounds fired
Foreign Office	6 pdr	9 rounds
Blackheath	3" 20-cwt	17 rounds
Honor Oak	3" 20-cwt	14 rounds
Barnes	3" 20-cwt	4 rounds
Waterloo	6 pdr	7 rounds
Nine Elms	6 pdr	5 rounds
Surrey		
Chilworth Anti-Aircraft Detachment, Sussex Royal Garrison Artillery (T)	Pom-Pom	77 rounds

Five Royal Flying Corps aircraft took off on operations. Only one pilot sighted a Zeppelin illuminated in searchlights, but lost sight of his target due to cloud. Two of the aircraft were wrecked on landing.

Events in the West End of London on 13 October 1915 were recalled by James Wickham, who was working as a call-boy at the Gaiety Theatre that evening:

> London was rather on edge – yet true to the 'carry on' policy of the British nation. The West End, it seemed, did not lack gaiety on that October night as I made my way along The Strand to the Gaiety Theatre, where I had recently secured the post of call-boy. Restaurants were crowded. From behind heavily-curtained windows of the big hotels, there came the sound of merry-making; the popping of champagne corks; the pulse of dance music; heady laughter. There were toasts, farewells, promises, tears and kisses. War! Tonight: Blighty. Tomorrow: Who cared? London – the capital of the Empire – had everything in the way of pleasure to offer her sons on leave. Theatres were flourishing; 'House Full' boards hung round their entrances every night. At the Gaiety Theatre, we had been playing '*Tonight's the Night*' to packed houses. What a contrast to the gloom and dimness of the streets was the glamour within the thronging theatres. Soft lights glowed in their auditoriums. There was the surge of lively tuneful music; bewitching choruses; frivolous songs; provocative dancing; smart quips; war burlesques – almost impossible amid all this light-hearted gaiety to realise the horrors being enacted a hundred miles distant. Had it not been for the ubiquitous khaki in stalls; in pit; in gallery; the war would have seemed even more remote. In the shadowy streets – for the Defence of the Realm Act in regard to lighting was being strictly enforced – crowds jostled and shouldered; khaki everywhere.
>
> I had been at the theatre for nearly an hour. 'Overture and Beginners' had been called. The curtain had risen on Act One. As I walked down the corridor

– breathing a sigh of relief that my duties were temporarily finished – the waves of laughter greeting the quips of Mr George Goldsmith and Mr Leslie Henson reached me. London was enjoying itself – but then London did not know that three hours earlier, an urgent message had been flashed from France to the War Office that five Zeppelins had been noticed making for the East Coast. I heard it from Jupp – the stage-door keeper. We often heard things of that kind at the Gaiety. Marconi House was next door. "Suppose they are coming again tonight," grumbled Jupp. I glanced out of the door across to the west. There was a perfect trellis of searchlight beams raking the blue-black sky. The pavements were still crowded. Shadowy groups gossiped at street corners. Omnibuses and taxi-cabs, dimly-lit, loomed up from and receded into the enshrouding gloom. A clock struck nine; 20 minutes to go for the first interval. A few minutes later, I heard my name being called. It was the stage manager who wanted me. "Just run across to the post with these letters, Jimmy," he said. "We've a special rehearsal call for the morning and they must go off tonight." As I went out of the stage door, I met Billy – the page. "Come over to the post with me, Billy," I said. He was a bright little lad of 15; I was three years older. Only too glad of a little relaxation, he readily agreed. The nearest pillar-box was at the top of Catherine Street – which lies immediately opposite the stage door of the Gaiety – and together we made our way alongside The Strand Theatre. I stopped a moment to light a cigarette – carefully screening the match. Billy waited. "They say Zepps are on their way, the swine," I remarked. As though my words had released 10,000 furies, there was a sudden crackle of anti-aircraft gunfire – and simultaneously, a dreadful sound that London only knew too well… a sound like no other on earth; it was the mournful wail created by the velocity of a descending bomb. In one brief terrible moment before the impact, I instinctively knew it was coming directly where we stood. I was not wrong. It exploded three yards from where we were standing. It flung me against the wall next to the pit entrance to The Strand Theatre. It sucked me back again; it dashed me to the ground; masonry fell; glass rained. I felt unhurt – only dazed – yet I had 22 lumps of shrapnel embedded in me. They carried me downstairs into the bar of The Strand Theatre. The streets were pandemonium. I asked for Billy, but he had been blown to pieces. I could hear screams in the street outside – the dull, vibrant thud of more bombs. Others were brought in and laid beside me. Some were moaning; some were calling for missing friends and relatives. Someone rushed in and said a London General omnibus had been blown to bits in Aldwych, opposite the Waldorf. More injured were brought in; they were carried on theatre boards. There was a ring of ambulance bells and the imperious clang of fire alarms – and above it all, a terrible, insistent thudding; more bombs; death, destruction. Would they never cease this agonising rain of death? They held every card up there. It was so easy for them.

26 October 1915
Parseval PL 26.
Germany.
Crashed on landing during its maiden flight and was burnt out. No casualties.

10 November 1915
Schütte-Lanz SL 6. Type D1.
Seddin, East Prussia.
Exploded on take-off; no survivors.
Kommandeur: Kapitänleutnant Fritz Boemarck +.

17 November 1915
Zeppelin L 18 / LZ 52. Type P.
Tondern, Belgium.
Caught fire while gassing up.
Kommandeur: Kapitänleutnant der Reserve Max Dietrich.

14 December 1915
Schütte-Lanz SL 4. Type C2.
Seddin, East Prussia.
Destroyed when the roof of the hangar that it was housed in collapsed under the weight of snow.
Kommandeur: Kapitänleutnant der Reserve Richard Wolff.

14 December 1915
1 Wing Royal Naval Air Service.

Tondern Airship Shed, with *Zeppelin L 18* ablaze inside.

All that was left of *Zeppelin L 18* having burnt out. Note how intact the structure of the shed is following the fire – allowing the damage to be rapidly repaired and the shed brought back into use.

Flight Sub-Lieutenant Graham (pilot), with Flight Sub-Lieutenant Ince (observer), Nieuport Scout no.3971. The pilot reported:

> I left the aerodrome in Nieuport Scout no.3971 – with Flight Sub-Lieutenant Ince – at 2.45pm to carry out hostile aircraft patrol between Dixmude, Nieuport and the vicinity of the stranded steamer off La Panne. Steering a course from Dixmude to pass slightly west of Nieuport, I sighted a German seaplane of a type very similar to a 'Short', but much longer. The hostile machine was some distance out to sea – and I at once altered course so as to intercept him as he made for Ostend immediately on sighting us. The Nieuport easily had the speed over the enemy and overhauled him rapidly – getting within a range of 100 yards at 3.45pm above the stranded steamer off La Panne. I dived and manoeuvred so as to take up a position – enabling my passenger to train his gun upwards under the enemy's tail (at about 50 yards' range) and he fired about 15 rounds. My passenger, on ceasing fire, clearly observed bullet-holes and an appearance of smouldering beneath the enemy observer's seat. The enemy carried a pilot and passenger – and beyond one slight alteration of course towards Ostend, did not appear to try to manoeuvre. I repeated my first manoeuvre twice – my passenger each time firing into the enemy – and finally, the German machine turned sharply down and dived vertically (nose first) into the water. After momentarily losing sight of the enemy, I then observed flaming wreckage on the water below and destroyers and minesweepers working towards it. I volplaned down to investigate and saw only the enemy's empennage above the water. My engine then failed – presumably owing to the petrol tank having been holed and emptied – and I made a forced descent in the sea close to HMS *Balmoral*. The Nieuport turned over in the water – and after some difficulty in trying to release my belt, I eventually succeeded in getting out of the machine and coming to the surface, where I joined Flight Sub-Lieutenant Ince, who was supporting himself on the fuselage.
>
> The officers of HMS *Balmoral* informed me that the German machine was in flames while nose-diving – and on striking the water, its bombs evidently exploded as it was hurled 30 feet up into the air in pieces.

For his actions, Flight Sub-Lieutenant Charles Walter Graham RN was awarded the DSO and Flight-Sub Lieutenant Arthur Strachan Ince RN the DSC; both gazetted 24 February 1916.[18]

18 The National Archives – (TNA) Air 1/629/17/122/19: report on destruction of a German seaplane.

18 December 1915
Zeppelin LZ 39 / LZ 39. Type O.
Luck, Ukraine.
Stranded following enemy action and decommissioned.
Kommandeur: Hauptmann Wilhelm.

Part 3: 1916

9 January 1916
Weather: fair, with a westerly wind; strength three.

At 1413 an enemy biplane was seen approaching Dover, Kent from a seaward direction at about 5,000 feet (presumably making for the Royal Naval Air Service Aerodrome at Langdon). As it crossed the breakwater, several anti-aircraft guns opened fire and the aeroplane turned 45° to its former course and made off. When it was about a mile off (over the sea), it dropped a bomb – probably aimed at a ship.

Anti-aircraft guns in action and reported use of ammunition:

Location of AA battery	Calibre or type of gun	Number / type of rounds fired
Dover Castle	Pom-Pom	70 rounds
Drop Redoubt	6 pdr	6 rounds
Langdon	3" 20-cwt	3 rounds

Six Royal Naval Air Service aeroplanes and one Royal Flying Corps aeroplane took off in pursuit, but only Flight Lieutenant B L Huskisson in Bristol Scout C, no.1258 sighted the enemy machine 10 miles off Dunkirk – flying in the direction of Ostend, Belgium – but had to abandon the chase.

12 January 1916
Schütte-Lanz SL 2. Type B1.
Luckenwalde, Germany.
Stranded due to lack of fuel.
Kommandeur: Hauptmann von Webster.

23 January 1916
Weather: wind from the west; strength one. There was a full moon, which had risen at 1910 with a bright and fine night.

An enemy aeroplane, a *Friedrichshafen FF 33b* of *See Flieger Abteilung 1,* appeared over Dover, Kent at 0047 and dropped eight HE and one incendiary bombs on the town. One bomb fell within a hundred yards of Garrison Headquarters, but nothing naval or military received any damage. The malthouse of a brewery and the Red Lion

Hotel were wrecked. One man was killed and two men, one woman and three children injured. The raider was last seen from St Margaret's flying east at 0103.

At 1252 two seaplanes, a *Friedrichshafen FF 33b* and a *Hansa-Brandenburg NW*, appeared over Dover, Kent – coming overland from the west – having crossed the English Coast between Dover and Folkestone while flying very high; they were unobserved. All anti-aircraft guns and ships moored in the harbour opened fire on the raiders, which then separated – one flying to the east; the other east-south-east. One of the raiders then circled and once more came in overland to the north – passing over Dover again at 1310 – but on again being engaged by the anti-aircraft guns, flew out to sea without dropping any bombs. The second aircraft circled to the south, came in overland near Folkestone and at 1323 dropped five HE bombs near to the naval aircraft hangars at Capel, but failed to do any damage. The aeroplane then passed to the west of Dover and out to sea at St Margaret's at 1355. It was seen, just off the coast, near to St Margaret's at about 1415 and then finally from the *North Goodwin Lightship* heading north-east at 1520.

Anti-aircraft guns in action and reported use of ammunition:

Location of AA battery	Calibre or type of gun	Number / type of rounds fired
Drop Redoubt	6 pdr	71 rounds
Dover Castle	3x 1 pdr	381 rounds
Langdon Battery	3" 20-cwt	30 rounds
Langdon Battery	Pom-Pom	118 rounds

The Royal Naval Air Service sent up two seaplanes and the Royal Flying Corps four aeroplanes, but none were able catch the raider.

24 January 1916

Weather: light westerly breezes were recorded over the Channel with variable sky.

At 1520 a German seaplane was reported to be five miles to the north-east of Dunkirk, France heading north-west. At 1545 it was seen near to the Royal Naval Air Service hangars at Capel, Kent and was engaged by a 6 pounder anti-aircraft gun. It thereupon turned north-east and at 1601 passed over Dover, where it was fired at by another two 6 pounder guns. No bombs were reported as having been dropped.

Anti-aircraft guns in action and reported use of ammunition:

Location of AA battery	Calibre or type of gun	Number / type of rounds fired
Capel	6 pdr	2 rounds
Dover	2x 6 pdr	20 rounds

The Royal Naval Air Service sent up two aeroplanes and the Royal Flying Corps also two aeroplanes to intercept the raider – one of which got to within 300 yards of the enemy aircraft, which it fired at with a Lewis gun, until it jammed and the enemy aircraft disappeared into cloud.

30 January 1916
Zeppelin LZ 79 / LZ 49. Type P.
Ath, Belgium.
Stranded following a direct hit by anti-aircraft fire during a raid on Paris, France.
Kommandeur: Hauptmann Gaissert.

31 January 1916
Weather: wind over the North Sea and Great Britain was negligible. The skies over the Midlands was clear, but on the East Coast there were large areas of mist and fog so thick in places that it was reported as drizzle. Over London, the inclination was towards mist and the sky was not clear. There was no moon.

Nine German naval airships crossed the North Sea – *Zeppelins L 11, L 13, L 14, L 15, L 16, L 17, L 19, L 20* and *L 21* – these representing the whole force of the new standardised type then available. They left the North German sheds in the morning and appeared off the English Coast in successive groups; the first two ships – *Zeppelin L 13* and *Zeppelin L 21* – arriving off the Norfolk Coast shortly before 1650 while *Zeppelin L 11* and *Zeppelin L 20,* which had the whole of The Wash to traverse, did not cross the coast until 1920. It was later established that the targets for the night's operation were the industrial towns and cities of the Midlands, but due to the fog and mist, navigation proved to be their undoing and none reached their intended targets of Manchester or Liverpool (although the German press subsequently claimed the targets had been bombed). The lack of effective anti-aircraft defence over the Midlands was also a notable point, along with the random nature of the blackout regulations from one town to another being enforced.

Zeppelin L 21 crossed the coast at 1650 north of Mundesley, Norfolk in company with *Zeppelin L 13* and headed east towards King's Lynn, Nottingham and Derby, where she changed her course to the south-west and headed towards Stafford. She was commanded by *Kapitänleutnant der Reserve* Max Dietrich. From Stafford she made a sharp turn to the south, passed over Wolverhampton and then hovered for a few minutes as if trying to fix her position before heading for Dudley and Tipton, where she dropped her first bombs. Three HE bombs landed in Waterloo Street – killing one person and destroying various outbuildings – while in Union Street 13 people were killed and another 10 injured, along with demolishing two houses and fracturing a gas main. Three incendiary bombs landed in Bloomfield and Barnfield roads, but all failed to ignite. Next, five HE bombs were dropped on the canal towpath at Lower Bradley near Bilston – killing one person and injuring another, who later died. At Bloomfield, three incendiaries fell on the brickworks – two failing to ignite and the third caused no damage. The Zeppelin then turned to the east to Wednesbury, where at 2015 she dropped 12 HE and eight incendiary bombs. In King Street – near to the Crown Tube Works – three houses were destroyed and 13 civilians were killed, while three incendiaries which hit the roof of the Crown Tube Works killed one and damaged the roof and windows. At Mesty Croft Goods Yard, railway wagons and buildings were damaged and another person killed. It was then the turn of Walsall, which was hit by seven HE and four incendiary bombs. Although damage was not severe, three people were killed – including the Mayoress – and nine injured. The airship then made off towards the east – dropping six incendiary bombs on the Islip Furnaces at Thrapston as she passed overhead, but all missed their target. The raider finally passed out to sea between Pakefield and Kessingland at 2335.

Zeppelin L 13, commanded by *Kapitänleutnant* Heinrich Mathy, followed a similar, but more undulating course than *Zeppelin L 21* – crossing the coast north of Mundesley, Norfolk and passed Nottingham and Derby – but continued directly for Stoke-on-Trent, where at 2015 she dropped six HE bombs on the Fenton Colliery, but caused only minor damage. The airship then headed towards Newcastle-under-Lyme and dropped a flare at Madeley before circling – her commander apparently unsure of his position. At 2115 she was over Burton-on-Trent and dropped about 15 HE bombs on the town that had already been bombed by *Zeppelin L 20*. Still unsure of her position, she headed north-west over the Peak District towards Manchester, but over Buxton gave up the attempt to reach her intended target and turned due east – passing out to sea near Ingoldmells, Lincolnshire at 2315.

Zeppelin L 15 crossed the coast at 1750 at Mundesley, Norfolk and proceeded in a south-westerly direction until reaching Swaffham, when she headed south towards Mildenhall. She was commanded by *Kapitänleutnant* Joachim Breithaupt. Over West Row Fen, three HE and 15 incendiary bombs were dropped – although only three of the incendiaries ignited and caused no damage. Again, her captain seemed very unsure of his position as a flare was dropped – followed by 22 HE bombs that fell on the fen near Isleham; 15 exploding – wrecking a chicken coop and killing 16 chickens. At this point, the airship followed a fairly erratic course to the north-west to Lincolnshire, where she dropped nine incendiary bombs at Wellbourn Hill Top (south of Lincoln) before heading east as far as Skegness and then following the line of the coast towards Boston – dropping an incendiary bomb on Holland Fen. She then proceeded across The Wash back into Norfolk and finally passed out to sea at Corton at 0035.

Zeppelin L 16, commanded by *Leutnant zur See* Werner Peterson, crossed the coast at Hunstanton on the southern coast of The Wash at 1810 and proceeded south towards Swaffham, where she dropped two HE bombs – one failing to explode, but caused no damage. After this, she appeared to have drifted over Norfolk for about two hours before passing out to sea north of Lowestoft (having dropped no further bombs).

Zeppelin L 14 came in north of Holkham, Norfolk at 1815 and pursued a south-westerly course – dropping an incendiary bomb on Wisbech as she passed towards

Thorney – whereupon she turned north-west and headed towards Grantham – passing Knipton and dropping an HE bomb before turning due east and finally reaching Shrewsbury at 2205. She was commanded by *Kapitänleutnant der Reserve* Alois Böcker (later to be captured at Little Wigborough when commanding *Zeppelin L 33*). Here she followed an erratic course – gradually working her way back towards the east – and passed over Ashby-de-la-Zouch, where attracted by the fires of some pipe furnaces, dropped an HE and an incendiary bomb, but caused no damage; then four HE bombs were dropped on Overseal and three on Swadlincote a few minutes later – causing only minor damage. Ten minutes later, the raider reached Derby and dropped 21 HE and four incendiary bombs on the town. Nine of the HE bombs fell on the Midland Railway Works – damaging engine sheds, killing three and injuring two workmen. Three HE bombs fell on the Metalite Lamp Works – causing a considerable amount of damage to the works – but another four HE bombs that fell on the Rolls-Royce Works caused no damage to the plant. A further two HE bombs fell on a gas company and three on a lace factory – again without causing damage. The four incendiary bombs fell on various streets – setting a house on fire, but caused little other damage. In all, five people lost their lives and two were injured. The airship then followed a rambling course to the north-east and crossed the coast at Alford, Lincolnshire at 0210.

Zeppelin L 19 crossed the English Coast at 1820 just above Sheringham, Norfolk and headed south – gradually swinging towards the west as she proceeded on her way and making several loops between Stamford and Leicester as if her commander (*Kapitänleutnant* Odo Lowe) was unsure of his position. The airship then made for Burton-on-Trent – presumably being attracted by the fire already started by the previous two Zeppelins – and added a couple more incendiary bombs to the carnage before heading south towards Birmingham. Having missed Birmingham which was in total darkness, an HE bomb was dropped on the Monway Works at Wednesbury – causing slight damage to buildings and machinery. The airship then turned its attentions on Dudley, where five HE bombs were dropped on Ocker Hill Colliery before releasing 17 incendiaries over Dudley – all but one landing in fields (the one on target landing on a grain shed at the railway station). Tipton was the next target, with 11 HE bombs (which landed between the London and North-West Railway Station and Bloomfield) causing considerable damage to property; then proceeding to Walsall (at 0025), a further three HE bombs fell – one landing in the church garden and another killed a horse and several pigs. Having expended all her bomb load, the raider made off towards the east – following a circuitous route as if her commander was still unsure of his position – and eventually crossed the coast near Marham, Norfolk at 0525. Due to her protracted journey across England, fuel was getting short – and it was not until 1700 on 1 February was she sighted over the island of Borkum, Northern Germany (at which point, her engines gave out and she was seen drifting westwards out to sea).

Zeppelin L 17, commanded by *Kapitänleutnant* Herbert Ehrlich, drifted in over Sheringham, Norfolk at 1840 and was immediately illuminated by a searchlight stationed at the Royal Naval Air Station at Bayfield (two miles south of Cley). The

Premises in Union Street, Tipton was the recipient of one of *Kapitänleutnant* Odo Lowe and his crew's 11 high-explosive bombs that were dropped on the town – although none of them were to live to be able to report their results.

airship immediately dropped 10 HE bombs that fell about 200 yards from the station. Another five fell in a field to the south-east and a further five fell to the south. Five more HE and one incendiary bomb fell on a farm house and premises of Bayford Lodge – destroying a barn and greenhouse. The airship then turned south towards Letheringsett – on the way dropping 14 incendiary bombs near Bayfield Hall and one HE bomb fell on Letheringsett, but none caused any damage. The airship drifted around over Norfolk for a while before departing out to sea south of Yarmouth at 2030.

Zeppelin L 11, accompanied by *Zeppelin L 20*, crossed overland at the southern end of The Wash at 1910 and there parted company; *Zeppelin L 11* heading westwards – under the command of *Kapitänleutnant* Freiher von Horst Buttlar – and dropped an incendiary bomb at Holbeach at 1940 before setting a north-westerly course towards the manufacturing districts of South Yorkshire. She dropped three HE and an incendiary bomb at Digby and four HE bombs at Bloxholme Park – two failing to explode, but no damage was caused by any of the devices. Passing Lincoln, the airship hovered over East Retford as if her commander were deciding to head for Sheffield – and in the end turned back towards Lincoln, dropped a flare at Hackthorn and then turned once more north for Scunthorpe, where just before 2300 dropped 16 HE and 48 incendiary bombs on the Frodingham Iron and Steel Works (which had received no warning of the impending raid and were in full production). All bombs missed the works – several falling on the Redbourne Iron Works and killing two workmen. In the town, four houses were destroyed and railway sidings damaged, along with one killed and seven injured. Having expended its entire load, the airship made off towards the east and crossed the coast at North Somercotes, Lincolnshire – being fired at by a Pom-Pom located at Waltham Wireless Station as she passed by.

Zeppelin L 20 – having crossed the coast in company with *Zeppelin L 11* – at Sutton Bridge headed south-west and dropped an HE bomb on Uffington (near Stamford) and then proceeded to Loughborough (which was not under blackout conditions, unlike nearby Leicester and Nottingham), where she dropped four HE bombs – one falling on the Empress Crane Works, which had failed to douse its lights. Considerable damage was caused to the town, with 10 being killed and 12 injured. Leaving Loughborough, the airship dropped an HE bomb in a field (which failed to explode) before heading north-west to Trowell, where seven HE bombs fell – damaging a railway signal box. At 2030 the airship appeared over Ilkeston, where 15 HE bombs fell on the Stanton Iron Works, Hallam Field – killing two and injuring two, along with causing a considerable amount of damage. The Zeppelin then did an about-turn towards Burton-on-Trent, where 12 incendiary bombs were dropped at 2045 – causing extensive damage to the breweries of Messrs Bass, Allsopps, Inn and Coope & Co and Worthington's (although no one was killed). The greatest amount of damage was caused in Wellington and Shobnall Streets, where nine houses were destroyed, five persons killed and many injured. In the High Street, two shops were wrecked; the Grammar School House partly destroyed (two persons being killed there); while at Christchurch Mission Room and Vicarage, four were killed. Other bombs fell on a billiard hall – killing one – and at the Midland Railway Company's Goods Depot (a warehouse, sidings and goods trucks were destroyed). Also, Moor Street Crossing and Leicester Junction were hit and damaged – an empty train being destroyed. Eight incendiary bombs failed to ignite. It was impossible to plot exactly which bombs from which Zeppelin caused the most damage this night, but in all 15 were killed and 70 injured in Burton. Taking a wide sweep to the north of Nottingham, the airship headed back towards Norfolk and passed out to sea near Blakeney at 2345. Her commander was *Kapitänleutnant* Franz Stabbert.

Partially-collapsed houses in Wellington Street, Burton-on-Trent which were hit by an incendiary bomb – causing extensive damage.

It may look harmless and innocuous, but the tar and rope-wrapped incendiary bombs (when they did ignite) had great potential to cause far more damage than the much heavier high-explosive bombs.

2 February 1916
Zeppelin L 19 / LZ 54. Type P.
North Sea off Ameland.
Came down in the sea off Holland due to engine failure and loss of hydrogen following the raid upon Britain on 31 January.
Kapitänleutnant Odo Loewe +. NKG.
Obermaschinist Wilhelm Köppen +. NKG.
Leutnant zur See Erwin Braunhof +. NKG.
Obersignalmaat Kurt Kröner +. NKG.
Obermaschinistenmaat George Baumann +. NKG.
Obermaschinistenmaat Otto Kruse +. NKG.
Segelmachermaat Andreas Busch +. NKG.
Bootsmannsmaat Artur Rinken +. NKG.
Obermaschinistenmaat Hans Constabel +. NKG.
Steuermann Bruno Rödmann +. NKG.
Steuermannmaat Johannes Dreyer +. NKG.
Obermaschinistenmaat Heinrich Specht +. NKG.
Obermaschinistenmaat Arnold Flade +. NKG.
Funkentelegraphistenobermaat Otto Uhle +. NKG.
Maschinistenmaat Wilhelm Kähler +. NKG.

The airship – having been forced to land on the sea – fired off a number of distress signals which were sighted by the seaman on watch, Mate George Denny of the Grimsby trawler *King Stephen*, who alerted his skipper. The trawler, registered *GY 174*, made off in the direction of the flares. On reaching *Zeppelin L 19* at 0730 it was found half-submerged, with the surviving crew clinging to the upper portion of the airship. It was decided by the skipper, William Martin, that rescuing the crew of the Zeppelin would mean that the crew of the trawler could have been overpowered by their prisoners – and therefore, the decision was taken to sail away and leave the Zeppelin and its crew. This decision sparked an international debate as to whether William Martin made the right decision – although in Britain, opinion was divided as to whether the 'Baby Killers' should have been left to their fate, or that for those in distress upon the sea, every effort should be made to rescue them.

Skipper Martin returned to the home port of Grimsby and reported the incident to the authorities, but the incident was repeated to a journalist on the *Grimsby Evening Mail* and also reached the national and international press, where it was picked up by the German authorities.

The crew of *Zeppelin L 19* wrote out a message and threw it into the sea in a bottle, which was picked up by a Swedish fisherman at Marstrand six months after the incident. A translation of the message read:

> With 15 men on the top platform and backbone girder of the *L 19* – floating without gondolas in approximately three degrees east longitude. I am attempting

> to send a last report. Engine trouble three times repeated; a light wind on the return journey delayed our return – and in the mist carried us over Holland, where I was received with heavy rifle fire; the ship became heavy and simultaneously, three engines broke down. 2nd February 1916 towards one o'clock will apparently be our last hour. Lowe.

The *King Stephen* was subsequently commandeered by the Royal Navy and refitted as a Q-Ship – commanded by Lieutenant Tom Phillips, Royal Naval Reserve, with a Royal Navy crew. During a subsequent action, the *King Stephen* was sunk by a torpedo fired from the German torpedo boat SMS *G41* and the Royal Navy crew captured. Once the identity of the ship had been divulged to the Germans, Lieutenant Tom Phillips and his crew were taken to Berlin and charged with war crimes by the German authorities for failure to rescue the crew of *Zeppelin L 19*. It was only after news of the charges being brought against Lieutenant Phillips were brought to the attention of the British Government was a picture of William Martin published in the press. The Germans then realised that they had the wrong man and the charges were dropped.

A graphic depiction by a German artist of the Grimsby trawler *King Stephen* sailing away from the wreck of *Zeppelin L 19* – leaving her crew to drown. The German press made much out of this event to counter the label given by the British press that the Zeppelin crews were 'Baby Killers'.

As a propaganda tool, a special medallion was struck in Germany to commemorate the loss of *Zeppelin L 19* and her crew.

9 February 1916

The weather was deteriorating over the North Sea; the wind being high, with unsettled weather.

Two German seaplanes – one a *Friedrichshafen FF 33e* and the other a *Hansa-Brandenburg NW*, piloted by *flugzeugführer Leutnant* Friedrich Christiansen – were observed passing over the *North Goodwin Lightship*, steering west, at 1530. On reaching the English Coast, one turned north towards Broadstairs, Kent while the other flew over Ramsgate, Kent. The first aircraft bombed Broadstairs from a height of about 6,000 feet, with four HE bombs falling into a girls' school – one of which exploded in the upper storey of the building. Portions of the ceiling below fell into a class of young children – one girl sustaining slight cuts and a maid was slightly injured. Three other bombs fell in the school grounds – two of them exploding without causing any damage beyond broken windows. Two other bombs were dropped on outlying parts of the town, with one woman receiving slight cuts. The second machine missed Ramsgate town, but appeared to target a tram which was travelling along the Broadstairs Road, as one bomb fell on the roadway just behind the tram, but caused no serious damage (the driver of the tram having pulled up and alighted his passengers). The enemy aircraft dropped three more HE bombs, but these fell into adjoining fields. The raiders then were seen to make off out to sea.

The Royal Naval Air Service sent up 10 aircraft from local aerodromes, along with the Royal Flying Corps scrambling five aircraft from Dover. The Royal Naval Air Service also sent up four aircraft from Dunkirk, France to try and intercept the raiders on their return journey, but all aircraft failed to engage the enemy machines.

Summary for 9 February 1916:

Location	**Number and type of bombs dropped**	**Casualties**	**Damage**
Broadstairs	9× HE		
Near Ramsgate	4× HE		
Total	13× HE		

One of the regular visitors over Kent skies was *Leutnant* Christiansen, seen here recovering from a head injury.

20 February 1916
Weather: fine, with light winds.

Lowestoft, Suffolk was raided at 1055 when a seaplane circled to the south of the town for five minutes – dropping bombs from about 5,000 feet before heading out to sea; then at 1110 a second seaplane flew over the town for six to eight minutes dropping more bombs – again from about 5,000 feet – before also heading out to sea. It was noted that the first machine was painted brown; the second either white or pale green. In all, 19 HE bombs were dropped on the town – of which one failed to explode and two more were seen to fall in the sea. The only damage of military value was caused by a bomb which fell on a greenhouse near the 5th Provisional Brigade Headquarters and broke the telephone line. The staff captain and a clerk were cut by pieces of flying glass – otherwise no serious damage was done.

Anti-aircraft guns were in action in Suffolk, with a 6 pounder gun at Lowestoft and a 12 pounder naval gun manned by a military crew on Gun Hill engaging the aircraft. HMS *Halcyon*, which was moored in Lowestoft Harbour, fired one round from a 4.7 inch gun.

Royal Naval Air Service Yarmouth sent up five aircraft to try and engage the raiders, but they were too late to catch the retreating German aircraft.

At 1121 a German aeroplane aimed bombs at shipping five miles south of the Kentish Knock and was later sighted off the Galloper at 1135. At 1130 another German aeroplane approached Walmer, Kent from the east and circled over the town at a height of about 3,000 feet – dropping six HE bombs (one of which fell on the Marine Barracks; one on Dover Road; one on Beach Road; and three into the sea). In Beach Road, one boy was killed and another seriously injured. Numerous windows were broken in Dover Road, but there were no casualties to military personnel. At 1440 two enemy aircraft – believed to have been the same ones that raided Kent – passed over Dunkirk, France from the north and dropped six bombs.[1]

In Kent, no anti-aircraft guns were in action.

Eight RFC aircraft took to the air, but were again all too late to engage the raiders.

Summary for 20 February 1916:

Location	Number and type of bombs dropped	Casualties	Damage
Lowestoft, Suffolk	19× HE		
Walmer, Kent	6× HE		
Dunkirk, France	6× HE		
Total	31× HE		

21 February 1916

Zeppelin LZ 95 / LZ 65. Type Q.

Namur, Belgium.

Severely damaged during first operation and force landed near base.

Kommandeur: Hauptmann George.

22 February 1916

Zeppelin LZ 77 / LZ 47. Type P.

Near Brabant le Roi, Révigny, France.

1 Two *Friedrichshafen FF 33* and one *Hansa Brandenburg NW* were operating on this day, but which aircraft attacked which target is not recorded. Cole, Christopher & Cheeseman, E F. *The Air Defence of Britain 1914-1918*. Putnam (London). 1984.

Shot down by French anti-aircraft fire during a raid on Révigny rail marshalling yards at the start of the Verdun Offensive and crashed in flames.
Hauptmann Alfred Horn +.
Oberleutnant der Reserve Hans Papperitz +.
Obersteuermann Friedrich Fischer +.
Luftschiffer Fritz Baerenreuth +.
Unteroffizier Frank Gurke +.
Luftschiffer Gottfried Koerfer +.
Vizefeldwebel Johann Link +.
Luftschiffer Hans Lockermann +.
Obersteuernmann Martin Löchel +.
Maschinist Reinhard Müller +.
Fahrer Ingenieur Paul Schlick +.
Untersteuermann Fritz Sieger +.

On the night of 21 February 1916 *Zeppelins LZ 77, LZ 95, LZ 88* and *Schütte-Lanz SL 2* – along with four aeroplanes – were engaged in bombing operations against Révigny and its vital railway junction in support of the forthcoming German assault against the French fortress town of Verdun and its surrounding fortresses.

Ernst Lehmann, commander of *Zeppelin LZ 90* (having made a number of successful raids against Paris and Antwerp in the proceeding weeks), subsequently recorded:

> The crews were full of confidence. Until then, the risks had not been so great – even against the very violent and accurate fire of the artillery. The chance of having one's ship blown to pieces or fired by a full hit was remote. Imagine then the complete surprise awaiting us when we made our initial sally against the French during the first siege of Verdun. Only a few days before, while we were still busy getting our new engines into shape, the *LZ 77* had been shot down – a blazing, twisted wreck. She had attacked a railway junction close to our objective, which was Bar-le-Duc, south-west of Verdun. We had not attached any special significance to the accident. The surface artillery always had an excellent chance to hit an airship while it is attacking a single objective – such as a railway yard – because the target is so small and the range easily secured.

Ernst Lehmann was to later to die in the *Hindenburg* (*Zeppelin LZ 129*) crash of 6 May 1937.

At 2030 the French 17th AA Battery – consisting of two 75 mm truck-mounted anti-aircraft guns and a number of truck-mounted searchlights commanded by Lieutenant Grameling – was positioned 500 metres from the Vautrombois Crossing (in the village of Sainte Menehoulde) when *Zeppelin LZ 77* was caught by a cone of five searchlights as it followed the railway line from Vouziers to Bar-le-Duc.

Captain Charles Delvert of the French 101st Infantry Regiment recorded:

> We saw in the sky a dark cylinder with its ends rounded like those of a cigar. A Zeppelin! It seems very high. It must be 2,000 metres up. The airship glitters like a shining, golden fish. Five searchlights grab it and won't let go.

Opening fire with six shrapnel shells, one definitely hit *Zeppelin LZ 77* – which was estimated to have been flying at about 2,500 metres – and set it alight. The airship immediately released its bomb load and headed in the direction of Brabant-le-Roi – taking about two minutes to hit the ground. One of the crew members fell or jumped from the burning airship; the others died in the wreck.

Lieutenant Grameling's 17th Anti-Aircraft Battery also claimed to have secured a hit on *Hauptmann* George's *Zeppelin LZ 95*.

The British were soon informed of the crash and were quick to despatch intelligence personnel to the site to inspect and recover portions of the wreckage for further analysis – even though the crash occurred within an area under French military control.

For further details, see appendix I.

1 March 1916

Weather: unsettled and overcast, with rain falling over Kent. Wind from the south-west, strength one.

At 1810 an enemy seaplane – a *Friedrichshafen FF 29* – approached Margate, Kent from the north-east, but due to the failing light (and only flying at 1,500 feet), it was not initially identified as hostile. It turned east over Margate, passing over Cliftonville, where it dropped three HE bombs in Norfolk Road – killing a baby and badly damaging two houses. Soon after, four HE bombs fell in Percy Avenue, Kingsgate – shattering windows of eight houses – and another two HE bombs fell on the golf links, but caused no damage.

Summary for 1 March 1916:

Location	Number and type of bombs dropped	Casualties	Damage
Cliftonville	3× HE		
Kingsgate	4× HE		
Total	7× HE		

It was later recorded that the *Friedrichshafen FF 29, no.201* was damaged by fire from patrol boats over the North Sea and was compelled to land on the sea near the

A memorial still stands at the position where the French anti-aircraft gun that was responsible for bringing down *Zeppelin LZ 77* was sited – and within a mile of the crash site.

Many postcards were produced showing the wreckage of the Zeppelin to give the French and British public the perception that the monsters that rained death upon their towns and cities were not impregnable.

Middelkerke Bank, Belgium. The crew were *flugzeugführer Flugzeugmatrose* Huth and *beobachter Flugzeugmeister* Johann Jacobs.[2]

5 March 1916

Weather: strong north-easterly wind overland, with localised sleet and snow conditions.

Three airships (*Zeppelins L 11*, *L 13* and *L 14*) left their sheds situated near the Heligoland Bight just before midday – crossing the North Sea in formation – making for Flamborough Head. The original intention was to attack Sheffield, Derby and Nottingham, but the problems of navigation in snowy conditions precluded this.

Zeppelin L 14 – after first having been heard out to sea off Flamborough Head, Yorkshire – circled to obtain her bearings and dropped flares on the beach at 2230 (so as to locate the land). She then headed south – following the coast from the landward side as far as Aldbrough – before turning out to sea and heading back up the coast as far as Barmstown. She then turned west to come overland again at 2325 – dropping an incendiary bomb as she went in a field near Gembling. Heading south following the railway, three HE and three incendiary bombs were dropped near Beverly – falling in open fields in the parish of Woodmansey. The commander, *Kapitänleutnant der Reserve* Alois Böcker, must have sighted Hull and bore directly down southwards on the city – passing slowly over the western part and dropped seven HE bombs which fell in a line. The first and second fell in the grounds of Hymer College and on a nearby railway embankment, while the following three bombs destroyed houses in Regent, Linnaeus and Day Streets along with wrecking a grocer's shop in Bean Street. The seventh bomb landed on the quay of Albert Dock – wrecking a crane. A further nine incendiaries were dropped on the town and another four landed in the river. The crew subsequently stated that the recent snowfall highlighted many of the buildings in the city – allowing for perfect visibility over the target.

The airship then continued south for a while – following the River Humber, where she was fired at by an anti-aircraft gun situated at Killingholme (at which point, the raider turned back to the north-east and dropped an HE bomb on Burstwick, followed by another four HE and two incendiary bombs at Owstwick – all of which burst harmlessly). The raider then passed out to sea at 0045 over Tunstall.

Zeppelin L 11 crossed the Yorkshire Coastline between Tunstall and Withernsea at about 2145 and after loitering for some time, made off south – reaching as far as Waddington – before the commander, *Kapitänleutnant* Freiherr von Buttlar, [3] apparently decided not to venture further south, but turned about and headed north-west

2 Cole & Cheeseman: *The Air Defence of Britain 1914-1918* records the observer being drowned and the pilot being captured.

3 Cole & Cheeseman: *The Air Defence of Britain 1914 -1918. Korvettenkapitän* Viktor Schütze is attributed to commanding *Zeppelin L 11* on this operation.

towards Doncaster before turning north-east towards the coast (as the weather conditions had deteriorated and snow clouds prevented the crew from pinpointing their position). Having reached the Humber, the airship then followed the river up to Hull – which was approached from a height of about 3,000 feet – and for a time, hovered over the city. An HE bomb was first dropped in the river opposite Earle's Shipyard – damaging a half-built 3,000 ton steamer – and which collapsed the following day. An incendiary bomb then fell harmlessly into the river. The airship then passed north-west over the city – passing the mouth of the Hull, where another incendiary fell across Prince's Dock and over the Paragon Station – dropping a further eight HE and 10 incendiary bombs as she passed. The CRA's Office in Queen Street was badly damaged. Other damage included houses and broken water mains in Queen and Collier Streets; a fire at the Mariner's Almshouses in Carr Lane; and another fire on the quay of Prince's Dock, but was soon extinguished. Following the Humber to the south-east, the raider was fired at by the gun situated at Killingholme, and in reply dropped four HE bombs – one of which struck a railway siding and killing one man. Continuing her course, the airship passed over the Spurn at 0140 and out to sea.

The total casualties caused by both raids on Hull were 17 killed and 52 injured.

Zeppelin L 13 crossed the Lincolnshire Coast at North Coates Fitties at 2114 and headed south-west towards Newark – dropping a flare at Branston and then more

An unusual close-up view of *Zeppelin L 13* as she nears the ground – giving an idea of the immense size of these great leviathans of the air.

flares to the south of Newark – before circling round Bilsby and then proceeding in a south-easterly direction. Near Whatton, another flare was dropped; the commander, *Kapitänleutnant* Heinrich Mathy, obviously being unsure of his position – and in the face of a strong northerly wind and snow, decided that it was better to return via Belgium rather than attempt to reach Germany via the North Sea. Having made his decision, the aim was probably to lighten the load and expend the bomb load on any target of opportunity that presented itself – and thus, at 2315, 32 incendiary bombs fell in open fields between the village and church of Sproxton – causing no damage; then at 2330, 14 HE bombs fell in fields near to Thistleton (eight miles north-east of Oakham) before then circling and dropping a further HE bomb at Edmundthorpe. With the wind behind her, the airship sped south-east and reached Burnham-on-Crouch, Essex at 0113 and proceeded to circle before passing Shoeburyness (where she was fired at by a 3 inch anti-aircraft gun) before crossing the Thames Estuary to the Isle of Grain – where she again circled to pinpoint her position. Here she hovered for about 10 minutes at a height of 9,000 feet – dropping four HE bombs at Ripley Hill Marshes and Danley Farm. All the anti-aircraft guns at Sheerness fired at her as she hovered almost motionless for about five minutes – standing with her bows into the wind; fully illuminated by searchlights. She then made off over Harty Ferry and was fired at by a 3 inch gun – and over Faversham, three rounds from a 6 pounder Hotchkiss were fired at her. She was next sighted over Canterbury – apparently drifting with her engines off at 0200 – and when over Adisham, dropped a small fan-driven oil pump before passing out to sea near Deal at 0225. At 0310 she was sighted by the SS *James Fletcher* mid-Channel (apparently drifting) before finally making Belgium. Supposition that she had been damaged by anti-aircraft fire was that she remained in Belgium for four days – presumably undergoing repairs.

Summary for 5 March 1916:

Location	**Number and type of bombs dropped**	**Casualties**	**Damage**
Yorkshire, East Riding			
Gembling	1× IB		
Beverly	3× HE, 3× IB		
Hull	16× HE, 25× IB	17 killed, 52 injured	4 terraces of houses destroyed; several houses and shops; a café, public house and CRA's Office; Paragon Station damaged; dock shed and crane destroyed
Burstwick	1× HE		

Location	Number and type of bombs dropped	Casualties	Damage
Owstwick	4× HE, 2× IB		
Lincolnshire			
Killingholme	4× HE	1 killed	Slight damage to railway
Leicestershire			
Sproxton	32× IB		
Edmundthorpe	1× HE		
Rutlandshire			
Thistleton	14× HE, 1× IB		
Kent			
Minster-in-Sheppey	4× HE		
Total	47× HE, 63× IB	18 killed, 52 injured	

Anti-aircraft guns in action and reported use of ammunition:

Location of AA battery	Calibre or type of gun	Number / type of rounds fired
Killingholme	1 pdr Hotchkiss (field mount)	11 rounds
Killingholme	1 pdr Hotchkiss (naval mount)	49 rounds
Killingholme	2× 6 pdr Hotchkiss (fixed)	14 rounds
Shoeburyness	3" 20-cwt	2 rounds
Sheerness		
Dummy Battery	2× 6pdr Hotchkiss (military)	27 rounds
Albemarle Battery	2× 6 pdr Hotchkiss (military)	25 rounds
Bartons Point	2× 6 pdr Hotchkiss (military)	12 rounds
Sheppey		
Naval Recreation Ground	2× 6 pdr Hotchkiss (naval)	27 rounds
Harty Ferry	3" 20-cwt	11 rounds
Faversham	6 pdr Nordenfeldt	3 rounds

One Royal Naval Air Service aeroplane took off in pursuit from Eastchurch Aerodrome, Kent, but failed to spot the airship.

19 March 1916

Weather: an easterly breeze, strength two, with some rain and mist.

In the afternoon, six German seaplanes – consisting of four *Friedrichshafen FF 33b-fs*, one *Hansa-Brandenburg NW* and a *Gotha Ursinus WD* – approached the Kent Coast. Three of the machines ('A', 'B' and 'C') appeared over Dover at 1350 – passing over the town centre from east to west. They dropped 24 HE bombs during their passage over the town and caused considerable damage to private property. About 100 shops and houses were damaged, with the bulk of the bombs falling into the centre of the town. Two fell within 50 yards of the Priory Railway Station in Folkestone Road, whilst six fell into the harbour – doing no damage. Two men, a woman and a child were killed, with 17 men and four women being injured (13 of the men being soldiers of the 5th Royal Fusiliers). Anti-aircraft guns opened fire on the raiders and three aeroplanes took off to try and intercept, but were too late. The enemy machines then separated, with 'A' turning south over Hougham and passing out to sea between Folkestone and Dover, while aeroplanes 'B' and 'C' headed north to Deal, where at 1405 nine HE bombs were dropped – all in a direct line from south to north (apparently from one machine). There were no casualties, but a great number of windows were broken.

Both aircraft 'B' and 'C' made out to sea, but 'C' turned back to Ramsgate, where it was joined by the fourth machine ('D'), which had earlier been spotted in the company of a fifth machine ('E') off the North Goodwins at 1400 steering for the North Foreland.

Ramsgate was over-flown at 1412 and bombed by 'C' and 'D' – each approaching the town from different directions. They appeared to meet over the town – on which 14 HE bombs were dropped; the Canadian Special Hospital being slightly damaged, along with some private property. Nine of the bombs fell around the gas works, but caused no significant damage, while another fell on the driving seat of a motor car which was crossing St Luke's Square – blowing the car and occupant to pieces. The same bomb killed four children who were on their way to Sunday school and wounded nine others. Another bomb fell nearby and injured a woman standing outside her house.

The raiders were fired at by anti-aircraft fire from drifters moored in Ramsgate Harbour and also attacked by a British aeroplane from Westgate, but they separated. 'C' headed west and was spotted over Westgate at 1420 while machine 'D' turned north to Margate and at 1415 dropped a single HE bomb on a house in Fort Crescent, Cliftonville, which was used as the headquarters of the 9th Provisional Cyclist Company (little damage being done and no casualties).

The fifth raider ('E') was not plotted overland and did not appear to have dropped any bombs.

Aircraft 'A', which passed out to sea at Dover, was claimed to have been brought down in flames over the Channel by Second Lieutenant R Collis of the Royal Flying Corps, who was flying overseas from Folkestone at the time and joined the chase. It later transpired that Second Lieutenant Collis and his observer, Flight Sergeant A C Emery, managed to damage the coolant system of the *Hansa-Brandenburg NW, no.521* of *See Flieger Abteilung 1* (*flugzeugführer Leutnant* F Christiansen and *beobachter Oberleutnant zur See* von Tschirschky und Bogendorff), but eventually managed to limp back to Zeebrugge, Belgium.

Flight Commander R J Bone also managed to damage and force *Friedrichshafen FF 33, no.537* (*flugzeugführer Flugmeister* Ponater and *Leutnant* Herrenknecht as *beobachter*) to land on the sea about 30 miles east-north-east of North Foreland. Another aircraft landed close by to rescue the crew and the aircraft was later towed into Ostend,[4] Belgium.

Summary for 19 March 1916:

Location	**Number and type of bombs dropped**	**Casualties**	**Damage**
Dover	24× HE	4 killed, 21 injured	
Deal	9× HE		
Ramsgate	14× HE	5 killed, 10 injured	
Margate	1× HE		
Total	48× HE	9 killed, 31 injured	

Anti-aircraft guns in action and reported use of ammunition:

Location of AA battery	**Calibre or type of gun**	**Number / type of rounds fired**
Langdon Battery	3”	103 rounds
Langdon Battery	6 pdr Hotchkiss	214 rounds
Dover Castle	6 pdr Nordenfeldt	94 rounds
Fort Burgoyne	6 pdr Hotchkiss	262 rounds
Drop Redoubt	6 pdr	211 rounds
Capel	6 pdr	21 rounds
Prince of Wales Battery	6”	6 rounds
Eastern Arm	6”	11 rounds
Drifters in Ramsgate Harbour	6 pdr	–

Three aircraft from Dover and two from Westgate were sent up to intercept the raiders.[5]

4 Cole & Cheeseman: *The Air Defence of Britain 1914 -1918*.
5 Cole & Cheeseman: *The Air Defence of Britain 1914 -1918* records 30 sorties.

31 March 1916

Weather: clear and calm, with wind over the North Sea coming from the west at 25 miles per hour. South of The Wash wind was practically dead calm.

Naval airships *Zeppelins L 13, L 14, L 15, L 16* and *L 22* left Northern Germany, with one targeting the Humber area and the rest to bomb ammunition factories at Waltham Abbey, Woolwich (as well as targets of opportunity to the east of London). *Zeppelins L 7* and *L 11* also started out, but turned back before crossing the coast. Two army Zeppelins were also operating this night (though they could not be identified with any certainty and did not drop any bombs).

Zeppelin L 15 crossed the coast at Dulwich, Suffolk at 1945 – dropping two HE bombs in the sea. At 1950 she dropped a fuel tank and an incendiary bomb at Yoxford, Suffolk before proceeding at a speed of 35 miles per hour to Ipswich Docks, Suffolk where two HE and one incendiary bomb were dropped – hitting two houses, killing three and injuring two people. At 2045 Colchester, Essex was hit by one HE bomb before the airship turned south-west towards the Thames (flying at about 8,000 feet). Upon reaching Erith, Kent (on the south bank of the Thames) heavy anti-aircraft fire was experienced from the 3 inch anti-aircraft guns of the Purfleet Battery, which fired 24 rounds of shrapnel – tearing a hole in the outer envelope and puncturing three of the airship's gas bags. The airship was also spotted by Second Lieutenant C A Ridley in a BE2c of 19 Squadron Royal Flying Corps, who managed to lose off 20 rounds at the airship, but lost her in the darkness. Numerous searchlights illuminated the airship – and anti-aircraft guns from numerous batteries along the Thames now opened up. The Zeppelin attempting to escape turned northwards – and at 2143 dropped 20 HE and 24 incendiary bombs over Rainham and Wennington, Essex. The airship then turned east, but at 2155 over Brentwood (at 9,000 feet), the airship was attacked from above by Second Lieutenant A de B Brandon in a BE2c of Home Defence Detachment, 19th Reserve Squadron, with Ranken explosive darts (with no obvious effect). While flying alongside the airship, de B Brandon experienced return fire before climbing once more to drop an incendiary bomb – and more explosive darts – before losing sight of the airship (Second Lieutenant de B Brandon, on landing, found three bullet-holes in his aircraft). The Zeppelin crew – in an attempt to lighten the load – threw overboard two machine-guns and a variety of moveable objects that landed in fields at Stock, South Hanningfield and Woodham Ferrers, Essex prior to circling twice over Foulness (as if the commander was pondering whether his ship would be able to cross the Channel) – heading out to sea at 2225. Thirty-five minutes later, the airship broke its back and fell into the sea from 2,000 feet – south-east of the *Kentish Knock Lightship* (the crew being rescued by two trawlers at midnight). An attempt was made to tow the airship back to land, but she sank off Westgate, Kent.

Markings: *L 15* was painted on either side of the bow, with a large black cross painted under the bow.

There was a strong white light fitted in the bow of the forward gondola.

Zeppelin L 15 is secured having just landed at Nordholtz, with *Zeppelin L 14* in the background.

Zeppelin L15 / LZ 48. Type P.
Kapitänleutnant Joachim Breithaupt: Repatriated via Rotterdam, Holland (15 April 1915).
Leutnant zur See C W F Kuhne: Second-in-command; repatriated via Switzerland (4 December 1916).
Oberbootmannsmaat Martin Frandsen: Directional steersman.
Obersteuermann Karl Thamm.
Obermaschinist Max H L Martens.
Bootsmannsmaat Friedrich C Kant: Directional steersman.
Obersignalmaat Erich Grund: Elevating steersman; repatriated via Switzerland (December 1916).
Oberbootmannsmaat Willi Albrecht +. NKG: Elevating steersman; drowned when the airship hit the water.
Funkentelegraphistenmaat Martin Roscher.
Obermaschinistenmaat Oscar Mittelstenschee: Engine staff.
Obermaschinistenmaat Oscar Pfeiffer: Engine staff.
Obermaschinistenmaat Eugen Hoyler: Engine staff.
Obermaschinistenmaat Otto K R Vogler: Engine staff.
Maschinistenmaat Willy Brubach.
Maschinistenmaat Otto Wulfert: Injured in crash; engine staff.
Maschinistenmaat Georg Blocher: Engine staff.
Obermatrose Alex Maraun.
Obermaschinistenmaat Otto Schulz: Engine staff.

Lieutenant Day, RNR of HMS *Kitty George* – the first ship to reach the wreck – stated that the hull of the airship was practically intact and partially submerged by a couple of feet. The crew had gathered at the forward observation platform, but in order to be rescued, they had to pass along a walkway to the aft end and then through a hole torn in the canvas of the tailplane. Towing of the airship commenced at the stern, but this collapsed and a new tow was taken up from the bow, which had risen out of the water.

Zeppelin L 15 with her back broken – clearly showing the hole torn in the aft structure from where her crew were rescued.

Kapitänleutnant Joachim Breithaupt pictured soon after his capture.

The last message transmitted from the airship was:

> To Chief of Staff: 10pm; have successfully bombed a battery at Stowmarket; have been hit; am turning; shall land at Hague about 4am. *L 15*.

Under interrogation, the airship's wireless operator admitted that he had sent two wireless messages (one at 2225 and the other at 2250) with information regarding the damage to the ship – and would have been picked up by the other airships which were operating.

Report by Second Lieutenant Alfred de Bathe Brandon regarding his actions:

> I left Hainault Farm at 9.25pm and circled round the aerodrome until I got to a height of 6,000 feet at about 9.40pm. I then saw the Zeppelin high up on my right in the light of the searchlights. She appeared to be heading to a point directly in front of me, so I continued in my direction. After about five minutes, the searchlights lost the Zeppelin and I continued in its direction until it was 5-600 feet over my head. I circled round in front and climbed – and passed over the Zeppelin (I think at about 3-400 hundred feet) and dropped no.1 lot of darts. I heard three reports and thought that I had made a hit. Shortly after this, I heard more reports (which probably were from a machine-gun) – and this made me uncertain whether I had made a hit or not. I continued and circled in front of the Zeppelin and turned round to get in its rear – and on going past, there was a tremendous amount of machine-gun-firing going on. At this point, I switched off my lights and continued in my direction for 2-300 yards and then turned and got in a direct line with the Zeppelin; I was then about 500 feet above it. I closed the throttle and volplaned towards the Zeppelin. The nose of my machine was pointing about quarter-way from the rear. I then got out an incendiary bomb – and in trying to get it into the tube, I had to take my eyes off the Zeppelin – and on looking up again, I was astonished to find that in a very few seconds I would have passed the Zeppelin, so I quickly placed the incendiary bomb in my lap and let off no.2 and 3 lots of darts. I did not hear any report from this. I conclude that the Zeppelin was, in reality, coming towards me, so I opened up the engine again and turned completely round and followed a southerly course (continuing for some considerable time, as I thought the Zeppelin had got a good start). In the meantime, I turned my lights on again – and I was at 8,000 feet. I cruised round at 8,000 feet for some time and saw nothing, and then dropped to 6,000 feet and cruised around for some considerable time without also seeing any sign of the Zeppelin. At this height, I saw one lot of flares – which subsequently, turned out to be Faningham. An examination of the machine shows that one Holt landing flare and wing skid were broken in landing – and there were three bullet-holes in the right aileron, the left tail and the right elevator respectively. I arrived down at 11.10pm.
>
> When I first saw the Zeppelin, I was flying at 6,000 feet. The flashes from our shells appeared to me to be about 6,500 feet – and I should say, the Zeppelin was 8-9,000 feet up. I first saw the Zeppelin at 9.40pm and lost sight of it at 10.05pm. The searchlights were on it for some four to five minutes; one flashed across it twice, but did not seem to pick it up.

Leutnant zur See C W F Kuhne asked his captors to send a telegram to his sister, one Mrs Barrett of Bungay, Suffolk.

The second-in-command of *Zeppelin L 15*, *Leutnant zur See* C W F Kuhne, was later repatriated to Germany and spent the rest of the war serving as an officer on the ground staff of the airship service.

Zeppelin L 15 – having been towed towards Westgate, Kent – finally disappeared below the waves, but not before some wreckage had been salvaged.

Zeppelin L 13, commanded by *Kapitänleutnant* Heinrich Mathy, crossed the coast at Sizewell, Suffolk at 2000 and proceeded south-west (heading towards Ipswich), but turned to the north-east and headed for Stowmarket – dropping two flares over Badley. At this point, the searchlight and anti-aircraft guns (situated at the new explosive works) opened up – and in response, 12 HE bombs landed very close to the guns and the works. The airship then completed a wide loop to the west and returned to Stowmarket at 2115 when she was hit by an anti-aircraft tracer shell. This was recorded by the anti-aircraft battery, but also by a message picked up the next morning, which had been written by the airship commander to be sent by the wireless operator, but had blown overboard. The message stated that the airship had been hit over Stowmarket and that he hoped to reach his shed in Northern Germany by four o'clock the next morning. In obvious trouble, the Zeppelin headed off east-north-east – and over Stoham dropped three large fuel tanks. She was not sighted again until near Wangford, when at 2210 the headlights of the cars of the Machine-Gun Section of the Royal Naval Air Service Anti-Aircraft Section were seen and 11 HE and five incendiary bombs were dropped, but all missed; then as she passed over the aerodrome at Covehithe, seven HE and 20 incendiary bombs were dropped, but again no damage was caused. At this point, the airship was no more than 2,000 feet up, but with the release of the bombs she climbed rapidly and finally made Germany at 0200 (having crossed the North Sea and hugged the Dutch Coast).

Zeppelin L 14, which was commanded by *Kapitänleutnant* Karl Böcker, crossed the Norfolk Coast at Palling at 2015 and circled over Coltishall while the commander got his bearings. She then passed to the west of Norwich and proceeded to follow the Great Eastern Railway Line south to Stowmarket. She continued on in the same vein to Sudbury, where at 2230 eight HE and 19 incendiary bombs were dropped on the town – killing five and injuring one when a pub and a number of houses were hit. The airship continued on her progression to the south – and on passing Braintree at 2305 three HE bombs were dropped, which demolished a house and partially wrecked four more, along with killing four and injuring three. Carrying on towards London, the airship was fired on by a Pom-Pom situated at Kelvedon Hatch – and illuminated by searchlights, Karl Böcker presumably abandoned his drive on London and turned his airship on the reciprocal course. He again passed over the Kelvedon Hatch anti-aircraft gun and dropped two HE bombs in response (which landed north of Doddinghurst), and then another nine HE bombs, which landed at Blackmore at 2345. Flying back north-eastwards over Chelmsford as far as Great Yeldham, the commander once more had a change of heart and turned through 108° and headed south for London – once more passing Chelmsford – and dropped an HE bomb that fell at Springfield at 0055. On passing Brentwood again, the airship turned to the south-east towards the oil storage tanks at Thames Haven and released an incendiary bomb over Stanford-le-Hope; then five HE and 12 incendiary bombs landed on the Asiatic Oil Company's Works at Thames Haven – destroying two empty oil tanks and causing a small fire on the pier. In response, the anti-aircraft guns at Thames Haven, Kynochstown and Pitsea opened fire on the raider, but with no apparent results, which then headed off back towards the north-east – dropping a dud flare on Canvey Island – and finally passed out to sea at Dunwich, Suffolk at about 0300.

Zeppelin L 16 passed the *Would Lightship* at 2120 and crossed the coast at Winterton Ness, Norfolk at 2210 and followed a weaving course towards Bury St Edmunds. When passing East Harting, she dropped a fuel tank at 2305. On reaching her goal, she was fired at by a mobile Pom-Pom section of the Royal Naval Anti-Aircraft Corps without visible results, but the commander of *Zeppelin L 16*, *Oberleutnant zur See* Werner Peterson, aimed his bombs at his opponents – scattering 21 HE and five incendiary bombs across the town – killing six and injuring six. Two cottages were wrecked and six badly damaged – the incendiaries falling in open fields. The airship then headed east as far as Ipswich before turning to the north-east and Lowestoft, where she passed out to sea – dropping a 100 kg HE bomb as she passed and damaging a tramcar-shed. She was fired on by a naval 12 pounder gun at Pakefield and by a 6 pounder gun at Lowestoft, with the only result being that the raider climbed higher.

Zeppelin LZ 90 (or *LZ 93*) crossed the North Sea from Belgium and approached the Suffolk Coast, but did not appear to have come inland and was reported to be back in its shed at Namur, Belgium by 1000 the next morning.

Zeppelin LZ – (possibly *LZ 88*) was sighted crossing the coast near Alderton, Suffolk and then followed a course of Wickham Market, Woodbridge. She then circled Ipswich at 0118 where she was fired at by a Pom-Pom of the Royal Naval Anti-Aircraft Corps before disappearing. The airship did not drop any bombs, so she may have been on a reconnaissance or practice flight, for two nights later, *Zeppelin LZ 88* steered almost the same course.

Zeppelin L 22, commanded by *Kapitänleutnant* Martin Dietrich, was sighted off the *Inner Dowsing Lightship* at 0015, 1 April and reached the Lincolnshire Coast at Mablethorpe at 0100. Following the coast north, she passed Donna Nook (where she dropped an incendiary bomb) and continued along the South Bank of the Humber towards Grimsby – dropping 14 HE and 12 incendiary bombs on Humberston at 0135 (although five of the HE bombs did not explode). Continuing to Cleethorpes, six HE bombs were dropped at 0148 which hit a chapel that was being used as a billet for men of the 3rd Manchester Regiment. Twenty-nine men were killed and 53 wounded. A wing of the Town Hall, houses and shops were badly damaged. The airship then circled twice over the town before heading out to sea at 0210 – being fired upon by an anti-aircraft gun mounted on a paddle minesweeper moored in the Humber.

Summary for 31 March 1916:

Location	Number and type of bombs dropped	Casualties	Damage
Lincolnshire			
Donna Nook	1× IB		
Humberston	14× HE, 12× IB		Windows of a farmhouse shattered
Cleethorpes	6× HE	29 killed, 53 injured	Chapel destroyed; Town Hall damaged
Suffolk			
Lowestoft	1× HE		Tramcar-shed damaged
Wangford	11× HE, 5× IB		
Covehithe	7× HE, 20× IB		
Yoxford	1× IB		
Stowmarket	12× HE		Glass in explosive works broken; railway slightly damaged
Bury St Edmunds	21× HE, 5 IB	7 killed, 5 injured	2 houses wrecked, 9 badly damaged, 26 slightly damaged; shed and stabling wrecked

Location	Number and type of bombs dropped	Casualties	Damage
Ipswich	2× HE, 1 IB	3 killed, 2 injured	2 houses damaged
Sudbury	8× HE, 19 IB	5 killed	Inn and 2 houses demolished
Essex:			
Braintree	3× HE	4 killed, 3 injured	1 house demolished; 4 wrecked
Blackmore	9× HE		
Doddinghurst	2× HE		
Colchester	1× HE		Glass roof of a printing works broken
Springfield	1× HE		
Rainham	6× HE, 12× IB		
Wennington	14× HE, 9× IB		
Stanford-le-Hope	1× HE		
Thames Haven	2× HE, 12× IB		Slight damage to pier and two empty oil tanks
Total	121× HE, 97× IB (2 HE bombs fell in the sea at Dunwich)	48 killed, 63 injured	

Anti-aircraft guns in action and reported use of ammunition:

Location of AA battery	Calibre or type of gun	Number / type of rounds fired
Eastern Mobile Section, RNAAC		
Bury (Position 198)	2× Pom-Pom	–
Wangford	3× Pom-Pom	–
Ipswich (Position 180)	1½ Pdr Pom-Pom	–
Ipswich (Position 180)	3× MG	–
London and Thames Defences		
Beacontree Heath	2× 13 pdr	2 rounds
Kelvedon Hatch	Pom-Pom	75 rounds
Thames Haven	2× 6 pdr	4 rounds
Kynochstown	2× 6 pdr	31 rounds
Kynochstown	1 pdr	24 rounds

Location of AA battery	Calibre or type of gun	Number / type of rounds fired
Pitsea	2× 6 pdr	22 rounds
Purfleet (3)	3" 20-cwt	24 rounds
Purfleet (3)	1 pdr QF	122 rounds
North Woolwich	3" 5-cwt	8 rounds
Erith, South Outfall, Northumberland Heath	13 pdr	10 rounds
Erith, South Outfall, Northumberland Heath	3" 20-cwt (AA mobile)	25 rounds
Erith	2× 6 pdr QF	34 rounds
Erith Marshes	6 pdr QF	24 rounds
Dartford	3× 3" 20-cwt	24 rounds
Abbey Wood	2× 3" 20-cwt	17 rounds
Plumstead Common	3" 20-cwt	4 rounds
Plumstead Common	13 pdr	11 rounds
Plumstead Marshes	1 pdr QF Pom-Pom	34 rounds
Royal Arsenal	2× 6 pdr QF	4 rounds
East Anglia		
Stowmarket	2× 6 pdr QF	26 rounds
Pakefield	2× 12 pdr (naval)	2 rounds
Lowestoft Pier	3× 6 pdr (naval)	29 rounds
Lowestoft Northend	2× 12 pdr (naval)	2 rounds
Humber Defences		
Waltham	Pom-Pom	202 rounds
Paddle Steamer on Humber	–	–

Actions of aeroplanes of the Royal Flying Corps:

Nine aircraft took off to try and intercept the raiders, with Second Lieutenant C A Ridley – flying from Joyce Green – catching sight of an airship in a searchlight beam and fired about 20 rounds. Second Lieutenant A de B Brandon, flying from Hainault Farm, saw and attacked airship – dropping three lots of Ranken darts. He was fired at and found three bullet-holes in his aircraft.

Second Lieutenant J W Bailey[6] took off from Northolt in pursuit, but crashed soon after and was killed.

6 Second Lieutenant John Winkworth Bailey, RFC, aged 33: buried Ruislip (St Martin) Cemetery Extension, Middlesex.

1 April 1916

Weather: calm and fine, with little cloud and no mist or fog until just before sunrise.

On the evening of 1 April two airships – *Zeppelins L 11* and *L 17* – were sighted off the Yorkshire Coast.

Zeppelin L 11, commanded by *Oberleutnant zur See* von Buttlar, crossed the coast at Seaham at 2305. At 2310 she passed over Eppleton Colliery, Durham where two HE bombs were dropped – landing on refuse heaps and causing no damage; then at 2312 when over Hetton Downs, two more HE bombs fell near some houses – destroying some wooden outhouses and shattering windows. The airship then turned north towards Sunderland and at 2315 a further two HE bombs were dropped on Philadelphia – breaking glass in the windows of 35 houses, but caused no other form of damage. Following the River Wear to Sunderland, the raider reached the city at 2320 and dropped 14 HE and seven incendiary bombs which destroyed four shops and 15 houses, along with a workmen's hall and three stables; a railway goods yard; and a tramcar (including its shed), which were wrecked. The toll of casualties for this incident was 22 killed and five seriously injured – including two soldiers – and 103 slightly injured. The Zeppelin was then picked up by a searchlight situated at Hylton and the 6 inch anti-aircraft gun at Fulwell Quarry fired one round before the airship was lost by the searchlight crew. The Zeppelin then crossed out to sea and followed the coast south towards Middlesbrough – and at 0005 dropped an HE bomb aimed at Messrs Sell's Works at Port Clarence, but it landed on a heap of steel billets. Crossing the River Tees, another two HE bombs fell in the mud – followed by another two on vacant land (adjoining the Cargo Fleet Steel Works) which shattered a number of windows in the area and injured two men. The airship then followed the railway line to Eaton Nab and then passed onto Saltburn before circling for a while before heading to Skinningrove, where a final two HE bombs were dropped, but they landed in open fields at Cattesty Farm before passing out to sea at 0030.

Zeppelin L 17, commanded by *Kapitänleutnant* Herbert Ehrlich, was spotted out to sea from Flamborough Head heading in a southerly direction at 2100 following the coast – dropping bombs as she went. Seventeen explosions were heard at about 2123 from Tunstall and the last sounds of aero-engines were heard at 2220 from Hornsea, Yorkshire.

Summary for 1 April 1916:

Location	Number and type of bombs dropped	Casualties	Damage
Durham			
Eppleton	2× HE		
Hetton Downs	2× HE		Several outhouses destroyed; windows broken
Philadelphia	2× HE		Windows broken in 35 houses
Sunderland	1×4 HE, 7× IB	22 killed, 128 injured	4 shops, 15 houses, workmen's hall, tram shed, tram and 3 stables destroyed; 2 shops, 36 houses badly damaged; 71 shop fronts blown in; fire in French polishing shop of Messrs Blumer; railway goods yard damaged
Port Clarence	1× HE		
River Tees	2× HE		
Yorkshire, North Riding			
Middlesbrough, Cargo Fleet	2× HE	2 injured	Windows broken in 93 houses, a shop and hotel
Brotton (Cattesty)	2× HE		
Yorkshire, East Riding			
Sea, off Tunstall	17× HE		

Anti-aircraft guns in action and reported use of ammunition:

Location of AA battery	Calibre or type of gun	Number / type of rounds fired
Fulwell Quarries, Sunderland	6" AA gun	1 round
Seaham	Maxim	–

Two Royal Naval Air Service aircraft – one from Whitley Bay and one from Redcar – took off, but were unable to locate the raiders. Another two aircraft took off from Cramlington, but likewise were also unsuccessful in sighting the airships.

2 April 1916

Weather: calm and fine, with practically no cloud, mist or fog until just before sunrise.

During the evening, it was reported that four airships – *Zeppelins L 13*, *L 14*, *L 16* and *L 22* – were approaching the northern coast of Britain (although *Zeppelin L 13* appeared to have turned back before crossing the coast).

Zeppelin L 22, commanded by *Kapitänleutnant* Max Dietrich, was heard off the coast near to Bamburgh at 2000 but finally crossed the coast just north of Berwick-upon-Tweed, Berwickshire at 2100. Here she dropped nine HE and five incendiary bombs near Lamberton Farm before proceeding inland for about six miles – dropping two HE and four incendiary bombs near Chirnside at 2115. A further three HE and five incendiary bombs fell in open fields near to East Blanerne Farm – causing no damage. The airship then turned east and followed the River Whiteadder towards the sea (dropping a flare over Clarabad Mill) and crossed the coast near Lamberton – dropping another five HE bombs in the sea (presumably aiming at a ship). Steering northwards along the coast (past St Abb's Head), the Zeppelin came inland once again at North Berwick (on the Firth of Forth) at 2230 and followed the southern coast of the estuary – dropping an incendiary bomb on the links near Archerfield House; she next appeared over Edinburgh. At the same time, *Zeppelin L 14* was engaged in bombing the city (but at a much greater height than the other airship) and hovered – slowly drifting towards the south. At 2350 *Zeppelin L 22* dropped an HE bomb at Slateford, followed by another at 0010 on Colinton and a third at 0020 on Bridgend near Craigmillar – all of which caused no damage. The airship then headed eastwards down the Firth of Forth and out to sea.

Zeppelin L 14, commanded by *Kapitänleutnant* Alois Böcker, was first sighted off St Abb's Head at 2130 and followed the coast northwards – crossing the Firth of Forth – and having located the Isle of May, turned west towards Edinburgh. Passing over Edinburgh Docks, she dropped an HE bomb that sank two small boats and damaged a couple of Danish steamers; then two incendiary bombs followed, which fell in the Albert Dock – causing no damage. A fourth bomb – an HE – fell on the roof of a grain warehouse (causing some damage), while a further HE bomb damaged the quay wall. A sixth HE fell in Commercial Street – damaging a building and killing a man (who was asleep in it). The next bombs to fall were incendiaries and fell in Commercial and Sandport Streets – one falling through the roof of 14, Commercial Street (passing through an upstairs room, occupied by an old lady, and bursting in the room below). The old lady calmly got out of bed and poured water through the hole where the bomb had passed and put out the fire. The eleventh bomb was an HE which fell on the bonded whisky warehouse of Messrs Innes and Grieve – destroying it, along with all the spirit (estimated to be worth £44,000). Next, two incendiary bombs fell through the roofs of two houses – one being the manse of St Thomas Kirk – and setting both buildings on fire, although all the residents escaped unharmed. Three more incendiaries and an HE bomb followed, but fell harmlessly; but the next – an HE bomb – fell in Bonnington Road and killed a child. The nineteenth HE bomb fell on a railway line close to Bonnington Tannery, but failed to explode, while the next HE landed on the tannery – causing extensive damage. The airship had followed the course of the Water of Leith (presumably clearly visible to the *Steuermann* [helmsman] Wilhelm Jensen) – and on reaching Edinburgh, dropped an HE bomb at 2350 on a piece of waste ground at Bellevue Terrace. The next bomb – an incendiary – fell in the road at Mound; then a third – an HE – fell on the roof of a house in Lauriston Place and seriously injured a man who was in the street below; he subsequently died of his injuries. An HE bomb was then dropped in the grounds of George Watson's College and an incendiary fell in meadows to the south. Another HE bomb fell on tenement houses in Marchmont Crescent – passing through to the basement, but causing only minor damage. Passing to the east, the airship then dropped an HE bomb on a tenement at Causewayside – wrecking the building and injuring six people – while an incendiary bomb fell in a garden at Hatton Place (causing no damage). Heading back for the centre of the city, the raider then dropped an incendiary that fell in the grounds of the Royal Infirmary, followed by an HE bomb that landed on the pavement of The Grassmarket in front of the White Hart Hotel – injuring four (one of whom subsequently died). Another HE bomb fell on the south-west corner of the Castle Rock – followed by another, which landed near the County Hotel in Lothian Road, along with damaging the Prince's Street Terminus of the Caledonian Railway (injuring one). Circling to the west, the airship dropped three HE bombs near Haymarket Station, but they caused no damage. Passing over the centre once again, an HE bomb fell on the pavement of Marshall Street – destroying a house and killing six and injuring seven. The eighteenth bomb (an HE) fell on a spirit store in Haddon's Court, Nicholson Street – wrecking the building and injuring three. The next HE bomb landed in St Leonard's Hill – destroying a tenement and killing a child and injuring two. The time was now 0015 and the airship passed off eastwards over the southern slopes of Arthur's Seat – from where she was being fired at by machine-guns – and in response dropped three HE bombs that fell in the southern part of King's Park and an incendiary that fell in the grounds of Prestonfield House. The airship then headed to the east – finally passing out to sea at 0100 over Cockburnspath.

The commander and the helmsman of *Zeppelin L 14* were subsequently captured when *Zeppelin L 33* was brought down and interrogated regarding the raid on Edinburgh. They admitted that having been unable to find the Rosyth Dockyard, they had made for Edinburgh and had come down as low as 2,200 feet to make sure the bombardment was effective. *Kapitänleutnant* Alois Böcker had been an officer of the Hamburg-American Line – and as a ship's captain, had visited Edinburgh prior to the war.

Zeppelin L 16, commanded by *Oberleutnant zur See* Werner Peterson, crossed the coast of Northumberland between Creswell and Druridge at 2300. Meandering slowly south-west towards Newcastle-upon-Tyne, the commander was possibly confused by the flares of the airfield at High West Houses (near Ponteland) as 12 HE and 11 incendiary bombs were dropped nearby at 2335. The airship then circled and

Crowds gather at The Grassmarket, Edinburgh to view the damage caused by the high-explosive bomb that landed on the pavement in front of the White Hart Hotel – blowing in many of the windows and doors.

then made for the flares of the aerodrome at Cramlington, where at 2340 five HE and six incendiary bombs fell – causing a small amount of damage. She then steered to the north-west (following the railway line) until she dropped a number of HE bombs near Broomhill Colliery – three landing near Hadstone and four on Togston Barns Farm – before passing out to sea over the mouth of the River Amble at 0020.

While the naval airships were raiding Scotland and Northumberland, two army airships crossed the North Sea from Belgium and carried out a raid on the East Coast.

Zeppelin LZ 90 was first sighted heading towards the coast by the *Kentish Knock Lightship* and crossed at the mouth of the River Colne at 2240 – continuing east as far as Witham before turning to the south-west in the direction of London. As she passed Great Baddow, the airship was fired at by an 18 pounder gun of the Kirkcudbrightshire Territorial Artillery – causing her to deviate round Chelmsford before resuming her course towards London. Passing Kelvedon Hatch at about 2335 the airship was engaged by Pom-Poms (but no hits were observed) and she continued on her way – gradually bearing to the west as if to approach London from the north. At 2350 she was picked up by a searchlight at Chingford – and the guns at Waltham Abbey opened up on her. She replied by dropping 25 HE and 65 incendiaries in a line from Woodridden Farm and Windmill Hill (near Waltham Abbey), with four houses being damaged (but there were no casualties). Having released her bomb load, the airship rose rapidly and made off towards the north-east – crossing the coast at Clacton at 0100. *Zeppelin LZ 90* was commanded by *Oberleutnant* Ernst Lehmann.

Zeppelin LZ 88, commanded by *Hauptmann* Falk, crossed the Suffolk Coast at Orfordness at 2330 but appeared to follow a very erratic course inland (as if her commander were unsure of his position). She was sighted over Wickham Market at 2347 – where she turned south towards Woodbridge – and was engaged by four machine-guns of the Mobile Section, Royal Naval Anti-Aircraft Corps and by a Lewis gun of the 58th Division. Reaching Ipswich, the Zeppelin circled the town and made off east towards the coast – being engaged by the guns of the Royal Naval Anti-Aircraft Corps. She passed over the River Deben and dropped 10 HE and 53 incendiary bombs in the vicinity of Ramsholt and Alderton; then a final HE bomb near Hollesley before passing out to sea at Orfordness at 0120.

Summary for 2 April 1916:

Location	Number and type of bombs dropped	Casualties	Damage
London MPD			
Waltham Abbey	25× HE, 63× IB		4 houses damaged
Suffolk			
Alderton	2× HE, 17× IB		
Ramsholt	8× HE, 46× IB		
Hollesley	1× HE		
Northumberland	12× HE, 11× IB		
Ponteland			
Cramlington	3× HE, 6× IB		Aeroplane shed damaged
Broomhill	7× HE		
Berwickshire			
Lamberton	9× HE, 5× IB		
Chirnside	2× HE, 4× IB		
East Blanerne	3× HE, 5× IB		
Haddingtonshire			
Direton	1× IB		

Location	Number and type of bombs dropped	Casualties	Damage
Edinburgh			
Leith	9× HE, 11× IB	2 killed	3 houses and bonded store destroyed; grain store and tannery damaged
Edinburgh	18× HE, 6× IB	11 killed, 24 injured	Princes Street Station, 4 houses, spirit store and 3 hotels damaged
Colinton	2× HE		
Liberton	1× HE		
Sea off Lamberton	5× HE		
Total	109× HE, 177× IB	13 killed, 24 injured	

Anti-aircraft guns in action and reported use of ammunition:

Location of AA battery	Calibre or type of gun	Number / type of rounds fired
Waltham Abbey Control		
Enfield Lock	3" 20-cwt	19 rounds
Waltham Abbey, Farm Hill	3" 5-cwt	4 rounds
Monkhams Hill	6 pdr Hotchkiss	46 rounds
Cheshunt	6 pdr Hotchkiss	22 rounds
Hayes Hill Farm	13 pdr (mobile)	6 rounds
Grange Hill	1 pdr Pom-Pom	62 rounds
Essex		
Kelvedon Hatch	Pom-Pom	75 rounds
Great Baddow (2nd Kirkcudbright Battery)	18 pdr QF	2 rounds
Suffolk		
Rushmere Heath (58th Division)	1 MG (Lewis)	-
Rushmere Heath (Mobile Section, RNAAC)	2× MG	-
Levington Heath (Mobile Section, RNAAC)	MG	-
Scotland (Edinburgh), Arthur's Seat	2× MG (1 Lewis, 1 Vickers)	-

Aeroplanes of the Royal Naval Air Service took off from East Fortune and Dundee to intercept the northern raiders, but failed to sight their quarry.

Two aeroplanes of the Royal Flying Corps took off from Cramlington Aerodrome, but again failed to locate the Zeppelin. One aircraft struck a ditch on landing, overturned, caught fire and was blown up by its own bombs; the pilot escaped safely.

Two Royal Flying Corps aeroplanes took off from Hounslow; one from Croydon; two from Sutton's Farm; and another two from Hainault, but only one pilot sighted an airship, which it was unable to catch. Three aircraft were damaged on landing.

3 April 1916

Weather: initially calm, but a northerly breeze of about 25 to 30 miles per hour sprang up along the East Coast during the latter part of the night. The skies were clear, but mist began to develop towards the morning over the East Coast.

There were reports of a number of airships heading for Britain, but only *Zeppelin L 11* crossed the coast.

Zeppelin L 11, commanded by *Oberleutnant zur See* Horst von Buttlar, was heard off the Norfolk Coast at Weybourne around 0130 heading east. The airship crossed the coast at Sheringham and at 0200 dropped an incendiary bomb near Hanworth Hall, Gunton – and then drifted south (with her engines off) for about half an hour. At 0230 she dropped two incendiary bombs at Buxton Lamas and then followed the course of the River Bure to Salthouse, where another incendiary bomb fell in a field. The airship then meandered towards the coast – which she crossed at Caister at 0305 – but when a mile out to sea, dropped nine HE bombs (probably aimed at a ship).

Summary for 3April 1916:

Location	Number and type of bombs dropped	Casualties	Damage
Hanworth Hall	1× IB		
Buxton Lamas	2× IB		
Salthouse	1× IB		
At sea (off Caister)	9× HE		
Total	9× HE, 4× IB		

4 April 1916

Weather: there was a north-westerly wind; 15 to 20 miles per hour at 1,500 feet. The skies were overcast, with rain falling on the continent.

A number of airships were operating during the night over the North Sea – including *Zeppelins L 7, L 13, L 14, L 16* and *L 17* – but none of them crossed the English Coast (possibly due to the changing nature of the weather conditions) and returned to their bases.

5 April 1916

Weather: the Eastern North Sea was calm, but off the British Coast there was a northerly breeze of 25 to 30 miles per hour, which increased over the North Sea during the day. Mostly fine; a few cloudy patches, with no mist.

It was reported around 2100 that two airships were operating – with one making for Spurn Head and the other towards Flamborough Head.

Zeppelin L 11, commanded by *Oberleutnant zur See* Horst von Buttlar, crossed the coast at 2110 at Hornsea Mere, Yorkshire and steered directly for Hull – following the railway line. Near Sutton (at 2117), one HE bomb fell in a field – slightly damaging a nearby farmhouse. At this point, the Hull anti-aircraft guns went into action and the raider veered away to the south-east to East Park, where she dropped three HE bombs which broke a few windows in Holderness Road. As the anti-aircraft fire was obviously causing some consternation to the crew of the Zeppelin, she passed out to sea at Aldbrough at 2150 on a northerly course – following the line of the coast. Although a house in Park Avenue, Hull was damaged by a blind anti-aircraft shell (and four people were wounded by falling shrapnel), it was thought that the airship may have been damaged – and that the time spent off the Yorkshire Coast was while the crew carried out urgent repairs. At 0229, 6 April *Zeppelin L 11* once more crossed the coast at Skinningrove – possibly attracted by the glow from tipping slag from the iron works. After circling round the iron works at a height of no more than 3,000 feet, the raider dropped nine HE and 14 incendiary bombs before heading south-east – heading out to sea over Hinderwell at 0250. The laboratory of the iron works was wrecked, along with a few broken windows (which was all the damage that was caused).

Zeppelin L 16, commanded by *Oberleutnant zur See* Werner Peterson, passed Hartlepool from the south and hovered for some time over the sea to determine her position before heading inland over the Black Hall Rocks at 2330. Taking a south-westerly course, the airship passed Bishop Auckland at a fast pace before carrying out a complete about-turn and heading back along her tracks – dropping 13 HE and 10 incendiary bombs on Evenwood and Randolf Colliery. Fifteen miners' cottages were destroyed and 70 damaged, but there were only two injuries. Proceeding on her way, the Zeppelin was then sighted at 0015 over Auckland Park Collieries at Close House, Eldon. A single HE bomb was dropped at Coronation Colliery – followed by 16 more – and 10 incendiary bombs at Close House and Eldon. Two miners' cottages were destroyed and 11 badly damaged, with windows of 28 cottages and 18 shops blown in by the blast from the bombs. No damage was caused to the colliery works, with 11 of the HE bombs falling on a cycle track and slag heaps. The airship then proceeded as far as West Hartlepool before circling and following the coast north – finally passing out to sea at Seaham Harbour at 0115.

Summary for 4 April 1916:

Location	Number and type of bombs dropped	Casualties	Damage
Durham			
Evenwood	13× HE, 10× IB	2 injured	15 cottages seriously damaged; 70 slightly damaged
Close House and Eldon	17× HE, 10× IB	1 killed, 3 injured	2 cottages destroyed; 11 seriously and 28 slightly damaged; windows in 18 shops broken
Yorkshire, North Riding			
Skinningrove	9× HE, 20× IB		Laboratory of iron works wrecked; Council School, Co-operative Society building and houses damaged
Yorkshire, East Riding			
Sutton	1× HE		Farmhouse slightly damaged
East Park, Hull	3× HE	4 injured by AA shrapnel	Windows broken; house damaged by AA shell
Total	43× HE, 40× IB	1 killed, 9 injured	

Anti-aircraft guns in action and reported use of ammunition:

Location of AA battery	Calibre or type of gun	Number / type of rounds fired
Sutton	12 pdr	8 rounds
Dairycoates Crossing	6 pdr	3 rounds
Hornsea	12 pdr	8 rounds
Hull Cricket Ground	12 pdr	7 rounds
Cottingham	13 pdr (mobile)	19 rounds
Marfleet	13 pdr (mobile)	13 rounds
Immingham Halt	12 pdr	6 rounds

Aeroplanes took off from Beverly and Scarborough aerodromes, but failed to locate the airship; one crashed on landing. Aeroplanes were also sent up from Cramlington, but one collided with a house and the pilot – Lieutenant J Nichol,[7] Royal Flying Corps – was killed.

23 April 1916

Weather: fair, with a south-westerly wind; strength three.

A German aircraft was spotted flying very high – passing over the Naval Pier at Dover, Kent at 1228 – heading in a south-westerly direction. Two minutes later, it was spotted over Gunston heading south. Seven British aircraft (three from the Royal Naval Air Service and four from Royal Flying Corps at Dover Aerodrome) were dispatched in pursuit, but made no contact.

24 April 1916

Weather: bright, clear and cloudless day, with a southerly wind; strength four.

At about 1135 a German aeroplane – identified as an *Albatros* – flew over the town of Dover, Kent from the south-east and then turned towards the Langdon Battery. All the anti-aircraft guns in range opened fire for over eight minutes, while the aircraft flew a small circle over the battery before disappearing north over Ringwold and out to sea at Kingsnorth. Its speed was estimated at 50 miles per hour and its height about 7,000 feet. As the aircraft passed over Ringwold, a German newspaper was dropped. Four Royal Flying Corps aeroplanes from Dover were also were sent up in pursuit, but failed to make contact.

Anti-aircraft guns in action and reported use of ammunition:

Location of AA battery	Calibre or type of gun	Number / type of rounds fired
Langdon Battery	3"	48 rounds
Langdon Battery	6 pdr	18 rounds
Fort Burgoyne	2× 6 pdr	84 rounds
Dover Castle	6 pdr	73 rounds
Drop Redoubt	2× 6 pdr	160 rounds
Prince of Wales Pier	6" naval mk 7	3 rounds
Eastern Arm	6" naval mk 7	1 round

Leutnant Ilges – the pilot of the aircraft on this raid [Ilges was subsequently captured during a raid on London on 28 November 1916] – stated that he was purely

7 Captain John Nichol, 36 Squadron RFC, aged 22: buried Margate Cemetery, Kent.

on a reconnaissance mission, but that the anti-aircraft bombardment at Dover was the heaviest he had experienced (yet he considered it negligible).

24 April 1916

Weather: a moonless night, with a south-westerly wind over the North Sea; velocity at 1,500 feet was 40 to 50 miles per hour, while further west it was even greater, with rain falling as far east as Nottingham.

In the morning, eight airships – *Zeppelins L 9, L 11, L 13, L 16, L 17, L 20, L 21* and *L 23* – left the north coast of Germany, along with *Zeppelins L 6* and *L 7*, which turned back halfway across the North Sea for operations (in conjunction with the German naval forces) against Great Britain.

Zeppelin L 16, commanded by *Oberleutnant zur See* Werner Peterson, crossed the Norfolk Coast at Trimingham at 2215 and pursued a winding course in a south-westerly direction towards Newmarket. In the vicinity of Wymondham (at Kimberley), a small parachute was dropped with a bundle of German-illustrated papers attached. The airship then continued to the Thetford area, where she circled for about 20 minutes (presumably while the crew tried to establish their location) before continuing the south-westerly course. Reaching Newmarket, the Zeppelin turned 108° to follow the reciprocal course – passing over Newmarket Heath – and was fired at by two machine-guns. In retaliation (at 0035), 18 HE bombs fell along a line across the middle of the town from the Heath to Warren Hill Station – and an incendiary bomb fell beyond the station at the junction of the Bury and Norwich roads. Several houses in St Mary's Square (in the centre of the town) were badly damaged – where one person was severely injured – along with a racing stables (where the racehorse 'Coup-de-Main' was killed). Outside the limits of Newmarket, an HE and an incendiary bomb fell on a training ground (known as The Limekilns) in the parish of Snailwell. At Honnington, five incendiary bombs were dropped, but caused no damage. The airship then pursued a course to the coast and crossed out to sea at 0135 near Mundesley.

Zeppelin L 21, commanded by *Kapitänleutnant der Reserve* Max Dietrich, reached the English Coast at Kessingland, Suffolk at about 2310 having dropped two HE bombs in the sea. The airship made straight for Eye before turning south to Stowmarket, but on nearing the town was engaged by the mobile anti-aircraft guns of the Royal Garrison Artillery at Badley Park and Stowupland (Thorney Green), along with the fixed guns at Stowmarket. This caused the airship to rise rapidly – and at 0016 dropped nine HE bombs on two farms at Old Newton, but caused no damage. The Zeppelin then headed swiftly north towards the coast, which she crossed at 0135 having dropped an HE bomb at Witton five minutes earlier. The Zeppelin later turned around and joined with the German Naval Fleet – being sighted off the *Haisboro Lightship* at 0430.

Zeppelin L 23, commanded by *Kapitänleutnant* Otto von Schubert, crossed the coast at Caistor, Norfolk and immediately dropped three HE bombs, but only one exploded. Following a wide arc northwards across Norfolk, she passed Ridlington, where at 0030, nine HE bombs were dropped – breaking the windows of a church and partly wrecking a cottage. As she passed near the Royal Naval Air Service Aerodrome at Bacton, another six HE bombs were dropped – damaging two houses and a searchlight as she passed out to sea.

Zeppelin L 11, commanded by *Korvettenkapitän* Victor Schütze, came in close to Bacton, Norfolk at 0030 and passed over Honing Hall – where four HE bombs were dropped – and then to Dilham, where at 0100, 19 HE and 26 incendiary bombs fell – one of the HE bombs failing to explode. Slight damage was caused to a few cottages – and a woman apparently died from shock. The airship then headed north for the coast – which was crossed at 0118 – but followed the coast as far as Bacton, where she was fired on by a section of 3 pounder anti-aircraft guns of the Royal Naval Anti-Aircraft Corps. Subsequently, it was established that the airship had been hit by one's shell that punctured one of her hydrogen gas bags.

Zeppelin L 13, commanded by *Kapitänleutnant* Eduard Prölls, followed a diverse course over North Norfolk – having crossed the coast at Cromer at 2220. She was sighted in company with *Zeppelin L 16* over Hanworth before heading west and then back, before crossing the coast once more at Sheringham around 2308 – having dropped no bombs (presumably being on a reconnaissance operation).

Zeppelin L 17, commanded by *Kapitänleutnant* Herbert Ehrlich, crossed the coast much further north than the other raiders at Chapel St Leonards, Lincolnshire – passing a short way inland over Anderby – and at Alford dropped three HE bombs at 0155 from a height of about 10,000 feet before immediately heading out to sea at Sutton-on Sea at 0205.

Herbert Ehrlich and Kuno Manger's photographs appeared in the German newspaper *Der Tag* on 19 April 1916 – praising them and other airship commanders for their previous attacks on Sheffield, Leeds, Hull and Grimsby.

Zeppelin L 9, commanded by *Hauptmann* August Stelling, accompanied the German naval forces and was sighted between 0325 and 0350 north-east of the *Cross Sand*, *Newarp* and *Cockle Lightships* heading in a south-easterly direction. She was sighted off the *St Nicholas Lightship* at 0410 (around the time of the bombardment of Yarmouth and Lowestoft) before heading off to the east.

Zeppelin L 20, commanded by *Kapitänleutnant* Franz Stabbert, was scouting for the German naval forces towards the south of their area of operations and did not approach the English Coast.

Zeppelins L 6 and *L 7*, commanded by *Hauptmann* Kuno Manger and *Kapitänleutnant* Karl Hempel respectively, headed out over the North Sea with the rest of the fleet and were reconnoitring to the north of the German naval forces and turned back before reaching four degrees east longitude towards Germany.

Summary for 24 April 1916:

Location	Number and type of bombs dropped	Casualties	Damage
Norfolk			
Caister	3× HE (2 u×)		Windows broken
Bacton	6× HE		2 houses damaged
Ridlington	9× HE		Church and farm windows broken; cottage partly wrecked
Dilham	19× HE (1 u×), 26× IB	1 died from shock	Farm and 4 cottages damaged
Honing Hall	4× HE		
Honingham	5× IB		Straw stack burnt
Witton	1× HE		
Suffolk			
Old Newton	9× HE (1 u×)		Window broken
Newmarket	18× HE, 1× IB	1 injured	5 houses wrecked; 100 houses slightly damaged; racehorse killed
Cambridgeshire			
Snaiwell	1× HE, 1× IB		1 window broken
Lincolnshire			
Alford	3× HE		
Anderby	1× IB		
Total	75× HE, 34× IB	1 died, 1 injured	

Anti-aircraft guns in action and reported use of ammunition:

Location of AA battery	Calibre or type of gun	Number / type of rounds fired
Eastern Mobile Section, RNAAC		
Bacton	3 pdr	18 rounds
Newmarket Heath	Machine-guns	70 rounds
Anti-Aircraft Section, RGA		
Needham Market (Badley)	13 pdr (mobile)	2 rounds
Stowmarket (Stowupland)	13 pdr (mobile)	8 rounds
Stowmarket	6 pdr (fixed)	5 rounds

Three aircraft took off to intercept the Zeppelins, but none of the pilots sighted the raiders.

24 April 1916

0410: A formation of four German battle cruisers (SMS *Lützow*, SMS *Derfflinger*, SMS *Moltke* and SMS *von der Tann* of the 1st Scouting Group, commanded by *Rear-Admiral* Friedrich Bödicker), along with six light cruisers and a torpedo flotilla, opened fire on Lowestoft, Norfolk for 10 minutes and destroyed about 200 houses and two coastal defence batteries – killing three civilians and injuring 12. The ships then moved onto Yarmouth, but due to fog, could not sight their target and only fired a few shells at the town – killing one and injuring seven civilians before departing.

A display of ordnance that landed in Lowestoft fired by the German cruisers – although the incendiary bomb must have been picked up on a previous occasion.

Some of the damage caused to a house in Yarmouth Road, Lowestoft by the German naval bombardment.

25 April 1916

Weather: the wind varied from 30 to 40 miles per hour over East Anglia during the day and diminished to less than 15 miles per hour over the North Sea during the evening. The skies were cloudless south of The Wash, but misty or overcast further north, with a tendency towards improvement.

The raid during the night was carried out by five military airships – *Zeppelins LZ 87* [*81*], *LZ 88*, *LZ 93*, *LZ 97* and *Z XII* – but the older airship (*Z XII*) turned back before reaching the English Coast.

Zeppelin LZ 87, commanded by *Oberleutnant zur See* Barth, was sighted off The Downs, Kent at 2150 – and at 2155 dropped eight HE bombs aimed at the steamer *Argus* in Deal Harbour, but all missed. The airship was then spotted off Walmer, where she was fired at by anti-aircraft guns and turned out to sea – heading north along the coast and turning east to cross the Channel at Ramsgate – and returned to Belgium.

Zeppelin LZ 97, commanded by *Hauptmann* Erich Linarz, reached the English Coast over Mersea Island, Essex at 2200 (passing north of Chelmsford) and followed the course of the River Roding – dropping 47 incendiary bombs in a line from Fyfield to Ongar (although the only damaged caused was to a shed at Ongar). Continuing on her course to the south-west towards the capital, the airship reached Barkingside (having been fired upon by the anti-aircraft gun sited at Dog Kennel Hill) and dropped 12 HE bombs – four falling at Forrest Farm, one at Fairlop Railway Station and one in the road at Fairlop (causing only slight damage to some cottages). The seventh bomb fell in a field at Monk's Well; the next at Barkingside Station Bridge; followed by one in a field and three near Aldborough – one hitting a well and two failing to explode. The airship then turned to the south and dropped an HE bomb at Newbury Park before coming under heavy anti-aircraft fire and heading back towards Chelmsford – dropping a final two HE bombs (one of which hit a house between Goodmayes and Chadwell Heath). Eight aircraft took off in pursuit of the raider (three from Sutton's Farm, three from Hounslow and two from Halnault Farm aerodromes), but only two pilots were able to get within 2,000 feet of the Zeppelin before it climbed out of range. The airship crossed the English Coast near Clacton at 0034 – following the coast as far as Harwich before proceeding out across the North Sea.

Zeppelin LZ 93 was sighted off the mouth of the River Orwell, Essex and dropped two flares on the sea before crossing the coast at Landguard Fort and releasing an HE bomb on the common (as well as three incendiary bombs into the mud on the northern side of the river). The airship then headed up to Harwich, where two HE bombs fell close to Government House, but neither exploded; then onto Shotley, where three HE and four incendiary bombs fell near the Royal Naval Training Barracks, but only shattered a few windows. A fifth incendiary fell in the mud west of the barracks, followed by a large HE bomb (probably 120 kg) near Parkstone Quay before the airship passed over Harwich and Landguard – dropping a further four flares in the water as she passed out to sea at 2245. Passing the *Sunk Lightship*, a number of bombs were aimed in its direction before the raider finally departed. The Zeppelin's commander was *Hauptmann* Wilhelm Schramm.

Zeppelin LZ 88, commanded by *Hauptmann* Falk, crossed the North Kent Coast near to Whitstable at 0030 on 26 April – and soon after, shut off her engines and drifted southwards over Sturry. She passed Canterbury before turning to the north-east to Wingham, where she altered course to the north. At 0120 she dropped nine incendiaries in a line west of Preston, but caused no damage. Five minutes later, a further 13 incendiary bombs (two of which did not ignite) fell at Sarre and Chislet Marshes, followed by an HE bomb that landed in the vicarage garden at St Nicholas at Wade – uprooting two trees. The airship then proceeded towards Birchington, where four HE bombs fell in fields between St Nicholas and Shuart's Farm, with another falling north of the farm and a further four on the marshes. Two further incendiary bombs fell; one landing near the railway line and the other hit the sea wall at Minnes Bay before the raider passed out to sea at 0135 – dropping a further three HE bombs in the bay as she went.

Two of the raiders were sighted off the coast of Belgium (near to Ostend) on their return flight and were chased by a French aeroplane piloted by Captain Mandinaud, with Lieutenant Deramond as observer.

Zeppelin Z XII was hard-pushed to escape her pursuer and was unable to rise above 8,000 feet, so when over Zeebrugge, the French aviators dropped small incendiary bombs on her – to which she replied with sustained machine-gun fire from guns mounted on an upper, forward platform. It was estimated that around 3,000 rounds were fired during the action (which lasted 20 minutes) and damaged the French aeroplane. The action moved north to the Dutch Frontier – where the French airmen had to disengage due to a punctured fuel tank – and landed near Flushing. The airship then made for Brussels, but after an hour was compelled to land in the open (to the east of Ghent). She was later moved to the airship shed at Etterbeek (near Brussels) and later to the shed at Cognelee (near Namur) to be fully repaired.

Summary for 25 April 1916:

Location	Number and type of bombs dropped	Casualties	Damage
Suffolk			
Landguard	1× HE		
Shotley	3× HE, 4× IB		
Essex			
Harwich	2× HE (ux)		
Parkestone Quay	1× HE (ux)		
Fyfield	11× IB		

Location	Number and type of bombs dropped	Casualties	Damage
Shelley	15× IB		
High Ongar	17× IB		Shed damaged
Chipping Ongar	4× IB		
Metropolitan District			
Fairlo and Barkingside	13× HE (1 ux)		Cottages damaged; a well was destroyed
Chadwell Heath	2× HE		House destroyed
Kent			
Preston Marshes	9× IB		
Sarre	1× IB		
Chislet Marshes	12× IB		
St Nicholas at Wade and Shuart's Farm	10× HE		Vicarage damaged
Minnes Bay	2× IB, 3× HE (in sea)		
Total	32× HE, 75× IB	One man injured due to AA fire	

Anti-aircraft guns in action and reported use of ammunition:

Location of AA battery	Calibre or type of gun	Number / type of rounds fired
Temple House, Waltham	3" 20-cwt	5 rounds
Victoria Park	2x 3" 20-cwt	18 rounds
North Woolwich	3" 5-cwt	10 rounds
North Woolwich	13 pdr	6 rounds
Purfleet	3" 20-cwt	25 rounds
Purfleet	Pom-Pom	3 rounds
West Ham	3" 20-cwt	13 rounds
Wanstead	75 mm	17 rounds
Clapton	3" 20-cwt	21 rounds
Dartford	2x 3" 20-cwt	21 rounds

Location of AA battery	Calibre or type of gun	Number / type of rounds fired
Park	2x 3" 20-cwt	40 rounds
Plumstead	2x 3" 20-cwt	89 rounds
Southern Outfall	2x 3" 5-cwt	84 rounds
Abbey Wood	2x 3" 20-cwt	67 rounds
Erith	2x 6 pdr Nordenfeldt	5 rounds
Arsenal	2x 6 pdr Hotchkiss	79 rounds
Blackwall	2x 3"	3 rounds
Blackheath	3"	10 rounds
Honor Oak	3"	–
Northumberland Heath	3"	9 rounds
Billericay	13 pdr	2 rounds
Kelvedon Hatch	Pom-Pom	88 rounds
Brentwood	13 pdr	2 rounds
Dog Kennel Hill	13 pdr	11 rounds
Shooter's Hill	13 pdr	2 rounds
Felixstowe	6" on railway mounting	1 round
Parkestone	2x 6 pdr	80 rounds
Landguard Common	2x 6 pdr	30 rounds
Landguard Fort	1 pdr	73 rounds

Nine aircraft took off to intercept the raiders. Lieutenant Robinson – of Sutton's Farm – engaged an airship with machine-gun fire, but as she was 2,000 feet above him, there was no effect.

Captain Harris – flying out of Hounslow – engaged an airship, but his machine-gun jammed and his aircraft was hit by machine-gun fire and shrapnel balls.

Note: There is some doubt as to exactly which airships were operating during the night – and there is the possibility that *Zeppelin LZ 87* was in fact *Zeppelin LZ 81* and that either *Zeppelin LZ 93* or *Zeppelin LZ 97* may actually have been *Zeppelin LZ 95*.

26 April 1916

Weather: the wind over the North Sea was light and the sky cloudless – except off the Scottish Coast. There was rain over Wick and the Orkneys. During the night, a mist developed off the North-East Coast at Yarmouth and London, but the Kent Coast was clear. Wind was no more than 15 miles per hour at 1,500 feet.

Zeppelin LZ 93, commanded by *Hauptmann* Wilhelm Schramm, was first sighted off Nieuport, Belgium heading along the coast towards Calais, France at 2105 and was fired upon as she passed La Panne, Dunkirk. She was next sighted crossing the Kent Coast at Kingsdown heading south – having first dropped three HE bombs in the sea off Deal, where she was again fired at. On reaching Kingsdown, the airship turned to the north and followed the coast from a distance of two miles inland – passing over Sandwich at 2240 – and then at 2248 was fired at by two anti-aircraft guns at Westgate; a hit being claimed. The Zeppelin then passed out to sea at Margate – heading in the direction of the *Tongue Lightship*, which she passed at 2305 with her engines making an unusual noise.

Summary for 26 April 1916:
Three HE bombs dropped in the sea, but no bombs fell on land.

Anti-aircraft guns in action and reported use of ammunition:

Location of AA battery	Calibre or type of gun	Number / type of rounds fired
Westgate	2× 6 pdr	12 rounds

One aeroplane took off from Westgate, but the pilot failed to locate the Zeppelin.

1 May 1916
Schütte-Lanz SL 3. Type C1.
Near Riga, Latvia.
Stranded due to degradation of fabric and woodwork due to the sea air.

2 May 1916
Weather: a depression over Brittany was moving quickly north-east and by 1800 it was centred over the Straits of Dover – causing rain over Spurn and Nottingham and a thunderstorm at Flushing. A secondary depression over Scotland, coming eastward, was causing rain at Wick and Nairn – but over the North Sea, north of the line from the Tyne to the Helder, the weather was still fine, so that the airship commanders on nearing the Yorkshire and Scottish Coasts would have had little idea of the approaching conditions.

On the morning of 2 May 10 naval airships left the North German sheds (*Zeppelins L 7, L 9, L 11, L 13, L 14, L 16, L 17, L 20, L 21* and *L 23* – although *L 7* and *L 9* had returned to their sheds by early afternoon). The eight airships that crossed the North Sea came over in three groups: the first group consisting of one; the second of five; and the third of two Zeppelins. The single airship (*Zeppelin L 23*) – in advance of the others – made straight for the Yorkshire Coast, while *Zeppelins L 11, L 14, L 17, L 20* and *L 21* kept together until 90 miles off St Abb's Head before *Zeppelins L 11,*

L 14 and *L 20* continued east, while the other two made off south for Flamborough Head (the act of separation being observed by the master of the Danish ship, SS *Hermia*, who noted the number of *L 20*). Of the third group of airships, *Zeppelins L 13* and *L 16* started together from Germany, but the latter was sighted by a trawler at 1618 – 100 miles north-east-north from Spurn – with the former being sighted by the same trawler three hours later over the same spot. *Zeppelin L 16* hovered in the area for about two hours (probably waiting for her consort), as at 2030 the two airships were sighted by another trawler heading west at a point 58 miles north-east of Flamborough. *Zeppelin L 16* then forged ahead again and reached the Yorkshire Coast shortly before 2200, while *Zeppelin L 13* crossed the coast at about 2230. In combination with the naval airships, one army airship (*Zeppelin LZ 98*) operating from Belgium and commanded by *Oberleutnant zur See* Ernst Lehmann of the *Kaiserliche Marine* [German Navy], hovered off the coast of Lincolnshire for an hour-and-a-half without ever crossing the coast. She approached the Humber and passed Spurn Head at about 1925 – heading south-west at a height of 5,000 feet and at a speed of about 40 miles per hour. She was engaged by a gun battery at Spurn Head for about 10 minutes as she headed south – discharging water ballast as she went so as to rise out of range. When off Sutton-on-Sea (near the *Inner Dowsing Lightship*), she completed an about-turn and headed back up the coast – and after hovering off Spurn Head for 25 minutes, made off across the North Sea at 2015 in the direction of Germany.

Zeppelin L 23, commanded by *Kapitänleutnant* Otto von Schubert, appeared over Robin Hood Bay at 2115 and headed directly east over the Yorkshire Moors as far as Danby High Moor, where a single incendiary bomb was dropped (which set fire to a large expanse of heather). The Zeppelin then turned north to Skinningrove – and at 2205 dropped seven HE and four incendiary bombs on the iron works, but only set fire to a store house. A searchlight, situated at Huntcliffe, located the airship and anti-aircraft fire was opened on her by the 6 inch gun at Brotton, which claimed a hit. Passing along the coast, six incendiary bombs were dropped at Easington at 2210 – one of which damaged a house and injured a child. At 2225 the raider was heard over Whitby, where from the sounds of her engines it appeared that there may have been some damage to the airship, but she left the coast and was last seen dropping flares in the direction of Scarborough.

Zeppelin L 21, commanded by *Kapitänleutnant de Reserve* Max Dietrich, came overland at Cloughton (north of Scarborough) at 2140 before heading directly towards York. Passing over Dringhouses, five HE and 13 incendiary bombs were dropped, but only shattered some windows and injured two soldiers. Over York, one incendiary bomb fell on the Knavesmire at 2240 – followed by three HE and two incendiary bombs which fell at Nunthorpe Hall (one incendiary falling on the building where the VAD Hospital was housed – destroying the roof). An HE bomb then fell in Nunthorpe Avenue – badly damaging four houses; then another fell in Upper Price Street, which destroyed one house and damaged several others – killing two. A further two HE bombs fell in Nunthorpe Road, another in Victoria Street and one in Price's Lane – damaging a large number of houses. Another HE bomb fell on Newton Terrace – wrecking four houses and injuring three civilians – followed by one in Kyme Street, where windows and doors were blown in and a woman injured. The last HE bomb landed in St Saviourgate, which blew out the fronts of several houses – killing six people and injuring others. The airship then headed off eastwards – following a meandering course towards the sea – and dropping an incendiary bomb at Kirkby Grindalythe as she passed. She crossed out to sea at 0010.

Zeppelin L 16, commanded by *Oberleutnant zur See* Werner Peterson, made landfall near Scarborough, Yorkshire at about 2200 – and after heading west for a while, turned north (making for the heath fire on Danby Moor – dropping a number of HE and about six incendiary bombs on the fires). At 2255 she dropped five HE bombs at Lealholm – causing slight damage to a farm building – and at 2315 dropped five incendiary bombs at Moorsholm before passing over Skinningrove and out to sea at 2325.

Zeppelin L 17, commanded by *Kapitänleutnant* Herbert Ehrlich, came in over the coast near Saltburn at 2250 – and making directly for Skinningrove, dropped 13 HE and four incendiary bombs on Carlin How – destroying six houses at 2300. Her captain, having sighted the fires on Danby Moor, then made straight for them and added some more HE bombs to the conflagration before heading out to sea north of Whitby.

Zeppelin L 13, commanded by *Kapitänleutnant der Reserve* Eduard Prölls, came in over Whitby at 2230 – and after heading east for a few miles, turned south. At 2350 she dropped two flares over Pocklington and an incendiary bomb at Fridaythorpe before heading towards Scarborough and dropping another incendiary at Seamer before passing out to sea at 0050. As only two bombs were definitely accredited as having been dropped by *Zeppelin L 13* during her flight over Yorkshire, it is possible that she also added to the total dropped on Danby Moor, which was known to be 39, but more may have fallen into boggy ground and disappeared.

Zeppelin L 11, commanded by *Korvettenkapitän* Viktor Schütze, was engaged at 2040 – 10 miles east of St Abb's Head – by HMS *Portia* and HMS *Semiramis*, which fired 13 rounds at the airship (which was flying low and broadside), but failed to secure a hit. The airship turned out to sea again and then returned to the Northumberland Coast near Beal at 2220 – dropping an incendiary bomb at Goswick and another on the sands between Holy Island and the mainland. The airship followed the coast southwards before passing out to sea at 2315 and then tracking back northwards up the coast – dropping a flare off Alnwick prior to heading for Germany.

Zeppelin L 14, commanded by *Kapitänleutnant der Reserve* Alois Böcker, came in over the coast near Eyemouth, Berwickshire at 2025 (heading north) and immediately went out to sea again – passing the Firth of Forth – and finally made landfall at 2250 north of Arbroath, Forfarshire. She headed south along the coast, but her commander – being unsure of his position – circled for about half an hour before once more heading south and dropping three HE bombs in a field at Bonhard (and 10 minutes later, two in a field at Panlathie). Crossing St Andrew's Bay, more bombs were dropped in the sea – and the airship was last seen passing to the north of the Isle of May.

Zeppelin L 20 / LZ 59 Type P – commanded by *Kapitänleutnant* Franz Stabbert – reached land at Redcastle, Lunan Bay to the north of Arbroath, Scotland at 2155 and steered a north-westerly course in the direction of the Cromarty Firth. She finally crossed Loch Ness at midnight before turning back towards the east. Crossing Castle Craig (which was beyond the restricted lighting area and was lit up), six HE bombs were dropped – breaking a few windows – and at 0200 four incendiaries and an HE bomb fell at Knockenbaird and Scotstown (north of Insch). Three more HE bombs were dropped in a field near Freefield House, Rayne (three miles from Knockenbaird) soon afterwards, but again no damage was caused. The airship finally went out to sea south of Peterhead at 0240. Her journey to the Caledonian Canal had brought the airship to the extreme range – and with the unfavourable weather, the airship was sighted at 0500 (95 miles due east of Aberdeen). With insufficient fuel to reach Germany, her commander steered the Zeppelin towards Norway, where at about 1000 on 3 May the airship came ashore – low down – over the coast of Jaederen (south of Stavanger). Some of the crew – including the second-in-command, *Leutnant zur See* Schirlitz – jumped into the sea, while the rest of the crew remained on board until the Zeppelin collided with a hill (the Jaataaberg, near Sandnaes). The impact wrenched the whole after-part of the airship up almost at a right angle before rising and then falling again into the water at Hafrsfjord, where she broke in two. The rest of the crew were rescued. Those crew who swam to land were treated as shipwrecked sailors and sent back to Germany, while those who were captured after the airship had crossed Norwegian territory were interned. Her commander, *Kapitänleutnant* Franz Stabbert, later escaped and returned to Germany via Sweden, while *Leutnant* Schirlitz was to serve on *Zeppelin L33* and was captured on 25 September 1916.

Summary for 2 May 1916:

Location	Number and type of bombs dropped	Casualties	Damage
Yorkshire, East Riding			
Fridaythorpe	1× IB		
Kirkby Grindalythe	1× IB		
Yorkshire, West Riding			
Dringhouses	5× HE, 13× IB	2 injured	Windows broken
City of York	12× HE, 4× IB	9 killed, 27 injured	Hospital and 18 houses destroyed
Yorkshire, North Riding			
Skinningrove	7× HE, 4× IB		Storehouse destroyed
Carlin How	13× HE, 4× IB		6 houses destroyed
Easington	6× IB	1 injured	House damaged

Location	Number and type of bombs dropped	Casualties	Damage
Moorsholm	5× IB		Slight damage to buildings
Leaholm	5× HE		
Danby High Moor	39× HE		Heather set on fire
Seamer	1× IB		
Northumberland			
Goswick	1× IB		
Holy Island	1× IB		
Forfarshire			
Arbirlot	5× HE		
Aberdeenshire			
Rhynie	6× HE (1 ux)		
Knockenbaird and Scotstown, Insch	4× HE, 1× IB		
Rayne	3× HE		
Total	99× HE, 49× IB		

Anti-aircraft guns in action and reported use of ammunition:

Location of AA battery	Calibre or type of gun	Number / type of rounds fired
Spurn	3 pdr	31 rounds
Brotton (near Skinningrove)	6"	3 rounds

Six aircraft took off to intercept the raiders, but there were no sightings.

3 May 1916

Weather was settled and fine but cloudy, with wind strength two from the south-west.

At 1530 an enemy aircraft – a *Hansa Brandenburg NW* – was sighted over Deal, Kent flying from the direction of Ramsgate. Due to the cloudy sky, the aeroplane was not seen until it had reached its objective. It circled the town for about two minutes before dropping nine HE bombs. One bomb fell on an outhouse near the railway station – a ticket collector being badly wounded by shrapnel. Another bomb fell on a road (not far away), along with a third, which hit the roof of a house where an invalid lady was lying in bed – severely injuring her. Another six bombs also fell close to the station, while another bomb fell on a public house opposite the parish church.

Another two bombs caused negligible damage. The raider then proceeded to fly out to sea. Three men and one woman were injured in the raid.

Anti-aircraft guns did not go into action.

One aeroplane from Dover was sent up to intercept, but failed to find the raider.[8]

4 May 1916

While German airships were bound for raids on Britain, elements of the British Grand Fleet set sail to try and draw the German High Seas Fleet out of their anchorage and into action using three seaplane carriers. The carriers were used to launch 11 Sopwith Baby seaplanes for an attack on the Zeppelin sheds at Tondern, Germany. Only one aircraft reached the target – dropping two bombs; the results not being observed due to mist. *Zeppelin L 7* came out and approached the British Fleet – and was fired upon by the British cruisers HMS *Galatea* and HMS *Phaeton* with their 6 inch guns at 12,000 feet; the Zeppelin, being hit, fell blazing into the sea – breaking her back as she fell. The survivors were rescued by the submarine HMS *E31.*

Zeppelin L 7 / LZ 32. Type M.
Sea: near Horns Rev, Eastern North Sea.
Maschinistermaat Hugo Hoyer, *Seewehr II*: Repatriated via Switzerland 23 November 1917.
Steuermann Klaus Schulz: Reserve.
Maschinist Paul Schmidt: Active.
Signalmaat Georg Fullner: Active.
Bootsmannsmaat Erich Ernecke: Active.
Bootsmannsmaat Fritz Reuter: Active.
Maschinistenmaat August Strassburger: Active.
Kapitänleutnant Karl Hempel +. NKG.
Oberleutnant zur See Friedrich Wenke +. NKG.
Obermaschinistenmaat Paul Grober +. NKG.
Maschinistenmaat Gustav Grosse +. NKG.
Obermaschinistenmaat Gustav Heller +. NKG.
Obermaschinistenmaat Wilhelm Kraatz +. NKG.
Funkentelegraphistenmaat Emil Kress +. NKG.
Maschinistenmaat Wilhelm Moll +. NKG.
Signalmaat Artur Ophey +. NKG.
Maschinistenmaat Paul Stolze +. NKG.
Obersegelmacher Friedrich Weise +. NKG.

8 Cole & Cheeseman: *The Air Defence of Britain 1914 -1918* records 12 sorties by the Royal Naval Air Service.

A British submarine – similar to the one that rescued the survivors of *Zeppelin L 7* (WW1 images).

HMS *Agamemnon's* anti-aircraft guns were responsible for the demise of *Zeppelin LZ 85*.The 12 pounder gun can be just discerned situated behind the rear mast superstructure (WW1 images).

5 May 1916

While on operations over the Balkans in support of Bulgarian forces, a shell from a 12 pounder anti-aircraft gun – mounted on HMS *Agamemnon* in the Adriatic Sea – managed to puncture a number of gas bags and forced *Zeppelin LZ 85* to carry out a forced landing in the Vardar Marshes. A great deal of interest was taken in the wrecked airship by the locally-based troops, who had to wade out to the wreck (and procured many souvenirs). The wreckage was later collected by barge – and an attempt was made to reassemble the airship on the dockside at Salonika.

Zeppelin LZ 85 / LZ 55. Type P.
The Vardar Marshes, Salonika, Greece.
Shot down by anti-aircraft fire from HMS *Agamemnon* and crashed into the marshes; the crew setting fire to the remains of their airship. All the crew were taken prisoner.
Oberleutnant Ernst Scherzer.
Oberleutnant Werner Nippe.
Leutnant Bernhard Noack.
Obermaschinist Peter Bürvenich.
Untermaschinist Hermann Kuck.
Untermaschinist Wilhelm Mertens.
Untermaschinist Wilhelm Lautenbach.
Steuermann Anton Katzemaier.
Untersteuermann Heinrich Kaiser.
Obermaschinist Adolf Ehrlich.
Sergeant Fritz Streyreiff.
Steuermann Schmidt.

Allied soldiers wade out to the wreckage of *Zeppelin LZ 85* in the hope of obtaining souvenirs. The airship lies at the centre left of the photograph.

An attempt was made to reassemble some of the recovered framework of *Zeppelin LZ 85* beside the White Tower at Salonica. Significant parts of the Zeppelin were later shipped to Barrow-in-Furness, England for further examination.

20 May 1916

Weather: wind north-east, strength one, with a fine and cloudless sky. There was brilliant moonlight, but a certain amount of mist at Sandwich.

Aeroplanes raided Dover, Deal District and St Peter's near Broadstairs, Kent by moonlight. Judging by the number of bombs dropped, five machines were employed – but as the machines were not actually seen, their number could not be stated with certainty. They appeared to have acted in two main groups – and their courses deduced from the fall of the bombs.

One machine came overland at Margate at 0200; three others crossed the coast at Sandwich Bay at 0208; and the fifth aeroplane appeared to have made landfall at Kingsdown at about 0220. The first aircraft ('A') steered south-east over St Peter's – and at 0205 dropped five HE bombs near Victoria Avenue. In all, 12 bombs were probably dropped by this machine, which went out to sea at Dumpton Gap. No casualties were reported – and the only damage caused was broken windows.

The second machine ('B') crossed over to land near Sandwich at 0208 and headed north along the coast – dropping several bombs (probably nine) in the sea opposite Small Down Coastguard Station – and then coming overland. She then passed behind Ramsgate and dropped three HE bombs at 0212 before following 'A' out to sea at Dumpton Gap.

The third aeroplane ('C') came in at Sandwich at the same time as 'B', turned south and came over Dover from the north-west at 0215. It dropped its full cargo of 12 HE bombs and then made out to sea.

Aeroplane 'D' followed 'C' at a five-minute interval – and at about 0215 dropped nine HE bombs south-west of the Chequers Inn (in the parish of Sholden), north-west of Deal, Kent. These bombs fell no more than 50 yards apart in a direct line going south-south-west from the coast. No damage was done. The aeroplane then went on to Dover and dropped four more HE bombs before passing out to sea.

In all, 16 HE bombs were dropped on Dover by 'C' and 'D', but surprisingly, little damage was done (only the public house in Snargate Street being at all seriously damaged). The whole of the remaining damage was merely broken glass. There were, however, some casualties: a soldier of the 3rd Battalion, East Surrey Regiment was killed; a seaman off a drifter badly wounded; and a woman slightly wounded.

A fifth aeroplane ('E') came in over Kingsdown and went towards Walmer; then turned on its tracks (south-east over Ringwold), where at 0225, 10 HE bombs were dropped in open fields. They did no damage and caused no casualties. The aeroplane then made off.

There was no action by the anti-aircraft guns as due to their invisibility, the hostile machines were not fired at. There was a brilliant moonlight, but a certain amount of mist at Sandwich.

Three British aeroplanes took off in pursuit of the raiders, but made no contact.

The conclusion of the British authorities was that aeroplane 'D' appeared to carry one more bomb than the normal load of 12 – unless, as was more probable, the sixteenth bomb dropped on Dover (which fell in the harbour) was dropped by 'E' going south from Ringwold. In this case, 'E' may have dropped a twelfth bomb in the sea.

The British claimed that two of the returning raiders were shot down into the sea by the British Air Patrol; one off Blankenberghe, Belgium; and one off Dunkirk, France – although the Germans claim all machines returned safely.

Summary for 20 May 1916:

Location	Number and type of bombs dropped	Casualties	Damage
St Peter's	15× HE		
In sea	9× HE		
Dover	16× HE		
Sholden	9× HE		
Ringwold	10× HE		
Total	59× HE		

Anti-aircraft guns did not go to action due to the height of the raiders – and they were deemed invisible.

Four Royal Naval Air Service aeroplanes – one from Westgate, two from Grain and one from Eastchurch aerodromes – took off to intercept, but all failed to find the raiders.

Two of the raiders were claimed to have been shot down off the French and Belgian Coasts, but German records confirmed all their aircraft returned safely.

Lull in air raids on Great Britain: During the summer period, three months elapsed without any attempt being made by the Germans to attack Great Britain from the air – mainly due to the summer nights, which were neither dark enough nor long enough to allow raiding airships to clear the coastline without the risk of being seen by pursuing aircraft.

9 July 1916

Weather: wind was fresh from the south-east; strength three; fine, mostly cloudy.

At 1040 an aeroplane was sighted off the north coast of Kent – coming from a north-easterly direction at a height of 12,000 feet. It crossed the coast between Westgate and Birchington, flew to Manstone, turned back when over the aerodrome and returned to Westgate. Three rounds were fired by 6 pounder mobile anti-aircraft guns, but these burst short. After circling over the guns (visible only between masses of cloud), it went off due east – following the coastline – and pursued by aeroplanes from Westgate and Manston. It then disappeared eastwards to the north of Deal at about 1105. No bombs were dropped. One of the pursuing aeroplanes, piloted by Flight Sub-Lieutenant F S Mills (who was piloting Bristol Scout D 8957 of the Royal Naval Air Service), over-hauled the enemy machine about 40 miles out to sea. Two trays of ammunition for the Lewis gun were fired without apparent effect. The German gunner returned fire – likewise without effect – and the combat was broken off when nearing Ostend, Belgium.

At 2350 an enemy aeroplane crossed the coast at Aycliff between Folkestone and Dover, Kent – and then flew west to Folkestone, where it turned inland and was reported by the anti-aircraft gunners at Capel, Kent. It proceeded east by St Radigund's Abbey over Buckland, across Dover (and south of the castle) and out to sea in a south-easterly direction. The moon was setting as it reached Dover. When over Dover, the raider dropped seven HE bombs along a line between a quarter and half a mile in length between Castlemount Cottages, the face of the cliff by Trevanion Street and Douro Place. No damage was caused beyond the breaking of windows in about 20 houses – and no casualties were reported. The aeroplane was estimated to have travelled at only a height of 800-1,000 feet – thus passing below the searchlights – and as its engines were throttled back, it made very little sound.

The first raid of the day was probably intended to be a photographic reconnaissance of the new Manstone Aerodrome.[9] As the day's second raider appeared over Capel,

9 Manstone is the name given to Manston Aerodrome near Folkestone, Kent in official documentation during the 1914 to 1918 War.

while he could still be seen by the setting moon, his reconnaissance may not have been unconnected with a reconnaissance of the airship sheds at that station. The fact that he dropped bombs on Dover showed that the raid included aggressive action against the fortress.

29 July 1916

Weather: the wind was light, with a considerable amount of sea fog on the East Coast of Britain.

Ten naval airships left the North German sheds in the afternoon of 28 July: *Zeppelins L 11, L 13, L 14, L 16, L 17, L 21, L 22, L 23, L 24* and *L 31*. The first nine ships came over in company – followed after an interval of about three hours by *Zeppelin L 31* – while four airships (*Zeppelins L 14, L 21, L 22* and *L 23*) did not cross the coast (having turned back on encountering fog).

Zeppelin L 24, commanded by *Kapitänleutnant* Robert Koch, made for the northern shore of the Humber Estuary, where she was sighted by the SS *Montebello* flying low at about 0040 east of Withernsea. At 0110 six HE bombs were dropped on Stallingbrough Marsh close to the Immingham Electric Railway. The airship was engaged by a fixed 12 pounder gun at Immingham Halt, but after two rounds being fired, the airship went off swiftly eastwards across the Humber and onto Withernsea. She crossed out to sea at 0125 and was fired at by a 3 inch anti-aircraft gun and a 6 inch mobile gun without result. The airship then turned north – until at 0155 she turned west in Bridlington Bay and once more crossed overland. Following a southerly arc, she crossed over Hornby – and at 0300 dropped two bombs aimed at the Swedish ship SS *Thor* from Kalmar (which was lying at anchor off the town) before the Zeppelin then made off eastwards towards Germany. After *Zeppelin L 24* had passed over Withernsea, a number of explosions were heard from the east.

Zeppelin L 17 appeared near Grimsby at 0010 and headed north-west in search of her objectives on the south shore of the estuary, but appeared that due to the fog, was unable to drop her bombs with any accuracy. Eight HE and four incendiary bombs were dropped at Killingholme – causing no damage. Continuing northwards in the direction of Hull, at 0048 two HE and two incendiary bombs were dropped at East Halton, which destroyed a straw rick, damaged some outbuildings and killed a cow. The airship then passed out to sea between Hornsea and Withernsea at 0110 but when a few miles south-west of Flamborough Head, she dropped three bombs that fell about 100 feet astern of the SS *Frodingham*. The airship was commanded by *Kapitänleutnant* Herbert Ehrlich.

Zeppelin L 13, commanded by *Kapitänleutnant der Reserve* Eduard Prölls, came in over North Somercotes on the Lincolnshire Coast at 0037 and steered a direct course for Lincoln. It appeared that the airship commander mistook Fiskerton for Lincoln and dropped one HE and one incendiary bomb, but caused no damage. The airship then proceeded in the direction of Newark – and at 0122 a single incendiary bomb fell at Bassingham; then at 0130 the raider dropped another single incendiary at Long

Bennington, followed by two HE bombs at Stubton at 0145 and four HE bombs at Dry Doddington at 0152. Turning east, the airship then dropped four HE and 17 incendiary bombs at 0200 that landed within 200 yards of the railway station at Hougham. The Zeppelin continued east and passed out over The Wash at Old Leake at 0230 before tracking along the Norfolk Coast – dropping a bomb as she passed a ship – before heading out into the North Sea at 0310.

Zeppelin L 16 made for the Norfolk Coast at Brancaster Bay at 0050, passed inland over Thornham and dropped a water-indicating bomb at Ringstead before passing out over The Wash. She then returned to drop two incendiary bombs on Snettisham before passing once more out to sea over Thornham at 0145. Her commander was *Kapitänleutnant* Erich Sommerfeldt.

Zeppelin L 11, commanded by *Leutnant zur See* Otto Mieth, appeared off the Norfolk Coast off Sheringham at 0235 where she dropped an HE bomb in the sea before coming inland at Weybourne a few minutes later – dropping another HE bomb which fell on the cliff edge and killed a cow. Passing to the south-west, the raider dropped a flare over Holt – and then another HE bomb at Sharrington at 0245. A few minutes later, a fourth HE bomb fell at Gunthorpe (again without causing any damage) before the airship turned abruptly east and dropped an HE bomb at Paston at 0320 before passing out to sea at Mundesley – flying very high and dropping a further HE bomb and an incendiary. She was last seen off Happisburgh by the Danish steamer *Rai* heading north-east.

Zeppelin L 31 came in over Corton, Norfolk at about 0115 heading in a south-easterly direction – and after travelling about 15 miles inland, turned east and headed out to sea north of Kessingland at 0150. She was last seen over Flushing, Holland at 0355; then near Antwerp, Maastricht and then on into Germany. The Zeppelin was commanded by *Kapitänleutnant* Heinrich Mathy.

Summary for 29 July 1916:

Location	Number and type of bombs dropped	Casualties	Damage
Yorkshire, East Riding			
Hornsea (in harbour)	2× HE		
Lincolnshire			
East Halton	2× HE, 2× IB		Straw rick burnt; outbuildings damaged; cow killed
Killingholme	8× HE, 4× IB		Horse wounded
Stallingborough (Immingham Halt)	6× HE		
Fiskerton	1× HE, 1× IB		Windows broken

Location	Number and type of bombs dropped	Casualties	Damage
Bassingham	1× IB		
Long Bennington	1× IB		
Stubton	2× HE		
Dry Doddington	4× HE		
Hougham	6× HE, 17× IB		
Norfolk			
Ringstead	1× flare		
Snettisham	2× IB		
Sheringham (sea)	1× HE		
Weybourne	1× HE		Cow killed
Holt	1× flare		
Sharrington	1× IB		
Gunthorpe	1× HE		
Paston	1× HE		
Mundesley	1× HE, 1× IB		
Cromer (sea)	1× HE		
Total	37× HE, 30× IB, 2× flare = 69; plus 3× HE in sea by *L 17*		

Anti-aircraft guns in action and reported use of ammunition:

Location of AA battery	Calibre or type of gun	Number / type of rounds fired
Withernsea	6" mobile QF	1 round
Waxholme	3" 20-cwt	1 round
Immingham Halt	12 pdr (fixed)	2 rounds

One Royal Flying Corps aeroplane took off from Bramham Moor Aerodrome, but was forced to land due to fog.

Also lost on 29 July 1916:
Schütte-Lanz SL 10. Type E 3.
Sevastopol, Russia.
Missing during an attack (presumably lost over the Black Sea due to the weather).
Kommandeur: *Hauptmann* von Wobeser +.
All crew missing.

30 July 1916
During the night, reports were received from units of the Northern Army, Home Defence that two Zeppelins were seen north-east of Wells-next-the-Sea, Norfolk between 1950 and 2020. There were indications that at least one enemy airship was far out in the North Sea during the afternoon – and she may have reached the British Coast in company with another on a reconnoitring cruise at about the time given. At the same time, there was a lot of sea mist – and it was suggested that two of the funnels of motor patrol boats showing beyond the mist (in the form of a mirage) may have accounted for the report. Two aircraft were sent up from Yarmouth – one from Bacton and one from Holt – to investigate the reports, but all failed to find any signs of airships. At 0515 on 31 July a Blackburn BE26, 100 hp, no.8612 – piloted by Flight Sub-Lieutenant J C Northrop – took off from Covehithe Aerodrome and engaged an enemy airship about 30 miles from the airfield. The seaplane was armed with four 16 lb bombs, 48 Ranken darts and a Lewis gun firing vertically upwards. The pilot engaged the Zeppelin with the Lewis gun and had fired two trays of explosive and tracer bullets (and four rounds from a third tray) when the tray came away and hit him in the face – stunning him. When he had recovered control, the airship had disappeared and the pilot returned to Covehithe.

31 July 1916
Weather: Over East Anglia and the Low Countries, the barometer stood high – and there was very little wind except in the Bight of Heligoland, where the velocity at 1,500 feet was about 20 miles per hour. The skies were fine, but there was some sea fog near the Humber. A depression, which spread in from the west over Scotland during the night, caused the wind to increase to about 40 miles per hour over the north-west part of the North Sea, but the southern part was not affected by this system.

On the afternoon of 31 July 10 naval airships – *Zeppelins L 11, L 13, L 14, L 16, L 17, L 21, L 22, L 23, L 30* and *L 31*- left their sheds in Northern Germany and flew towards England. Four of the airships were sighted by the trawler *Adelaide* at 2030 about 50 miles south-east of the *Humber Lightship*, while the trawler *Lilac* also sighted four Zeppelins at 2100 about 45 miles south-east of the *Humber Lightship*, with *Zeppelin L 11* manoeuvring over the ship. The trawler *Exeter* also reported four Zeppelins in the same area at the same time, but also added that the airships remained almost motionless for about one-and-a-half hours before heading west at 2200. It appeared that *Zeppelins L 21* and *L 30* turned back late in the evening and did not cross the English Coast.

Zeppelin L 16 came in over the Lincolnshire Coast near Skegness at 2335 and headed inland towards Newark – and en route dropped two incendiary bombs at Caythorpe at 0135 and one incendiary at Skinnard at 0140. The airship, commanded by *Kapitänleutnant* Erich Sommerfeldt, appeared to hover for some time in the neighbourhood of Newark before turning north-east and dropping another incendiary at Langford Common at 0155. Heading for the coast, she dropped further single incendiary bombs at Metheringham at 0215 and West Ashby at 0225 – passing out to sea in the region of Mablethorpe at 0245.

Zeppelin L 14 crossed the Lincolnshire Coast at Wainfleet and followed the northern coastline of The Wash – crossing the coast at Holbeach. She continued in a southerly direction until she reached March, where she dropped two HE and two incendiary bombs which landed close to the railway at Whitemore Junction, but caused no damage. Turning east, the airship then dropped an incendiary bomb at Hockwold and then seven HE and one incendiary bomb on Croxton Heath, near Stanford, at 0130. Five minutes earlier, *Zeppelin L 22* – passing to the north of Thetford – had dropped a flare which had set fire to heathland (and therefore, the commander of *Zeppelin L 14* had presumed there was something important beneath him). Continuing on her course, at about 0145 the raider dropped two incendiary bombs on Bunwell; then another incendiary fell 15 minutes later half a mile east of Buckenham Station (near Acle), followed by four HE bombs on Reedham at 0205 – prior to passing out to sea south of Yarmouth at 0215. The Zeppelin was commanded by *Hauptmann* Kuno Manger.

Zeppelin L 13 came in over The Wash, Norfolk and was first sighted near Sutton Bridge at 2355 – dropping her first bomb (an incendiary) at midnight on Walpole St Peter before sweeping round to the north. She passed over King's Lynn and onto Newton (near Sandringham), where at about 0015 she released another incendiary bomb before turning east. On the way, she dropped a third incendiary bomb at West Rudham at 0025; then an HE bomb at Guist, near Cawston, at 0040 was followed by a further two HE and one incendiary bomb. The Zeppelin, commanded by *Kapitänleutnant der Reserve* Eduard Prölls, then turned north and crossed the coast at Cromer before looping back. She then headed out into the North Sea at 0105. It was noted that the airship appeared to be travelling at speeds of no less than 60 miles per hour during her exploits across Norfolk.

Zeppelin L 11, commanded by *Korvettenkapitän* Viktor Schütze, cruised off the Norfolk Coast for some time before venturing inland at Cley at 0204 on 1 August – dropping an incendiary bomb on the sands at Warham Hole before proceeding south to Binham, where an incendiary bomb was dropped. Heading in a south-easterly direction, a flare was released over Field Dalling, followed by an incendiary at Gunthorpe; an HE bomb at Briningham and a fourth incendiary at Briston; then an incendiary and HE bomb at Thurning; a sixth incendiary at Wood Dalling; and a seventh at Cawston. Turning east, the raider then dropped an incendiary at Wroxham at 0245 and another at Hoverton St John – followed by a final one at Neatishead before the airship passed out to sea between Horsey and Winterton at 0300.

Zeppelin L 17 passed over the *Cross Sand Lightship* at 2325 and came overland at Ormesby, Norfolk at 2345. She followed the River Yare to Lodden before turning towards Norwich, which she missed – passing to the south. An incendiary bomb was dropped at Bixley before the airship arrived over Tuddenham – and possibly attracted by the aerodrome flares, dropped 10 HE bombs before turning to the east and dropping seven more HE and five incendiary bombs between Tuddenham and

Honingham. The raider then passed on over Costessey and passed out to sea between Mundesley and Bacton at 0140. The airship was commanded by *Kapitänleutnant* Herbert Ehrlich.

Zeppelin L 22 passed near to the *Cross Sand Lightship* at 2215 and crossed the Suffolk Coast to the south of Lowestoft – heading in a south-easterly direction. She finally reached Stowmarket at 2335 where she hovered for about five minutes before heading to Poslingford, where at 2345 an incendiary bomb was dropped. At 0020 four HE bombs fell on West Wickham Aerodrome before the airship headed east – dropping six incendiary bombs near the gas works at Haverhill as she went and another five HE bombs at Withersfield (along with one HE bomb at Great Wratting at 0035). Making off in a north-easterly direction, the raider – commanded by *Kapitänleutnant* Martin Dietrich – found Thetford Aerodrome, on which she dropped three HE bombs, but again caused no damage. Passing over Croxton Heath, a flare was dropped which set fire to the heath – which later attracted the bombs of *Zeppelin L 14*. Still pursuing a north-easterly course, the airship arrived over Hevingham where six HE and four incendiary bombs were dropped at 0200 – injuring a horse. Further on, an incendiary was dropped on Burgh-next-Aylsham – once more causing no damage – before the Zeppelin passed out to sea between Mundesley and Happisburgh at 0210.

Zeppelin L 23 came overland at Benacre, Suffolk at 2315 and travelled inland for a few miles before turning back to the south-east and passing over Southwold. She dropped an incendiary bomb at 2333 which fell on the common – 20 yards from the Military Ammunition Store. The Zeppelin, commanded by *Kapitänleutnant* Otto von Schubert, then passed out to sea and followed the coast southwards for a few miles before heading out to the east.

Zeppelin L 31 – commanded by *Kapitänleutnant* Heinrich Mathy – approached North Foreland, Kent and started dropping HE bombs at 2320 into the sea in groups of three in the vicinity of Kingsgate. The Zeppelin passed over Westgate and headed towards Ramsgate, where she was fired at by the anti-aircraft guns at Manston and Ramsgate. At 2335 three HE bombs fell in a field near Ramsgate – causing no damage (apart from breaking a few windows in 10 houses and also a greenhouse). The raider then passed out to sea – dropping bombs as she went. She passed Sandwich (where more bombs were dropped), but on approaching Dover, the anti-aircraft barrage opened up on her and she turned back to the north-east and headed out into the North Sea towards Germany – crossing part of neutral Holland as she went.

Zeppelin L 30 never crossed the English Coast – although she was sighted midway between Zeebrugge, Belgium and North Foreland, Thanet, Kent at 2250 before heading back to Germany.

Summary for 31 July 1916:

Location	Number and type of bombs dropped	Casualties	Damage
Lincolnshire:			
Caythorpe	2× IB		
Langford Common	1× IB		
Metheringham	1× IB		
Skinnard	1× IB		
West Ashby	1× IB		
Norfolk			
Binham	1× IB		
Bixley	1× IB		
Briningham	1× HE		
Briston	1× IB		
Buckenham	1× IB		
Bunwell	2× IB		
Burgh-next-Aylsham	1× IB		
Cawston	2× HE, 2× IB		
Croxton Heath	7× HE, 1× IB		
Guist	1× HE		
Gunthorpe	1× IB		
Hevingham	6× HE, 4× IB		1 horse injured
Hockwold	1× IB		
Honingham	7× HE, 5× IB		
Hoverton St John	1× IB		
Neatishead	1× IB		
Reedham	4× HE		
Snarehill (Thetford)	3× HE		
Thurning	1× HE, 1× IB		Slight damage to a farm
Tuddenham	10× HE		
Walpole St Peter	1× IB		
Warham Hole	1× IB		
West Newton	1× IB		
West Rudham	1× IB		
Wood Dalling	1× IB		
Wroxham	1× IB		

Location	Number and type of bombs dropped	Casualties	Damage
Suffolk			
Great Wratting	1× HE		
Haverhill	6× IB		
Poslingford	1× IB		
Southwold	1× IB		
Withersfield	5× HE		
Cambridgeshire			
March	2× HE, 2× IB		
West Wickham	4× HE		
Kent:			
Ramsgate	3× HE		
Total	57× HE, 46× IB; an uncertain number of bombs were dropped in the sea		

Anti-aircraft guns in action and reported use of ammunition:

Location of AA battery	Calibre or type of gun	Number / type of rounds fired
Manstone, Kent	2× 12 pdr 12-cwt	16 rounds
Ramsgate, Kent	2× 12 pdr 12-cwt	2 rounds

Eleven Royal Naval Air Service aeroplanes took off, but failed to find any of the raiders.

One Royal Flying Corps aeroplane took off, but crashed – seriously injuring the pilot.

1 August 1916
During the afternoon, three airships – *Zeppelins L 14*, *L 24* and *L 30* – were making a reconnaissance over the Heligoland Bight.

Zeppelin L 30 was identified cruising in the area north of Ameland, North Friesian Islands, Holland from 1923 to 1945.

Zeppelins L 14 and *L 24* began to fly further west – and by 2115 they were respectively about 90 miles due east of Spurn Head and about 120 miles east by north of Flamborough Head. Here they turned and returned to their sheds in Germany.

The purpose of this operation could not be established (unless it was connected with naval activity).

2 August 1916

Weather: the wind was very light, except between the north of Scotland and Norway – with the wind speed over the central portion of the North Sea at 1,500 feet being little more than five miles per hour; generally fine, but somewhat misty.

During the afternoon, six naval airships left their sheds in Germany and flew westwards over the North Sea. These were *Zeppelins L 11*, *L 13*, *L 16*, *L 17*, *L 21* and *L 31*.

Zeppelin L 21, which was commanded by *Hauptmann* August Stelling, cruised out to sea off the North Norfolk Coast for a few hours before coming inland at Wells-next-the-Sea at 2355 and heading south – flying very fast until reaching Thetford Aerodrome (probably attracted by the flares there). Here she dropped five HE bombs at 0045 before turning to the east and reaching the coast at 0135 at Covehithe. Here two HE and two incendiary bombs were dropped – with another eight HE bombs falling in the sea.

Zeppelin L 13 crossed the Norfolk Coast at Bacton, Norfolk at 2345 but was immediately fired upon by the anti-aircraft guns sited at Bacton Coastguard Station. This drove the airship to the south along the coast, where there were reports of explosions from the sea – possibly from bombs. The airship came again overland at Happisburgh at 2352 and headed in the direction of Norwich – passing to the east – and dropped an incendiary bomb at Panxworth and then three HE bombs over Mundham at 0025. A further five HE and three incendiary bombs were then dropped over Ditchingham, followed by four incendiaries over Earsham. The total damage was a few panes of glass broken at Grange Farm, Mundham and Ditchingham Hall. Passing round to the north, the Zeppelin passed over Shelton at 0045 where she dropped three HE bombs (which again broke a few windows) before arriving at Tacolnestone at 0055. Here she dropped six HE and one incendiary bomb. Five minutes later, the airship crossed over Fundenhall, where two incendiary bombs fell. Still bearing north-west, she passed Silfield at 0110 – dropping three HE bombs – before passing onto Wymondham, where one incendiary bomb fell. The bombs at Silfield damaged two farm houses and two cottages. Between 0115 and 0125 the Zeppelin was seen circling round Stoke Holy Cross, Shotesham All Saints, Saxlingham Thorpe, Shotesham Saint Mary and back to Stoke Holy Cross (possibly while the crew tried to locate Norwich). From this point, the airship made straight northwards and passed out to sea at Trimingham at 0210. The Zeppelin was commanded by *Kapitänleutnant* Eduard Prölls.

Zeppelin L 16, being commanded by *Kapitänleutnant* Erich Sommerfeldt, crossed the British Coast over Hemsby, Norfolk at 0025, 3 August and travelled in a south-westerly direction to Hempnall. Here she was sighted heading west at 0100 – and then at 0110 dropped three incendiary bombs at Long Stratton before next being sighted at Burnwell heading north-west. All trace was lost of her until she appeared over Ashby St Mary at 0135 where four HE and three incendiary bombs were dropped – breaking most windows in the village. She then went out to sea over Yarmouth at 0210 and was heard flying in a north-easterly direction at an estimated height of 10,000 feet.

Zeppelin L 17, whose commander was *Kapitänleutnant* Herbert Ehrlich, came in between Caister and Yarmouth, Norfolk just north of the Yarmouth Lighthouse at 0020, 2 August – having passed the *Cockle Lightship* at midnight. At 0030 she was seen near to Ormesby St Margaret in company with *Zeppelin L 16*. She then turned south-west – passing to the north of Bungay – and on reaching Pulham, dropped three HE bombs before following the valley of the River Waveney to Eye. She then turned west to Mellis on the Great Eastern Railway, where she dropped an incendiary bomb at 0103. Retracing her course to Eye (and again following the River Waveney), she passed over Thorpe Abbot and at 0115 and dropped two HE and three incendiary bombs on Billingford – killing six horses and damaging a farm house at Brockdish. Turning north, the Zeppelin was over Hardwick at 0130 where she dropped a further five HE bombs; then another two at Long Stratton. At Forncett St Mary, an incendiary bomb was dropped near an up-starting signal on the Great Eastern Railway – again causing no significant damage – before turning south-east again towards the Waveney Valley. Here she dropped two HE bombs at Starston at 0145 – killing three horses; then onto Redenhall – dropping one HE bomb there and six incendiary bombs on Denton at 0150. Turning north-east to Broome, three incendiary bombs were dropped on the village before turning towards Southwold and the sea. She was last seen over the Southwold Lighthouse at 0215.

Zeppelin L 11, being commanded by *Korvettenkapitän* Viktor Schütze, was first sighted about 10 miles off Orfordness, Suffolk at 0040, 3 August heading in a southerly direction. She crossed the coast at Hollesley at about 0048 – and on reaching the River Debden, followed it in the direction of Woodbridge (two bombs being dropped at Bawdsey Ferry and one near Bawdsey). Turning south towards Kirton, she dropped a flare [*Blendbombe*] on Kirton Marshes, followed by one large and three small HE bombs on the village. Six cottages were seriously damaged and a boy was slightly injured. After bombing Kirton, the Zeppelin appeared to have shut off her engines and drifted down the River Debden – passing out to sea at around 0125 (without being seen or heard of until out to sea off Felixstowe). The raider was fired upon by the naval guns of the Shingle Street Gun Position between 0125 and 0130. At 0154 she was seen off Landguard and fired a star-light while hovering over the sea. At 0200 she came in over the entrance to Harwich Harbour, but was immediately engaged by the anti-aircraft guns while flying at about 6,000 feet. She immediately turned north to Landguard, where two HE and four incendiary bombs fell in the sea, and one HE bomb landed on the parade ground – damaging a few tents. The airship then went out to sea before repeating the manoeuvre twice more – each time being engaged by the anti-aircraft guns – before finally heading out to sea at 0235.

Zeppelin L 31, commanded by *Kapitänleutnant* Heinrich Mathy, was first reported by Dover-based seaplanes as being 35 miles north-west of Dunkirk, France at 2215 while cruising over the Straits of Dover before turning westward at 0050 towards the East Coast of Kent. The coastguard at Kingsdown reported seeing an airship heading north in a semi-circular sweep, which crossed the coast at Deal at 0100 – having just dropped 20 HE bombs in the sea in response to three rounds of anti-aircraft fire being aimed at her by the steamer *Duchess of Devonshire.* Turning south from Deal, she followed the outline of the coast until just off Dover at 0110 where she was picked up by the searchlight at St Margaret's. She was then heavily fired upon by the anti-aircraft batteries – hence, she turned east and was believed to have dropped some further bombs over the sea before turning north-east and heading steadily back to Germany.

Summary for 2 August 1916:

Location	Number and type of bombs dropped	Casualties	Damage
Norfolk			
Thetford	5× HE		
Mundham	3× HE		Windows broken
Ditchingham	5× HE, 3× IB		Windows broken
Thwaite	3× IB		
Earsham	4× IB		
Long Stratton	2× HE, 3× IB		
Shelton	3× HE, 1× IB		Windows broken
Tacolnestone	6× HE, 2× IB		
Fundenhall	2× IB		
Silfield	3× HE		2 farmhouses and 2 cottages damaged
Wymondham	1× IB		Windows broken
Ashby St Mary	4× HE, 3× IB		Windows broken
Billingford	3× HE		8 horses killed, 2 injured
Brockdish	3× HE, 3× IB		Farmhouse damaged
Redenhall	1× HE		
Sarston	2× HE		3 horses killed, 1 injured
Denton	6× IB		
Broome	3× IB		
Forncett	1× IB		
Hardwick	5× HE		
Pulham	3× HE		
Panxworth	1× IB		
Sea (off Happisburgh)	6× HE?		

Location	Number and type of bombs dropped	Casualties	Damage
Suffolk			
Covehithe	2× HE, 2× IB		
Sea (off Covehithe)	8× HE		
Melis	1× IB		
Bawdsey	2× HE		
Kirton	4× HE	1 injured	6 cottages damaged
Landguard	1× HE		Broken windows; tents damaged
Sea (off Landguard)	2× HE, 4× IB		
Kent			
Sea (off Deal)	20× HE		
Sea (off Dover)	?		
Total	93× HE, 49× IB	1 injured	

Anti-aircraft guns in action and reported use of ammunition:

Location of AA battery	Calibre or type of gun	Number / type of rounds fired
Harwich Defences		
Shingle Street (naval)		16 rounds
Felixstowe		
Golf Club House	12 pdr	9 rounds
Trimley Heath	12 pdr	13 rounds
Felixstowe	6" QF (converted naval)	8 rounds
Landguard	3" QF	19 rounds
Dovercourt	3" QF	19 rounds
Great Oakley	6 pdr	1 round
Dover Defences		
Frith Farm	2× 12 pdr Hotchkiss A/1	10 rounds
Frith Farm	2× 12 pdr Hotchkiss A/2	7 rounds
Drop Redoubt	2× 6 pdr Hotchkiss A/1	25 rounds
Drop Redoubt	2× 6 pdr Hotchkiss A/2	14 rounds
Fort Burgoyne	2× 6 pdr 'A' Group	21 rounds

Location of AA battery	Calibre or type of gun	Number / type of rounds fired
Fort Burgoyne	2× 2 pdr 'B' Group	14 rounds
Langdon Battery	3"	18 rounds
Langdon Battery	6 pdr	18 rounds
SS *Duchess of Devonshire*	6 pdr Hotchkiss AA	3 rounds
Admiralty Pier and Eastern Harbour	2× 6"	-
Norfolk		
Bacton (North Walsham)	2× 3 pdr	9 rounds

The Royal Naval Air Service sent up three aeroplanes from Killingholme (two from Cranwell, one from Holt) and two from Bacton aerodromes to intercept the raiders, but none of the pilots saw any of the Zeppelins.

Royal Naval Air Service Station Yarmouth reported the following:

2 August 1916
Operations against hostile aircraft on 2-3 August 1916.
Royal Navy Air Station, Great Yarmouth.

> Sir, I have the honour to submit the following report on the operations carried out against hostile aircraft:
>
> 6.27pm: Flight Lieutenant Wood on Sopwith Clerget Schneider 8132 left to attack Zeppelin airship reported 30 miles due east of Yarmouth. Lieutenant Wood flew south-east for 30 minutes, cruised round at a height of 7,000 feet for 20 minutes and returned to Yarmouth having seen nothing. Visibility above 5,000 feet good; bad looking down.
>
> 6.40pm: Flight Sub-Lieutenant Bittles in Sopwith Clerget Schneider 8149 left HMS *Brockesby* on sighting a Zeppelin 10 miles to the north-west.
>
> 6.45pm: Flight Sub-Lieutenant Smith in Sopwith Schneider 3736 (100 hp – Monosoupape) left to attack the same Zeppelin.
>
> I consider this engine missing due to the pilot not properly adjusting his petrol supply – having had little experience with this type of machine.
>
> 6.45pm: At this time, sounds of continual firing was heard to the eastward. Flight Commander Nicholl left in BE2c RAF [Royal Aircraft Factory] aeroplane no.8417, proceeded 15 miles to seaward due east, cruised at a height of 8,000 feet for about 20 minutes and returned to Yarmouth – landing at 7.45pm.
>
> 7.18pm: Flight Lieutenant Galpin in Sopwith Schneider Seaplane no.3776 (100 hp – Mono) left to attack hostile aircraft reported 10 miles north of Yarmouth. Sighted a Zeppelin 25 miles north of Yarmouth hanging over a cloud bank at 6,000 feet. Turned north in pursuit. At 8.05pm dived into a cloud

bank – and owing to failing light, descended. Flew south-west for 40 miles and picked up by the Danish steamer *Alberbrika* four miles north-east of Cromer.

7.20pm: Flight Lieutenant Kilner on BE2c RAF aeroplane no.8420 left and cruised in vicinity of Yarmouth at 8,000 feet for one hour.

7.15pm: Bacton: Flight Lieutenant Cadbury left in aeroplane 8618 BE2c RAF and cruised in the vicinity of Bacton Aerodrome for one-and-three-quarter hours.

Burgh Castle: At approximately 10.15pm Zeppelins were reported approaching the vicinity of Yarmouth and Lowestoft.

Flares were lit at Burgh Castle Night Landing Ground and Flight Sub-Lieutenant Pulling left in BE2c RAF aeroplane no.8418, ascended to a height of 7,000 feet and proceeded to cruise round this lighted area. At approximately 11.30pm a Zeppelin approached Burgh Castle at a height of about 8,000 feet and was sighted by Flight Sub-Lieutenant Pulling, who attacked it with machine-gun fire – using three trays of ammunition.

I have reason to believe that this Zeppelin was seriously damaged.

10.47pm: On Zeppelin approaching Bacton, Flight Lieutenant Cadbury on BE2c 8418 left Bacton in search of hostile airship. This officer cruised over Norfolk at an approximate height of between 7,000 and 8,000 feet for two-and-a-half hours, but did not sight the Zeppelin and returned to his aerodrome.

I would bring to your notice the conduct of Flight Sub-Lieutenant Pulling, who made a most determined attack upon this airship in spite of difficulties with his machine-gun – and I have reason to believe, causing serious damage. This officer has made frequent and determined attempts to attack airships at night.

I consider Flight Lieutenant Cadbury's flight was very creditable.

I have the honour to be, Sir,
Your obedient servant,
Squadron Commander, Royal Naval Air Service.

Flight Lieutenant Charles T Freeman took off from the deck of HMS *Vindex* – a seaplane carrier – in Bristol Scout D8953 at 2050 and reported:

Climbed to 5,000 feet – steering south-east. Saw two Zeppelins: one at 8,500 feet, 10 miles away; the second rather higher, about 10 miles further off. Attacked the nearer Zeppelin from 500 feet above her. Dropped Ranken darts, which apparently missed. By altering her course, the airship avoided the second attack, but the third more successful – and one of the darts hit the Zeppelin.

The pilot observed a puff of smoke from the airship. He dropped to 5,000 feet and, having expended all his ammunition, returned west by north to rejoin his ship. His engines failing, he came down onto the sea and was in the sea for some hours before finally being picked up by a ship – and landed at the Hook of Holland. While attacking the airship, the pilot was subjected to fire from a machine-gun – forward – on the roof of the airship.

Three aeroplanes of the Royal Flying Corps also took off to intercept the raiders, but all pilots failed to sight the enemy raiders.

8 August 1916

Weather: the wind over the North Sea was practically calm, with a slight increase in an easterly wind in the southern part of the North Sea. South of the latitude of Yarmouth, the east wind reached a velocity of 20 miles per hour at lower levels, but at greater heights, it was considerably less – decreasing towards the morning. It was fine, with very little mist or fog.

Eleven naval airships left the North German airship sheds on the afternoon of 8 August for operations over England. They were *Zeppelins L 11, L 13, L 14, L 16, L 17, L 21, L 22, L 23, L 24, L 30* and *L 31*. *Zeppelin L 23* was first – located north of Ameland at 1726 – and the others were located in succession during their flight (with the exception of *Zeppelin L 14*, which was not identified until she was on her way home). Of the 11 airships, nine reached Great Britain – with *Zeppelin L 17* (possibly being on picket duty) as a lookout for warships and *Zeppelin L 23* may have been damaged.

Zeppelin L 14 was commanded by *Hauptmann* Kuno Manger. After passing northward along the coast of Northumberland, she came overland at Berwick at 0025 and went west over Chirnside and Duns. At 0037 she dropped an incendiary bomb on a farm at Fallside Hill, near Gordon. Course was changed to the south-east – and at 0118 three HE bombs were dropped at Grahamslaw (south of Kelso), along with a flare. A minute later, an incendiary bomb fell at Kersknowe and three minutes afterwards, two more incendiary bombs fell at Clifton. The raider then made off east over the Cheviots – dropping an incendiary bomb on the hills half a mile south of Southernknowe as she went past Alnwick and Alnmouth at 0200 and out to sea.

Zeppelin L 11 came in over Whitley Bay near Cullercoats, Northumberland – and after a flare had been dropped, eight HE and five incendiary bombs were dropped. The first seven HE bombs fell in a line from Whitley Road across Albany Gardens and Clarence Crescent to the railway. The last HE and five incendiary bombs fell further on between the corner of Alma Place and Burnfoot Terrace, and across Lish Avenue and the corner of Carlton Terrace and Marden Crescent. A man, a woman and three children were injured, along with one house being wrecked and three shops seriously damaged. Slight damage was caused to signals and telephone and telegraph wires at the railway station. The bombs fell practically simultaneously with the opening of fire from the Whitley Bay anti-aircraft gun – although the searchlights, being hampered by mist, caused the gun to fire blind. The second shell burst under the tail of the airship, which immediately dropped a bouquet of bombs which fell into the sea. The airship then rose and went out to sea and dropped what was described as a burning petrol tank, which fell into the sea and burnt for some time (so was probably an acetylene flare). The airship was commanded by *Korvettenkapitän* Viktor Schütze.

Zeppelin L 31 – after dropping a number of bombs in the sea off Seaham and Sunderland between 0015 and 0115 – came inland near Whitburn, Northumberland. She passed over Boldon and Cleadon – and at 0145 went north-east to Marsden, where at Salmon's Hall, six HE bombs were dropped on miners' houses at 0200. Apart from a horse being killed and a few windows broken, very little damage was done. The Zeppelin – whose commander was *Kapitänleutnant* Heinrich Mathy – by then went on north and circled over the mouth of the Tyne two or three times, but as the whole area was completely blacked-out, the airship commander probably failed to realise he was over a river. The airship passed over South Shields and Tynemouth – and unable to find any definite objective, went out to sea at 0300.

Zeppelin L 13, being commanded by *Kapitänleutnant* Eduard Prölls, crossed the coast at Denemout (north of Hartlepool, Durham) at 0133 and passed over Castle Eden. She followed the Hartlepool-Ferryhill Railway to Wingate, where at 0145 an HE bomb fell in a field – causing very little damage. Probably attracted to the Coxhoe District by a burning waste heap at Kelloe Colliery, the Zeppelin made in that direction and dropped 12 HE and 14 incendiary bombs on the colliery at Quarrington Hill and at Bowburn. At Kelloe, 30 feet of colliery railway was destroyed and windows were shattered in a weigh cabin. At Quarrington, windows were broken in about 40 houses and a shop. The airship then went off to the north-east – passing out to sea at Easington at 0205.

Zeppelin L 30 was heard approaching Skinningrove, Yorkshire from the north-east at around 0020 and was picked up by the no.2 searchlight at Skinningrove. After being held in the beam for about one-and-a-half minutes, she turned out to sea – dropping bombs into the sea as she went. She was next heard off Hartlepool at 0050 heading north – and at 0055 (having turned a half-circle west) was over the town, but the blackout – being total – failed to drop any bombs. At 0058 she turned south and dropped six HE bombs in a field to the west of Seaton Carew Iron Works and three HE on a slag tip at the iron works themselves. A minute later, an incendiary bomb fell at the zinc works at Seaton Snook, but caused no damage. At 0105 the no.9 searchlight at Port Clarence illuminated the airship – and she immediately turned east, crossed the River Tees and thence, out to sea. The commander of the airship was *Kapitänleutnant* Horst von Buttlar [10].

Zeppelin L 22 approached Redcar, Yorkshire from the direction of Hartlepool at 0055 – her commander, *Kapitänleutnant* Martin Dietrich, possibly attracted by three flares that had been used to guide a seaplane that took off at 0030 and had not been extinguished. She dropped five HE bombs on the grass fields forming

10 Von Buttlar's full title was *Kapitänleutnant* Horst Freiherr Treusch von Buttlar-Brandenfels. His memoirs, entitled *Zeppelins over England*, were published in English by George G Harrap & Co Ltd (Kingsway, London 1931).

part of the Redcar Aerodrome. The airship proceeded south and dropped four HE bombs on a camp east of Wheatlands Farm – again causing no damage. When the Zeppelin arrived over Saltburn, she was sighted by the crew of the Huntley Hall anti-aircraft gun, which fired one round before the airship was out of range. Heading for Skinningrove, she then turned round – and apparently, with the aim of attacking the anti-aircraft gun at Huntley Hall, passed over the site again. The gun opened fire and she then turned again to the south – continuing to Howlsyke – where at 0135 an incendiary bomb was dropped on the moor. She then turned east – following the River Esk and the railway to Whitby – and was last seen from Robin Hood Bay going out to sea at 0150. The airship was pursued from Redcar to Skinningrove – and farther by a Royal Naval Air Service aeroplane.

The commanding officer of the Royal Naval Air Service Aerodrome Redcar reported:

> Sir, I have the honour to submit the following report on last night's aerial activities in the neighbourhood of this station: Having received warning messages from the Admiralty, London and the naval centres at Hull and the Tyne, I ordered pilots and men to stand by their machines at 2215. Towards midnight, incessant bomb-dropping appeared to be taking place well to the north of this station [Royal Naval Air Service Redcar] and growing nearer. At 0010 Flight Lieut de Roeper was ordered to make a reconnaissance on BE2c aeroplane no.1109, which was armed with four 16 lb bombs and 12 grenades.
>
> Shortly after he left the ground, a Zeppelin was observed steering towards us from the direction of West Hartlepool. The night was a particularly fine one, with a light north-easterly wind. The Zeppelin could be distinctly seen and appeared to be of a very large type – flying at 8-10,000 feet. At 0035 – when immediately over the aerodrome – the Zeppelin commenced to drop bombs. In all, six high-explosive bombs were dropped – all of which exploded in the aerodrome (making conical-shaped pits three feet deep and 12 to 15 feet in diameter). The first four bombs were dropped in pairs. After passing over the aerodrome, it appeared to steer over Skinningrove, where anti-aircraft guns engaged her. Heavy bombing was heard at intervals both to the northward and southward of us, but nothing further of importance occurred at the station.
>
> No casualties of any kind occurred. Flight Lieut de Roeper returned at 0245 – making a very good landing. All officers and men at duty on this station conducted themselves in an exemplary manner – and I wish to call your special attention to the fine performance of Flight Lieut de Roeper, who made a particularly fine flight of two hours, 40 minutes.

Flight Lieutenant B P H de Roeper submitted the following account on the pursuit of the Zeppelin:

Sir, I have the honour to submit the following report on reconnaissance flight and pursuit of Zeppelins last night:

The first imitation we received of a Zeppelin in the immediate vicinity was the sound of high-explosive bombs bursting at Hartlepool and Teeside. The time – as near as possible – was 0015. It was decided a suitable time to go up; the only machine available on the station was an old-type BE2c fitted with an 80 hp Rolls-Royce Renault. The armament consisted of four 16 lb bombs and 12 grenades. A height of 6,000 feet had been attained. When I observed bombs bursting at South Bank, I immediately altered course with the idea of meeting the Zeppelin, which remained invisible. I had covered about two miles in this direction when bombs were observed to burst on the aerodrome behind me. The recognition lights on the aerodrome were then put out – and my landmark was gone. However, I again turned in my tracks – having by this time attained a height of 8,000 feet – and proceeded in the track of the bursting bombs (some more of which were dropped in the sea just off Saltburn). On arriving at the latter place, the Zeppelin was easily discernible at an estimated height of 10,000 feet. Just about this time, she was caught in the ray of the anti-aircraft searchlight stationed at Skinningrove, but the operator lost her again after a few seconds. The Zeppelin then described a large semi-circle and climbed to about 12,000 feet. She then followed the coastline down to a point midway between Flamborough Head and Spurn – steering about 120 degrees – when she altered course to the east. I had taken station on her starboard quarter and slowly climbed until I had reached an altitude of 8,300 feet. The BE at this height would not climb anymore – and I therefore released my four bombs in the sea. This gave me a further 1,500 feet – increasing my height to just 11,000 feet. The Zeppelin, however, had the advantage in position and was about three-quarters of a mile ahead of me. I continued the chase from Flamborough about 20 miles out to sea, when the Zeppelin lost altitude and disappeared in the mist. I then returned to Redcar and landed safely after having been in the air for two hours, 40 minutes. I beg to submit that if an effective machine had been available, say a 1½ Strutter or RAF BE with a quick climb to 15,000 feet and about 20 knots faster than the machine used, bombs could effectively have been dropped on the Zeppelin. The Zeppelin appeared to be of the newest type – presumably about 600 feet in length.

I have the honour to be, Sir,
Your obedient servant,
De Roeper. Flt Lt.[11]

11 The National Archives (TNA) – Air 1/632/17/122/76: report of seaplane attack on Zeppelin off Spurn Head.

The Royal Aircraft Factory BE2c was used by the Royal Flying Corps as a night fighter from 1915 until the end of the war. It was the type piloted by many of the airmen charged with the task of combating the threat posed by the German airships and aircraft.

Zeppelin L 21, commanded by *Hauptmann* A Buttlar, was sighted in company with *Zeppelin L 23* [which never came in overland] 12 miles north-east of Scarborough at 2300, 8 August when both airships were fired on by the armed trawler *Itonian*. The trawler reported that one of the airships appeared to drop 23°. This was, in all likelihood, *Zeppelin L 23*, which probably received some damage (which necessitated repairs) and prevented her coming overland. *Zeppelin L 21* had a further encounter with naval forces as she approached Skinningrove, Yorkshire as at 0045 she was heard by HM yacht *Miranda* (stationed two miles north-east of Skinningrove). At 0058 *Zeppelin L 21* attacked the *Miranda* – dropping three HE bombs (one of which exploded 400 yards from the ship). In reply, the *Miranda* fired five 3 pounder shells when the airship was about 6,000 feet overhead. The third shell was claimed as a hit, but not verified. On being fired at, the airship passed over the cliffs east of Skinningrove – and at 0117 three HE bombs fell in a quarry before the raider passed directly over the town. At 0120 she dropped seven HE bombs, which destroyed a small wooden office. The Zeppelin then passed out to sea – dropping more bombs as she went to lighten her load.

Zeppelin L 24 came in over Flamborough Head, Yorkshire at 0015 and headed in a south-westerly direction towards Beverly before turning west and then south – picking up the Hull-Selby Railway at 0110. Over Hessel, she dropped eight HE and two incendiary bombs in open fields near the town. At 0120 the airship reached the north-west portion of Hull – steering over the golf course, where three HE bombs fell on the Hull and Barnsley Railway by Spring Bank Junction. Here, one HE and four incendiary bombs – one of which buried itself in the railway without exploding – were dropped. The Zeppelin passed on by Anlaby Road and the North-East Railway Line at the bottom of Walliker Street and turned north-east – circling round West Park, over Hymers College and the neighbourhood of Newland. Eight HE and 28 incendiary bombs were dropped on the city – causing considerable damage in Walliker Street, where two houses and a shop were wrecked. Two houses were also wrecked – and others damaged – in Granville and Sandringham Streets. Lesser damage was caused to Park Avenue – where fires were started – and also in Arnold Street, where a haystack was set alight. The total casualties were 10 killed and 11 injured – most of those being killed were out in the streets. The airship was fired at by the anti-aircraft guns at Harpings, sited to the north of the city, which fired eight rounds of shrapnel without apparent effect. At 0130 the airship – commanded by *Kapitänleutnant* Robert Koch – went off eastwards and was heard passing out to sea at Hornsea at 0140 before crossing back slightly further north. She finally passed out to sea over Filey Bay at 0210.

Zeppelin L 16 was spotted by the master of the *Inner Dowsing Lightship* flying very high and crossed into The Wash – finally making landfall over Brancaster at about 0030. She passed south-south-west to Fring and Dersingham, where at 0040 she dropped 10 HE and 10 incendiary bombs – the concussions shattering windows in various properties, but causing very little other damage. Five minutes later, eight HE and seven incendiary bombs were dropped on Wolferton – causing no damage. The airship then went north along the coast and out to sea at Hunstanton at 0109. Her commander was *Kapitänleutnant* Erich Sommerfeldt.

With the exception of *Zeppelin L 24* – which bombed Hull – and *Zeppelin L 14*, none of the raiders penetrated far inland (with the airships flying very high) and were not prepared to make a stand against anti-aircraft fire. Also, a large quantity of bombs were dropped into the sea and little damage was caused – apart from in Hull. One feature of the raid was the two airships *Zeppelins L 21* and *L 22*, which appeared to have exhibited some combined method of attack at Skinningrove. Where *Zeppelin L 21* was bombing the works, *Zeppelin L 22* was attempting to locate and bomb the anti-aircraft batteries engaging her consort.

Summary for 8 August 1916:

Location	Number and type of bombs dropped	Casualties	Damage
Roxburghshire			
Fallside Hill	1× IB		
Grahamslaw	3× HE		
Kerskowe	1× IB		
Clifton	2× IB		
Northumberland			
Southernknowe	1× IB		
Whitley Bay	8× HE, 5× IB	5 injured	1 house wrecked
Durham			
Marsden	6× HE		Horse killed; windows shattered
Wingate	1× HE		Windows damaged
Kelloe and Quarrington, Coxhoe	12× HE, 14× IB		Colliery railway damaged
Seaton Carew	9× HE		
Seaton Snook	1× IB		
Yorkshire, North Riding			
Redcar	9× HE		
Howlsyke	1× IB		
Skinningrove	10× HE		Small office destroyed
Yorkshire, East Riding:			
Hessle	8× HE, 2× IB		
Hull	12× HE, 32× IB	10 killed, 11 injured	Houses and shops destroyed and damaged
Norfolk			
Dersingham	10× HE, 10× IB		
Wolferton	8× HE, 7× IB		
Total	96× HE, 77× IB	10 killed, 16 injured	
Kelso	1× illuminating bomb		

A large number of bombs – mainly HE – were dropped in the sea off Sunderland, Seaham and the coast of the North Riding.

Anti-aircraft guns in action and reported use of ammunition:

Location of AA battery	Calibre or type of gun	Number / type of rounds fired
Hunley Hall, Saltburn	6" naval gun on railway mounting	3 rounds
Harpings (near Hull)	3" AA gun (mobile)	–
Whitley Bay	3" AA gun	4 rounds

12 August 1916

Weather: wind light to moderate; hazy and cloudy to overcast – the clouds being very high.

At 1230 an aeroplane of the Roland Scout type passed over Dover, Kent from north-north-west to south-south-east. It was later established that *Leutnant* Ilges was the pilot. The aircraft came in near the South Foreland Lighthouse, but was not observed, with the result that the first intimation of its arrival was the fall of a bomb. Four HE bombs were dropped: one near a shed on the naval aerodrome at Guston Road; another fell by the officers' mess of the 5th Battalion, Royal Fusiliers, North Fall Meadow – wounding one officer and five men. A third bomb fell on the edge of the cliff near the castle – wounding a man belonging to the Royal Defence Corps – and the last fell in the sea. No damage was done other than a few broken windows. The raider was fired upon by the anti-aircraft guns from as soon as he was detected until he had flown out of range.

Anti-aircraft guns in action and reported use of ammunition:

Location of AA battery	Calibre or type of gun	Number / type of rounds fired
Frith Farm	2× 12 pdr	26 HE rounds
Drop Redoubt	2× 6 pdr Hotchkiss	8 day tracer rounds, 2 common rounds
Dover Castle	6 pdr Nordenfeldt	11 day tracer rounds, 13 night tracer rounds
Langdon Battery	3"	2 shrapnel rounds, 24 HE rounds
Langdon Battery	6 pdr	19 common rounds
Prince of Wales Pier	6"	1 shrapnel round

Seven aircraft were sent up by the Royal Naval Air Service to intercept the raider, but only Lieutenant Hore – who was piloting BE12a no.6146 – came close to the enemy aircraft, but lost it in cloud.

Along with aircraft such as the Royal Aircraft Factory BE2c, the British Isles were defended by a wide range of calibres of anti-aircraft guns on a variety of mountings (with some types having been rapidly modified and pressed into service to accommodate the guns in their new role to allow for high angle elevation). This wide range of calibres and types presented quite a contingency problem for the supply of ammunition and spares. Alongside the guns were various forms of searchlight; some powered by acetylene, others taking their power from the electricity main – a supply that was often cut in the event of air raids to increase the blackout (much to the distain of the searchlight crews).

So as to give it the ability to relocate rapidly to counter the threat posed by airships and aircraft from whichever part of the country that may be immediately threatened, many of the anti-aircraft guns were mounted on any suitable chassis that came to hand. Here, a 3 pounder Vickers quick-firing gun has been mounted on a Lancia lorry chassis.

A 3 inch quick-firing gun is seen on a 20-cwt fixed mounting near to the centre of London. Of interest is the detail to be seen in the sighting and breach operating system.

19 August 1916
Report on the attack on a Zeppelin off Spurn Head by Flight Sub-Lieutenant F M Fox in a Sopwith Baby Seaplane no.8131 of Royal Naval Air Station, Killingholme:

20 August 1916
Sir, I have the honour to submit the following report on the mid-day patrols carried out from this station yesterday, August 19th:

> At 12.15 (BST) a signal was received from the rear admiral commanding East Coast reporting a Zeppelin 30 miles E by S from Spurn. In accordance with usual practice, two Baby seaplanes and two 225 hp Sunbeam Short machines were ready on the slipway and were dispatched by Flight Lieutenant Hards DSC – who was, at the time, the commanding officer at the air station – as follows:
>
> Flight Sub-Lieutenant F M Fox – Baby Seaplane no.8131 – to the position indicated by signal; thence to search to the SE. Left at 12.20.
>
> Flight Sub-Lieutenant K N Smith – Baby Seaplane no.8154 – to same position; thence to search to the north. Left 12.21.
>
> Both machines were armed with four 16 lb bombs and two boxes of darts.
>
> Flight Sub-Lieutenant Arundel – with observer Petty Officer Homer in Short Seaplane no.8375 – to a position 60 miles ENE of the Spurn and ordered to work to the south. Left 12.26pm.
>
> Flight Sub-Lieutenant Simpson – observer Petty Officer Kershaw in Short Seaplane no.8391 – 40 miles E by S of the Spurn and thence to the south. Left 12.23pm.
>
> Both these machines were fitted with sending and receiving W/T gear and their instructions were to locate and report positions of any hostile aircraft, ships or submarines.
>
> Flight Sub-Lieutenant Fox was the only one to sight and attack the Zeppelin – and I attach his report.
>
> I submit that he carried out his attack with great skill and determination – and from the report, it would appear quite certain that the Zeppelin was damaged; whether sufficiently to prevent her reaching one of the Zeppelin bases cannot be stated.
>
> I submit that the disadvantage of the limited slipway accommodation was very marked on this occasion. Though the times of despatch of machines after the signal was received were quite quick, this was from the fact that they were already on the slipway in the order mentioned above – and the two Baby shorts could not have changed positions with two more Baby seaplanes without considerable delay.
>
> Signed: Wing Commander, Commanding Officer Royal Naval Air Service Station, Killingholme, Lincs.

Sir,
I have the honour to report that at 12.15 BST I was ordered to proceed in chase of a Zeppelin reported to be about 35 miles east of Spurn.

I started in Sopwith Baby Seaplane no.8131 at 12.20 BST – passing over Spurn at a height of 3,000 feet at 12.31. I then steered course E by N to allow for wind. At 12.50 I sighted a Zeppelin directly ahead of me at a distance of about 15 miles – steering east at a height of 9,000 feet. I steered for the Zepp – keeping behind a cloud bank and rising to a height of 11,000 feet. I do not think the Zeppelin sighted me until I was quite close.

I attacked her from 1.1 to 1.8 BST – passing at about 1,000 feet over the Zeppelin from stern to bow. I dropped four 16 lb bombs in succession and two boxes of Ranken darts – during which time I was doing S-turns over her bows. I felt four violent concussions underneath my machine and consequently concluded that the Zeppelin was hit. She immediately turned a complete circle – her nose dropping very considerably. I kept her under observation for about five minutes – and during this time, she appeared to right herself; losing about 1,000 feet.

I then returned – landing at 2.5pm.

My left float was punctured by what, on examination, I first considered was an explosive bullet, but this may possibly have been from a broken valve rocker which 'went' during my return. The machine, after alighting, gradually sank by the left float, but was kept up by the right float – assisted by my sitting on the right wing tip – and was salved.

I have the honour to be, Sir,
Your obedient servant,
Signed F M Fox, Flight Sub-Lieutenant.[12]

23 August 1916

Weather: wind velocity was very light – probably less than five miles per hour over the North Sea. There was a great deal of low stratus cloud.

Army *Zeppelin LZ 97* crossed the North Sea from Belgium. She was reported by the *Long Sands Lightship* at 2316 and the *Sunk Lightship* at 2317 as overhead and bearing north-north-west – flying very high. She crossed the English Coast at Bawdsey Ferry, Suffolk – turning south-west at 2355 – and passed over the anti-aircraft gun at the Golf Club House. She dropped one HE bomb about 200 yards north of Old Felixstowe and then another at Low Pasture Farm (about 600 yards north of Walton Church). She then turned south-west towards Landguard, but did not keep her course – veering round northwards over Blowfield Hall towards Trimley Station (short of

12 The National Archives (TNA) – Air 1/632/17/122/58: report of Zeppelin raid on RNAS Station Redcar and subsequent pursuit of Zeppelin by BE2 aeroplane.

which five HE bombs were dropped). An incendiary bomb was then dropped, which narrowly missed the station buildings. The airship then went on to Trimley – dropping four incendiary bombs on the way. The airship then circled over Trimley – dropping 10 incendiary bombs at 0003 hrs on the village. The only one that caused any damage was one that fell through the roof of a barn and landed in a bath. The raider then passed over Mill Farm – where a further HE bomb was dropped – before flying eastwards over Hill House (beyond which 11 HE bombs were dropped in a north-easterly direction (towards Kingsfleet) in the parish of Walton). The airship then passed near to the golf course's anti-aircraft gun again and went out to sea near Orfordness at 0012.

Summary for 23 August 1916:

Location	**Number and type of bombs dropped**	**Casualties**	**Damage**
Old Felixstowe	1x HE		
Trimley	6× HE, 15× IB		Barn slightly damaged
Walton	12× HE		
Total	19× HE, 15× IB		

The airship was neither seen nor fired upon, but the engines could be heard from about eight miles away.

24 August 1916

Weather: there was practically no wind south of a line from the Firth of Forth to the mouth of the Elbe – and as far south as the East Coast of Kent. In the Straits of Dover, the direction of the wind was from west-south-west; velocity at 1,500 feet being 15 miles per hour. There was a good deal of cloud throughout the night over both England and the continent.

Twelve naval airships – one of which was believed to have been a Schütte-Lanz type – left the North German sheds and were first located over the North Sea. They were *Zeppelins L 11, L 13, L 14, L 16, L 17, L 21, L 22, L 23, L 24, L 31, L 32* and possibly *Schütte-Lanz SL 8*. Of these airships, *Zeppelins L 11, L 17* and *L 24* were detected heading home during the evening, while *Zeppelins L 13, L 23* and *Schütte-Lanz SL 8* approached to within 60 miles of the English Coast before turning back. *Zeppelin L 22* was located about 45 miles off Yarmouth, but never crossed the coast.

Zeppelin L 16, her commander being *Kapitänleutnant* Erich Sommerfeldt, was the first airship to cross the coast – crossing at Aldeburgh, Suffolk at 2305 and heading west-north-west before turning to the south-west and Ipswich. She hovered over Wickham Market for about 10 minutes before continuing in the direction of Ipswich, but turned east and dropped an incendiary bomb on Woodbridge at midnight. She then dropped one incendiary bomb at Martlesham – followed 10 minutes later by six HE and three incendiary bombs on Kelsgrave. At 0015 five HE and four incendiary bombs were dropped on Playford. The last two HE bombs fell within 20 yards of one of the searchlights of No.9 (Tyne) Anti-Aircraft Brigade at Bealings. After this incident, the airship headed off in a north-easterly direction towards Aldeburgh and then followed the coast north for a few miles before heading out to sea.

Zeppelin L 21 was first heard off Orfordness – heading south a little way off the coast. As she passed Felixstowe, Suffolk at 0121 she dropped some HE bombs into the sea. She finally crossed the coast at Frinton at 0143 and headed north-west – arriving over Pewit Island at 0155. Eighteen HE bombs were dropped in the area between Great Oakley, Little Oakley, Pewit Island and the coast (about a mile to the south of Dovercourt) – and a further incendiary bomb fell on the mud-flats at Crabknowe Spit. Two houses were slightly damaged in the outskirts of Little Oakley, while a granary and a cow house were wrecked in a farm. On Bramble Island, just to the west of Pewit Island (and between it and Great Oakley), were the Explosive and Chemical Products Company's Explosives Works – and these may have been the raider's objective; her commander being *Oberleutnant zur See* Kurt Frankenburg. From Crabknowe Spit, the airship travelled north-east along the coast – being heavily fired at – and finally went out to sea from the mouth of the River Deben at 0215. The airship was engaged during her course by no fewer than seven anti-aircraft guns from Great Oakley to Golf House, Felixstowe and was thought to have been hit, but the seaplane sent out to search for her found nothing in the form of wreckage.

Zeppelin L 31 (commanded by *Kapitänleutnant* Heinrich Mathy) and *Zeppelin L 32* left their sheds in company and travelled overland across Belgium – having London as their final goal (and carrying an especially large bomb load for the purpose). The two airships passed over Furnes, Belgium at 2200 and *Zeppelin L 31* dropped bombs on St Pol at 2215. Soon after 2300 both airships were heard cruising off the North Foreland – and it was here that they separated, with *Zeppelin L 31* proceeding along the Thames. The raider clung to the Kentish Coast as far as the Swale – having circled off Birchington and Herne Bay. She then flew over the *Nore Light Vessel* in the direction of Southend – following the river as far as Canvey Island before crossing overland and heading west. On reaching the unmistakable landmark of the West India Docks, the airship turned to the south and began dropping bombs along a course curving south-west, south-east and north-east – which passed over Millwall, Deptford, Greenwich, Blackheath and Eltham to Plumstead (where she crossed the river again into Essex). During her 10 minutes' course south of the river, *Zeppelin L 31* dropped 35 HE and eight incendiary bombs. Of the HE bombs, 16 were of an unusually large type – weighing at least 120 kg; the remainder being the normal weight of 50 kg. Of the bombs dropped, three landed on the Cyclops Iron Works at Millwall – causing considerable damage – while three more fell in the river at Millwall as the airship crossed. One landed on the London Electric Supply Corporation's Works at Deptford – stopping the working of the Deptford searchlight; one on a supply reserve depot at Deptford, which destroyed a quantity of flour; and three fell on a military camp at

Blackheath. The rest of the bombs fell on waste ground or on suburban residential districts between Blackheath and Plumstead – most damage being done at Eltham (primarily on private houses). One house was completely destroyed by a bomb of the heavy type which fell on its roof; nothing being left of it or its occupants but the outline of its foundations. The number of deaths recorded was eight (three men, three women and two children). Twenty-four men – including 14 privates of No.2 HT Depot, Army Service Corps, Blackheath – 11 women and five children were injured.

The searchlights appeared to have been unable to pick up the airship during her course, as they could not pierce the cloud and mist until the airship reached Shooters Hill (after leaving Eltham) at 0135. It was here that she was picked up in the direction of Erith – and the anti-aircraft guns of the London defences opened fire on her at 0137. Swiftly crossing the river north of Plumstead at 0140 she dived into a heavy cloud bank in the direction of Rainham. Travelling down wind at 60 miles per hour, she eluded the shells. At Rainham, she released her last HE bomb at 0445 – causing no further damage. The airship then made for the sea – following her inward course closely as far as Vange; then going along the north shore of the estuary as far as Southend, which she passed at 0200 (and Southend at 0215). Off North Foreland at 0240 she was fired upon by naval ships – and at 0255 she was stationary one mile off Ramsgate, where she showed coloured lights as a signal to *Zeppelin L 32* to join her before heading out across the Channel (where an aviator – Captain John Woodhouse of 50 Squadron, flying from Dover – fired one-and-a-half drums of ammunition at her without result). The two airships headed for Ostend, where they separated; *Zeppelin L 32* going home along the Dutch Coast and *Zeppelin L 31* overland across Belgium.

Zeppelin L 32, commanded by *Oberleutnant zur See* Werner Peterson, was seen from the North Foreland Lighthouse at about 2317 working her way into the Thames Estuary – having made sure of her position off the coast of Thanet, Kent. Her commander's anxiety to avoid the defences appeared evident – and at 2342 the North Foreland Lighthouse again reported her being on a north-north-west course (having seemingly abandoned the projected joint attack on London). At 0048 she was over the Straits of Dover and approaching the French Coast. At 0130 she was eight miles north of Gravelines, France but then turned for England again – being reported off Folkestone Harbour at 0210 before venturing over the town and being engaged by the anti-aircraft guns at Capel. The airship then went out to sea, but returned again almost immediately. At 0218 she was over Dover, where about five HE bombs were dropped in the sea, and then at 0255 she dropped about 18 HE bombs in The Downs (two miles out to sea off Deal) – causing no damage to shipping, but was fired on by Royal Naval Guard ships before heading off to meet *Zeppelin L 31*.

Oberleutnant zur See Werner Peterson, commander of *Zeppelin L 32*, is seen here posing with his wife. He was to meet a fiery death on 22 September 1916.

Summary for 24 August 1916:

Location	Number and type of bombs dropped	Casualties	Damage
Suffolk			
Woodbridge	1× IB		
Martlesham	1× HE		
Kesgrave	6× HE, 3× IB		Telegraph and telephone wires broken
Playford	5× HE, 4× IB		
Essex			
Oakley area	18× HE, 1× IB		Damage to 2 houses, granary and cow house
Rainham	1× HE		
Kent			
Deal	18× HE in sea		
Dover	5× HE in sea		
London:			
Millwall			
West Ferry Road, Millwall	1× 250kg HE		Damage to houses, shops, church and school
Cyclops Engineering Works	1× 250 kg HE, 1× 50 kg HE, 1× IB		Fire; iron foundry damaged

Location	Number and type of bombs dropped	Casualties	Damage
In River Thames (opposite, above and on barge *Cambria*)	3× 250 kg HE, 1× IB		Slight damage
Deptford			
Deptford Market	1× 250kg HE	1 killed, 4 injured	Considerable damage to buildings
ASC and RE offices, Deptford Market	1× 250 kg HE		Severe damage
Deptford Dry Dock	1× 250 kg HE		Engineering workshops, offices and stores severely damaged
London Electric Supply Corporation	1× 250 kg HE		Serious damage to machinery; switchboard destroyed
Woods' Wharf, Deptford; barge *Margaret*	1× IB		
Greenwich			
17, Straightsmouth	1× IB		Slight damage to house
Station Yard, Greenwich (SE and C Railway)	1× HE	3 injured	Railway station damaged
Almshouses, Greenwich	1× HE		Considerable damage.
South Street	1× HE	3 injured	Houses and roadway severely damaged; water main broken; 2 horses killed
86, King George Street	1× IB		
58, King George Street	1× IB	1 injured	House damaged
New Gutta Percha Co., Grove Hill	1× IB		Slight damage

Location	Number and type of bombs dropped	Casualties	Damage
8, The Grove, Blackheath	1× HE		Windows broken
No.2 HT Depot, ASC	1× 250 kg, 1× 50 kg HE, 1× IB	14 soldiers injured	Storage and YMCA hut damaged; iron fencing blown away
Roadway (near Hare and Bullet Inn, Blackheath)	1 HE		Windows broken
32, South Vale Road	1 HE	1 killed, 1 injured	House destroyed; 1 damaged
Allotments	1× HE		
Eltham			
23, Dickson Road and Well Hall Road	1× HE	5 injured	Roadway and several houses damaged; gas main shattered
Sandly Green	1× 250 kg		Slight damage to roofs and windows
210, Well Hall Road	1× 250 kg	4 killed	House destroyed; 2 damaged
Lovelace Green	1× 250 kg		Houses damaged
215, Grange Hill Road	1× 250 kg		House destroyed; others severely damaged
Jackwood	2× HE		
Plumstead			
Kingsdale Road	2× HE	Police Constable injured	2 houses partly destroyed
Plumstead Common	1× 250 kg, 2× HE		Houses damaged
3, Bostall Hill, Plumstead	1× 250 kg	3 killed, 8 injured	House destroyed; other damaged
Cordite Street	2× HE		House partly destroyed
Total	16× 250 kg, 72× HE, 17× IB	9 killed, 40 injured	

Anti-aircraft guns in action and reported use of ammunition:

Location of AA battery	Calibre or type of gun	Number / type of rounds fired
Harwich		
Ramsey	3" 20-cwt	19 rounds
Great Oakley	6 pdr	4 rounds
Dovercourt	3" QF	18 rounds
Shotley	3" 20-cwt	8 rounds
Felixstowe		
Landguard	3" QF	25 rounds
Golf Club House	12 pdr	2 rounds
Felixstowe	6" QF CN	9 rounds
London		
North Woolwich	3" 5-cwt	8 rounds
Danson Park	3" 20-cwt	16 rounds
Plumstead	3" 20-cwt	45 rounds
Abbey Wood	3" 20-cwt	20 rounds
South Outfall	3" 5-cwt	9 rounds
Erith	4" BL	11 rounds
Crayford	75 mm	5 rounds
Shoeburyness	3" 20-cwt	2 rounds
Shoeburyness	3" on experimental ranges	3 rounds
Dover		
Little Cauldham Farm	2× 6 pdr Hotchkiss	70 rounds
Frith Farm	12 pdr 12-cwt	49 rounds
Langdon Battery	12 pdr 12-cwt	56 rounds
Langdon Battery	3" 30-cwt	52 rounds
Fort Burgoyne	2× 6 pdr Hotchkiss	40 rounds
P of W Pier	6" HA (naval)	1 round
Eastern Arm	6" HA (naval)	7 rounds
Deal	12 pdr 12-cwt	11 rounds
Ramsgate	12 pdr 12-cwt	2 rounds

The Royal Naval Air Service sent up eight aeroplanes to intercept the raiders. Two pilots sighted the airships – which were held in searchlight beams – but lost them when searchlights were extinguished.

The Royal Flying Corps sent up seven aeroplanes to intercept the raiders – and one pilot fired one-and-a-half drums of ammunition at *Zeppelin L 31*, but lost her while reloading. Another airman pursued *Zeppelin L 31* over the Channel, but lost her when she entered clouds. One aircraft crashed on landing.

2 September 1916

Weather: slight rain, with a good deal of cloud and mist in South-East England, with wind at 10 miles per hour.

Sixteen airships consisting of 12 navy Zeppelins and four army Schütte-Lanzes took off to attack the city of London in one mass attack, but *Schütte-Lanz SL 8* and *Zeppelin L 17* turned back. Naval *Zeppelins L 11, L 13, L 14, L 16, L 17, L 21, L 22, L 23, L 24, L 30* and *L 32* took off from Germany, while the army *Schütte-Lanz SL 11* and two others left from bases in Belgium – crossing the English Coast over Foulness, Essex at 2240 on 2 September. Army *Zeppelins LZ 90, LZ 97* and *LZ 98* may have also been involved in this operation, with *Zeppelin LZ 97* turning back while still over the North Sea.

An army airship – which was not identified, but was possibly *Zeppelin LZ 98* (commanded by *Oberleutnant zur See* Ernst Lehmann) – passed through the Straits of Dover and was sighted off Deal, Kent at 2335. She crossed the coast at Littlestone just after midnight and headed in a north-westerly direction – hovering over Maidstone. On reaching Sevenoaks, the airship turned to the north and Gravesend, where she was illuminated by the Harley and Southfleet searchlights at 0111 – and the Southfleet and Dartford anti-aircraft guns opened fire. The airship reached the railway north of Hartley at 0113 – crossing it west of Fawkham Station and dropping six incendiary bombs at Longfield (immediately north of the junction of the Gravesend Branch Line). Twelve more incendiary bombs fell east of the branch line slightly further on before the airship went directly over and attacked the Southfleet searchlight – dropping three HE bombs just beyond it. Continuing towards Gravesend, the Zeppelin dropped two HE bombs at 0120 at Northfleet Green Farm – destroying a coal shed, pollard house and stable. These were followed by an HE and an incendiary bomb falling on the Gravesend Golf Course before the airship crossed the Thames east of Gravesend – dropping one incendiary in the river. The Essex searchlights were illuminated and the Tilbury anti-aircraft gun opened fire – compelling the airship to rise steeply as the Fobbing gun joined in the barrage. The raider retaliated by dropping two incendiary bombs at Corringham and three HE bombs on Fobbing. Next, eight incendiary bombs fell at Vange at 0130 before the airship headed northwards at high speed – passing Billericay and Chelmsford and onto Great Waltham, where one HE bomb fell. Turning north-east, she passed Colchester and Ipswich – and on the boundary of Rushmere and Playford parishes, destroyed some crops with two HE bombs at 0213. She passed out to sea north of Aldeburgh at 0235.

Another army airship (probably *Zeppelin LZ 90*) crossed the Essex Coast shortly after 2300 north of Clacton – and at 2320 reached Mistley (south-east of

Manningtree), where she stopped her engines and lowered an observation car. For some reason, the wire cable from which the car hung broke. It was probable that the pawls of the winch – by which the car was lowered – had become disengaged and had allowed the cable to run out suddenly and uncontrollably. Some marks on the teeth of the gear-wheels of the winch, which was itself dropped later on and found near Postlingford, might have been caused by a bar having been thrust between the teeth in order to prevent the car dropping further and avoid it becoming entangled on the ground. It was supposed that the wire broke under the sudden strain, as the car was found the next morning with about 5,000 feet of wire attached. At 2345 the airship restarted her engines and went off in a north-westerly direction to Foxearth, west of Sudbury, where two incendiary bombs were dropped. She then went on westward to Wixoe, where at 0030 hrs 21 HE and 16 incendiary bombs were dropped – merely breaking windows in two houses and a school. The airship then turned north-east to Poslingford, where at 0040 the damaged winch of the observation car was thrown out to save weight; then following a north-westerly course, passed out to sea between Caister and Yarmouth at 0145.

The observation car was made of light aluminium; streamline in form and of about 14 feet in length, with horizontal and vertical fins at the tail in order to keep its head onto the direction of the ship. It contained a mattress – on which the observer lay at full length and carried out his observation through celluloid windows in front of the car. He communicated with the ship by means of a telephone – the wire of which was contained in the centre of the suspension cable. There was no indication that there was an observer in the car at the time of the accident.[13]

Schütte-Lanz SL 11 approached Foulness Island at 2240 and crossed the Blackwater at 2255 – heading in a north-westerly direction before bearing to the west. She passed over Saffron Walden, circled over Great Chesterfield and then on to Royston, which she passed at 0030. At 0120 on 3 September *Schütte-Lanz SL 11* dropped three HE and three incendiary bombs on London Colney, Hertfordshire; then two HE and two more incendiary bombs on South Mimms; then one HE and two incendiary bombs at 0128 on Littleheath, where a water main was broken and two houses damaged. One HE bomb fell at Northaw; one incendiary bomb fell at Temple House, Ridgeway Road; and two more incendiary bombs on Gordon Hill Station, Hertfordshire at 0129. At 0135 two HE and seven incendiary bombs fell at Stud Farm, Clayhill – setting some stables alight and killing three horses – followed by three incendiary bombs at Cockfosters (near the Enfield Isolation Hospital, Hertfordshire) before the airship crossed the Great Northern Railway Main Line just south of the Hadley Wood Tunnel. At 0145 she dropped two incendiary bombs before turning back towards the east. At 0150 three incendiary bombs fell at Southgate. At 0212 six HE and two incendiary bombs fell on Edmonton (one bomb in the grounds of Messrs

13 The recovered observation car is, at the time of writing, on display in the Imperial War Museum, Lambeth, London.

The cloud car from *Zeppelin LZ 90* that was unceremoniously dropped on British soil survived relatively intact.

The winch that controlled the cloud car's descent – and was to follow its charge shortly after.

The damage to the cloud car winch (presumably caused by a member of *LZ 90's* crew thrusting a bar into the mechanism in an attempt to stop it unwinding completely).

Eley's Explosive Works) before the airship, which came under heavy anti-aircraft fire, dropped two more HE bombs at Ponders End and six HE bombs along the Enfield Highway, Hertfordshire – one of which failed to explode, but 15 houses were damaged. Three BE2c aircraft (piloted by lieutenants Robinson, Mackay and Hunt) were chasing the airship – and at 0217, 12 HE bombs (two of which failed to explode) fell at Turkey Street. At this point, the greater part of the anti-aircraft guns of North and Central London – including those of Regent's Park, Paddington and Green Park (which were out of range) – were firing at the airship even as Lieutenant William L Robinson in BE2c no.693 of 39 Home Defence Squadron closed in – firing three drums of ·303 into the airship from his Lewis gun before the airship fell in flames; the mainly wooden wreckage burning for over two hours.

Schütte-Lanz SL 11. Type E 4.
0225: Castle Farm, Cuffley, Hertfordshire.
Hauptmann Wilhelm Schramm +. CC.
Oberleutnant Wilhelm Vohdin +. CC.
Leutnant Hans Geitel +. CC.
Obermaschinist Jakob Baumann +. CC.
Vizefeldwebel Rudolf Goltz +. CC.
Feldwebel-Leutnant Karl Hassenmüller +. CC.
Gefreiter Bernhard Jeziorski +. CC.
Untermaschinist Fritz Jourdan +. CC.
Untermaschinist Karl Kachele +. CC.
Obersteuermann Fritz Kopischke +. CC.
Obermaschinist Friedrich Modinger +. CC.
Obermaschinist Reinhold Porath +. CC.
Unteroffizier Heinrich Schlichting +. CC.
Obersteuermann Rudolf Sendzik +. CC.
Unteroffizier Anton Tristram +. CC.
Untermaschinist Hans Winkler +. CC.

Later, a letter was received via Berlin from the sister of *Obersteuermann* R Sendzik asking for details of his burial.

Lieutenant William Leefe Robinson wrote to the commanding officer of 39 HD [Home Defence] Squadron following his combat:

> Sir,
> I have the honour to put before you the following report: On my night patrol on the night between the 2nd and 3rd September, I took to the air about 11.8 in the evening of the 2nd with orders to patrol between Suttons Farm and Joyce Green. I climbed to 10,000 feet in 53 minutes. I counted what I thought to be 10 sets of London flares. There were some clouds underneath, but altogether it was a beautiful clear night. I saw nothing till 1.10 a.m. when two searchlights

Much propaganda was made of postcards reputedly showing *Schütte-Lanz SL 11* falling in flames – and making Lieutenant Robinson a household name.

discovered a Zeppelin about south-east of Woolwich. Clouds had accumulated in this direction and the searchlights had some difficulty to keep the airship. By this time I had succeeded in climbing to a height of 12,000 feet and I made off in the direction of the Zeppelin, which was fired on by some anti-aircraft guns, with the hope that I should be able to cut it off on its return journey eastwards. I gained on it slightly in the next 10 minutes. I considered the Zeppelin to be about 800 feet under me – and I sacrificed speed to retain my height when it went behind some clouds and I lost sight of it. After 15 minutes searching without any result, I returned to my patrol. I succeeded in detecting and recognising my own London flares at Sutton's Farm. About 1.50 I noticed a red kind of glare in the north-east of London. Taking it for granted that it was the outburst of a fire, I made in that direction. At 2.5 a.m. the Zeppelin was detected by the searchlights over the east of London. Remembering my first failure, I now sacrificed height for speed and put my nose downwards in the direction of the Zeppelin. I saw shells bursting and tracers passing round the airship. Coming nearer, I noticed that the anti-aircraft guns either fired too high or too low; also many shots about 800 feet behind. Some tracers went straight off. I could hear the explosion when I was about 3,000 feet from the Zeppelin. I flew about 800 feet under it from the bow to the tail and fired a drum alternately of

The hero of the hour: Lieutenant William Leefe Robinson, VC.

the new Brock and Pomeroy ammunition. This did not seem to have any result. I then steered aside and fired a whole drum on the airship's side, but also this without apparent result. I then flew behind the tail. I was now very near – about five feet under – and concentrated a whole drum on the aft part of the lower part of the ship. I was now, when attacking the Zeppelin, 11,800 feet up. I had only fired a few shots when I saw from the aft part of the ship a glowing glare. In a few seconds, the whole ship was one mass of flames. Then a third drum was used. There were no searchlights on the Zeppelin and no anti-aircraft guns were firing. I came very quickly out of the way of the falling Zeppelin – and as I was very much excited, I fired off a red light and threw off the parachute flare. As I had very little oil and petrol left, I returned to Sutton's Farm and landed at 2.45. On landing, I found that the wire netting of my Lewis gun had been destroyed. The aft part of my central top plane had also been hit several times.
I have the honour to be, Sir,
Your obedient servant,
W L Robinson. Lieut. No.39 Sqdn. RFC.[14]

14 Lieutenant William Leefe Robinson, later promoted to Captain, was awarded the Victoria Cross two days later by King George V at Windsor for his actions in bringing down the first enemy airship over the British Isles. Captain W L Robinson later became a Flight Commander with 48 Squadron and was shot down over the Western Front in April 1917 and captured. He died from the effects of the Spanish flu on 31 December 1918 and is buried in All Saints' Churchyard Extension, Harrow Weald, Middlesex.

As the framework of *Schütte-Lanz SL 11* was mainly manufactured from a wooden box section and formers tensioned with wire, the remains burnt very well – leaving only the few metal parts to be recovered and inspected.

One of the few clearly identifiable parts of *Schütte-Lanz SL 11* is one of the engines being closely inspected by members of the Royal Flying Corps.

Zeppelin L 16, being commanded by *Oberleutnant zur See* Kurt von Friemel, crossed the Norfolk Coast at 2240 at Salthouse and initially headed south. She dropped an incendiary bomb at Kimberley at 2328 before joining company with *Zeppelin L 21* for a while (still heading south). She dropped three HE bombs at Little Livermere and then parted company with her fellow raider as they passed over Bury St Edmunds, with *Zeppelin L 16* heading south-west, while *Zeppelin L 21* took a more westerly route. Passing Saffron Walden, the raider turned west towards Luton before looping around and heading south towards London. Moving more slowly – as if feeling her way – she dropped one HE bomb on Harpenden and five HE bombs on Redbourn. Of the latter bombs dropped, one was found to be a cast-iron type from an obsolete mortar, as it was dated 1884, while another was a 2-cwt naval bomb of the latest design; the rest were ordinary 1-cwt types. Changing course to the south-east, the airship passed over South Mimms before turning northwards towards Hatfield, but then turned south again – passing over Potters Bar at 0215 (possibly with the aim of crossing the defences in the wake of *Schütte-Lanz SL 11*) – but decided that the response was so formidable that the Essendon searchlight posed a more opportunist target. Therefore, at 0220 the airship circled slowly over the searchlight – dropping 16 HE and nine incendiary bombs, which resulted in serious damage to the village. The church was badly damaged, along with the vicarage; three cottages were destroyed; and a number seriously damaged. A telephone operator and a child were killed and two people injured – although the nearest bomb to the searchlight was within 100 yards. The commander of *Zeppelin L 16* at this point must have seen *Schütte-Lanz SL 11* falling in flames and turned to the north-east – dropping an incendiary bomb on Aston as he went. At 0250 the airship passed Cambridge and at 0310 passed Fordham before circling for a while. She then headed eastwards – dropping an incendiary bomb at West Stow – and while passing over Raveningham at 0410 a German blue naval cap was dropped before passing out to sea at 0420 near Yarmouth.

Zeppelin L 32 was heard north-west of Cromer at 2130 – although she did not cross the coast for another half an hour (having cruised just off the Norfolk Coast). Heading in a south-westerly direction, she dropped a flare at Whinburgh and her first bombs fell at Ovington and Saham Toney, where three HE bombs fell at each location at 2310. Proceeding at a slow pace, the airship stopped a couple of times and hovered – presumably to verify her position; then at 2345 two incendiary bombs fell at Two Mile Bottom (near Thetford). On reaching Hake Bottom (near Mildenhall, Suffolk), a petrol tank was dropped before proceeding to Newmarket – and at 0005 again hovered for 20 minutes to verify position. At 0150 the airship formatted on *Zeppelin L 21* and they proceeded in a south-westerly direction for a number of miles. At 0200 the airships parted with *Zeppelin L 32* – heading for Leighton Buzzard, where she turned south-west along the railway line of the London and North Western Railway at Tring. The airship turned due east, but as at this point in time, the commander cannot have failed to observe the fate of *Schütte-Lanz SL 11*. He must have decided that it was a safer option to head for home rather than continuing to follow the railway line to the capital and face the fully-alerted defences of London. At 0254 five

HE and 11 incendiary bombs were dropped at Hertford Heath – killing two horses; then 16 HE and eight incendiary bombs fell on Great Amwell, which killed a pony. Two minutes later, two more HE bombs dropped near Ware – causing no damage. The airship then made off in an east-north-east direction – finally passing out to sea at 0415 at Corton. Although she stopped over the sea to verify her position, her engines were heard to stop and restart by the crew of the *Cross Sand Lightship* at 0420. The Zeppelin's commander, as usual, was *Oberleutnant zur See* Werner Peterson.

Zeppelin L 21 crossed the coast at Mundesley, Norfolk at 2220. Being invisible in the clouds, she was not fired at. Her commander was *Oberleutnant zur See* Kurt Frankenburg. Steering a slow south-westerly course, she formatted with *Zeppelin L 16* at Attleborough for a while – dropping a petrol tank at Stanton at 2345 before parting company near Bury St Edmunds. *Zeppelin L 21* took a more easterly course towards the south of Cambridge. On reaching Six Mile Bottom, *Zeppelin L 16* stopped and hovered for about a quarter of an hour (to presumably verify her position) before continuing on her course towards Biggleswade and then Bedford. Her commander turned her due south towards Hardington (presumably intending to approach London from the north-west), but at 0225 the crew must have seen the glow from the burning *Schütte-Lanz SL 11* as the airship turned west towards Hitchin; then north towards The Wash – dropping bombs as she went. Two incendiary bombs were dropped on Dunton at 0240; a third fell at Gamlingay. Heading north rapidly, the airship reached North Fen, Sutton at 0300 where an HE bomb fell; then an HE and an incendiary bomb fell in fields at Horselode Fen, Chatteris; then another HE and incendiary bomb were dropped on Tilney St Lawrence at 0335 – followed by two HE bombs to the west and two incendiary bombs to the north of Lynn (all of which caused no damage). Continuing north, an incendiary bomb was dropped at Wolferton and seven HE and two incendiary bombs fell at Dodshill (near Dersingham) – damaging four houses at 0347 and injuring three (one of whom subsequently died). Four HE and three incendiary bombs fell on Snettisham; six HE and four incendiary bombs at Sedgeford; and at 0400 one incendiary bomb fell at Thornham before *Zeppelin L 21* passed out to sea. The airship was engaged by a 75 mm gun at Sandringham, which fired 12 rounds – of which the second round was thought to have scored a hit, but was not subsequently substantiated.

Zeppelin L 14 crossed the Norfolk Coast east of Wells at about 2150 and dropped an incendiary bomb (presumably to confirm her position overland, or establish her speed) and headed to the east side of The Wash, but stopped her engines over Thornham and drifted for half an hour. She then dropped an HE bomb on Ringstead before passing out over The Wash to Terrington Marsh, where at 2255 she dropped an incendiary bomb. She circled south of Lynn and on to Gayton, where she dropped two HE bombs at 2330 and onto Wormegay Fen, where one HE bomb fell. This was followed by three more HE bombs on Shouldham Warren – none of the bombs causing any damage. Her commander, *Hauptmann* Kuno Manger (presumably having established his position), went off to the south-west towards Peterborough before turning to the south at 0010 on 3 September – dropping an incendiary bomb at Upwood at 0020. Passing over Huntingdon, the airship turned due west, but after a few minutes flying, her commander must have decided that he may be lost. He turned back to the south-east – arriving over Thaxtead, Hertfordshire at about 0225. It is presumed that it was here he witnessed the destruction of *Schütte-Lanz SL 11* 25 miles to the south-west, for he immediately turned the airship north-east for home – dropping the bombs he had saved for London as he went. One HE bomb fell at Little Bardfield and then another at Fincingfield at 0230; then two HE bombs on Lavenham (one at Thorpe Morieux and one at Brettenham). At 0250 two incendiary bombs fell near Drinkstone and then four HE and one incendiary bomb fell on Buxhall. Finally, five HE bombs fell near Haughley – none of which caused any damage. The airship crossed the coast at Bacton at 0405 hrs being pursued by an aeroplane.

Schütte-Lanz SL 8 crossed the Norfolk Coast north of Holkham at 2305, 2 September. At 2315 she dropped two incendiary bombs at Burnham Thorpe before going off towards the south-west. Her commander, *Kapitänleutnant* Guido Wolff, was probably doubtful of his position and decided to proceed slowly. At 0030, 3 September the airship passed Downham Market and turned south – dropping an incendiary bomb at Littleport. This was followed by six more on Oxlode Fen before the airship appeared to drift for an hour-and-a-half over the Fen district of Ely. It is possible that the commander saw the glow on the horizon of *Schütte-Lanz SL 11*, for the airship then made off to the north – following the straight line of the Bedford Level – and dropping bombs at random as she neared the coast. Three HE and three incendiary bombs fell on Congham at 0300 and one incendiary bomb at Harpley Dams, Flitcham. This was followed by three HE bombs at Syderstone and another two at South Creake. The only damage caused by these bombs was to cottages at Congham and South Creake, where windows and tiles were damaged. At 0315 one HE bomb fell at Great Walsingham and two more at Wighton. Finally, at 0320 one HE bomb landed at Cley as the airship passed out to sea, followed by another eight bombs falling into the sea.

Zeppelin L 24 came inland near Trimingham at 0030 and dropped a flare at Gunton before following a short and circuitous route over the north-east of Norfolk. She dropped two HE bombs at Briston at 0050 – followed by an incendiary bomb at Plumsted – before appearing over the coast at Bacton. The airship was fired at from Bacton by an anti-aircraft gun before turning north – and again was fired at from Mundesley at 0112. On being fired at, she circled and dropped five HE bombs which fell on the beach just below the high tide mark (below the cliff where the anti-aircraft gun was situated). The raider then turned inland and dropped two incendiary bombs at Trunch, followed by 13 HE and 27 incendiary bombs at Ridlington at 0130 – causing no damage. These bombs were presumably meant for Bacton Aerodrome, which had been lit up. The airship then approached Bacton again prior to going out to sea (and was once more fired at), but with poor visibility – due to low cloud and mist – was only momentarily sighted. The Zeppelin was commanded by *Kapitänleutnant* Robert Koch.

Zeppelin L 30, being commanded by *Kapitänleutnant* Horst von Buttlar, came overland at Southwold at 2240, 2 September and went west to Blythburgh. She then turned north-north-west to Bungay, where she was picked up by the Pulham searchlight, and immediately turned north-east – dropping nine HE and 12 incendiary bombs as she did so. Two farmhouses were damaged and one man was injured. Two minutes later, she passed Mettingham and dropped eight HE and one incendiary bomb on Bungay Common – killing two cows. At 2315 she dropped six HE bombs at Ditchingham, followed three minutes later by four HE bombs at Broome. Passing off to the north-east towards the coast, the airship was fired at by the anti-aircraft guns situated at Fritton before passing out to sea (south of Yarmouth) at 2325.

Zeppelin L 11 approached Yarmouth, Norfolk from the north-east at 2200 – passing over the *St Nicholas Lightship* at 2205, 2 September. Five minutes later, she began dropping her bombs into the sea – and at 2215 crossed the coast and dropped one HE and one incendiary bomb about half a mile north-west of Southtown Railway Station. She was then engaged by anti-aircraft guns and passed out to sea – dropping more bombs as she went. She passed along the coast and at 2330 came in once again north of Lowestoft – circling round to the north – and was fired at by the anti-aircraft guns of No. 5 Mobile Brigade at Fritton and Lowestoft. The airship then once again went out to sea and proceeded south, following the coastline – dropping one white and one red rocket east of Golf House Gun, Felixstowe before circling for a while. She then finally turned north at 0220 – and over Harwich Harbour, dropped three HE

For *Zeppelin L 11*, this was to be her last operational sortie over Great Britain. Declared to be obsolete, she was decommissioned in April 1917.

and one incendiary bomb that all fell in the water. When illuminated by searchlights and fired at, her commander – *Korvettenkapitän* Viktor Schütze – quickly turned the airship and disappeared into the clouds. He followed the coast up as far as Aldeburgh and turned out across the North Sea at 0250, 3 September.

Zeppelin L 23 came in from the North Sea following a southerly course into The Wash – passing the *Lynn Well Lightship* at 2200, 2 September and dropping a calcium flare as she went. Her commander was *Kapitänleutnant* Wilhelm Ganzel. She approached the Norfolk Coast at Snettisham, where she dropped at least three incendiary bombs that fell into the sea. The airship then made off across The Wash in a westerly direction – crossing the coast at Kirton Fen, where she dropped an HE bomb at 2240 which damaged a farmhouse and killed some poultry. This was followed by an incendiary bomb at Kirton Holme, two at Swineshead and one at Gosberton. The Zeppelin then turned north and dropped four HE and one incendiary bomb on Boston at 2254 which damaged the signal-box of the Great Northern Railway Station, a workshop and an office at the gas works. One house was destroyed and about 75 others were damaged to some degree. The pier at the sluice doors of the River Witham was also damaged. One man was killed and three people injured. The airship then went off to the south towards Wisbech; then back towards Spalding – dropping an incendiary bomb at Weston before once more heading to Holbeach and The Wash towards home. She dropped about 22 HE bombs into the sea as she went.

Zeppelin L 13's commander, *Kapitänleutnant* Eduard Prölls, took a much more northerly course across the North Sea – crossing the coast at Cleethorpes, Lincolnshire at 2256, 2 September – and dropped six HE and two incendiary bombs at Humberston. Turning south as far as Ludford, she then turned westward – dropping an incendiary bomb at Caenby – before continuing on her course. At 0010 she dropped five HE and five incendiary bombs at East Stockwith – destroying two cottages, with one woman being killed. The airship then turned south along the valley of the Trent to Morton, where at 0015 four incendiary bombs fell – causing no damage. Continuing on to Retford (and although the blackout was in place), 15 HE and four incendiary bombs were dropped. Two of the HEs fell on the Corporation Gas Works, with three gasometres being set alight and destroyed. Eight houses were wrecked, along with a fruit warehouse – and glass was broken in 67 houses and businesses in the town (although only three women were injured). The airship then went off towards Gainsborough – and at 0105 dropped an HE bomb on Lea (causing no damage); then continuing east, dropped an incendiary bomb at Aylesby before passing out to sea at Donna Nook at 0130.

Zeppelin L 22 was initially detected in the neighbourhood of Skegness and Wainfleet, Lincolnshire at 2210, 2 September. She appeared to have followed the coastline northwards – passing Sutton, where some bombs were dropped into the sea; then continuing to the north – crossing the coast around Donna Nook (almost simultaneously with *Zeppelin L 13*). At 2305 she appeared to have been near Laceby – and at 2310 in the neighbourhood of Stallingborough and Immingham. She then turned inland to the west and at 2335 was near Goole, where she hovered for some considerable time. She was next sighted near Scunthorpe at 0020, 3 September and then at Barton-on-Humber before crossing the Humber at Killingholme. At 0042 the airship was sighted east of Hull, where she was fired at by the anti-aircraft guns at Marfleet and Sutton. At 0046 she dropped three HE bombs on open fields in the parish of Flinton before passing Burton Constable. She left the coast at Aldbrough at 0055 – being heard to drop her remaining bombs out to sea. Her commander was *Kapitänleutnant* Martin Dietrich.

To summarise the night's events: A determined attack on London had been intended by eight or 10 airships of the 16 that had set out – although *Zeppelin L 11* was not intended to carry out a very prolonged raid as she was deemed to be an old airship (and was largely employed in training crews). *Zeppelin L 17* did not come overland at all, whilst *Zeppelin L 23* was content to make landfall and circle over the Fen areas before heading home before midnight. *Zeppelin L 22* conceivably made her right landfall to participate in the attack on London, but hesitated, turned north and carried out a deviating flight over Lincolnshire and Yorkshire with no apparent objective. *Zeppelin L 13* obviously intended to raid the Midlands as a diversion for the attack on London, but possibly mistook the town of East Retford for that of Sheffield. Meanwhile, *Zeppelin L 30* just managed to cross the coast before returning home. Likewise, *Zeppelin L 24* – perhaps coming under unexpected anti-aircraft fire near Bacton – wandered about the Norfolk Coast. Of the remaining nine airships, four made a very careful attempt to attack London from the north-west, with two others coming in from Huntingdonshire. The last airship of the nine approached London from the south-east in a slow and uncertain manner – possibly with the intention of crossing London from the south-east to the north-west.

The leading airship – the army *Schütte-Lanz SL 11* – had left her shed near Cologne with an unusual quantity of bombs for a ship of her capacity. When approaching Enfield, she began dropping bombs – seemingly with the intention of gaining buoyancy – and was circling at the time in order to make good her maximum height. When however, she finally came under the searchlight and anti-aircraft fire, her commander realised the tactic was too risky and turned back too late for him to escape. He could not stave off the aeroplane attack that brought him down at 0220. At the same moment, the crews of *Zeppelins L 21* and *L 32* saw the disaster that had overtaken *Schütte-Lanz SL 11* and made for home. The course steered by *Zeppelin L 16*, which was nearer to *Schütte-Lanz SL 11* at the moment of her downfall, was remarkably brave. Her commander, *Oberleutnant zur See* Kurt von Friemel,[15] followed *Schütte-Lanz SL 11* in close over London and into the barrage, but the sight of the burning airship nearby proved too much for the commander's nerve. *Zeppelin L 14* and *Schütte-Lanz SL 8* appeared to have given up their attempts to reach London even before *Schütte-Lanz*

15 *Oberleutnant zur* See Kurt von Friemel, who was previously second-in-command of *Zeppelin L 31* under Kapitänleutnant Mathy, probably imbibed much of his master's energy and boldness.

SL 11 had fallen, but then immediately turned for home. *Zeppelin LZ 90*, if not for the accident to her cloud car, probably intended to follow a similar course to that of *Schütte-Lanz SL 11* over London. As for *Zeppelin LZ 98*, that came in over Dungeness – as if her commander had not intended to attack London (he may have been intended as a diversion to the main intended attack by bombing Woolwich).

Summary for the night of 2-3 September 1916:

Location	Number and type of bombs dropped	Casualties	Damage
Yorkshire, East Riding			
Flindon	3× HE		
Lincolnshire			
Humberston	6× HE, 2× IB		
Aylesby	1× IB		
Caenby	1× IB		
East Stockwith	5× HE, 5× IB	1 injured	2 cottages demolished
Morton	4× IB		
Lea	1× HE		
Kirton Fen	1× HE		Windows broken
Gosberton	1× IB		
Swineshead	2× IB		
Boston	4× HE, 1× IB	1 killed, 2 injured	Railway signal-box, work-shop and offices at gas works damaged; 1 house destroyed; windows broken in 75 houses
Weston	1× IB		
Nottinghamshire			
Retford	15× HE, 4× IB	3 injured	3 gasometres destroyed; 8 houses badly damaged; 1 ware-house demolished; windows in a school and 67 houses broken
Norfolk			
Yarmouth	1× HE, 1× IB		
Ditchingham	6× HE		Windows and tiles broken
Earshain	9× HE, 12× IB	1 injured	2 farmhouses damaged
Broome	4× HE		Windows smashed

Location	Number and type of bombs dropped	Casualties	Damage
Mundesley	5× HE		
Ridlington	13× HE, 27× IB		
Trunch	2× IB		
Cley	1× HE		Windows broken
Great Walsingham	1× HE		
South Creake	2× HE		
Syderstone	3× HE		
Flitcham	1× IB		
Congham	3× HE, 3× IB		Windows broken
Briston	2× HE		
Gayton	2× HE		
East Rudham	3× HE		
West Lynn	2× HE		
North Lynn	2× IB		Windows broken
Wormegay Fen	1× HE		
Shouldham	3× HE		
Tilney St Lawrence	1× HE, 1× IB		
Terrington Marsh	1× IB		
Thetford	2× IB		
Saham Toney	3× HE		
Ovington	3× HE		Windows broken
Wolferton	1× IB		
Dersingham	7× HE, 2× IB	3 injured	6 houses badly damaged; 8 slightly damaged
Snetisham	4× HE, 3× IB		
Sedgeford	6× HE, 4× IB		
Thornham	1× IB		
Barnham Thorpe	2× IB		
Plumsted	1× IB		
Wighton	2× HE		
Isle of Ely			
Littleport	1× IB		
Oxlode Fen	6× IB		
Sutton	1× HE		

Location	Number and type of bombs dropped	Casualties	Damage
Chatteris	1× HE, 1× IB		
Cambridgeshire			
Hatley Park	1× IB		
Huntingdonshire			
Upwood	1× IB		
Bedfordshire			
Dunton	2× IB		
East Suffolk			
Bungay	8× HE, 1× IB		2 cows killed, 3 injured
Rushmere	1× HE		Crops damaged
Playford	1× HE		
Buxhall	4× HE, 1× IB		
Haughley	5× HE		
West Suffolk			
Little Livermere	3× HE		
Wixoe	14× HE, 16× IB		Windows in a school and 2 houses shattered
West Stow	1× IB		
Drinkstone	2× IB		
Brettenham	1× HE		
Thorpe Morieux	1× HE		
Lavenham	2× HE		
Essex			
Foxearth	2× IB		
Vange	8× IB		
Fobbing	3× HE		
Corringham	2× IB		
Great Waltham	1× HE		
Harwich	4× HE		
Little Bardfield	1× HE		
Finchingfield	1× HE		
Hertfordshire			
Aston	1× IB		

Location	Number and type of bombs dropped	Casualties	Damage
Redbourn	5× HE		
Harpenden	1× HE		
Essendon	16× HE, 9× IB	2 killed, 2 injured	Church and rectory severely damaged; 3 cottages destroyed, others damaged
Hertford Heath	5× HE, 11× IB		2 horses killed
Ware	2× HE		
Great Amwell	16× HE, 8× IB		
London MPD			
London Colney	3× HE, 3× IB		
North Mimms	2× HE, 2× IB		
Northaw	1× IB		
Littleheath	1× HE, 2× IB		Water main broken
Gordon Hill	3× IB		
Clayhill	2× HE, 7× IB		Stables burnt, 3 horses killed
Cockfosters	3× IB		
Hadley Wood	3× IB		
Southgate	3× IB		
Edmonton	6× HE		
Ponder's End	2× HE		Road and water main damaged; tramway and telephone wires down; slight damage to houses
Enfield Highway	6× HE		15 houses and greenhouses damaged
Forty Hill and Turkey Street	12× HE		Backs of three houses damaged
Kent:			
Longfield	6× IB		
Southfleet	3× HE, 12× IB		Wheatstack burnt; windows broken
Northfleet	2× HE		Coal house, pollard house and stable destroyed
Gravesend	1× HE, 1× IB		
In River Thames	1× IB		

Location	Number and type of bombs dropped	Casualties	Damage
Total	260× HE, 208× IB (at least 30 HE and 6 IB were known to have fallen in the sea)	3 killed, 12 injured	

Anti-aircraft guns in action and reported use of ammunition:

Location of AA battery	Calibre or type of gun	Number / type of rounds fired
London District		
Regent's Park	2× 3" 20-cwt	17 rounds
Paddington	2" 20-cwt	4 rounds
Green Park	3" 20-cwt	3 rounds
HAC Headquarters	2× 6 pdr	19 rounds
King's Cross	3" 20-cwt	4 rounds
Meath Gardens	2× 6 pdr	35 rounds
Tower Bridge	3" 20-cwt	6 rounds
Deptford Park	2× 75 mm	32 rounds
NE Sub-Control		
Beckton	4.7"	4 rounds
Palmers Green	4.7"	2 rounds
Victoria Park Gun	2× 3" 20-cwt	31 rounds
Finsbury Park Gun	3", 20-cwt	5 rounds
West Ham Gun	3", 20-cwt	10 rounds
Higham Hill Gun	4.7"	5 rounds
Clapton	3", 20-cwt	16 rounds
Wanstead	4.7"	2 rounds
Waltham Abbey		
Temple House	3" 20-cwt	20 HE rounds
Farm Hill	3" 5-cwt	1 shrapnel round
Enfield Lock	3" 5-cwt	13 HE rounds
Warleis Park	2× 3" 5-cwt	7 HE rounds

Location of AA battery	Calibre or type of gun	Number / type of rounds fired
Woolwich Sub-Command		
Southfleet	12 pdr 12-cwt	4 HE rounds
Dartford	2× 3" 20-cwt	47 HE rounds
Thames and Medway Garrison:		
Tilbury	12 pdr	8 shrapnel, 4 HE rounds
Fobbing	12 pdr	1 shrapnel round
"B" Battery, No. 5 Mobile AA Brigade		
Yarmouth (near Fritton)	2× 3 pdr Vickers	34 HE rounds
Harwich Garrison:		
Dovercourt	3" 20-cwt	12 HE rounds
Felixstowe	6" 20-cwt	1 CS round
Ramsey	3" 20-cwt	5 HE rounds
Landguard	3" 20-cwt	2 HE rounds
Shotley	3" 20-cwt	1 HE round
Golf Club House	12 pdr 12-cwt	1 HE round
Royal Naval Mobile Brigade, Cromer		
Sandringham	75 mm	12 HE rounds
North of Bacton	2× 75 mm	2 HE rounds
Bacton	3 pdr	18 HE rounds
Humber Garrison:		
Sutton	12 pdr 12-cwt	2 shrapnel rounds
Marfleet	3" 20-cwt	6 HE rounds

Events relating to actions of the Royal Naval Air Service and the Royal Flying Corps.

Four aircraft were sent up to intercept the raiders from the Royal Naval Air Service. Two pilots failed to find any sign of the raiders, but Flight Commander Arnold in Henry Farman no.9167 – flying from Grain Aerodrome – reported seeing an airship at Romford dropping bombs and under anti-aircraft fire. The machine was wrecked on landing at Romford – the pilot being slightly injured.

Flight Lieutenant Cadbury, flying BE2c no.8626 from Yarmouth Aerodrome, reported sighting an airship at 2300 when it was over Lowestoft – being fired at by anti-aircraft guns – but lost it in clouds.

The Royal Flying Corps dispatched nine machines on Home Defence flights; five of the pilots reported no contact with the raiders. Captain R C L Holme in BE2c no.2661 crashed on take-off from Beverly Aerodrome, but was unhurt. Lieutenant

Rose in a BE12 – no.6484 – crashed in a forced landing, but was unhurt. Lieutenant MacKay in BE2c no.2574 – flying from North Weald Bassett Aerodrome – reported seeing an airship caught in a searchlight north of London, but when he was within a mile of his quarry, it fell in flames.

4 September 1916
Zeppelin LZ 86 / LZ 56. Type P.
Szentrandas, Russia.
Crashed due to pilot error.
Kommandeur: Hauptmann W Wolf.

16 September 1916
Zeppelin L 6 / LZ 31. Type M.
Fuhlsbüttel, Hamburg, Germany.
Caught fire while being inflated and destroyed.
Kommandeur: Kapitänleutnant Joachim Breithaupt.

Zeppelin L 9 / LZ 36. Type O.
Fuhlsbüttel, Hamburg, Germany.
Caught fire while being inflated and destroyed.
Kommandeur: Oberleutnant zur See von der Haegen.

22 September 1916
Weather: cloudy to fine, with some local mist or haze. Wind south, strength one.

At 1500 hrs an enemy aeroplane, identified as an *Albatros* type, approached the Kent Coast at Kingsdown – heading towards Deal. It then changed course to the south and at 1505 hrs was observed going south-east over Dover – flying at about 50 miles per

A close-up of *Zeppelin L 6* showing damage to her forward section from a previous accident.

hour at an estimated height of 10,000 feet. It dropped three HE bombs – one falling in the Duke of York's School, where some windows were broken and telephone wires cut. No other damage and no casualties were reported. The aeroplane was heavily fired upon by anti-aircraft guns. One round was observed to burst near to it, but no result was observed as it continued out to sea pursued by two Royal Flying Corps aeroplanes – flown by Captain Williams and Major Christie – but lost the enemy in clouds at 11,000 feet. The raider was subsequently observed off Deal, where it was again fired upon by anti-aircraft guns.

Anti-aircraft guns in action and reported use of ammunition:

Location of AA battery	Calibre or type of gun	Number / type of rounds fired
Dover		
Frith Farm	12 pdr 12-cwt	27 HE rounds
Citadel	2" 20-cwt	6 HE rounds
Fort Burgoyne	2× 6 pdr Hotchkiss	29 day tracer rounds
Langdon Battery	3" (naval)	19 TNT rounds, 12 shrapnel rounds
East Arm (Naval)	6"	3 rounds
Prince of Wales (Naval)	6"	3 rounds
Deal		
No.1 Section	12 pdr	8 HE rounds

The Royal Naval Air Service launched eight aircraft from Dover, Maidstone, Grain and Westgate aerodromes, while the Royal Flying Corps sent up two aeroplanes from Dover.

23 September 1916

Weather: calm and fair, with a morning fog or mist. Wind over the southern part of the North Sea at 1,500 feet was between 10 to 15 miles per hour; direction south and south-east. During the night, the wind was calm on the East Coast.

Eleven Zeppelins – consisting of *Zeppelins L 13*, *L 14*, *L 16*, *L 17*, *L 21*, *L 22*, *L 23*, *L 30*, *L 31*, *L 32* and *L 33* – took to the skies from their bases in Germany to raid targets in England situated between the Humber Estuary and South Kent Coast, but *L 16* and *L 23* turned back before crossing the coast.

Kapitänleutnant Martin Dietrich – commanding *Zeppelin L 22* – was off Kilnsea, Yorkshire at 2225 on 23 September and dropped three bombs in the sea. He passed over the Spurn Lighthouse at 2235 and dropped two HE bombs close to the searchlight and three more near the Spurn anti-aircraft gun, which had just gone into action. The airship then went across the estuary to the Lincolnshire Coast – dropping three

HE bombs in the sea – and came in over Donna Nook (again dropping three more HE bombs in the sea). Passing over North Somercotes, two incendiary bombs were dropped at 2240. Steering west, she dropped five incendiary bombs at Grainthorpe and another one on Fulstow. She then turned south-west to Utterby, where another two incendiary bombs fell. The airship then drifted around over the area before dropping an incendiary bomb at Caistor at 2320. Turning east, she passed south of Donna Nook at 2335 and passed out to sea and onto Germany.

An unidentified airship (probably *Zeppelin L 23*, commanded by *Kapitänleutnant* Wilhelm Ganzel) came in over the Lincolnshire Coast near Mablethorpe at 2300 on 23 September having dropped some bombs in the sea at 2240. Her course was not tracked until at 2345 when she dropped an incendiary bomb at Glentham (10 miles east of Gainsborough). She then drifted between Grimsby and Gainsborough – evidently looking for a particular target. Two more incendiary bombs were dropped at Kingerby (north-west of Market Rasen) at 0025 before heading north. At 0035, 19 HE and 11 incendiary bombs fell at Scarthoe (south-east of Grimsby) – slightly damaging a few buildings. The airship was then engaged by the anti-aircraft guns situated at Scarthoe Top and Cleefields before going out to sea at 0040.

Zeppelin L 14, commanded by *Hauptmann* Kuno Manger, came in over between Mablethorpe and Skegness, Lincolnshire in company with *Zeppelin L 17* at 2200 on 23 September. Both airships headed west for Lincoln, with an HE bomb being dropped on Waddington on the way. As both of the airships approached Lincoln at 2245 the Washingborough searchlight and Canwick gun opened up on *Zeppelin L 14* (which did not attempt to cross over Lincoln, but emptied her whole cargo of bombs over the searchlight, which the commander may have presumed to have been Lincoln). The village of Greetwell received 15 HE bombs and Washingborough 12 HE bombs, while neighbouring Heighton received 17 incendiary bombs. At Greetwell, a few railway telegraph wires were broken and a sheep killed; at Washingborough, a fowl house was demolished, an orchard torn up and some outbuildings damaged. After this, the airship turned back to the east and passed out to sea at about 2330 at Sutton.

Zeppelin L 17, commanded by *Kapitänleutnant* Hermann Kraushaar (having parted company with *Zeppelin L 14*), continued over Lincoln at 2250 and then turned south-west towards Nottingham. Travelling slowly to make sure of her course, the Zeppelin circled in the neighbourhood of Newark at 2350 and at midnight dropped an incendiary bomb at North Muskham, but it fell in the River Trent. At 0034 two HE and four incendiary bombs were dropped in the region of the Great Northern Railway goods sidings at Colwick, but fell in fields. Soon after, six more HE bombs fell in fields between Colwick and Sneinton. The anti-aircraft defences at Nottingham were now fully prepared, but the Sneinton gun and searchlight lost their telephone lines due to one of the previous bombs severing the cable. The Zeppelin then proceeded to drop eight HE and 11 incendiary bombs on Nottingham – causing considerable damage (killing three and injuring 11). The Midland Railway Goods Station was seriously damaged along with the Great Central Station – and tracks suffered some damage. A chapel was set on fire; three houses were wrecked; and three more houses and three shops – along with a public house – were seriously damaged. Leaving Nottingham at 0049 the airship passed over Mapperley – dropping an HE bomb before returning to Lincoln (and continuing in a north-easterly direction to Grimsby) at 0120. Here she dropped a number of bombs in the Humber before turning east and passing out to sea over Spurn Head at 0200. It was estimated that during her flight over England, the airship was flying at about 9,000 feet as while she was over Nottingham, she was never sighted.

The fourth airship to visit Lincolnshire this night was *Zeppelin L 13*, which crossed the coast north of Skegness at 2230 on 23 September (following in the wake of *Zeppelins L 14* and *L 17*). Her commander, *Kapitänleutnant* Franz G Eichler, navigated her past Wainfleet and hovered in the vicinity of Boston for a while before making off in the direction of Sleaford. At 2350 she was engaged by an aeroplane that had been sent up from Cranwell Aerodrome and the Rauceby gun. On being fired at by the anti-aircraft gun, her response was to drop an incendiary bomb at Silk Willoughby and another four at Holdingham – followed by 13 HE bombs on Rauceby. The sole result of this barrage of bombs was damage to a house and some farm buildings at Rauceby. The airship then went about and after dropping seven incendiary bombs at Lesasingham, made off towards the East Coast – crossing out to sea near Wainfleet at 0015. She then followed the coastline northwards towards the Spurn, where at 0043 she was engaged by an anti-aircraft gun and a hit was claimed. She also probably dropped her remaining bomb load in the sea at this point, as a number of explosions were heard.

Zeppelin L 30, commanded by *Kapitänleutnant* Horst von Buttlar, appeared to make a half-hearted attack on the Norfolk Coast – having passed the *Haisboro Lightship* at 2035 on 23 September – and was heard dropping bombs in the sea north of Cromer at 2055. She then approached land and dropped a number of bombs at Overstrand – none of which fell on the shore. She was then heard to drop a further 10 HE bombs in the sea between 2055 and 2205 and then went off eastwards.

Zeppelin L 21, commanded by *Oberleutnant zur See* Kurt Frankenburg, was initially heard at sea east of Aldeburgh, Suffolk at 2135 on 23 September – steering south-west – and passed landward of Orfordness at 2140. Here she circled before heading on a westerly course – dropping a flare at Letheringham at 2200 and a fuel tank at Crowfield at 2223. Two minutes later, a second fuel tank landed at Stonham Parva before the Zeppelin turned south to Coddenham, where an HE bomb was dropped – causing no damage. She passed the River Gipping and then followed it north-west to Needham Market, where an incendiary bomb fell at 2237. Two minutes later, she dropped two HE bombs at Badley, crossed the river to the north and was engaged by the Stowmarket anti-aircraft guns (which fired 25 rounds at her) before she dropped 16 HE and 10 incendiary bombs at Creeting St Peter and five HE and one incendiary at Stowupland. Damage was caused to a farmhouse at Badley, while at Creeting St Peter, five pigs were killed and farm buildings damaged. The airship then went off directly east (to the coast to Saxmundham) before turning north and following the coast to Southwold – turning due east out to sea.

Zeppelin L 33 passed into the Thames Estuary (north of the *Black Deep Lightship*) at 2200 on 23 September and was fired at by a naval destroyer in the Edinburgh Channel before coming overland over Foulness, Essex at 2240 and dropping one incendiary bomb on South Fambridge and a flare over the south of Brentwood at 2335. At 2340 four incendiary bombs fell at Upminster Common. Ten minutes later, six HE bombs fell at South Hornchurch and at 2355 a flare was dropped over Chadwell Heath, Essex. While being subjected to heavy and accurate anti-aircraft fire as she neared London, the Zeppelin dropped a 100 kg HE and five incendiary bombs on St Leonards Street and Empson Street in Bromley, Kent – wrecking four houses, killing six people and injuring 11. Soon after, one 50 kg HE fell on Spratt's Dog Biscuit Factory, with one 300 kg, one 100 kg and two 50 kg HE bombs falling on the North London Railway Carriage Depot and the Overtime Tractor Company's premises at Bow. This caused considerable damage to sheds, a boiler house and railway rolling-stock. At 0012 a 50 kg HE fell on the Particular Baptist Chapel, Botolph Street and a 100 kg HE hit the Black Swan public house at the corner of Devons Road and Bow Road – wrecking the pub and neighbouring buildings and killing three women and two children (as well as injuring 11). At 0015 a 100 kg HE bomb fell at the junction of Old Ford Road and Wrexham Road near Stratford, Essex and an incendiary bomb fell in Brickfield Road (soon to be followed by a 100 kg HE bomb on Cook's Soap Works, but this failed to explode). Two 50 kg HE also fell on The British Petroleum Works at Marsh Gate Lane – causing severe damage and severing an 18 inch water main; then seven 50 kg HE bombs fell on the Stratford Marshes, with another 50 kg HE bomb and an incendiary bomb falling on Messrs Judd's Match Factory – setting fire to the building. At 0015 the Zeppelin made off in a north-easterly direction – passing over Buckhurst Hill with the sound of its engines running rough before being fired at by a 13 pounder anti-aircraft gun sited on Kelvedon Common, Essex while at 9,000 feet. At 0030 the airship was attacked by Second Lieutenant Alfred de Bathe Brandon in a BE2c of 39 HD [Home Defence] Squadron, Royal Flying Corps but the crew claimed to have failed to notice this – claiming that the ship had been punctured by an anti-aircraft shell. Rapidly losing gas, the crew started jettisoning cargo at Bromfield. Spare parts, two aluminium cartridge boxes and a leather machine-gun case landed at Boreham, while at 0100 a second machine-gun was dropped over the grounds of "Monctons", Wickham Bishops and a third machine-gun at Gate House Farm in Tiptree, Essex. At 0105 with the airship nearing the ground, a fourth machine-gun was jettisoned. At 0115 the Zeppelin passed over the coast near West Mersea, Essex but soon turned back and landed in a field – severely damaging the forward gondola. Following a small explosion, the ship caught fire, but only the outer envelope burnt away and the framework partly collapsed amidships. It was probable that many bombs had been dropped at the mouth of the Thames on her way over, as the 26 that were dropped overland was much less than was carried by this type of airship.

Lieutenant Alfred de Bathe Brandon was to join the small band of British heroes who were responsible for shooting down – or claiming a share in the demise of – the German airship raiders.

Kapitänleutnant Böcker and his crew were lucky to survive being brought down during operations – although in an attempt to destroy their airship by setting fire to it, they only managed to burn the outer envelope and gas bags (leaving much of the framework intact).

Some of the captured crew from *Zeppelin L 33* are led off under guard down a Suffolk street.

Zeppelin L 33 / LZ 76. Type R.
0120: Crashed at Knapps Field, Little Wigborough, Essex.
Kapitänleutnant Alois Böcker: Reservist; repatriated via Switzerland 27 November 1917.
Leutnant zur See Ernst Schirlitz: Active.
Oberdeckoffizier Carl Schunemann: Reservist.
Deckoffizier Wilhelm Jensen: *Seewehr II.*
Funkentelegraphistenmaat Peter Morsdorf: Active.
Unteroffizier Segelmacher Hermann Melchen: Active.
Obersignalmaat Max Emmerlich: *Seewehr II.*
Obersignalmaat Ernst Reiche: Active.
Maschinistenmaat Arthur Piepkorn.
Obermaschinistenmaat Adolf Schultz: *Seewehr I*; repatriated via Switzerland 14 December 1916.
Obermaschinistenmaat Max Tanzer: *Seewehr I.*
Obermaschinistenmaat August Bossler: Active.
Obermaschinistenmaat Johannes Herrmann: *Seewehr.*
Obermaschinistenmaat Heinrich Balzer: *Seewehr II.*
Obermaschinistenmaat Friedrich Wiese: *Seewehr I.*
Obermaschinistenmaat Emil Langmann: *Seewehr II.*
Obermaschinistenmaat Peter Wirth: *Seewehr I*; died 1 May 1917 (NKG).
Obermaschinistenmaat Karl Sogtrup: *Seewehr II.*
Maschinistenmaat Wilhelm Gartner: *Seewehr I.*
Oberbootsmannsmaat Emil Diercke: *Seewehr II.*
Oberbootsmannsmaat Hermann Wolff: Reserve.
Obermaschinistanwärter Joseph Niebus.

It was recorded in the 39 Home Defence Squadron history:

> At about half-past 12, when approaching Chelmsford, the *L 33* was attacked by 2Lt A de B Brandon of No.39 Squadron, who was up on patrol between Hainault and Suttons Farm. Brandon hung onto her for 20 minutes – firing at every available opportunity – but although he saw his shots bursting all along her body, the airship did not catch fire. After this combat, the *L 33* rapidly began to lose gas and height as a result of serious injuries from the guns of the London defences. She went out to sea at West Mercia at a quarter-past one, but came back and landed in a field between Little Wigborough and Peldon. There she took fire, but owing to the great loss of gas, she was not badly burnt.

Second Lieutenant Brandon, Hainault Farm, recorded in his report:

> I have to report that I left Hainault at 11.33pm on the 23rd instant with orders to patrol between Hainault and Suttons Farm. At 12.12 I saw a Zeppelin in

> the searchlights some distance away and made for it. Very shortly after this, it escaped from the searchlights and I lost it, but I continued on and picked it up again. I went on climbing and managed, with some difficulty, to keep it in view, as there were no searchlights on it and my automatic pump had failed and I had to work the cocking handle of the Lewis gun. After putting on a drum of ammunition, I came up behind the Zeppelin – and on raising the gun, jerked it out of the mounting; the gun and the yoke falling across the nacelle. I managed to replace the gun, but in the meantime, had passed under and past the Zepp. I turned and passed along it again, but from the bow, but we passed each other too quickly for me to aim. On turning, I came up from behind and fixed a drum of ammunition. The Brock ammunition seemed to be bursting all along it, but the Zepp did not catch fire. I was using Brock, Pomeroy and Sparklet. I turned again and put on a fresh drum and came up from behind and fired again. The gun jammed after about nine rounds. I now decided to get above the Zepp and went on climbing, but there was a large bank of grey cloud all around the horizon and it was impossible to see the Zepp against it after I had got level with the Zepp. I first saw the Zepp at 12.13 and lost it at 12.33. I continued to patrol in various directions owing to having lost my bearings. I was about 10,200 when attacking the Zepp – and I should say the Zepp was about 1,000 to 1,200 feet higher.

The Air Department report concluded:

> There can be little doubt that during the bombardment over East London, one propeller had been damaged and a shell had passed through her body. She also began to lose gas, though not rapidly, through punctures caused by shell splinters. In getting out of the rays of the searchlight at Kelvedon Common, she attempted to climb rapidly and appeared to release a smoke cloud. At about 12.30 she was attacked by 2nd Lieutenant (now Captain) A de B Brandon, Royal Flying Corps, but his bullets failed in their purpose of bringing her down. The majority of the prisoners of *L 33* were vague as to the aeroplane attack, which apparently passed more or less unnoticed by them, but are unanimous that the ship was pierced by a shell shortly after leaving the river (i.e. over East London).
>
> The crew of this ship had previously manned *Zeppelin L 14* – under *Kapitänleutnant* Böcker – and the *L 14* must certainly be looked upon as one of the most boldly-handled airships possessed by the German Navy between August 1915 and May 1916. Her record of raids throughout this period is a striking one: she had bombed Edinburgh, Skinningrove, Hull and the city of London – and had taken part in several other lesser raids. On 13 October 1915 she had nearly collided with *L 13* when near Woolwich. The loss of this commander to the German airship service is undoubtedly a serious one. He was a bold navigator and had a good crew with him – every man of which had undergone at least 12 months' service in the Naval Air Squadron.

The size of a Zeppelin is readily illustrated by this photograph in comparison to a house. Although the centre section of *Zeppelin L 33* collapsed under its own weight, much information could be obtained about the complex construction of the Zeppelin airships, which was to prove useful in the British post-war airship programme.

An illustration of how the fuel tanks of a Zeppelin were arranged (suspended either side of the central walkway) so, if needed, they could be quickly jettisoned to save weight.

A view of one of the rear engine gondolas of *Zeppelin L 33*.Notable points is the radiator, which could be raised or lowered into the slipstream to increase or decrease cooling, and also the shrouded exhaust pipe.

Zeppelins L 32 and L 31 followed the coast down from Germany and into Belgium before passing through the Straits of Dover at 2250 on 23 September. *Zeppelin L 32* crossed the English Coast at Dungeness, Kent – dropping six HE bombs (two of which fell in the sea, but the others wrecked a house). She then hovered for some time over Romney Marsh as if unsure of how to proceed before heading west – passing over Tunbridge Wells at 0010 and then bearing round to the north. She dropped an incendiary bomb at Ide Hill (near Sevenoaks) at 0030. Twenty minutes later, seven HE bombs fell near the Crockenhill Searchlight Battery, which had just illuminated the airship. The Zeppelin passed over Dartford, crossed the Thames east of Purfleet at 0100 and was at once picked up by the searchlights and anti-aircraft guns north of the river; the gunners claiming two direct hits. In response, the airship dropped nine 100 kg HE and six incendiary bombs – soon to be followed by 23 HE (including two of 300 kg and eight of 100 kg) and 21 incendiary bombs at South Ockendon, Essex. They caused limited damage – injuring two horses. At 0110 the airship was found and attacked by Second Lieutenant Frederick Sowery, Royal Flying Corps – in BE2c no.4112 of 39 HD Squadron – who, with his third drum of Lewis gun ·303 ammunition, set the airship alight in several places before it fell in flames; the wreckage burning for 45 minutes. Lieutenant Brandon, who saw the combat from his aeroplane some distance off (alluding to the airman's attack), said that the airship looked as if she were 'being hosed with a stream of fire'. The catastrophe was seen from a very great distance – being even observed by a British submarine in the Straits of Dover.

Zeppelin L 32 / LZ 74. Type R.
0110: Snail's Hall Farm, Great Burstead (near Billericay, Essex).
Oberleutnant zur See Werner Peterson +. CC.
Leutnant zur See Karl Brodrück +. CC.
Obersignalmaat Adolf Bley +. CC.
Obermaschinistenmaat Albin Bocksch +. CC.
Funkentelegraphistenobermaat Karl Bortscheller +. CC.
Oberheizer Wilhelm Brockhaus +. CC.
Maschinistenmaat Paul Dorfmüller +. CC.
Obermaschinistenmaat Richard Fankhänel +. CC.
Obermaschinistenmaat Georg Hagedorn +. CC.
Oberbootsmannsmaat Friedrich Heider +. CC.
Funkentelegraphistengast Robert Klisch +. CC.
Obermaschinistenmaat Hermann Maegdlfrau +. CC.
Obersegelmachersgast Bernhard Mohr +. CC.
Matrose August Müller +. CC.
Bootsmannsmaat Friedrich Pasche +. CC.
Obermaschinistenmaat Karl Paust +. CC.
Obersignalmaat Ewald Picard +. CC.
Maschinistenmaat Walter Pruss +. CC.
Obermatrose Paul Schiering +. CC.
Steuermann Bernhard Schreibmüller +. CC.
Obermaschinistenmaat Karl Völker +. CC.
Obermaschinistenmaat Wilhelm Wirth +. CC.
Oberbootsmannmaat Alfred Zöpel +. CC.[16]

In his report of the action, Second Lieutenant F Sowrey wrote:

> At 11.25pm I received orders to patrol between Suttons Farm and Joyce Green – and at 11.30pm I left the aerodrome. The weather was clear, with a few thin clouds at 3,000 feet. At 4,000 feet, I passed another machine proceeding in a

16 All the crew are buried in a communal grave at the Deutschen Soldatenfriedhof, Cannock Chase, Staffordshire. German sources also stated that Steuermann Christian Jensen was also killed / missing.

Breaking into two major portions on the way down, the rear section of *Zeppelin L 32* fell on a tree – which is a prominent landmark in most photographs – while the forward section and control gondola fell close by in a field.

The forward portion – including the control gondola of *Zeppelin L 32*.

northerly direction. I was then flying due south. I continued climbing as hard as possible and at 12.10am I noticed an enemy airship in a southerly direction. It appeared to be over Woolwich. I made for the airship at once, but before I could reach it, the searchlights lost it. I was – at this time – at 8,000 feet. There was a certain amount of gun fire, but it was not intense. I continued climbing and reached a height of 13,000 feet. I was still patrolling between Suttons Farm and Joyce Green. At 12.45am I noticed an enemy airship in an easterly direction. I at once made in that direction and manoeuvred into a position underneath. The airship was well-lighted by searchlights, but there was not a sign of any gun fire. I could distinctly see the propellers revolving and the airship was manoeuvring to avoid the searchlight beams. I fired at it. The first two drums of ammunition had apparently no effect, but the third one caused the envelope to catch on fire in several places; in the centre and front. All firing was traversing fire along the envelope. The drums were loaded with a mixture of Brock, Pomeroy and tracer ammunition. I watched the burning airship strike the ground and then proceeded to find my flares. I landed at Suttons Farm at 1.40am, 24th instant. My machine was BE2c 4112. After seeing the Zeppelin had caught on fire, I fired a red Very's light.

Second Lieutenant Frederick Sowery, who was responsible for the demise of *Zeppelin L 32*, poses with Lieutenant W M L Robinson of *Schütte-Lanz SL 11* fame – both of 39 HD Squadron. Frederick Sowery remained in the post-war RAF – rising to the rank of Group Captain before retiring in 1940.

Zeppelin L 31, commanded by *Kapitänleutnant* Heinrich Mathy, crossed the English Coast near Rye, Sussex at 2300 on 23 September and followed a fairly west-south-west course towards London – passing Tunbridge Wells, Oxted and Mitcham (evidently reserving all her bombs for the capital). The airship was over Caterham at 0015 and was being illuminated by the searchlights of the south-eastern defences. In response, her commander dropped illuminating flares to blanket out the effects of the searchlights. A 4 inch quick-firing anti-aircraft gun at Croydon opened fire on her, but only at the rate of one round a minute, and was soon outranged as the airship appeared to be flying at about 12,000 feet – and fast. At 0025 the airship started her bombing by dropping four HE bombs on Kenley – damaging three houses and injuring two people. After dropping two HE and two incendiary bombs on two farms at Mitcham, the airship started her bombing of London – heading directly northwards. Streatham was hit by 10 HE and 22 incendiary bombs falling in quick succession. At Streatham Common Railway Station, a signal box, tracks and rolling-stock were damaged. Further serious damage was caused in the area to 14 houses (four of which were wrecked) and 10 shops, with seven killed and 27 injured. Six of those killed were in a tram which was hit by shrapnel from a 300 kg bomb on Streatham Hill. The airship then followed the line of the main road through Streatham and Brixton Hill to Kennington, with six HE (one being a 100 kg) and 17 incendiary bombs falling on Brixton – wrecking one house and seriously damaging a garage, 21 houses and 21 shops. A further 40 houses were slightly damaged. Seven people were killed and 17 were injured. At Kennington, an HE bomb fell – the blast shattering numerous windows. The airship now crossed over the Thames (east of London Bridge) at 0040 and at 0046 dropped 10 HE bombs on Lea Bridge Road and Leyton – causing serious damage to 12 houses; killing eight people and injuring 31. As the mist had risen, the airship was invisible to all the anti-aircraft guns north of the Thames and they did not open fire on her. She headed off in a north-eastern direction towards Norfolk and the coast – finally passing out into the North Sea over Yarmouth at 0215 (although she was fired at by the Fritton guns and a warship). At 0220 she was sighted by the crew of the *Cross Sand Lightship* – heading east at a great height.

A house near to Streatham Hill Railway Station received considerable blast damage from a 300 kg bomb that landed nearby and killed six civilians who were travelling in a tram.

Considerable damage was caused to properties in Brixton – a terraced house in Baytree Road being totally demolished.

Summary for the night of 23-24 September 1916:

Location	Number and type of bombs dropped	Casualties	Damage
London			
Streatham	10× HE, 22× IB	7 killed, 28 injured	4 houses wrecked; 10 houses and 10 shops, 2 railway stations and a signal box seriously damaged; 165 houses and shops slightly damaged
Brixton	6× HE, 17× IB	7 killed, 16 injured	1 house wrecked; 21 houses, 21 shops and 1 garage seriously damaged; 40 houses and shops damaged
Kennington	1× HE	1 injured	

Location	Number and type of bombs dropped	Casualties	Damage
Bromley East	1× HE, 6× IB	6 killed, 12 injured	4 houses wrecked; railway sheds and rolling-stock damaged; 60 houses damaged
Bow	9× HE, 1× IB	5 killed, 13 injured	2 houses wrecked
Kent			
Dungeness	4× HE		1 house wrecked; 1 damaged
Ide Hill	1× IB		Windows broken
Crockenhill	7× HE		
Surrey			
Kenley	4× HE	2 injured	3 houses seriously damaged
Mitcham	2× HE, 2× IB		9 houses slightly damaged
Essex			
Stratford	10× HE	1 injured	1 factory destroyed; 1 seriously damaged
Lea Bridge	4× HE	3 killed, 16 injured	125 houses and police station damaged
Leyton	6× HE	5 killed, 11 injured	11 houses seriously damaged
Aveley	9× HE, 6× IB		Windows broken
South Farnbridge	1× IB		
South Hornchurch	6× HE		
South Ockendon	23× HE, 21× IB		Windows broken; 2 horses injured
Upminster	4× IB		
Suffolk			
Coddenham	1× HE		
Needham Market	1× IB		
Badley	2× HE		Railway telegraph wires and farmhouse damaged
Greeting St Peter	16× HE, 10× IB		Farmhouse damaged; 5 pigs killed
Stowupland	5× HE, 1× IB		

Location	Number and type of bombs dropped	Casualties	Damage
Lincolnshire			
Silk Willoughby	1× IB		
Holdingham	4× IB		
Lessingham	7× IB		
Rauceby	13× HE		Farm buildings and house slightly damaged
Waddington	1× HE		
Greetwell	15× HE		Railway telegtraph wires and windows broken; 1 sheep killed
Washingborough	12× HE		Fowl house demolished; damage to orchard and outbuilding
Heighington	15× IB		
Glentham	1× IB		
Kingerby	2× IB		
Caistor	1× IB		
Utterby	2× IB		
Grainthorpe	5× IB		
Fulstow	1× IB		
North Somercotes	2× IB		
Scarthoe	19× HE, 11× IB		Slight damage to church roof; windows in village broken
Nottinghamshire:			
North Muskham	1× IB		
Colwick	2× HE, 4× IB		
Sneinton	6× HE		Glass broken; military telephone wires cut
Nottingham	8× HE, 11× IB	3 killed, 16 injured	MR goods yard seriously damaged; GCR station slightly damaged; 3 houses wrecked; 4 houses and 3 shops seriously damaged; 3 shops and 3 houses slightly damaged
Mapperley	1× HE		1 house seriously damaged

Location	Number and type of bombs dropped	Casualties	Damage
Yorkshire			
Spurn	5× HE		
Total	208× HE, 163× IB (at least 29 HE bombs were dropped into the sea at various points)	36 killed, 116 injured	

To the list of casualties must be added those attributable to anti-aircraft shells. These were all in the London District:

Location	Number and type of bombs dropped	Casualties	Damage
Leyton		3 injured	
Canning Town		2 killed, 5 injured	
Plaistow		2 injured	
Hoxton		1 killed, 3 injured	

A Royal Flying Corps pilot at Thetford, a soldier at Sandwich and another soldier stationed at Scarthoe Top were all slightly wounded by falling shrapnel. One soldier was killed and three were injured in a gun accident at Southern Outfall, with a further four injured in another gun accident at Nottingham.

Location	Number and type of bombs dropped	Casualties	Damage
Total casualties for			
London		28 killed, 80 injured	
Nottingham		3 killed, 20 injured	
Elsewhere		10 killed, 38 injured	
Total		41 killed, 138 injured	

Anti-aircraft guns in action and reported use of ammunition:

Location of AA battery	Calibre or type of gun	Number / type of rounds fired
Shenfield Common	2× 13 pdr 6-cwt.	2 HE rounds – 1 hit claimed
Kelvendon Common	13 pdr 9-cwt	4 HE rounds – 2 direct hits claimed
Victoria Park	2× 3"	34 HE rounds
Tunnel Farm	2× 3" 20-cwt	34 HE rounds – 2 hits claimed
Beckton	4.7" mark IVb	3 CS rounds
Wanstead	3" QF	11 HE rounds
Belhus Park	3" 20-cwt	10 HE rounds
Clapton	3" 20-cwt	3 HE rounds
West Ham	3" 20-cwt	18 HE rounds
Tilbury	12 pdr 12-cwt	14 shrapnel rounds
Fobbing	12 pdr 12-cwt	3 shrapnel rounds
Shonks	3" 20-cwt	17 rounds – 3 shrapnel, 14 HE
Tower Bridge	3" semi-automatic	9 shrapnel HE rounds
Meath Gardens	2× 6 pdr Hotchkiss	18 shrapnel CS rounds
Blackwall	2× 3" 20-cwt	21 shrapnel HE rounds
Deptford Park	2× 75 mm	23 shrapnel FHE rounds shrapnel – 2 hits claimed
Shooter's Hill	2× 3" 20-cwt	8 shrapnel HE rounds
Southern Outfall	2× 3" 5-cwt	10 shrapnel rounds (breech-block of gun blew out – killing 1 and wounding 3)
Southfleet	12 pdr 12-cwt	5 shrapnel HE rounds
Croydon	4" QF mark I×	2 CS rounds
Stowmarket	2× 3"	25 HE rounds
Fritton	2× 3 pdr	11 HE rounds
Yarmouth	2× 3 pdr	-
Cranwell (Sleaford)	2× 6 pdr Nordenfelt (mob)	23 CS rounds
Canwick (Lincoln)	12 pdr 12-cwt	19 HE rounds
Scarthoe Top	3 pdr 20-cwt	4 shrapnel rounds
Cleefields	12 pdr 12-cwt	3 shrapnel rounds
Spurn	3 pdr Vickers	128 HE rounds

The Royal Naval Air Service sent up 11 aeroplanes to intercept the raiders. The pilot of Seaplane no.8074 from Yarmouth reported attacking an airship 45 miles east of Yarmouth, but with no result. The pilot of Seaplane no.8149 – also flying from Yarmouth – attacked an airship 30 miles east of Lowestoft and fired one tray of bullets at it (possibly *Zeppelin L 21* or *L 23*).

The Royal Flying Corps sent up 12 aircraft and Second Lieutenant Sowery attacked and brought down *Zeppelin L 32* at Billericay. Second Lieutenant Brandon attacked *Zeppelin L 33* without success. Second Lieutenant Michael H Francis Thunderer,[17] Royal Flying Corps of 51 Squadron was killed in an accident on take-off from Thetford Aerodrome.

25 September 1916

Weather: a south-east wind along the East Coast increased slightly in force during the day, but died down again – being less than 15 miles per hour by midnight.

During the afternoon of 25 September eight airships left their sheds to attack England. These were *Zeppelins L 13, L 14, L 16, L 21, L 22, L 23, L 30* and *L 31*, but *L 13* returned to base while *L 23* and *L 30* confined their operations to manoeuvring off the Norfolk Coast. *Zeppelins L 30* and *L 31* came overland across Belgium – along with two army airships – and were sighted off the Straits of Dover and off the Belgian Coast during the early morning, which may have been a cover for U-boats entering the Channel.

Zeppelins L 14 and *L 16* crossed the Yorkshire Coast almost simultaneously at about 2205 at Bridlington Bay. *Zeppelin L 16* passed Driffield, Huggate and Malton – but at this point, her commander (*Kapitänleutnant* Erich Sommerfeldt) decided to return to the coast and dropped an incendiary bomb on Velmire Farm, Whitwell-on-the-Hill at 2250 and another on Langtoft at 2300. She then headed in the direction of Scarborough – dropping a few flares; then turning south and dropping a third incendiary bomb at North Burton at 2330. At 2340 the airship was engaged by the Bessingby gun, which fired a single round even though the Zeppelin was invisible. It was estimated to be flying at 12,000 feet – only being located by sound. She made her way to Speeton, Filey Bay where she passed out to sea at 2355 (probably dropping the rest of her bomb load in the sea).

Zeppelin L 14, being commanded by *Hauptmann* Kuno Manger, crossed the coast at Atwick, Yorkshire and appeared to follow the railway line towards York. At 2245 the raider approached the city from the north-east and dropped an HE bomb at Heworth before passing south over the eastern part of the city. Here, seven HE and two incendiary bombs were dropped en route, which wrecked a house. Still heading south, a further two HE and five incendiary bombs were dropped on Fulford, which damaged telephone wires. The airship was then engaged by the 3 inch anti-aircraft gun at Acomb, which fired five rounds – causing her to turn to the north – and at 2315 an incendiary bomb fell at Pilmoor. The airship then turned to the south-west and

17 Second Lieutenant Michael Hubert Francis Thunderer, Royal Flying Corps, aged 34: buried Ramsgate (St Augustine) Roman Catholic Churchyard, Kent.

dropped one HE bomb at Newby-with-Mulwith and four HE bombs on Ripon rifle ranges at Wormald Green at 2340; then turning south, she passed Killinghall Camp (near Harrogate) just after midnight and dropped four HE bombs at Dunkeswell at 0015 on the Royal Flying Corps landing ground. At Harewood, 13 incendiary bombs fell at 0020 – causing slight damage to an outhouse. The airship, which was heading east, was then picked up by a mobile searchlight at Collingham and headed straight for the source of the beam -dropping three HE bombs (one of which broke telephone wires). The associated anti-aircraft gun fired nine rounds and the airship then went off to the north-east – passing out to sea at Scarborough at 0130.

Zeppelin L 21 crossed the English Coast at Sutton-on-Sea, Lincolnshire at 2145 and followed a course to the east and Sheffield, which she passed to the north and disappeared over the Peak District. She was next heard at Todmorden, Lancashire at 2355 and then between Lumb and Newchurch, where she dropped two incendiary bombs at midnight. Her commander, *Oberleutnant zur See* Kurt Frankenburg, then turned her south-west and bombed the railway at Rawtenstall with two HE bombs; then the airship headed to Haslingden and followed the railway line south – dropping seven HE bombs at Holcombe which damaged the post office and injured a woman. Further down the valley, two HE and two incendiary bombs fell at Holcombe Brook. The raider was next heard over Bolton, where she dropped nine HE and 11 incendiary bombs – killing 12 and injuring nine people at 0045. Six houses were destroyed and another six were badly damaged, along with a church. One small fire was also started at a mill, but soon brought under control. From here, the Zeppelin turned north to Blackburn before turning to the north-east – dropping an HE bomb at 0135 on Bolton Abbey (which failed to explode) as she continued her course towards the sea. She crossed the coast at Whitby at 0305.

Zeppelin L 22 came in over the Lincolnshire Coast at 2230 and dropped an incendiary bomb at Maltby-le-Marsh soon after before another incendiary bomb fell at Market Rasen at 2315. *Kapitänleutnant* Martin Dietrich guided her towards Sheffield, where she then dropped seven incendiary bombs near Tinsley Park Colliery at 0015. She then followed the railway towards Sheffield and passed diagonally across the Attercliffe and Brightside districts of the city – dropping 15 HE and 15 incendiary bombs (one dropping through the roof of a machine shop of Messrs John Brown & Company's Atlas Works – causing a slight fire). In all, nine houses and a chapel were destroyed and another 62 houses were damaged, with 28 people being killed and 19 injured. The airship was flying at a great height and was invisible from the ground – although the first five HE and three incendiary bombs dropped fell close to an anti-aircraft gun site. The 3 inch gun at Shire Green fired two rounds almost blindly in the direction of the raider – causing her to turn back to the east and the coast and altering course a couple of times as if verifying her position. At 0130 she was heard over Killingham steering towards Grimsby and at 0140 was fired at by the Chase Hill anti-aircraft gun, which fired one round. Two minutes later, when over the Humber, another single round was fired by HMS *Patrol*. The airship headed inland (presumably to avoid the warship) and crossed the river at Immingham – heading north-north-east and dropping bombs into the water as she went before being fired at by the Sutton, Marfleet and Harpings anti-aircraft guns. She eventually passed out to sea west of Grimston Hall at 0205.

Zeppelin L 23 was sighted about 30 miles out to sea off the Norfolk Coast at 2000 and five bombs were heard from Cromer to fall into the sea. No further sightings were made.

Zeppelin L 30 was also sighted off the Norfolk Coast at Cromer at 2015 and approached Yarmouth. She then proceeded to course up and down the coast a few times – dropping bombs as she went into the sea. At 0100 the airship was sighted off the Dutch Coast heading back towards Germany.

Zeppelin L 31 and *Kapitänleutnant* Heinrich Mathy came in down the Straits of Dover and passed Hastings, Sussex at 2205. She was sighted off Selsey Bill at 2316 before heading to the Isle of Wight, where she dropped a flare and turned north over Sandown. She passed Ryde and headed directly for Portsmouth Harbour, which she passed over at 2350 – coming under sustained anti-aircraft fire. Passing over Porchester and Fort Southwick (where a flare was dropped), she continued towards Petersfield before bearing round to the east – hovering over Burgess Hill at 0040 while her commander verified his position. The airship then followed the coast past Hastings, Rye and Dungeness into the Channel and the Straits of Dover to Belgium at 0225. At 0230 some bombs were dropped in the region of some warships.

Army *Zeppelin LZ ?* was sighted in the Straits of Dover at 2335 and followed the coast as far as Pevensey, Sussex before turning back towards the east without dropping any bombs.

Summary for the night of 25-26 September 1916:

Location	Number and type of bombs dropped	Casualties	Damage
Yorkshire			
York	7× HE, 2× IB		House wrecked
Heworth	1× HE		Windows broken
Fulford	2× HE, 5× IB		Windows broken
Pilmoor	1× IB		
Newby-with-Mulwith	1× HE		
Wormald Green	4× HE		
Dunkeswick	4× HE		
Harewood	13× IB		
Collingham	3× HE		
Bolton Abbey	1× HE		

Location	Number and type of bombs dropped	Casualties	Damage
Sheffield	15× HE, 15× IB	29 killed, 21 injured	9 houses and chapel destroyed; 62 houses damaged
Tinsley Park	7× IB		
Whitwell-on-the-Hill	1× IB		
Langtoft	1× IB		
North Burton	1× IB		
Lancashire			
Lumb	2× IB		
Rawtenstall	2× HE		
Ewood Bridge	5× HE, 2× IB		Damage to railway line and windows
Holcombe Brook	2× IB		
Holcombe	7× HE	1 killed	Post office, windows and telegraph wires damaged
Ramsbottom	2× HE		
Bolton	9× HE, 11× HE	13 killed, 10 injured	6 houses wrecked; 4 seriously damaged; 3 small fires; windows broken
Lincolnshire			
Maltby-le-Marsh	1× IB		
Market Rasen	1× IB		
Total	63× HE, 65× IB (at least 8 – and probably more – bombs were dropped in the sea)	43 killed, 31 injured	

Anti-aircraft guns in action and reported use of ammunition:

Location of AA battery	Calibre or type of gun	Number / type of rounds fired
York	3" 20-cwt	5 HE rounds
Collingham	13 pdr (mobile)	9 HE and shrapnel rounds
Sheffield, Shire Green	3" 20-cwt	2 HE rounds
Humber:		
Harpings	3" 20-cwt	8 HE rounds
Marfleet	3" 20-cwt	4 HE rounds
Sutton	12 pdr 12-cwt	4 HE rounds
Chase Hill	12 pdr 12-cwt	1 HE round (jammed)
Bessingby	6" on railway mounting	1 CS round
Portsmouth:		
Horseand	6 pdr Hotchkiss	3 CS rounds
Rowner	2 pdr Hotchkiss	15 CS rounds
Brockhirst	3" 20-cwt	9 CS, HE and shrapnel rounds
Lumps	6 pdr Hotchkiss	14 CS rounds
Blockhouse	4" (naval) QF, mk IV	10 shrapnel and day tracer rounds
Fort Cumberland	6 pdr Hotchkiss	2 CF rounds
Gilkicker	6 pdr Hotchkiss	25 CF rounds
Bafins	3"	39 HE rounds
Hilsea	6 pdr Hotchkiss	2 CF rounds
Great Salterns	6 pdr Hotchkiss	12 CS rounds
Porchester	6 pdr Hotchkiss	7 CS rounds

The Royal Naval Air Service dispatched seven aeroplanes to intercept the airships, but only one pilot flying from Calshot sighted an airship, but was unable to overtake it.

The Royal Flying Corps dispatched eight aircraft – none of the pilots sighting an airship.

27 September 1916

Zeppelin LZ 81 / LZ 51. Type P.
Tirnowa, Bulgaria.
Stranded following bombing raid on Budapest.
Kommandeur: Hauptmann Barth.

1 October 1916

Weather: calm, with a good deal of cloud, but not much mist or fog.

Eleven airships left their northern German sheds in the afternoon. These were *Zeppelins L 13*, *L 14*, *L 16*, *L 17*, *L 21*, *L 22*, *L 23*, *L 24*, *L 30*, *L 31* and *L 34* – although *Zeppelins L 13*, *L 22*, *L 23* and *L 30* never crossed the English Coast, with *Zeppelins L 14*, *L 16* and *L 21* raiding Lincolnshire.

Zeppelin L 13 apparently started out with the intention of raiding the north of England, but at 1930 turned south – as if to cross the North Norfolk Coast – but then turned north in the region of the Humber and hovered off the coast for about two hours before heading back to Germany at 0225.

Zeppelin L 22 was sighted off the Norfolk Coast in the region of the *Haisboro Lightship* at about 2130 but never crossed the coast – returning at once when fired at by the Bacton gun. She dropped four HE bombs into the sea as she went off in a north-westerly direction and straight across the North Sea to the Dutch Coast near Texel – following the Frisian Islands back to Germany. It may have been that she was damaged by the Bacton Gun and sought the safest route home.

Zeppelin L 23 returned early – having got no more than halfway across the North Sea.

Zeppelin L 30 reached the Yorkshire Coast and was sighted off Robin Hood's Bay at 2250 before returning slowly across the North Sea.

Zeppelin L 31 was spotted passing south of the *Cross Sand Lightship* and *South Sand Lightship* at 1940 before turning to cross the coast at Corton, Suffolk at 2050 and heading straight for London. At 2120 the airship's engines were stopped while her commander verified his position over Halstead before proceeding south-west. At 2145 she was picked up by a searchlight and altered course to the north-west to Buntingford; then at 2230 she turned south-west before turning east over Hatfield. On reaching Hereford, the airship's engines were again shut down and she drifted slowly in the direction of Ware before restarting her engines and heading south at speed for London. At 2340 the Zeppelin came under heavy fire from the anti-aircraft guns at Newmans and Temple House. Abandoning the idea of reaching London, she dropped most of her bomb load of 30 HE and 26 incendiary bombs at Cheshunt – wrecking four houses and damaging another 300. After she had dropped the first dozen HE bombs, the airship turned westwards very suddenly. Of the remaining bombs, five were of 300 kg HEs which landed on the recreation ground. Soon after – at 2354 – another HE bomb fell at Potters Bar, whereupon the Zeppelin was attacked by Second Lieutenant Wulstan J Tempest in BE2c no.4577 of D Flight, 39 HD Squadron at 12,700 feet and fell in flames – breaking in two during its descent (probably due to two or three bombs exploding) and leaving a trail of burning fragments as she went.

It was reported at the time that Heinrich Mathy jumped or fell from the gondola of the burning airship during its final descent and that he was found a little way from the wreckage barely alive; he died soon after.

Heinrich Mathy, one of the most successful of the German airship commanders, poses with members of the crew of *Zeppelin L 31.*

Zeppelin L 31 / LZ 72. Type R.
2354: Crashed at Oakmere Farm, Potters Bar, Hertfordshire.
Kapitänleutnant Heinrich Mathy +. CC.
Leutnant zur See Jochen Werner +. CC.
Obermatrose Karl Dornbusch +. CC.
Obermaschinistenmaat Karl Hiort +. CC.
Segelmachermaat Ernst Kaiser +. CC.
Funkentelegraphistengast Ernst Klee +. CC.
Steuermann Siegfried Körber +. CC.
Signalmaat Gustav Kunisch +. CC.
Maschinistenmaat Karl Mensing +. CC.
Obersteuermanmaat Friedrich Peters +. CC.
Obermatrose Heinrich Philipp +. CC.
Maschinistenmaat Friedrich Rohr +. CC.
Maschinistenmaat Hubert Stender +. CC.
Maschinist Josef Wegener +. CC.
Bootsmannsmaat Heinrich Witthöft +. CC.
Maschinistenmaat Eugen Boudanger +. CC.
Obermaschinistenmaat Viktor Woellert +. CC.
Bootsmannsmaat Artur Budwitz +. CC.
Maschinistenmaat Nikolaus Hemmerling +. CC.

The remains of *Zeppelin L 31* burnt for a number of hours – leaving very little information to be gleaned from the wreckage. In the foreground are the remains of an engine gondola and fuel tank.

Members of the public who have come to witness the spectacle are kept at a safe distance, while members of the General Staff closely inspect the shattered remains of *Zeppelin L 31*.

An account of the action was recorded in 39 HD Squadron history:

> 2nd Lieutenant W J Tempest of B Flight, 39 Squadron left North Weald Bassett at 10 o'clock in BE2c 4577 for the patrol Hainault Farm – Joyce Green. At 11.45pm he found himself over the south-west of London at an altitude of 14,500 feet. There was a heavy ground fog and it was bitterly cold; otherwise, the night was beautiful and starlit at the altitude at which he was flying. He was gazing over towards the north-east of London, where the fog was not quite so heavy, when he noticed all the searchlights in that quarter concentrated in an enormous pyramid. Following them up to the apex, he saw a small cigar-shaped object which he at once recognised as a Zeppelin about 15 miles away and heading straight for London. Previous to this, he had chased many imaginary Zeppelins – only to find they were clouds on nearing them. He rapidly drew near the airship – passing through a very inferno of bursting shells from the anti-aircraft guns below. The Zeppelin was now nearly 15,000 feet high and mounting rapidly, for although Tempest had a slight advantage in speed, the airship was climbing like a rocket. Tempest dived straight for the Zeppelin – firing a burst into her. He let her have another burst as he passed under her and then banking his machine over, sat under her tail – and flying along her, pumped lead into her for all he was worth; the airship replying with copious tracer bullets. Suddenly, he noticed her begin to go red inside like an enormous Chinese lantern and then a flame shot out of the front part of her. She then shot up about 200 feet, paused and came roaring down. Tempest had to dive full out to get out of the way. Thus perished Mathy – the most resolute and formidable airship commander of the German Naval Airship Service.
>
> Tempest then proceeded to North Weald to land and wrecked the machine on the aerodrome without injury at 12.10am.

Recollections of Wulstan J Tempest as recorded on 15 September 1920:

> In or about the month of September 1916 I held the rank of 2nd Lieutenant in the RFC and was stationed at Suttons Farm, Hornchurch in the county of Essex. I was one member of a flight of four other men who included Captain W L Robinson and Lieutenant F Sowery. Part of our duty was to go on patrol during air raids with the view of intercepting Zeppelins. On the night of September 30th-October 1st, I received orders to stand by about 7pm and at 10pm I received orders to patrol at an altitude of 8,000 feet. I may mention that in those days, the organisation of the London defences was practically nil. There were a few detached flights of RFC and AA batteries dispersed round the defended area and no form of co-operation was carried out between these two services. Beyond the fact that we were given stand-by orders – and that a certain armament was detailed to be carried by us – pilots practically had to use their own initiative. After many months – and guided by experience in previous

air raids – our flight had condensed our own plan of action to cope with the Zeppelin menace. We came to the conclusion that the most important factor was to attain the maximum possible altitude – and to do this, we decided to discard the major part of the armament laid down by the War Office such as Rankin darts, Carcass bombs, Le Prieur rockets which we regarded as so much unnecessary weight. We decided to rely entirely on the explosive ammunition fired by our Lewis guns. To do this, we had to [sic] many dodges to "throw dust in the eyes of the higher commands" when inspections of the aerodromes and machines were carried out. Thus, after many height tests and much experimenting, we got our machines able to attain altitudes of 15,000 feet.

An amusing incident occurred after I had sent in my report of my encounter of the Zeppelin, which I destroyed. I stated in this report that my armament consisted solely of a Lewis gun and drums of explosive bullets, as I had discarded the remainder – standardised by the War Office owing to its cumbersome nature – which greatly diminished the climbing efficiency of the aeroplane. For this, I was severely hauled over the coals. In fact, I had dared to destroy a Zeppelin without Le Prieur rockets.

Accordingly, I left the ground and proceeded to attain as high an altitude as possible. At about 11.45pm I found myself over SW London at an altitude of 14,500 feet. There was a heavy ground fog on and it was bitterly cold; otherwise, the night was beautiful and starlit at the altitude at which I was flying. I was gazing over towards the NE of London, where the fog was not quite so heavy, when I noticed all the searchlights in that quarter concentrated in an

An example of how Le Prieur rockets were fitted to the outer struts of aeroplanes – this being a Nieuport 16.

enormous pyramid. Following them up to the apex, I saw a small cigar-shaped object which I at once recognised as a Zeppelin about 15 miles away – and heading straight for London. Previous to this, I had chased many imaginary Zepps only to find that they were clouds on nearing them. At first, I drew near to my objective very rapidly, as I was on one side of London and it was on the other – and both heading for the centre of the town. All the time I was having an extremely unpleasant time, as to get to the Zepp, I had to pass through a very inferno of bursting shells from the AA guns below. All at once, it appeared to me that the Zeppelin must have sighted me for she dropped all her bombs in one volley, swung round, tilted up her nose and proceeded to race away northwards – climbing rapidly as she went. At the time of dropping her bombs, I judged her to be at an altitude of about 11,500 feet. I made after her at all speed at about 15,000 feet altitude – gradually overhauling her. At this period, the AA fire was intense and I – being about five miles behind the Zeppelin – had an extremely uncomfortable time. At this point, misfortune overtook me for my mechanical pressure pump went wrong and I had to use my hand pump to keep up the pressure in my petrol tank. This exercise at so high an altitude was very exhausting, besides occupying an arm – thus giving me 'one hand less' to operate with when I commenced to fire. As I drew up with the Zeppelin, to my relief I found that I was free from AA fire for the nearest shells were bursting quite three miles away. The Zeppelin was now nearly 15,000 feet high and mounting rapidly. I therefore decided to dive at her for though I held a slight advantage in speed, she was climbing like a rocket and leaving me standing. I accordingly gave a tremendous pump at my petrol tank and dived straight at her – firing a burst straight into her as I came. I let her have another burst as I passed under her and then, banking my machine over, sat under her tail – and flying along underneath her, pumped lead into her for all I was worth. I could see tracer bullets flying from her in all directions, but I was too close to her for her to concentrate on me. As I was firing, I noticed her begin to go red inside like an enormous Chinese lantern and then flame shot out of the front part of her – and I realised she was on fire. She then shot up about 200 feet, paused and came roaring down straight on to me before I had time to get out of the way. I nosedived for all I was worth, with the Zepp tearing after me, and expected every minute to be engulfed in flames. I put my machine into a spin and just managed to corkscrew out of the way as she shot past me – roaring like a furnace. I righted my machine and watched her hit the ground with a shower of sparks. I then proceeded to fire off dozens of green Very's lights in the exuberance of my feelings. I glanced at my watch and saw it was about 10 minutes past 12. I then commenced to feel very sick and giddy and exhausted – and had considerable difficulty in finding my way to ground through the fog and landing (in doing which, I crashed and cut my head on my machine-gun). I duly made my report to headquarters and later on was awarded the DSO.

W J Tempest, Major.

Wulfstan J Tempest (right) poses with other members of 39 (HD) Squadron (from left: Lt F Sowery DSO, Lt W L Robinson VC and Capt F R Stammer).

Zeppelin L 24 was sighted off the Norfolk Coast at Weybourne at 2205 – being commanded by *Kapitänleutnant* Robert Koch – and crossed the coast at 2215 following a south-westerly course in the direction of London. At midnight she was sighted over Waterbeach heading toward Cambridge, but her crew must have sighted the glow from the burning *Zeppelin L 31* as the airship turned west – travelling slowly towards St Ives. The commander must have decided that he needed to make some impression, in that the airship then turned to the south until reaching Hitchin, where she turned west. At 0114 she dropped 28 HE and 26 incendiary bombs between Willians and a point two-and-a-half miles to the east (presumably aiming at the flares of the night landing ground). No damage was done, but a soldier of the Royal Defence Corps who was guarding the aerodrome was killed [18]. At Weston, two-and-a-half miles to the east, a German cap was dropped overboard. The airship then headed off to the north-east at great speed – passing out to sea at Kessingland at 0235 and being sighted from the *St Nicholas Lightship*.

The newest airship of the German Naval Air Service, *Zeppelin L 34*, was on her maiden flight over England and was commanded by *Kapitänleutnant* Martin Dietrich. She was first heard over the *Haisboro Lightship* at 2136 and crossed the coast

18 Probably 26095 Private William Hawkes of the 56 Protection Company, Royal Defence Corps: buried Stopsley (St Thomas) Churchyard, Bedfordshire.

at Overstrand, Norfolk – heading west-south-west and dropping a flare at Kempstone before continuing to Stoke Ferry and turning west towards Market Harborough. When nearing Corby at midnight, the searchlight and anti-aircraft gun opened up on the airship, so the commander made directly for the gun position and dropped 17 HE bombs on a curving line between Kirby Hall and the southern entrance to Corby Railway Tunnel. She then sharply turned north-east and dropped 13 incendiary bombs that fell in a line east of the road from Rockingham to Gretton. The bombs fell in woods and fields (causing no damage), while the Zeppelin headed off to the north-west and crossed the coast between Palling and Horsey at 0140 – dropping a further three HE bombs into the sea.

Zeppelin L 21, commanded by *Oberleutnant zur See* Kurt Frankenburg, crossed the Norfolk Coast at Weybourne at 2120 and followed the coast as far as The Wash at Heacham, where she dropped two incendiary bombs. She then turned south along The Wash Coastline – turning west at Kings Lynn and again following the coast to Holbeach – dropping a flare at Gosberton as she passed at 2315. At 2320 an incendiary bomb fell in the vicinity of Buckminster and at midnight she was sighted near Oakham heading to the north-east (her crew possibly having seen the fate of *Zeppelin L 31*). At 0010 she passed Donnington and at 0030 she dropped an HE bomb at South Kyme – killing a sheep. Continuing on her course, the airship went out to sea near Donna Nook at 0110 and was heard from the Spurn Lighthouse dropping bombs in the sea soon after.

Zeppelin L 16 crossed the Lincolnshire Coast at Theddlethorpe, where an HE bomb was dropped at midnight before she turned to the south – following the coast some distance inland. At 0045 she dropped an incendiary bomb at Huttoft and at 0050 an HE bomb fell at Willoughby. Her commander, *Kapitänleutnant* Erich Sommerfeldt, pursued a course parallel with the coast. She turned inland at Wainfleet and then turned sharply inland in a north-westerly direction at 0110 – dropping three HE bombs between Westville and Stickford; then two incendiary bombs at East Kirkby. At 0120 four HE and two incendiary bombs fell at Hameringham, where a cow was killed and two horses injured. This was followed by one HE bomb at Scrafield and one incendiary bomb at Fulletby at 0130. The airship then turned off to the east and crossed the coast near Wainfleet at 0200. She made straight for the Dutch Coast and shortly before 0500 violated Dutch territory at the Helder and crossed the province of Noord Holland, the mouth of the Zuyder Zee and part of Friesland before reaching the German Islands and the Bight of Heligoland.

Zeppelin L 14 made landfall near Friskney, Lincolnshire at 0045 and was sighted north of Boston at 0130 where her commander, *Hauptmann* Kuno Manger, hovered for nearly an hour before heading inland in a north-easterly direction. He dropped five HE and seven incendiary bombs at Blankney Dales; then an HE bomb fell at Kirkstead at 0245. Turning north, the Zeppelin then (at 0250) dropped 11 HE bombs on Stixwould – five of which failed to explode, but a horse and three sheep were killed. An HE bomb then dropped in Bucknall, where course was altered to the north-east and an incendiary bomb fell in the neighbouring village of Horsington at

0255. Continuing on a north-easterly course, the airship then dropped four HE and two incendiary bombs at Hemingby at 0300 and four HE bombs on Goulceby. A further HE bomb was dropped on Stenigot – again causing no damage. The course of the airship then altered to the east and an HE bomb fell in Burwell Wood (south of Louth) at 0310 before the airship made for the sea and crossed over Mablethorpe at 0320 – passing over the *Inner Dowsing Lightship*.

Zeppelin L 17 came in over Weybourne, Norfolk at 0145 after dropping a flare and three HE bombs into the sea heading directly south – although her commander, *Kapitänleutnant* Hermann Kraushaar, was unsure of his whereabouts as he altered course a few times and hovered over Shipdam for a while. At 0246 – having verified her position when near Bingham – she turned north-east and at 0310 dropped an HE bomb at Marlingford and another at Easton (neither of which caused any damage). She then turned to the east and passed out to sea at Caister at 0335; then at 0345 she passed over the *Cross Sand Lightship* and dropped seven HE bombs into the sea.

Summary for the night of 1-2 October 1916:

Location	Number and type of bombs dropped	Casualties	Damage
Lincolnshire			
Blankney Dales	5× HE, 7× IB		
Kirkstead	1× HE		Windows broken
Stixwould	11× HE		1 horse and 3 sheep killed
Bucknall	1× HE		
Horsington	1× IB		
Hemingby	4× HE		Windows broken; rabbit killed
Goulceby	4× HE		
Stenigot	1× HE		
Burwell Wood	1× HE		
Theddlethorpe	1× HE		
Huttoft	1× IB		
Willoughby	1× HE		
Westvile	1× HE		
West Fen	1× HE		
Stickford	1× HE		
East Kirkby	2× IB		
Hammeringham	4× HE, 2× IB		Cow killed; 2 horses injured
Scrafield	1× HE		
Fulletby	1× IB		

Location	Number and type of bombs dropped	Casualties	Damage
Kirkby Underwood	1× IB		
South Kyme	1× HE		Sheep killed
Northamptonshire			
Gretton	17× HE, 13× IB		Telegraph wire broken
Norfolk:			
Heacham	2× IB		
Easton	1× HE		
Marlingford	1× HE		
Hertfordshire:			
Willians	28× HE, 26× IB	1 killed	
London MPD			
Cheshunt	30× HE, 26× IB	1 injured	4 houses wrecked; 343 slightly damaged; 40 glass-houses wrecked
Potters Bar	1× HE		House and 3 cottages damaged
Total	117× HE, 84× IB (at least 17 bombs were dropped in the sea)	1 killed, 1 injured	

Anti-aircraft guns in action and reported use of ammunition:

Location of AA battery	Calibre or type of gun	Number / type of rounds fired
Mundesley	3 pdr Vickers mk 1	5 CS rounds
Corby	2× 6 pdr Nordenfelt QF	8 rounds
Waltham Abbey		
Newmans	2× 3" 20-cwt	44 rounds
Temple House	3" 20-cwt	50 rounds
Farm Hill	3" 5-cwt	–

The Royal Naval Air Service dispatched one aeroplane from Yarmouth, but the pilot did not see any airships.

The Royal Flying Corps dispatched 14 aeroplanes to intercept the raiders.

Second Lieutenant J I MacKay in BE2c no.2581 – from North Weald Aerodrome – saw an airship over West Ham, but it fell in flames before he could close on it.

Second Lieutenant Tempest in BE2c no.4577 – from North Weald Aerodrome – intercepted *Zeppelin L 31* and after firing one drum from his ·303 Lewis gun, set the airship alight. He crashed on landing – wrecking his aeroplane, but received no injuries himself.

Lieutenant L G S Payne in BE2c no.2736 took off from Hainault Aerodrome. Later seeing gun flashes beyond North Weald, he flew in their direction and saw a Zeppelin outlined in searchlights. He climbed to 9,000 feet and heard bursts of machine-gun fire – and a few seconds after, the Zeppelin fell in flames.

Second Lieutenant P McGuinness was patrolling between North Weald, Chingford and Hendon. He sighted a Zeppelin and went in pursuit – the airship bursting into flames before he could reach it.

22 October 1916

Weather: fair, but beginning to cloud over. Wind west-west-east, strength four.

At 1337 an aeroplane was heard very high over Sheerness, Kent – apparently moving in a northerly direction. It had not been observed on its inward flight and dropped four HE bombs – of which three fell in the harbour and the fourth into the dockyard railway station. A few telegraph wires, the windows of four railway carriages and a horse box standing on a siding were damaged. There were no casualties and no damage was done. At 1340 the machine was plotted heading north-west towards the Nore. Owing to the haze and height of the aeroplane, it could not be engaged by the anti-aircraft guns.

A second aircraft was heard off North Foreland at about 1500 and was fired at by a destroyer and a torpedo boat off the *Tongue Lightship*. The noise of the guns firing was mistaken on shore as the sound of bombs dropping. The aircraft then made off without crossing the coast. At 1530 hrs a single-engine, two-seater German seaplane coming from the direction of England was shot down off Blankenberg, Belgium by Flight Lieutenant Galbraithe, Royal Naval Air Service flying from Dunkirk who dived from 15,000 feet to 7,000 feet and fired two trays of Lewis gun ammunition into the enemy machine (which was seen to nosedive into the sea).

There is no record of a loss by the German Air Service on this date, at this location. This was not the aircraft that bombed Sheerness, as the latter was piloted by Leutnant Ilges, who returned unharmed to Mariakerke.

No anti-aircraft guns went into action due to the ranges involved.

Eight Royal Naval Air Service aeroplanes – six from Dover and two from Maidstone aerodromes – took off to intercept the raider.

23 October 1916

Weather: sky a quarter to half-clouded. Wind southerly, strength five.

At 1045 a German aeroplane passed over Margate, Kent and headed in a north-easterly direction. Four HE bombs were dropped – one falling in the sea. A servant girl and a male civilian were slightly wounded, although very little material damage was done. The anti-aircraft guns at Sackett's Hill, St Peter's opened fire as the aeroplane was approaching from Margate. The aeroplane then turned almost about for a short distance – as if to ascertain the position of the gun battery firing at it – before making off towards the south-east and Ramsgate. As the sunlight was dazzling to the ground observers – and the aeroplane was flying in the sun's rays – it was very difficult to distinguish (even with coloured glasses) and supposedly went out to sea near Ramsgate. Several Royal Naval Air Service aeroplanes took off in pursuit, but none caught up with the enemy (although one went all the way to Dunkirk and landed there).

Anti-aircraft guns in action and reported use of ammunition

Location of AA battery	Calibre or type of gun	Number / type of rounds fired
Sackett's Hill	12 pdr 12-cwt	16 HE rounds

7 November 1916
Zeppelin LZ 90 / LZ 60. Type P.
North Sea.
Broke away from its moorings and disappeared out to sea.
No crew on board.

Photos of some Zeppelin wreckage – attributed to being in the Faroe Isles – was found during research for this book. The islands are situated equidistant between Northern Scotland, Iceland and Norway. These may possibly be some of the remains of *Zeppelin LZ 90*.

Further photographs of the Zeppelin wreckage.

27 November 1916

Weather: winds up to 55 miles per hour over Scotland and speeds up to 40 miles per hour from the south-west over the Humber. Fine, with very little cloud.

Zeppelins L 13, L 14, L 16, L 21, L 22, L 24, L 30, L 34, L 35 and *L 36* left their sheds in Northern Germany to raid England – the last two airships being on their maiden voyages over Britain. *Zeppelin L 17* was absent on a cruise up the Jutland Coast and *Zeppelin L 23* did not leave her shed. *Zeppelins L 24* and *L 30* never reached the English Coast.

Zeppelins L 34, L 35 and *L 36* crossed the North Sea in formation – aiming for Durham.

Zeppelin L 34 came in over Black Halls Rock on the Durham Coastline at 2330 and at 2335 dropped 13 HE bombs aimed at Elwick Searchlight Battery, Yorkshire. However, they all missed and demolished a cow shed. The Zeppelin was then spotted by Second Lieutenant I V Pyott RFC (flying BE2c no.2738) of 36 Squadron in the Hutton Henry searchlight beam coming towards him and attacked at a height of 9,800 feet – passing below the airship amidships and firing as he went. He then turned and followed his quarry at 70 miles per hour, which at this point was bombing the Elwick searchlight. He concentrated his fire at one point, and after 71 rounds – directly over West Hartlepool, Yorkshire – the envelope became incandescent; the fire spreading until the whole ship was in flames and falling almost vertically. As it fell, a gondola fell from the centre of the airship and the outer envelope separated from the framework – both falling into the sea 1,800 yards east of the Heugh Lighthouse. Portions of wreckage were still burning on the water just after midnight, but half an hour later, there was no trace. Just before the Zeppelin caught fire, 16 bombs fell on West Hartlepool, which wrecked 15 houses and killed four civilians. As she passed over the town, the airship was under heavy fire from the anti-aircraft guns at Hartlepool and Seaton Carew.

The flare of the burning airship was seen as far north as Matfen (near Morpeth) and as far south as Poppleton (north of York from the ground). From the air, it was seen by an aviator flying near Melton Mowbray 136 miles away.

A photograph of *Kapitänleutnant* Max Dietrich taken from a German newspaper which extolled the virtues of their airship commanders (not to be confused with *Kapitänleutnant* Martin Dietrich – commander of *Zeppelins L 22, L 38* and *L 42*).

Zeppelin L 34 / LZ 78. Type R.
2350: Sea – one mile off the mouth of the Tees, Durham.
Kapitänleutnant Max Dietrich +. NKG.
Oberleutnant zur See Christian von Nathusius +. NKG.
Maschinistenmaat Johannes Blunk +. NKG.
Maschinistenmaat Ernst Doering +. NKG.
Obermatrose Otto Ehlers +. NKG.
Obermaschinistenmaat Alexander Keller +. NKG.
Segelmachermaat Wilhelm Koberg +. NKG.
Funkentelegraphistenmaat Paul Nettlau +. NKG.
Obermaschinistenmaat Heinrich Oelbrich +. NKG.
Signalmaat Julius Petitjean +. NKG (body washed ashore at Middlesbrough).
Obermaschinistenmaat Wilhelm Pfirrnann +. NKG.
Signalmaat Heinrich Predel +. NKG.
Bootsmannsmaat Hermann Pufahl +. NKG.
Maschinistenmaat Alfred Rüger +. NKG.
Maschinistenmaat Josef Schydlo +. NKG.
Obermaschinist Franz Seemann +. NKG.
Matrose Friedrich Siegel +. NKG.
Matrose Adam Smieskol +. NKG.
Bootsmannsmaat Bernhard Wever +. NKG.
Obersteuermannmaat Hans Wüst +. NKG (body washed ashore at Middlesbrough).

Report by Ian V Pyott, Second Lieutenant Royal Flying Corps:

> At 9.50pm I had orders to leave on BE2c 2738 to patrol the whole of C Flight area for three hours and to get as high as possible. The latest information was that five Zeppelins had been seen over Seaham Harbour. I had been in the air for 20 minutes when I was recalled to the aerodrome. At 10.22pm I again had orders to go up on BE2c 2738 patrol as before till 12.50am. I had been in the air for approximately an hour when I sighted a Zeppelin between Sunderland and Hartlepool in the beam of a searchlight (Castle Eden) coming south and towards me. At this moment, I was at 9,800 and the Zepp seemed a few hundred feet below me. I flew towards the Zepp and flew at right angles to and underneath him amidships – firing as I went under. I then turned sharp-east; the Zepp turned east also. We then flew on a parallel course for about five miles – firing 71 rounds at the Zepp. I estimate his ground speed to be approximately 70 miles per hour. I was aiming at his port quarter and noticed first a small patch became incandescent where I had seen tracers entering his envelope. I first took it for a machine-gun firing at me from the Zepp, but this patch rapidly spread and the next thing was that the whole Zepp was in flames. I landed at 12 midnight – engine and machine ok. The Zeppelin, which fell into the sea at the mouth of the Tees, was still burning when I landed.

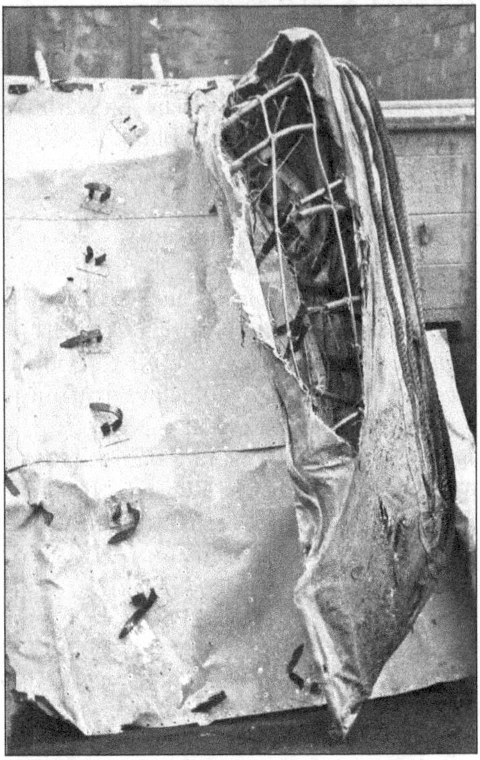

Attempts were made to recover some portions of *Zeppelin L 34* over the following few days – and a number of bodies of the crew were reported to have been washed up on the coast, but records of their burial were subsequently lost. Here is a portion of one of the gondolas.

The remains of one of *Zeppelin L 34's* propeller blades, which was recovered from the sea.

Zeppelin L 35 came in at Hawthorn, Durham at 2336 and went inland for 10 minutes – passing over Hesledon and then turned round and went out to sea again north of Easington at 2345. It was presumed that on witnessing the destruction of *Zeppelin L 34*, her commander – *Kapitänleutnant* Herbert Ehrlich – turned for home without releasing any bombs.

Zeppelin L 36 never came overland (being about 15 miles off the mouth of the Tyne) when her commander (*Korvettenkapitän* Viktor Schütze) and crew witnessed the destruction of *Zeppelin L 34* and turned northwards – dropping a number of bombs in the sea off Alnmouth at 0030 before making for home.

The North Midlands attack

Zeppelin L 13, commanded by *Kapitänleutnant* Franz Georg Eichler, came overland in company with *Zeppelin L 22* at Flamborough Head at 2205 – the two airships passing Bridlington and Barton Agnes before separating (*Zeppelin L 13* passing Langtoft and heading south-west). At 2305 an incendiary bomb was dropped at Yapham, followed by 21 HE and three incendiary bombs in open fields at Barnby Moor. At 2315 the airship approached York from the south-east and was engaged by the Acomb anti-aircraft gun. She was driven off to the east, but not before two HE and 21 incendiary bombs were dropped on the outskirts of the city. One house was wrecked and several others damaged – injuring two civilians. At 0010 the airship was sighted over Wold Newton (where five incendiary bombs were dropped) before heading out to sea north of Scarborough – being fired at by anti-aircraft guns and dropping a number of bombs into the sea.

Zeppelin L 22 was commanded by *Kapitänleutnant* Heinrich Hollender – and after parting company with *Zeppelin L 13* near Burton Agnes, Yorkshire headed south. After passing Holme-on-Spalding-Moor at 2245 she was picked up by the Willitoft searchlight and anti-aircraft gun. After two rounds being fired, the airship circled round and headed off to the south-east. Her commander seemed uncertain of his position and proceeded to drift with the engines cut off. At 2316 the airship was spotted by an aeroplane near Goole, where she crossed the Humber, but recrossed it soon after near Hessle. She was next heard near Leven at 0004. At 0015 she passed near to Skirlaugh (heading east) and passed out to sea near Hornsea at 0020 – being fired at by the Cowden anti-aircraft guns. No bombs were dropped overland by this airship.

Zeppelin L 14 came in at Tunstall at 2110 and approached Hull before turning north-east back towards the coast, where she was engaged by the mobile anti-aircraft guns at Cowden. In response, she dropped 18 HE and 26 incendiary bombs – all of which fell between the villages of Mappleton and Rowlston Hall. The airship immediately went off towards the west and made a wide circle towards Barnstown, where the mobile anti-aircraft guns went into action and the airship turned south – dropping two petrol tanks as she went (one falling at Moortown and the other at Brandesburton). The commander, *Hauptmann* Kuno Manger, then shut off the engines and drifted towards Hull – being picked up and fired at by the Sutton anti-aircraft gun at 2215. The Zeppelin gradually turned to the east and passed out to sea north of the Spurn at 2225 – dropping bombs into the sea off Cromer.

Zeppelin L 16 crossed the English Coast at Filey Bay, Yorkshire at 2120 and proceeded south-west – reaching the line of anti-aircraft guns sited between Howden and Selby and being fired at by the Hemingborough Grange gun. She then turned north-west and was fired at by the Cliffe gun, so her commander – *Kapitänleutnant* Hans-Karl Gayer – turned her to the south-west, but was fired at by the Woodhouse gun. The airship then passed over the Barlow Aircraft Works, turned south-east and increased speed in order to escape the area. At 2230 she approached Wakefield at a low level before heading to Sharlston, where at 2232 she dropped three HE and six incendiary bombs. She then proceeded to Cudworth, where at 2240 an incendiary bomb was dropped. She then headed west to Monk Bretton, where two HE bombs fell. Turning abruptly to the north-east, the Zeppelin dropped two HE and two incendiary bombs (neither of which ignited) at South Hiendley before continuing her course to Pontefract. Four HE and four incendiaries fell near to the town – causing no damage (with the incendiary bombs again failing to ignite). The airship then turned south-west towards Featherstone, where at 2310 she dropped six HE bombs. She then headed back to the north – dropping an incendiary bomb at Lumby and another at Monk Fryston. At 2335 the raider approached the city of York, but was fired at by the Acomb anti-aircraft guns and then sheared off to the north-west. She then turned back to the north-east – passing Birdsall's West Farm, Helperthorpe at 0025 and dropping an HE bomb there. Soon after, another fell at Jepson's Farm, Boythorpe – neither of which exploded as they had no fuses fitted. A further five HE bombs landed at Foxholes before the airship proceeded north-east to Seamer and went out to sea south of Scarborough – being fired at by anti-aircraft guns at 0035.

Zeppelin L 21 crossed the coast at Atwick, Yorkshire at 2120 hrs on 27 November and was immediately fired at by the Barmston guns. She then proceeded to drift across the North Midlands at 12,000 feet towards Leeds. At 2334 the Brierlands gun opened fire and fired 10 rounds (although visibility was poor) and the airship proceeded on her way. She was then engaged by the gun at Rothwell Haigh, which fired four rounds. At 2348 one HE bomb and two incendiary bombs fell at Sharlston (east of Wakefield) – causing no damage; then at 0015 on 28 November the airship dropped one HE bomb and two incendiary bombs at Dodworth (two miles south-west of Barnsley, Yorkshire); then at 0050 one incendiary bomb fell at Pott Shrigley (four miles south of Dursley, Cheshire); and at 0110 one HE bomb landed at Birchenwood (near Kidsgrove, Staffordshire). This was followed at 0115 by three HE bombs (including one unexploded 50 kg) at Goldenhill and three HE bombs at Tunstall, Staffordshire – demolishing two houses and injuring a man. At 0130 four incendiary bombs fell near Fenton and Trentham, Staffordshire (but three of these failed to ignite) before the airship headed off to the east and the coast. At Nottingham, the airship shut off her engines and drifted for a while, but was picked up by the searchlight at Ruddington; she immediately restarted her engines. At 0250 she approached the searchlights north of Peterborough, where she was picked up by two aeroplanes which attacked over Buckminster, Lincolnshire, but no results were observed (although the airship gunners returned fire and she climbed from 7,000 feet to 13,000 feet to escape). With fuel presumably getting low, the airship drifted with its engines off towards the East Coast and Belgium. At 0445 the airship was nearly caught by Lieutenant W R Gayner, who spotted the airship due to a light that she was showing, but the aircraft's engine failed just as the pilot was within striking distance of the raider and had to land. At 0600 hrs – just north of Yarmouth, Norfolk – the raider was spotted and fired at by an anti-aircraft battery before making out over the sea at 0630 hrs at a speed of 35 miles per hour and at a height of 8,200 feet. She was followed by Flight Lieutenant Egbert Cadbury in BE2c no.8625 and Flight Sub-Lieutenant Gerard Fane in BE2c no.8420. With the approach of daylight, the pursuing aeroplanes could readily follow their quarry – and they caught up with the ship a few miles east-south-east of Lowestoft, with Cadbury firing five drums of ·303 from his Lewis gun into the aft port side to no effect (apart from the speed of the Zeppelin increasing to 55 miles per hour and returning fire). Fane then closed in to 100 feet from the starboard side, but his Lewis gun jammed – at which point Flight Sub-Lieutenant Edward L Pulling in BE2c no.8626 of the Royal Naval Air Service approached to within 60 feet. He experienced intense machine-gun fire from the Zeppelin gunners before firing 10 rounds and the airship caught fire – soon becoming an intense fiery furnace, with its gunners still continuing to fire from their gondolas until their last moments. The Zeppelin fell stern-first into the sea and sank immediately – leaving a large area of oil-covered water.

Zeppelin L 21 / LZ 61. Type Q.
0642: Sea – eight miles off Lowestoft, Norfolk.
Oberleutnant zur See Kurt Frankenberg +. NKG.
Leutnant zur See. Hans-Werner Salzbrunn +. NKG.
Obermaschinistenmaat Alfred Brieger +. NKG.
Obersignalmaat Albert Carlsen +. NKG.
Oberbootmannsmaat Otto Gras +. NKG.
Obermaschinistenmaat Hans Hintzer +. NKG.
Obermatrose Theophil Kaczikowksi +. NKG.
Obermaschinistenmaat Wichi Kiel +. NKG.
Maschinistenmaat Walter Klann +. NKG.
Obermatrose Wilhelm Metzger +. NKG.
Funkentelegraphistenmaat Paul Petznick +. NKG.
Signalmaat Otto Prinke +. NKG.
Maschinist Anton Reisehel +. NKG.
Obermaschinistenmaat Theodor Schmidt +. NKG.
Maschinistenmaat Alfred Schwarz +. NKG.
Bootsmannsmaat Wilhelm Wittkugel +. NKG.

Account by Flight Sub-Lieutenant E L Pulling, Royal Naval Air Service:

> I have the honour to submit the following report of a hostile aircraft patrol carried out on the morning of the 28th instant from Becton: I left the ground at 4.55am with orders to patrol for one hour. At 5.35am I was patrolling to the north-west of the aerodrome at 9,000 feet. Nothing unusual was seen during this part of the patrol. At 6am I had descended to 6,000 feet preparatory to landing when I saw anti-aircraft guns in the direction of Yarmouth firing. I immediately steered a course south-east – hoping to intercept their target out to sea. At 6.10am I sighted a Zeppelin making out to sea and proceeded in pursuit – having by this time reached the height of 8,000 feet. A few moments later, I saw an attack being made on her by a machine which I was unable to see; the tracer ammunition was clearly visible. Some minutes later, the attack ceased – four trays of ammunition having apparently been fired. About five minutes after the attack ceased, I came level with the Zeppelin at 8,300 feet – approaching her at right angles on her port quarter. I then turned sharply to the left and passed about 50 feet beneath her – firing as I did so. The Lewis gun fired two shots, both hitting, and stopped – and she immediately opened fire with machine-gun apparently from the after gondolas. I turned sharply to the right – intending to keep out of range until I had cleared the jamb. A few seconds later, on looking over my shoulder, I saw that the Zeppelin was on fire by the stern. By this time I was to the south-east of the Zeppelin and apparently a good target against the dawn, for the fire was kept up for several seconds after she was alight. I flew parallel to the Zeppelin for a short time – a few hundred yards to the starboard of her – and watched her sink by the tail and dive into the sea. The flames spread with great rapidity. I was unable to discern any number on the airship as she was between my machine and the light. As I dived, I noticed her propellers working and also two black crosses – one on each side of her stern. During the greater part of the operations, she was canted up at an angle, which finally reached about 45 degrees. Thus, at the moment of passing under her, she appeared to be considerably foreshortened. After witnessing the fall of the Zeppelin, I steered due west – hitting the coast about two miles north of Southwold. I steered due north to Yarmouth and landed there at 7.12am. I am uncertain as to the locality in which the Zeppelin fell, but it appeared to me about 10 miles east of Lowestoft. The speed of the Zeppelin at the moment of attacking was about 55 knots.

Account by A Ellison, Commodore-in-Chief, Lowestoft and Great Yarmouth:

> Sir, be pleased to lay before Their Lordships the following account of the attack – and destruction – of a Zeppelin airship this morning:
>
> At 5.07am a report was received that a Zeppelin was over Swaffam at 4.40am and at Dereham at 5.03am. On receipt of this information, I ordered two

aeroplanes (one from Becton and one from Holt) to ascend in the hope of intercepting her before she got over the coastline. At 6.05am Yarmouth reported: "Zeppelin overhead." Aeroplanes were immediately dispatched from Burgh Castle and Yarmouth and, as by this time dawn was breaking, they could clearly follow the course of the Zeppelin, which was then steering SSE from Yarmouth. Flight Lieutenant Egbert Cadbury and Flight Sub-Lieutenant Gerrard William Reginald Fane, from Burgh Castle, proceeded immediately after her – and Flight-Sub Lieutenant Edward Laston Pulling (who had ascended at 5am from Becton night landing ground), attracted by the sound of firing from the anti-aircraft guns at Great Yarmouth, proceeded south at full speed. At 6.35 the Zeppelin, then being about nine miles ESE from Lowestoft Naval Base, Flight Lieutenant Cadbury and Flight Lieutenant Fane had overtaken her. The former got under her at about 700 feet distance and fired his Lewis gun into the after part of her – being at the time under heavy fire from the Zeppelin. The first tray, not having the desired effect of setting fire to her, he changed trays and repeated the evolution – still with the same result. This evolution, he performed altogether four times until his ammunition was exhausted. The Zeppelin at that time was proceeding at an estimated speed of 55 miles an hour – to which she had increased the moment Flight Lieutenant Cadbury opened fire on her (previously she had been proceeding at about 30 knots). On perceiving that Flight Lieutenant Cadbury had exhausted his ammunition and that the Zeppelin was still apparently intact, Flight Sub-Lieutenant Fane then approached to within 100 feet of the starboard side of the Zeppelin and tried to open fire, but his Lewis gun jammed – probably due to the intense cold and the oil having frozen. Flight Sub-Lieutenant Pulling, who had witnessed the two previous officers' attack, then approached. He advanced to within 60 feet of the Zeppelin. The Zeppelin, by this time, endeavouring to rise rapidly, had assumed an angle of about 45 degrees to the vertical. Flight Sub-Lieutenant Pulling opened fire within 50 feet of her – being under a continuous fire from the Zeppelin's machine-guns that would bear. After 10 rounds had been fired from his Lewis gun, the Zeppelin caught fire – and within a few seconds was nothing but a fiery furnace. Flight Sub-Lieutenant Pulling immediately dived to starboard to avoid the falling debris – and it is noteworthy that the crew of the Zeppelin continued to fire at him for some appreciable time after she was ablaze. She then fell stern foremost into the sea, where she was engulfed and entirely sank – leaving a large area of oil-covered water. The height at which these officers attacked the Zeppelin was 8,200 feet – and from my own personal observation from the pier, I estimate that it took about a minute from the time of her ignition to the time that she struck the water.

Summary for the night of 27-28 November 1916:

Location	Number and type of bombs dropped	Casualties	Damage
Durham			
Elwick	13× HE		Cow shed destroyed; 2 cows injured
West Hartlepool	16× HE	4 killed, 11 injured	15 houses wrecked, 30 damaged; windows broken; grandstand on football field demolished
Yorkshire, East Riding			
Barmby Moor	21× HE, 3× IB		Hay shed and telegraph wires damaged
Yapham	1× IB		
Mappleton	18× HE, 26× IB		
Boythorpe	1× HE		
Helperthorpe	1× HE		
Foxholes	5× HE		
Wold Newton	5× IB		Roof and windows damaged
Yorkshire, West Riding			
Cudworth	1× IB		
Dodworth	1× HE, 2× IB		
Monk Bretton	2× HE		
Featherstone	6× HE		
Pontefract	4× HE, 4× IB		Windows broken
Sharlston	4× HE, 8× IB		
South Hiendley	2× HE, 2× IB		
Lumby	1× IB		
Monk Fryston	1× IB		
York	2× HE, 21× IB		
Cheshire			
Pott Shrigley	1× IB		
Staffordshire			
Kidsgrove	1× HE		
Chesterton	16× HE, 7× IB		
Goldenhill	3× HE		

Location	Number and type of bombs dropped	Casualties	Damage
Trentham	1× IB		
Fenton	3× IB		
Tunstall	3× HE	1 injured	2 houses wrecked, 3 outhouses demolished; glass in 60 cottages blown out
Total	119× HE, 87× IB	4 killed, 16 injured	

Anti-aircraft guns in action and reported use of ammunition:

Location of AA battery	Calibre or type of gun	Number / type of rounds fired
Tyne		
Seaham	13 pdr 6-cwt	16 HE rounds, 18 shrapnel rounds
Tees		
Port Clarence	3" 20-cwt QF	2 night tracer rounds
Seaton Carew	3" 20-cwt QF	9 HE rounds
Scarborough	4x 13 pdr 6-cwt	44 night tracer rounds
Hartlepool (Cemetery)	3" 20-cwt mk III	18 night tracer rounds
Billingham	2x 6 pdr Hotchkiss	12 common plugged rounds
Humber		
Cowden	4x 13 pdr 9-cwt	44 night tracer rounds
Barmston	2x 13 pdr 9-cwt	14 HE rounds, 27 night tracer rounds
Sutton Fields	12 pdr 12-cwt	8 HE rounds
Wood House	3" 20-cwt	2 HE rounds
Hemingborough	3" 20-cwt	3 HE rounds
Cliffe	3" 20-cwt	5 HE rounds
Willitoft	3" 20-cwt	9 HE rounds
Leeds		
York	2x 3" 20-cwt	17 HE rounds
Brierlands	3" 20-cwt	10 HE rounds
Rothwell Haigh	3" 20-cwt	12 HE rounds
Yarmouth:		
Bradwell	2x 13 pdr 9-cwt	23 HE rounds

The Royal Naval Air Service sent nine aircraft up to intercept the raiders with:

Flight Lieutenant Cadbury in BE2c no.8625 from Burgh Castle: reported that he attacked an airship at 8,200 feet and fired four drums of ammunition, with no result.

Flight Sub-Lieutenant Fane in BE2c no.8420 from Burgh Castle Aerodrome: saw that Lieutenant Cadbury had exhausted his ammunition, attacked the airship to within 100 feet, but his Lewis gun jammed.

Flight Sub-Lieutenant Pulling in BE2c no.8626 from Bacton Aerodrome: attacked the airship from 60 feet, fired 10 rounds and the Zeppelin burst into flames.

The Royal Flying Corps sent up 13 aircraft to intercept the raiders with:

Second Lieutenant I V Pyott in BE2c no.2738 from Seaton Carew Aerodrome: sighted a Zeppelin in the beam of a searchlight at 9,500 feet between Sunderland and Hartlepool. After passing underneath amidships, he opened fire. He flew parallel for about five miles – firing about 71 rounds – the speed being about 70 miles per hour when the airship caught fire.

Captain Richardson in BE2c no.2665 flying from Elsham Aerodrome: while flying at 9,000 feet, he saw an airship in a searchlight beam at 12,500 feet over Hornsea, but later lost her.

Lieutenant J Willcox in BE12 no.6660 flying from Elsham Aerodrome: saw two airships several miles north at over 10,000 feet, but lost sight of them.

Lieutenant Brophy in BE12 no.6661 from Kirton Lindsey Aerodrome: while flying at 5,000 feet, he saw bombs explode near Beverly and an airship 3,500 feet above caught by a searchlight, but could not catch her up. On returning he saw bombs explode near York, but saw no other airship.

Captain G E Birley in a BE20 flying from Buckmaster Aerodrome: when at 11,500 feet, he fired at an airship which was 2,000 feet above him.

Second Lieutenant D S Allan in a BE no.6290 flying from Leadenham: while flying at 12,000 feet, he saw two airships at 13,500 feet, but could not get near them.

Lieutenant Gayner in FE2d no.7680 saw an airship east-south-east. When within a mile of it at 7,500 feet, his engine failed. On landing, his machine wrecked.

28 November 1916

Weather: fair to fine, with some mist or fog – and the wind was very light with hardly any definite direction. Owing to the haze, visibility was bad – and due to the height that the aeroplane was travelling, it was only twice observed during its trip to the capital (and even then not definitely identified as hostile).

At 1150 an enemy aeroplane appeared over London. The first intimation of its presence was with the fall of a bomb. Six 10 kg HE bombs were dropped and landed at:

1. 108, Brompton Road (a baker's shop): chimney blown down.
2. 13, Lowndes Square, SW on a roof at the back of the house: roof demolished, with fragments penetrating two floors down.
3. 15, Pavilion Road (Lord Rayleigh's Dairy) through the roof: office room wrecked.

4. Eccleston Mews, Belgrave Place: a roof damaged and glass broken.
5. Belgrave Mews, East (opposite no.23): one cobblestone was cracked and the galvanised iron shutters and brick piers of the garages of nos.22 and 23 were riddled with splinters. A large amount of glass was broken. Two men were slightly injured.
6. Victoria Palace Music Hall (opposite Victoria Station): destroyed about six to eight square feet of a dressing room roof – wounding a woman. A few windows in five adjoining houses were broken.

In all, four men and five women were injured – all very slightly.

The order in which the bombs were dropped could not be stated, but the general course of the aeroplane was from west to east. When over London, it was definitely seen by only two people. From London, the raider made the coast almost unseen and continued across the Channel in the direction of France. However, at 1415 the pilot was forced to land at Souverain-le-Moulin near Boulogne, France. The *beobachter* (*Leutnant* Walter Ilges) and the *flugzeugführer* (*Deckoffizier* Paul Brandt) of *1Marine Feldflieger-Abteilung* were captured. Statements made by them were examined and showed that they started from Mariakerke – with the intention of bombing the Admiralty Building – and also taking photographs of aerodromes, munitions works etc. *Leutnant* Ilges stated that they steered from the mouth of the Thames – making a wide detour in order to avoid being seen from Westgate (and so being cut off by the Westgate patrol aircraft on their return). They then made a wide curve round Sheerness, as they had flown over that part five weeks earlier (22 October); then flying parallel to the River Medway (well north, as the sky here was hazy and there being much mist north of the Thames – and also with the sun behind them – they could get good obtuse photographs of places south of the Thames). After following the Medway for some miles, the German crew turned west and flew parallel with the Thames, which could be distinguished on their right as far as Woolwich. They continued along the North Downs until there was an easily recognisable military camp due to the tents; then turning north, they headed straight for the West End of London. By this time, Ilges had taken 20 photographs of various places – one judged to be a new aerodrome. The remainder were either military hutments or munitions works. On reaching London, which neither Ilges nor Brandt had seen before, they depended on the map that they were captured with for picking out the Admiralty. The haze was such that *Leutnant* Ilges was unable to use the telescopic bomb sight – and he threw his bombs in a line for a building which he assumed to be the Admiralty. He had gained the impression since his capture that his nearest bomb fell within 300 yards of the Admiralty – and he expressed some disappointment on being told that this was not the case. After releasing their bombs, they flew off in a south-easterly direction without being able to distinguish any particular features. When well clear of London, they became anxious about their return – and finding themselves over an aerodrome from which two aeroplanes were seen rising, imagined that the alarm had been given and their retreat may be cut off. The two machines that were rising were no more than

1,500 feet up – and although there was no fear of being overtaken by them, Westgate and Margate may be more active. Therefore, they turned back towards the south-west for some miles to throw off any possible pursuers before turning due south and passed over a town (thought to be Hastings). The German crew then steered a course towards Abbeville, France from where they thought they could cross the Allied lines and land at Lille. Thus, they would have avoided the Dover and Dunkirk patrols and stood a fair chance of crossing the lines at a high altitude – thus avoiding detection. However, engine trouble set in, with the fuel feed pipe becoming blocked – thus forcing the crew to come down to 6,000 feet over the Channel. Realising that they would never have sufficient height to cross the lines in France, they opted to follow the French Coast in the hope of making Belgium. Keeping out to sea within the sight of the French Coast, the engine trouble became worse and they had to land north-east of Boulogne. The camera and plates had already been thrown into the sea – and on landing, the crew tried to set fire to their aircraft – burning all the maps and charts except for the map of London.

The aeroplane was a *LGV C-4* biplane no.272/16 with a 225 hp Mercedes engine: speed 80 miles per hour; radius of flight about 400 miles.

No anti-aircraft guns were in action. The Royal Naval Air Service sent up four aeroplanes and the Royal Flying Corps eight aeroplanes to intercept the raider, but all the pilots failed to see the enemy aircraft.

28 December 1916

Zeppelin L 17 / LZ 53. Type P.
Tondern, Germany.
Burnt out following collision with hangar door.
Kommandeur: Kapitainleutnant Hermann Kraushaar.

The remains of *Zeppelin L 38* lies amongst the winter snow.

Zeppelin L 24 / LZ 69. Type Q.
Tondern, Germany.
Burnt out.
Kommandeur: *Oberleutnant zur See* Kurt von Friemel.

29 December 1916.
Zeppelin L 38 / LZ 84. Type R.
Seerappen, Kurland.
Stranded and later decommissioned.
Kommandeur: *Kapitänleutnant* Martin Dietrich.

Appendix I

Zeppelin airships

The transcript of a lecture given by Count von Zeppelin – giving an insight into the development of the Zeppelin airships prior to the Great War (and the insight into the thoughts of an early aviation pioneer).

<u>Zeppelin airships</u>

Lecture by Count von Zeppelin and Engineer Dornier.
Summer meeting of the "Schiffbautechnische Gesellschaft", Stuttgart,
27 May 1914.

Translated by W H Hancock 1.10.14.

Your Royal Highness, ladies and gentlemen, you have honoured me by desiring that I deliver a lecture to you on the development of my airships.

Every development commences with the conception of the idea. The high value of airships capable of covering long distances and carrying profitable loads was particularly recognised by me from the lecture on "The World's Mails and Airship Traffic" by the Secretary of the Imperial Post Office, Stephan, which was published in 1874. This awoke in me the desire for the realisation of such ships. The few airships which at that time had made any trips – the best of them was the French military airship "*La France*" – were not able to serve as models for me on account of their small performances. When getting out my design, I knew nothing of the airship of the Austrian engineer Schwarz, which was ready before my first. It was, however, clear to me from the commencement that, in contrast with water ships, in the case of which a trunk of a tree used as a raft represented a serviceable vessel for primitive man, the first really practical airship had to be of very large dimensions.

As means of construction, the following were available.

For raising a load in the air: air rarefied by heating and the light, but very inflammable, hydrogen gas. The former was prohibitive on account of the great weight of the fuel necessary for the maintaining the heat. There remained only hydrogen gas.

I have frequently been blamed for constructing airships with which a gas so dangerous as regards fire must be used. As in several thousand trips, only one of my airships – and this in consequence of the unfortunate combination of several causes, which will be avoided in the future – has been burnt in the air, nobody will now estimate the danger so highly as to consider that on its account I should have given up their construction.

I intend to make the gas cells of silk covered on both sides with goldbeater's skin, or of goldbeater's skin only. As, however, means of keeping the goldbeater's skin flexible had not then been discovered, I used waterproofed cotton cloth, which was attempted to make gas-tight with the "Ballonin" discovered by Duttenhofer and Liwentaal.

Whether I should construct the airship of wood, steel or aluminium was not easy to decide. Only after long experiments under the direction of Professor, now State Councillor, von Back at Stuttgart did I decide on aluminium, which with equal strength proved not inconsiderably lighter than wood. Steel was given up because the plates would have been too thin for the necessary strength and could not have been attached to the edges nor firmly riveted – the employment of stronger plates not being possible on account of their too-great weight.

Naval constructor Pietzker, who lost his life in the "*L 2*" disaster, shortly before his tragic end prepared an able lecture for the "Schiffbautechnische Gesellschaft" on the "Connection Between Airship Construction and Ship Building", which gave evidence of clear views concerning airship construction and a thorough treatment of the subject. It is my duty to express here the thanks which we airship constructors all owe to the deceased for his services to our science. The following is to be found in Pietzker's lecture: "We rightly see one of the main difficulties of ship construction in contrast with all other domains of practical techniques, in that we must make exceptionally great efforts to get light weight." We have indeed called to our aid many branches of techniques solely from this point of view. In the domain of marine engine construction also, the development specially aimed at has been lightness. What does this signify, however, in face of conditions in which a cubic metre gives only a thousandth part of the lifting power. In water, a cubic metre equals 1,000 kilograms; in air 1 kilogram.

This small buoyancy in air necessitated at the commencement constructing vessels of such size that I foresaw the general doubts, which soon arose, as to my sanity. In order to be able to prove the correctness of my ideas, the first airship had to be able to lift its own weight, running materials for several hours, water ballast, various apparatus, ropes, anchoring gear, etc.; in addition, machinery for attaining a speed of at least nine metres per second (18.4 miles per hour) and, of course, the necessary crew. Nothing could be forgotten. As a further safeguard against failure, a surplus buoyancy was allowed in order to be able to fit additional things required – or to strengthen any parts requiring it. These demands corresponded with a gas supply of 11,300 cubic metres (398,890 cubic feet).

The covering of the metal framework, the outer skin, consisted in its upper part of waterproofed cotton cloth, and in its lower – on account of the greater lightness – of thin silk.

As the source of power for propulsion I selected the, at that time, most reliable and comparatively light Daimler engine. It weighed 30 kilograms (66 lbs) per hp and required 500 grams (1.1 lb) of benzene per bhp per hour; a 9 hp engine with 10 hours working required 200 litres (44 gallons) of cooling water. In order to determine the latter, as nothing was then known concerning it, I allowed the hot water from the engine in the Daimler works to run into an upper flat vessel from which it dripped through numerous small holes into a lower vessel – and from this, after cooling, was led back to the engine. For use in the airship, the cooling water flowed through long pipes – round which bands with pointed projections were wound, so that the temperature was immediately reduced through surface and air cooling. In the case of the second or third airship, it was possible to replace the arrangement by the cooling apparatus invented in France, such as in an improved form is still in use to-day.

In order to avoid too long – and therefore heavy – connecting gear, and also to keep down the width of the airship, four-bladed propellers 1.15 metres (3.8 feet) in diameter were selected. These, in spite of the necessarily somewhat hurried construction, had, according to the calculations of my engineer of that time, an efficiency of 71.3 percent.

The form of the airship, once the capacity was fixed, resulted from the practical requirements of smallest surface in order to keep the weight as low as possible and smallest cross-section in order to reduce the resistance. Considerations concerning the handling of the airship on the ground and the size of the construction shed at first only permitted a gas envelope less than 12 metres (39.4 feet) in diameter – actually 11.6 metres (38.1 feet); this meant a length 11.03 times great – namely 128 metres (420 feet).

It appeared impossible to maintain this extraordinarily-extended form solely by inner pressure, and thus, the rigid construction automatically followed. Even with this, however, the main loads could not be combined approximately under the centre; the longer the girder, which the gas envelope may be regarded as, the stronger must it be – and there is a certain limit of length with which the weight is greater than the buoyancy obtained from the increased gas capacity. I therefore divided the main weights, engines with propellers etc. and gondolas into two parts – one being suspended under the buoyancy centre of the fore half of the airship and the other under that of the after half.

From the considerations mentioned resulted the first airship, which was completed in 1900. This had the following dimensions:

Diameter	11.6 metres (38.1 feet)
Length	128 metres (420 feet)
Midship section	106 square metres (1,141 square feet)
Capacity	11,300 cubic metres (398,890 cubic feet)

Both ends of similar shape and each 16 metres (52.5 feet) in length.
The cross-section of the framework has 24 angles.

It is constructed like a spacious trellis-work, consisting of longitudinal girders and transverse frames. Intervals between transverse frames eight metres (26.2 feet) and four metres (13.1 feet) – through these the space for the gas is divided into 17 sections. The aluminium serving as building material has a specific gravity of 2.7 and a breaking strength of approximately 33 kilograms per square millimetre (46,936 lbs per square inch.). Plain lattice-girders are constructed from angle and T profiles – the fittings also form angle profiles. The weight of these girders is, according to position, .9 to 1.8 kilograms per metre (.6 to 1.2 lb per foot); the weight of the whole framework, 5,825 kilograms (12,842 lbs) – .516 kilograms per cubic metre (.03 lb per cubic foot).

Corresponding to the number of sections, the airship contained 17 gas cells of waterproofed cotton cloth, which weighed in the upper half of the ship .170 kilograms per square metre (.035 lbs per square foot) and in the lower half, because less waterproofed, .150 kilograms per square metre (.031 lbs per square foot).

The outer skin had a weight above of .130 kilograms per square metre (.027 lb per square foot), below of .085 kilograms per square metre (.017 lb per square foot), and therefore an average weight of .107 kilograms per square metre (.022 lb per square foot).

Whilst horizontal control was effected by means of planes – material stretched on wooden frames – placed underneath at both ends, for vertical control there was a movable weight which at first was suspended at some distance, but later was rolled along the gangway. On the third ascent, however, a rudder for vertical control was fitted under the bow – an alternative method thus being provided for greater safety as in the case of all other controls.

Underneath the first and second quarters of the vessel's length – and also underneath the third and fourth quarters – there was a rigidly suspended gondola, containing a powerful Daimler engine of 14.7 hp.

By means of double bevel-wheel gear, aluminium casting, raw-hide and inclined shafts, the two engines each drove two propellers fitted to right and left of the framework on a level with the centre of resistance.

The total weight of the engine installation was 1,970 kilograms (4,343 lbs); that is 67 kilograms (148 lbs) per horse power.

This first rigid airship, with all its weaknesses and defects, formed a reliable basis for the development of the rigid system.

A comparison with one of the latest airships will show what improvements have already been made – and then we can see what further development is possible for the rigid type.

When once an airship that could proceed under its own power – and was capable of being controlled – had been constructed, it was a question of building one suitable for commercial and military purposes.

Greater lifting power made possible, in particular, more powerful engines to give greater speed, and fuel supplies for longer voyages – as well as a larger number of persons as crew or passengers, living quarters, W/T equipment, mooring gear, spare parts etc.

A lighter gas to give increased buoyancy was not available – nor at that time a lighter material to reduce the weight. On the contrary, the weight of the gas cells, which were much too leaky, had to be increased from 170 grams per square metre (.035 lb per square foot) to 230 grams per square metre (.047 lb per square foot), until finally the correct treatment of the goldbeater's skin was found, when the cell weight was again reduced to 170 grams per square metre (.035 lb per square foot). The impermeability has become almost perfect. The weight of the outer cover was also increased because the silk used for the lower half in the case of the first ship proved too weak and too extensible – for which reason it had to be replaced by cotton material.

In order to increase the lifting capacity, there remained therefore, generally speaking, only the enlargement of the gas space and a more economical use of the aluminium.

The enlargement of the gas space finds its limit in the difficulty of handling the colossus and in the construction of sheds to take it.

The introduction of the triangular girder in place of the flat girder – and the general employment of stamped and processed parts – meant a much better utilisation of the material.

The important gain in buoyancy – obtained mainly through an increase in the volume – now permitted the speed to be improved. The automobile industry in particular, by always demanding better, more reliable and more powerful engines, made this possible. It was a great handicap to the development of aerial navigation that it was not profitable for engine builders to expend time and money in producing an engine specially suitable for aircraft as regards reliability, accessibility and low weight per hp. There remained no alternative but to take up the manufacture of engines, which was done most successfully by the firm of Maybach & Son, with the type designed and gradually perfected by them (the much lower petrol consumption of the engines is particularly noticeable).

It was now necessary to proceed with the construction of more pointed ships in order to reduce the resistance – although this involved a less favourable ratio between capacity and surface area.

The most important improvements made possible by the gain in buoyancy were the fitting of the third engine, the W/T Station, the comfortable living rooms, the ascents through the balloon to platforms on top, the searchlight equipment etc.

Thus the modern airship, of which the "*Sachsen*", built last year and lengthened a short time ago by eight metres (26.2 feet), is a representative, has gradually been arrived at.

A comparison of this vessel with the first of my rigid airships shows progress in the 14 years intervening between the two similar to that which took place in steamships in the previous century.

The diameter increased from 11.6 metres (38 feet) to 14.8 metres (48.6 feet) and the length from 128 metres (420 feet) to 149 metres (489 feet). The length now is only

10 times the diameter, as compared with 11 times previously. The capacity of 20,800 cubic metres (734,240 cubic feet) instead of the former 11,300 cubic metres (398,890 cubic feet) – an increase of 8,200 cubic metres (289,460 cubic feet) – which gives an additional lifting power of from 8,500 to 10,000 kilograms (18,739 to 22,046 lbs) according to the position of the barometer and the temperature of the air.

The transverse section has 17 angles as compared with 24 angles formerly; the head, which was blunt, is now 28 metres (92 feet) long and the stern 32 metres (105 feet). The "*Sachsen*" is divided into 17 compartments. Method of construction and material have remained the same.

What considerably greater strength the new lattice girders possess in spite of the, on an average, lower weight of .13 kilograms per metre (.087 lb per foot) is shown by the fact that the framework of the first airship showed considerable alterations of form (up to 25cm = 9.8 inches) with comparatively small bending moments; whereas in the new ships, alterations of form are not perceptible with the stresses arising during a voyage.

Corresponding with this much greater strength, the weight of the framework could be kept comparatively low.

The gradual improvements described above have been accompanied, in a gratifying manner, by corresponding progress in the performances of the airships. In the first airship, there were, of course, many small defects: rudders got caught, valves opened involuntarily etc. It could only obtain a speed of nine metres per second (18.4 miles per hour) and carry running materials for a voyage of about 10 hours. The second ship, however, had a speed of 12 metres per second (26.8 miles per hour) and the fifth covered a distance of 1,194 kilometres (742 miles) in a run of 38 hours, which came to end at Birnbaum near Göppingen, but not on account of any defect in the ship: there were still running materials on board for two hours – and both engines were in the best condition; only the crew being overstrained. In the meantime, several thousand voyages have been made by Zeppelin airships under the most varied – and frequently most difficult – conditions. These show that the calculated performances of the airships have also been the actual. The diagram in the first instance permits it to be recognised to what really fine efficiency the first ship had been brought by the removal of the small defects mentioned and, we say it openly, a few large ones; a passage through the air of up to 1,800 kilometres (1,118 miles) in 67 hours would have been very noteworthy for the first ship – especially as the atmospheres would have considerably extended these distances by the direction and strength of its own motion.

And now the "*Sachsen*"! With a speed of 72 kilometres (44.7 miles per hour), 1,000 kilograms (2,205 lbs) crew and 3,000 kilograms (6,614 lbs) useful load, it covers a distance of 2,200 kilometres (1,367 miles); and with a contrary wind, which would not have allowed the first ship to move, 1,480 kilometres (920 miles). The more economical its fuel consumption, that is, the slower its speed, the longer is the distance it can cover. With half power, 1,000 kilograms (2,205 lbs) crew, and 3,000 kilograms (6,614 lbs) useful load, the distance rises to 2,900 kilometres (1,802 miles). If the "*Sachsen*" only proceeded at the speed at which the first ship travelled 1,800 kilometres (1,118 miles), it would cover a distance which cannot be shown on the diagram – namely about 30,000 kilometres (18,614 miles). Such, without accompanying wind, slow and, with contrary wind, unreliable voyages are indeed not of much value. If airships are to find useful employment for traffic purposes, they must be able to cover fixed distances in unfavourable weather and carrying a profitable cargo of passengers, mails etc. more rapidly, more conveniently and at least as safely as the means of conveyance on the ground – and, particularly, in the water. From the experiences already obtained, one is justified in assuming that as soon as rotating sheds are available, this distance limit for airships of the "*Sachsen*" class will be approximately 1,000 kilometres (621 miles). With modern airships, therefore, a regular service might be institutes – for example, between Berlin and London or Stockholm; between Stockholm and St Petersburg; Constantinople and Alexandria; Genoa and Algiers etc. which would pay as soon as the conviction has become general that one cannot travel more comfortably, with more freedom from sickness, more rapidly, or with less danger.

That which has been attained represents, however, only one stage of the development which I have had in mind for aerial navigation from the commencement. Only when quite long voyages with profitable freight, in which weeks are saved as compared with other means of communication, have been safely made will the object have been achieved.

Should one continue at the work, however? In a lecture in 1896 before the Württemberg District branch of the Society of German Engineers, I prophesised that: 'to the wing-frame for independent flight there could be fitted an engine by which the foundation would be laid for proceeding with continually larger flying machines' – and to-day, only 18 years later, I have to place before myself, in common with the whole flying world, the question whether aeroplanes will not take over the tasks of my airships, which have originated in the meantime, and take away from these their raison d'être?

I could not be content with my own negative answer to this question; as I have always done, I had the correctness of my conclusions confirmed by science – of which I myself have not sufficient knowledge. I beg permission to present to you my co-worker, Engineer Dornier, who, on the basis of his investigations, will sketch for you the possibilities of future development – and at the same time compare, as far as is practicable, the performances of the airship and the aeroplane.

* *

Your Highness, ladies and gentlemen!

The development possibilities of rigid airships can best be given with the aid of an equation, which can rightly be termed the 'fundamental equation of the airship'.

To understand the following, it is necessary to briefly trace back this equation.

If V is the useful gas space of an airship in cubic metres, s the difference between the weights of one cubic metre of air and the gas used for filling – that is, the buoyancy, then the lifting capacity H of the airship is obtained as follows:

$$H = V.s \text{ in kilograms.}$$

The empty weight of the ship, Le, is composed of the weight of the framework, gas cells, outer covering, steering gear and balancing planes, gondolas, structures, apparatus and other equipment.

The empty weight is mainly that of the gas cells and framework.

The total weight of the gas cells is essentially influenced by the sub-division of the gas space – that is, the number of cells.

The weight of the framework depends, with given dimensions, on the stresses on the body of the airship and the safety with which they are taken up. The weight, Gm, of the propelling machinery consists of the weight of the engines and their appurtenances, the tanks and pipes, the gearing and the propellers. If km is the weight for 1 hp in kilograms, then the weight of the whole machinery installation of Ne hp is obtained as:

$$Gm = km.\ Ne \text{ kilograms.}$$

The fuel consumption per hp per hour, kb, can for practical purposes be assumed as constant; the weight B of the running material carried for t hours is obtained as:

$$B = kb.\ Ne.\ t \text{ kilograms.}$$

If the empty weight, the weight of the machinery installation and the weight of the running materials carried are deducted from the lifting capacity, the useful load is obtained – that is, the weight available for carrying persons, goods, ammunition etc. We get the formula:

$$Nu = H - Le - Ne\ (km + kb\ .\ t).$$

If the resistance of a ship at an actual speed of v metres per second is W kilograms, then the power Ne in hp necessary for the attainment of this speed is:

$$\frac{Ne = W.v}{\eta_o\ 75}$$

Where the total efficiency of the machinery installation is η_o.

It was established by a large number of experiments on voyages – and with models – that for the resistance W, which is experienced by a body moved through the air in a straight line at the speed v, can, with sufficient accuracy for practical purposes, be written:

$$W = V v^2$$

Where C is a coefficient independent of the speed. We thus obtain:

$$\frac{Ne = Cv3}{\text{˥}\ 0.75}$$

If we insert this value of Ne in the expression for the useful load then we get:

$$Nu = H - Le - \frac{\text{˥}\ 0.75}{v^3}(km + Kb.t)$$

On account of its outstanding importance for estimating the value of dirigibles, I desire to call this the fundamental equation of the airship.

The fundamental equation contains in the values H, Le, C, ˥o, km and kb the principal development possibilities of airships – and will throw light on all questions concerning them. We will consider in the first instance the prospects for the improvement of the performances of rigid airships without an enlargement of the gas space.

The lifting capacity with volume constant could only be increased by the employment of a lighter charging gas. In the most favourable case (a vacuum), there would be an increase of only about seven percent. Practically, therefore, nothing more is to be expected here as regards the increase of the useful load.

Moreover, the weight empty with the present dimensions can only be reduced to an inconsiderable extent.

The most effective means offered to the airship industry to increase the performances of the ships without adding to the volume is the reduction of the resistance. This has to be done by giving the body of the ship a favourable form, by reducing the harmful resistances and diminishing the friction.

Diagram no.4 shows what can be attained with a ship of approximately the same dimensions as the "*Sachsen*" by reducing the air resistance figure by 10 percent. As abscissa of the diagram are laid out the useful loads in kilograms as ordinates; the lengths of the voyages in kilometres. The "ausgezogenen" [? continuous] lines correspond with present conditions. The "gestrichelten" [? line of small dashes] lines give the conditions if the resistance figure C is reduced from 3 to 2.7. We read off from the diagram, for example, with 4,000 kilometres (2,486 miles) voyage length, the following useful loads:

> At 54 kilometres per hour: 5,100 kilograms as compared with 3,400 kilograms in the case of the "*Sachsen*" class.

At 63 kilometres per hour: 4,000 kilograms as compared with 2,200 kilograms in the case of the "*Sachsen*" class.

At 72 kilometres per hour: 2,700 kilograms as compared with 770 kilograms in the case of the "*Sachsen*" class.

At 81 kilometres per hour: 1,200 kilograms as compared with 0 kilograms in the case of the "*Sachsen*" class.

In addition, of course, as is seen from the figure written at the side, the power necessary has fallen. The diagram should have shown the importance of the reduction of the resistance.

The efficiency of the driven-gear is already so high that noteworthy improvements are not to be expected here. On the other hand, it appears possible to improve the total efficiency of the propeller installation, which now, in consequence of the reciprocal influence of the propellers, lies approximately between .65 and .70.

A considerable increase in the power of the engines is to be expected from the motor industry. Diagram no.5 shows for the same ship, for which diagram no. 4 was drawn, the influence of the alteration of the power, in case ˥0 = .80 instead of .70, kmt = 4 instead of 6 kilograms per horse power, and kb** = .2 instead of .24 kilogram per horse power per hour. The improvement of the power, as will be seen from the diagram, would be extraordinary. We read, for example, with 3,000 kilograms (6,614 lbs) useful load:

At 54 kilometres (33.6.miles) per hour: 8,750 as compared with 4,500 in the case of the "*Sachsen*" class.
At 63 kilometres (39.1 miles) per hour: 6,450 as compared with 3,300 in the case of the "*Sachsen*" class.
At 72 kilometres (44.7 miles) per hour: 4,850 as compared with 2,500 in the case of the "*Sachsen*" class.
At 81 kilometres (50.3 miles) per hour: 3,800 as compared with 2,000 in the case of the "*Sachsen*" class.

These figures speak for themselves.

Note: t. in the case of aeroplane's km amounts approximately to 3 kilograms per horse power.

** On the occasion of the competition for the Emperor's prize in 1913, a fuel consumption of kb = .210 kilograms per hp per hour was attained.

Although much work is still required before vessel and driving-gear attain such a high degree of perfection – as was assumed for the "gestrichelten" lines [lines of small dashes] of the two diagrams, the combined efforts of the airship and motor industries will certainly soon result in these figures being reached approximately.

Up to now, we have examined in what manner and to what extent an increase of the capabilities can be obtained with the present dimensions of the ship.

We will now show how the conditions shape themselves if the dimensions of the ship are increased.

We will limit our examination to a number of similar ships having a diameter to length ration of 1 : 10 as is now usual. The outer form of the ships is also similar to the present design.

On the basis of experience with completed ships 11 to 16.6 metres (36 to 54.5 feet) in diameter, and with the aid of accurate weight investigations for ships 22 to 25 metres (72 to 82 feet) in diameter, lifting capacity and empty weight were ascertained for ships with diameters ranging from eight to 30 metres (26 to 98 feet), corresponding with lengths of 80 to 300 metres (262 to 984 feet).

Measurements with completed ships and model experiments enabled the resistance figures for these ships to be determined with sufficient accuracy.

After lifting capacities, empty weights and resistance figures for the ships had been determined, the fundamental equation could be applied.

In order to put forward the conditions as clearly as possible, diagram no. 6 was prepared. This is based on the following assumptions: buoyancy 1.1 kilograms per cubic metre (.069 lb per cubic foot), ᒣ0 = .70 km = 6 kilograms (13.2 lbs) per hp, kb = .24 kilograms (.53 lb) per hp per hour.

As abscissa, there are shown on the right the speeds in metres per second and on the left the useful loads in kilograms. The right portion of the diagram contains the line of the weights of the machinery installation – as well as the lines of the fuel consumption for voyages of five to 300 hours. In the left portion are drawn the characteristic lines for ships eight to 30 metres (26 to 98 feet) in diameter. It is to be remembered that the length of the ship is 10 times the diameter; the diameter figure is, therefore, sufficient to give a definite idea of the dimensions of the ship.

A few examples will make clear the influence of the increase of the dimensions on the performances of the ship:

1. Given – length of voyage, or time for which running and speed; required – the useful loads that can be carried by the ships. The following figures are assumed: length of voyage, 7,200 kilometres (4,474 miles); mean speed, 72 kilometres (44.7 miles) per hour. The time endurance is then 7,200 ÷ 72 = 100 hours. The speed in metres per second is 72 ÷ 3.6 = 20. We seek the point of intersection of the lines V = 20 and t = 100 and go parallel to the abscissa axis up to the intersection with the characteristic lines of the individual ships. We read, for example:

D =	18	20	22	25	30	metres
	(59.1	65.6	72.2	82.0	98.4	feet)
Nu =	600	3,400	7,300	15,200	33,300	kilograms

(1,323	7,496	16,094	36,510	73,414	lbs)

The extension of the diameter from 18 to 30 metres (59.1 to 98.3 feet) therefore increases the useful load 55 times.

2. Given – useful load and speed; required – the endurance (time and distance) of ships of various sizes. The following figures are assumed: useful load, 15,000 kilograms (33,069 lbs); speed V = 18 metres (59 feet) per second = 65 kilometres (40.4 miles) per hour.

We want the points of the ships' characteristic lines which correspond with the useful load of 15,000 kilograms (33,069 lbs). The diagram shows us that a useful load of 15,000 kilograms (33,069 lbs) can generally only be obtained with ships over 16 metres (52.5 feet) in diameter. If, for example, we go from the points of intersection with the characteristic lines of the ships of 20, 22, 25 and 30 metres (65.6, 72,2, 82 and 98.4 feet) up to the ordinates with V = 18 metres (59 feet per second (= 40.4 miles per hour), then we find:

D =	20	22	25	30	metres
	(65.6	72.2	82	98.4	feet)
t =	10	23	39.5	57.5	hours
s =	900	2,070	3,660	5,180	kilometres
	(559	1,286	2,274	3,219	miles)

Where D = diameter
t = time endurance
s = distance endurance

But not only the useful load and distance increase with rising volumes. The diagram also shows clearly that with equal useful load and time endurance, the large ship is faster than the small one.

After these examples from the diagram of the influence of increasing dimensions have been made clear, it should be generally shown what is the effect – if, in addition to the increase in the volume, there is an improvement of H, Le, ˥o, C, km and kb – as was done at first for constant volume.

Every point between the characteristic line of the weight of the machinery installation and the ordinates axis represents a definite distance. If a parallel line to the abscissa axis is drawn through a desired point of the right portion up to the intersection with the characteristic lines of the ships, then the abscissa of these points of intersection are the co-ordinated useful loads.

The points of intersection of the characteristic lines of the individual ships with the abscissa axis correspond with the values H – Le. If, therefore, H or Le should be improved, then these points would fall further to the left, which means greater useful loads would be obtained. The inclinations of the ships' characteristic lines towards the abscissa axis are determined by the ships' resistance figures C and the assumption of the value ηo = .70. If these values should be altered, the characteristic lines would enclose larger angles with the abscissa axis – and therefore, so to speak, become erect; with equal useful load greater speeds or endurances are then obtained.

An improvement of the values of km and kb should result in the lines of the weight of the machinery installation and of the fuel consumption approaching nearer to the abscissa axis; with equal speed and endurance – therefore, the useful loads would increase.

How great is the influence of these factors is shown by the fact that with an increase of the total efficiency from η0 = .70 to η0 – .75 with 30 metres (98.4 feet) per second (= 67 miles per hour) and 25 hours endurance, the useful loads with, for example, diameters of 25, 26 and 28 metres (82, 85.3 and 91.8 feet) would undergo the following increases:

D=	25	26	27	metres
	(82	85.3	91.8	feet)
Nu with η0 = .70=	1,200	2,200	4000	kilograms
	(2,648	4,850	8,819	lbs)
Nu with η0 = .55=	4,900	6,300	8,600	kilograms
	(10,803	13,889	18,960	lbs)

It must be pointed out in connection with this that the costs of manufacture and maintenance increase very rapidly with the dimensions. If, however, these costs are given in percentages of the useful load, then the large ship is seen to be superior to the small one.

In practice, increases in the volume, improvements in the machinery installation and reduction of the resistance go hand in hand.

If this is borne in mind, it may be said, on the basis of the foregoing considerations, that the airship is not at the end, but only the beginning, of its development.

We have become acquainted with the development possibilities of the rigid airship, so far as they can be dealt with in this paper.

In conclusion, it is proposed to briefly compare the performances of aeroplanes with those of airships.

Messers Bendemann and Everling of the German experimental establishment for aeronautics at Adleshof give, in no. 8 of the *Journal for Flying Techniques and Airship Navigation*, a 'work equation; for aeroplanes, which corresponds with that here put forward for airships.

We propose, with the aid of this equation, to compare aeroplane and airship:

Nu = Ne (η0.75/km. 1/V – (km+kb.t);

The following values are taken: km = 3 kilograms (6.6 lbs) per hp; kb = .30 kilogram (.66 lb) per hp per hour; η_0 =.70; k = W/N = .13; the weight constant m = 1.8 (in the case of the dotted line m = 1.0).

Diagram no.7 gives the connection between speed and distance endurance in the case of aeroplanes when the total carrying capacity as regards fuel is made use of: the "ausgezogene" [? continuous] line with an efficiency of 70 percent: greatest distance 2,200 kilometres (1,367 miles); the "gestrichelte" line [? line of small dashes] with an efficiency of 100 percent: greatest distance 3,200 kilometres (1,988 miles); and the "strichpunktierte" [? dotted] line also with an efficiency of 100 percent and Le = 0: greatest distance 5,700 kilometres (3,542 miles). These limits can of course never be attained in practice. They show us, however, that even these most favourable imaginable assumptions the limits for the endurance in the case of aeroplanes are comparatively narrow.

The limits for the useful load are as narrow for aeroplanes as for airships.

Of course, the dimensions of aeroplanes – and particularly the power necessary – increase very rapidly with a rise in the useful load, so that the great advantage of the handiness of the present machine is lost as soon as useful loads of 1,000 kilograms (22,046 lbs) have to be transported.

In order to enable a direct comparison to be made between airship and aeroplane, diagram no.8 has been drawn. This shows the performances at various speeds of a ship of the "*Sachsen*" type – equipped with machinery installations of various powers, and those of aeroplanes of equal engine power and at the same speeds.

It is seen from the diagram that so long as it is a question of great distances and moderate speeds, the airship is to be preferred to the aeroplane. If, on the other hand, short distances have to be covered at high speeds, the aeroplane is far superior to the airship.

Even at 90 kilometres (55.9 miles) per hour, the characteristic lines of airship and aeroplane cut one another. At 108 kilometres (67.1 miles) per hour, the airship can no longer compete with the aeroplane.

In order to avoid misconceptions, it may be specially pointed out that the results given by the diagrams must not be taken as absolute values, but only as comparative figures.

His Excellency Count von Zeppelin:
Your Royal Highness, ladies and gentlemen!
The statements which we have just heard give us a surprising view into the future.

It is true the figures found by calculation for the distances travelled undergo important limitations through the influence of the air currents which may increase or reduce the speed; in practice, only those objects can be attained which are easily within the capacity of an aircraft in spite of possible winds checking the flight. With the arrow-like progress of the aeroplane, the air currents have much less influence than in the case of the airship.

In spite of this qualification, the statements made establish the rigid law concerning the development possibilities of both types of aircraft that, independently of the load to be carried, the aeroplane must reach the limit as regards endurance very much sooner than the airship. The aeroplane, moreover, needs an engine installation of the power necessary to leave the ground and must make comparatively high demands on it during the whole of its flight in order not to drop down. Consequently, they cannot lengthen as desired their time in the air by and economical consumption of fuel. Airships, on the other hand, as they rise without engine power like a balloon, can do this to a very great extent. Aeroplanes also, much more than the airship, are dependent for their safety on the working of their machinery installation – for example, on the propeller blades not getting damaged or the engine not failing. For comparatively short journeys – up to about 1,000 kilometres (621 miles), when it is required to cover this distance in the shortest possible time – they will always be superior to airships on account of their much greater speed; for which they also have an advantage owing to their flying capabilities not being affected by rising to great heights.

If it is a question of covering distances of over 3,000 kilometres (1,864 miles) where no stopping places can be arranged – for example, across the Atlantic Ocean, from the heart of Europe to Colombo, or between China and Japan – then, in the near future, airships will alone come into consideration.

Our generation must not take such a narrow view as to neglect, because of the, at present, truly astonishing progress made with aeroplanes, the steady development of airships, which will permit the complete conquest of this domain.

At the commencement of my lecture, I spoke of the danger of hydrogen gas on account of its inflammability. The discovery of a non-inflammable, though somewhat less light, substance for filling the cells is not excluded. For this reason, the gradual development of airships to such dimensions that they would be lifted by the non-inflammable substance must not be neglected.

In this way the safest imaginable vessel would then be produced.

The National Archives (TNA) Air 1/626/17/33.

Appendix II

List of German airships 1914

At the commencement of the Great World War, Germany was known to possess the following airships:

Airship	Locality	Radius of action in miles
Naval:		
L III	Hamburg	
L IV (Schütte-Lanz)	Doing trials	
L V	Friedrichshafen	Under construction
Military:		
Z II	Cologne	950
Z III	Metz	950
Z IV	Allenstein	1,200
Z V	Posen	1,200
Z VI	Leipzig	1,200
Z VII	Dresden	1,200
Z VIII	Leipzig	1,500
Z IX	Friedrichshafen	1,500
SL II	Liegnitz	1,500
Private:		
Viktoria Luise	Friedrichshafen or Potsdam	950 (Under alteration)
Hansa	Dresden	950
Sachsen	Potsdam	1,000

National Archives (TNA) Air1/2099/207/201.

Appendix III

Specification of Zeppelin airships by type

Type	Length	Diameter	Gas capacity	Performance	Service height	Range	Payload	Engines
	m/ft	m/ft	m³/ft³	kmph / mph	m/ft	km/m	tonnes/ tons	No. of/type/ hp
G	148	14.0	18,700	80		1,100	6.5	3× Maybach 170
	486	46	660,384	50		683	6.4	
H	140	14.9	19,500	72		2,700	7.0	3× Maybach 170
	459	49	688,636	46		1,678	6.9	
K	148	14.9	20,900	76		1,900	7.8	3× Maybach 170
	486	49	738,077	47		1,181	7.7	
L	156	14.9	22,100	72		2,000	8.8	3× Maybach 180
	512	49	780,454	45		1,243	8.7	
M	158	14.9	22,500	81	2,500	2,200	9.0	3× Maybach 210
	518	49	794,580	50	8,202	1,367	8.9	
O	164	16	25,000	79	3,200	2,800	10	3× Maybach 210
	539	53	882,886	49	10,500	1,740	9.8	

Type	Length	Diameter	Gas capacity	Performance	Service height	Range	Payload	Engines
	m/ft	m/ft	m^3/ft^3	kmph / mph	m/ft	km/m	tonnes/ tons	No. of/type/ hp
P	164	19	31,900	96	3,200	4,300	16.2	4× Maybach 210
	536	61	1,126,537	60	10,500	2,672	15.9	
Q	179	19	35,800	95	3,500	4,900	17.9	4× Maybach 240
	586	61	1,264,265	59	11,483	3,045	17.6	
R	198	24	55,200	100	4,000	7,400	32.5	6× Maybach 240
	650	78	1,949,369	62	13,125	4,598	31.9	

Figures from: *Zeppelin! The German Airship Story* by Manfred Griehl and Joachim Dressel (Arms & Armour, London 1990) and www.onlineconversion.com

Appendix IV

The properties of hydrogen gas

The lifting capacity of hydrogen gas is about 1.2 grams per litre of gas at standard temperature and pressure – or one cubic foot of hydrogen gas will lift about 0.0749 lbs.

Hydrogen – being the first element in the Periodic Table of Elements – consists of very small molecules, and hence, is very difficult to contain and will easily pass through materials used to contain it; the rate of escape increasing with the increase in pressure. Hence, the higher an airship rises due to the lower atmospheric pressures, the greater the loss rate of hydrogen. Hence, airships that operated at much higher altitudes so as to avoid the defences would lose hydrogen at a far greater rate than those choosing to operate at lower altitudes.

Hydrogen is an odourless, colourless gas and will burn in air at concentrations between four and 75 percent with an almost invisible flame; the orange glow often described as having been seen from a burning airship is due to the combustion of other material from which the airship is made, such as the outer envelope.

Hydrogen gas was first recognised as a substance by the scientist Henry Cavendish in the late 18th century – its name being derived from the Greek for 'water former' as it produces water when burned with oxygen.

Hydrogen gas can be produced by the electrolysis of water or by the reaction of acids on metals, although during the Great War, hydrogen was mainly produced by passing steam over red-hot iron to give iron oxide and hydrogen by the use of the Lane Hydrogen Producer (or similar apparatus).

The means of making the gas bags of airships impervious to hydrogen gas was to use goldbeater's skin, which is the membrane found on the outer part of a cow's intestine, and it required about 200,000 sheets (80,000 cows) per airship. When wetted, the goldbeater's skin really adheres to itself or other sheets – although becomes slightly brittle when dry, so usually was applied to a muslin cloth or similar fabric to add to the strength and resilience.

There were about 18 gas bags, or ballonets, in each airship – meaning that even if three or four of the gas bags were punctured and deflated, the airship would still be able to remain aloft and have a good chance of making it to friendly territory.

Appendix V

Further details regarding the air raid of 15 June 1915

The fact that such an important target could be attacked with impunity stimulated an investigation into the circumstances by the Admiralty. Some of the correspondence reproduced below gives an indication as to concerns and an insight into the defence systems in place at this time:

Captain Superintendent, Tyne District to the Secretary of the Admiralty:

The loss of life and casualties appear to be chiefly due to lack of organisation, by which no warning of the attack was conveyed to the yards and workshops. It will have a serious effect on our new construction and refits if the men become reluctant to carry out refit work for fear of overhead attack. In view of the extreme importance of this district to us (more especially since the advent of floating dock), it would appear that its defence against air attack requires reconsideration and reorganisation of a much larger and more efficient scale.

Copy of telegram 709 from Flamborough Head to Admiralty.

Date 15.6.15. Sent 8.23pm. Received 8.54pm.

Following received from Yorkshire Mounted Brigade, Scarborough:

"Zeppelin approaching Flamborough Head; two of our aeroplanes have gone up from Hull to attack it. Hull Aberdeen informed."

To the officer commanding Tyne Defences and copied to the Secretary of the Admiralty, Whitehall, London, SW.

Report on the air raid by Palmers Shipbuilding & Iron Co Ltd, Hebburn-on-Tyne. Dated 17 June 1915:

Zeppelin airship attack; our Jarrow Works

We have the honour to place before you the following report with regard to an attack by an enemy airship upon our Jarrow Works on Tuesday evening, the 15th instant:

Arrangements for notice of probable attack and extinguishing of lights

We would, in the first place, state that in connection with arrangements for meeting an attack by aircraft, our first arrangement was that we would put out our lights whenever we received intimation of the presence of Zeppelins and send the men home. This, however, was occurring so frequently with a manifest loss of progress on our Admiralty work that, on the intervention of the interested parties, the under mentioned arrangement was come to, we being instructed to keep our lights on and our men at work until the given signal was supplied us. We were notified to this effect by a communication dated 1st May 1915, Tyne R/253, signed by Captain C Spearman, General Staff, Tyne Garrison. It was therein stated that we should receive the code word 'Prepare' when time allowed, which word would indicate that hostile aircraft had been reported in the vicinity, and that preparations should be made to extinguish lights eventually on getting the further message 'Extinguish', which it was arranged to send us in the event of the attack becoming imminent. At 8pm on 15th instant, the nightshift manager at our Jarrow Shipyard received a message from the Tyne Defences stating the War Office reported a Zeppelin seen 100 miles off Flamborough Head at 6.28pm steering west. No further message was received at Jarrow, and we may add that no messages at all were sent to our Hebburn Shipyard, which is occupied with Admiralty work.

Attack

Our nightshift manager records that about 11.40pm a loud report was heard coming from the direction of our steel works. He immediately ran towards our power station to order the lights out, but before anyone could possibly get there, bombs were dropped all over the shipyard and our engine works. All the electric lights were burning when the first bombs were dropping, but were switched off before the last bomb was dropped. A fire was found on the jetty at the dock entrance, but was put out before any serious damage was done.

Steel works

The Zeppelin dropped the first bomb in the pond outside the works and a further three bombs were dropped near the roll stock – parallel with the hot bank. The next bomb was dropped in the excavation for the new soaking pits. After that, three bombs were dropped near the "A" furnace, and three at the bottom of the stairs near the 15" mill. Two further bombs were dropped near the pickling tanks – after which the Zeppelin went in the direction of the engine works. The first bomb dropped at 11.40pm and the last about 11.50pm.

All the bombs appear to have been incendiary in this department, except that dropped in the soaking pit excavation; the explosion of this shell causing the death of one of our workmen, named Frederick Pinnock, who was employed at the band saws – he having been struck on the head by a piece of shell.

The total number of bombs dropped in the rolling mills and steel works was 12. No damage was caused to these departments by the bombs.

Jarrow Shipyard

There would appear to have been four bombs dropped in the Jarrow Shipyard – one of which was an incendiary bomb – and the material damage in the shipyard consists of the distorting and piercing of a few piles of plates and bars, 14 dents and small holes pierced in the shell plating of the monitor HMS *Marshal Ney*; practically the whole of the windows of the shipyard offices and stores were broken by concussion, and one wooden structure splintered. No loss of life took place in the shipyard department.

Engine works

The most serious damage was done in our engine works, where a sad loss of life occurred. A bomb dropped in the passage between the pattern shop and the blading room – spreading out into the heavy machine shop and extending into the tool room and medium machine shop – bringing down several of the principals of the roof, abutting against the pattern shop, and practically destroying all the glass roofs in the vicinity – together with the glazing in the pattern shop. Another bomb was dropped in the centre of the main erecting shop – destroying several of the principals of the roof – and damaging beyond further use the following destroyer turbine casings: Two low-pressure bottoms and one top, one hp bottom; also two gland sleeves, two gland covers and guide columns and a large quantity of blading. One hp rotor received damage to the blading, and also other minor damage. The glass of the building is all destroyed; the gateways have been thrown down, and a great deal of glass in the iron foundry and a few panes in the brass foundry are destroyed. A tool room lathe has had the saddle broken and the leading screw damaged. There is also considerable damage to the stock of turbine blading – both finished segments and material.

Two bombs were dropped in the neighbourhood of the boiler shop – one dropping in a field close by, and the other at the colliery company's crossing.

In the engine works department, a number of men were killed and wounded; the number killed up to the present time being 15 and wounded (most seriously) 11 – in addition to about 20 minor cases.

Hebburn Shipyard

No attack was made upon our Hebburn Shipyard, but the manager reported as follows:

> "Shortly after 11.30pm last night, an explosion was heard by those working in the yard. The foreman in charge and the electrician at once proceeded to turn out the lights. Five or six more reports were heard by the time this was done. The men working on the monitor, being under cover, remained there until explosions ceased. No damage has been done in the yard. The men who were working remained and resumed work after their midnight meal. The men at work were shipwrights fastening the slope deck armour plating."

Conclusion

We have thought it well to give the above details our experience, and would beg to add that we feel, as the lives of these men were lost and damage done to the Jarrow Works, was caused owing to the establishment being in a full blaze of light, which would have been extinguished had we received the pre-arranged signal. Some explanation is, we think, due to us, while, in addition, it will also be necessary, before we can approach our workmen to resume night work, for us to have some assurances and guarantee for the future in regard to the carrying out of arrangements for reasonably ensuring their safety.

We have the honour to be, Sir,
Your obedient servants,
A B Gowan; Managing Director.
Palmers Shipbuilding & Iron Co Ltd.

A copy of a letter from Captain Superintendent, Tyne District to the Admiralty sent on 16 June 1915:

As verbally reported this forenoon, an enemy airship visited this district between 11.30pm and midnight on the 15th instant, and caused considerable damage. The facts, as far as I have been able to gather them, are as follows:

The senior naval officer (*Patrol*) was informed that about 11.25pm, an airship was passing over Blyth – proceeding rapidly in the direction of Newcastle. He made the prearranged signal of blowing short blasts on the siren. Reaching the river in the neighbourhood of Wallsend, the vessel, apparently a Zeppelin, dropped eight or nine bombs on the premises of the North Eastern Marine Engineering Company – setting fire to a stack of timber and a large quantity of patterns, wrecking the roof of the foundry, doing various other minor damage in the yard and narrowly missing the large tower crane and two sets of 15" mountings awaiting shipment in monitors. There were no casualties here.

One bomb was dropped in the admiralty barge, *Y.200*, lying at the jetty – causing some damage – and she will have to be hauled up for repair.

The airship then crossed to Hebburn and after dropping one or two bombs in the steel works, appeared to have hovered almost stationary over Palmer's Jarrow Yard – completely wrecking the roof of the engine shop, where at least three bombs were dropped – and doing much damage to stacks of steel plates in the yard. The yard clock stopped at 11.40pm.

Very slight damage was done to HMS *Marshal Ney*, which will cause one day's delay in launching, but at the present moment, it is impossible to state the extent of the damage done to destroyer turbines in the machinery shop; the fall of glass – besides the actual explosion of the bombs – having to be considered.

During the whole of this time, the airship was at a considerable height – estimated at 5,000 to 7,000 feet. At Messrs Palmer's Jarrow, 15 men were killed and 30 to 40 wounded – of whom two or three have since died.

About six bombs were dropped here altogether. Apparently the vessel then passed over South Shields, dropped a bomb which set fire to a circus, and then descended considerably and made off.

She was fired at by the high angle gun (military) at Hebburn – also by HMS *Brilliant* – and the *Patrol*, used her searchlights as far as the elevation would allow.

The managing director of the North Eastern Marine Engineering Company spoke in terms of high appreciation of the prompt arrival of fire brigades sent by Captain Alan C Bruce, (SNO) from ships present, and for the very great assistance they rendered in extinguishing the blaze.

I understand that in both these firms, there will be some delay in recommencing work owing to the enormous mass of rubbish to be cleared out and roof to be reglazed, but probably in neither case will the delay be serious.

An unfortunate feature is that the men are showing considerable reluctance to doing night work – and I enclose for your information a copy of a letter I am sending to the military authorities.

He followed up with later on 16 June 1915:

To the General Officer, commanding North East Coast:

With reference to last night's attack by enemy airship, various firms employed on admiralty work in the district inform me that they received no warning that an attack was imminent.

As far as I am able to gather, (a) a message was received about 8pm that an airship had been sighted in the neighbourhood of Flamborough Head; (b) The Lord Mayor was informed by a friend at Cullercoates about 10.30pm of the presence of an airship on the coast. The chief constable of Newcastle apparently knew nothing of this.

The senior naval officer informs me that he received intimation of the airship being over Blyth, moving rapidly in the direction of Newcastle, about 11.25pm. He thereupon gave the usual warning on the siren, but this warning had hardly been given when the attack commenced.

The firms state that this signal was not heard, which is highly probable considering the nature of work in shipyards and machinery shops.

It therefore seems necessary to arrange for some more direct and efficient method, by further co-operation between the naval and military authorities, and it is suggested that some direct electrical signal between the garrison commander at Tynemouth, the senior naval officer and firms concerned should be installed – which ought not to be a difficult matter.

The continuance of admiralty work by night – as well as by day – is of the utmost importance, but naturally workmen are showing some reluctance to continue night work unless they can rely on receiving due warning of danger.

Report by Captain (D), 9th Flotilla, HMS *Patrol* regarding the events of 15-16 June 1915:

In reply to Admiralty telegram no.2130 of 19th June, I beg to submit that Flamborough Head 709 message was the first intimation received of approach of hostile airships.

This message was:

Handed in	8.20pm
Received at Newcastle Naval Centre	8.41pm
Received by *Patrol*	8.50pm
Made general	8.55pm

It was passed by Naval Centre to:

Military Centre
Whitley Air Station
Senior naval officer (*Patrol*)
Captain-in-charge (*Satellite*)
Naval Centre, Rosyth

The next information was from Blyth by telephone and W/T at 11.30pm and 11.32pm that airship was over Blyth. At same time, Port War Signal Station, Tynemouth, reported seeing airship. This information was passed by Naval Centre to me at 11.35pm and was also passed to:

Military Centre
Whitley Air Station
Captain-in-charge (*Satellite*)

And on its receipt by me, the pre-arranged siren alarm signal was immediately sounded.

At 11.52pm, when the Zeppelin was passing over HM ships at Jarrow, her position was reported from *Patrol* to Naval Centre and passed by them to Military Centre, Whitley Air Station and captain-in-charge, but by this time, the only two available aeroplanes had left.

All my arrangements for transmission of information worked satisfactorily and all HM ships at Jarrow were informed by signal and telephone between 11.30pm and 11.35pm – and I then endeavoured to assist the military by warning some of the shipyards by telephone; but from 11.35pm, when the siren warning was sounded, no reply could be got from Jarrow exchange; the operators having apparently taken refuge.

A full report on the raid was transmitted to the Admiral of Patrols yesterday.
Captain (D), 9th Flotilla.

From: Captain (D), 9th Destroyer Flotilla, HMS *Patrol*.
To: The Admiral of Patrols.
Date: 18th June 1915.

Air raid on Tyne night of 15-16th June

In continuation of my telegram 0015 of 16th June, I beg to report the following:

At 11.32pm on the 15th June the following signal was received from HMS *Panther* at Blyth:

"Zeppelin passing overhead, steering SW."

I at once gave the alarm siren signal, and ascertained that the Naval Centre and Whitley Air Station had been informed. The W/T Station at Tynemouth PWSS intercepted *Panther's* signal and reported that the Zeppelin could be seen steering inland.

The next report was by telephone from submarine officer at Blyth at 11.38pm:

"Zeppelin altered course towards south – apparently making for Newcastle."

Almost at the same time, the airship was sighted from *Patrol* coming towards the river from the northward – and apparently steering straight for Palmer's blast furnaces. It was very high up, but the night was very clear – and there were exceptionally few clouds.

Several bombs were dropped on the North Eastern Marine Engineering Company's Works at Wallsend – and one of them, falling among a large quantity of wooden patterns, immediately caused a large conspicuous fire. The airship then crossed the river to Palmers going quite slowly, and dropped a further six or seven bombs – apparently all high-explosive. At least two of these struck the large fitting shop, doing considerable damage. It was in this shop that nearly all the casualties occurred.

From Palmers, it altered course down the river; passed over HM ships at Jarrow to South Shields, where more bombs were dropped. The only gun that could be brought to bear here was a 3-pdr on a temporary HA mounting on board *Brilliant,* which has a very limited arc of fire directly overhead. Fire was opened from this and maintained as long as possible.

From South Shields, the airship altered course to southward and passed out to sea over Whitburn.

Having ascertained that the big fire was at the NE Marine Engineering Co's Works, I ordered fire parties to be landed at once from ships not at short notice. It was found on arrival that one of the new motor lighters – *Y.200* – had been struck by a bomb and was in a sinking condition. A collision mat was placed round her, and Elswick fire float telephoned for. She was eventually pumped out, the holes plugged, and the captain superintendent arranged for her to be hauled up for repairs. This work was carried out by a party from *Brilliant* under Lieutenant James C F Lewis, whose prompt action undoubtedly saved the lighter from sinking.

Whitley Air Station was kept informed of the airship's movements, and she was well-lit-up by *Patrol's* searchlights as soon as they would bear, in the hope that the aeroplanes might be able to attack. It will be seen from Captain Robinson's report, however, that there was only one reliable machine out of three, and that the Zeppelin was never seen. It is submitted that there should be sufficient machines at Whitley to allow of three being always ready. Had there been even two, there would have been a chance of attacking in the present case.

It is further submitted that the 6-pdr gun allowed to *Patrol* under CIO 491/1915 may be supplied and fitted as early as possible. The Tyne is too good an attraction not to be visited again, and the absence of a properly mounted A-A gun was badly felt in the present case, where the hostile airship hovered in the vicinity for quite an appreciable time.

Apart from any arrangements made by the military for notifying the approach of aircraft, *Patrol* endeavoured to warn some of the principal firms, but after the sounding of the siren signal, no response could be obtained from Jarrow exchange. At Palmers, a bomb dropped between two monitors on the slips, and small bits of metal pierced the hulls – making holes like bullet-holes.

Signed, Alan C Bruce, Captain (D), 9th Flotilla.

From: Commanding Officer, R.N.Air Station, Whitley Bay.
To: The Senior Naval Officer, Tyne.
Date: 16th June 1915.

Submitted:

Herewith report on action taken at this air station during attack by hostile aircraft on night 15-16th June 1915.

At 11.32pm the following message was received from the Military Headquarters, Tyne Defences:

"Tynemouth Castle report Zeppelin flying SW in direction of Blyth. Blyth people can see it as well."

At 11.40pm a message was sent from here reporting that aeroplane no.1101 had left the aerodrome.
At 11.50pm a message was sent to headquarters reporting that aeroplane no.1099 had left the aerodrome.
The respective pilots and passengers were:

Aeroplane	No.1101
Pilot	Flight Commander Robinson
Observer	Leading Mechanic Hinkler

Aeroplane	No.1099
Pilot	Flight Lieutenant Savory
Passenger	Nil

Armament carried:

No.1101
- 2 Hale's 20 lb bombs
- 4 petrol bombs
- 1 short rifle and 3 Hale's grenades.
- 1 Martini-Henri rifle and 20 rounds incendiary bullets

No.1099
- 2 Hale's bombs
- 2 petrol bombs

Aeroplane no.1101 on leaving the station observed fires (the effect of bombs dropping) in a westerly direction and a course was steered for these – and at the same time, the machine was climbed as rapidly as possible.

Soon after this, a searchlight was observed searching the sky in the same direction.

After reaching a height of 1,000 feet, nothing could be seen owing to getting into banks of cloud.

Above 2,000 feet I got out of the clouds but could see nothing of the ground owing to clouds being below me – and after flying about for some time, lost my bearings and decided to steer an easterly course in the hope of perhaps cutting off the hostile aircraft.

Nothing was seen of the aircraft or the ground either by myself or my passenger, except occasionally a fire (now believed to have been Palmer's Works).

After flying for some time in an easterly direction, I throttled down my engine and glided down about 800 feet (i.e. under the clouds) to pick up my bearings, and found myself to be between Whitburn and Sunderland. When and where I originally crossed the Tyne I have no idea, as I had lost my bearings in the clouds. I then steered a northerly course and seeing nothing, returned to the aerodrome about 12.30am.

On leaving the aerodrome, I hit one of the firing butts on this rifle range with my chassis and carried away two of the left-hand struts. On landing, the aeroplane was considerably damaged (having no chassis to land on).

Aeroplane no. 1099 steered south on leaving the aerodrome and then up the Tyne towards Newcastle, but keeping north of the river. The engine was going badly at the start, and so after reaching Newcastle, the pilot returned to the aerodrome as his engine was failing rapidly. Lieutenant Savory also saw nothing of the airship and when over 1,000 feet also got lost in clouds (i.e. when near large fire – probably Palmer's).

We have now two aeroplanes here, vix., nos. 972 and 1099 (both BE2c). No. 972 should be ready to-night and no.1099 is awaiting two cylinder leads to replace cracked ones.

I therefore submit that you apply for more aeroplanes to be sent here owing to the great difficulty of locating hostile aircraft at night – especially when there is only two aeroplanes available.

Signed: C E Robinson. Flight Commander.

The National Archives (TNA) Air 1/635/17/122/114.

Appendix VI

Bombs

During the early airship raids on Great Britain, the bombs employed by the Germans were already of two distinct classes or types, viz. those used by naval airships and those used by army airships.

The bombs carried by the naval airships, as far as could be ascertained, were the same type as was used subsequently by those ships (i.e. pear-shaped, round-bottomed, fitted with percussion fuse in the neck). These bombs were almost all about 50 kg in weight, and until the month of June 1915 the number carried was usually nine – giving a total weight of 990 lbs of high-explosive projectiles. These were supplemented by a varying number of incendiary bombs, which never exceeded 50 in number, and usually totalled about 30. This gave an average load of about 1,740 lbs per ship.

The HE bombs carried by army airships, as far as can be ascertained, were all of the spherical type with percussion fuse – similar to those employed on subsequent raids by army airships. The average weight was 50 kg each – or about 1cwt. The military ships usually carried a much larger number of incendiary bombs than the naval ships.

There were, however, two raids in which the spherical HE bomb carried by the army airships were replaced by hand-grenades (Taube) weighing about 5 lbs each. Their effect was practically negligible and their use was never repeated. They were intended for use against troops or crowds of civilians in the streets. The two raids in which these hand-grenades were employed were carried out by *Hauptmann* Linnarz in *LZ 38*. The first was against Southend on 26 May 1915 – when a total load of 1,290 lbs was carried – and the second against London on 31 May 1915 – when the total load was estimated at 2,375 lbs.

The incendiary bombs carried by all these ships, both naval and army, were the conical type -weighing about 25 lbs – standardised later by the military air service.

An army airship, *LZ 38*, on 10 May 1915 – when raiding Southend – carried about 90 incendiary bombs of the above type, in addition to four HE bombs – a total load of 2,690 lbs; again on 29-30 April 1915 *LZ 37* carried 66 incendiary bombs in addition to 10 high-explosive – a total load of 2,750 lbs.

The first marked increase in the weight of bombs carried by the early raiders occurred on the raid of 15-16 June 1915 when *Kapitänleutnant* Hirsch in *L 10* raided Newcastle-upon-Tyne. On this raid, a total of 3,450 lbs of bombs was carried – made up of 25 HE and 28 incendiary bombs.

The National Archives (TNA) Air 1/2123/207/73/2.

Appendix VII

22 February 1916: Zeppelin *LZ 77* – British report on wreckage

Report on the remains of *LZ 77*:

ROYAL NAVAL AIR SERVICE REPORT ON THE REMAINS OF LZ 77

In accordance with orders, we proceeded to France on the 22nd February to inspect the wreck of the German airship *LZ 77*, which had been brought down by the French at Revigny during the night of February 21st. The following is the report of our inspection:

We reached the scene of the wreck on the morning of the 24th and spent the whole of that day and the following morning inspecting the remains. With the consent of the French authorities, representative portions of the girder work, engines, fabric, &c. were brought back to England.

It is understood that the airship was brought down at night by a 75mm gun mounted on a motor trolley, and firing incendiary projectiles. The height at which the airship was flying has been estimated at 1,200 metres. It appears that, after a number of shots had been fired, a hit in the stern was made, and that this caused a small fire, which was immediately extinguished. A further shot hit the airship amidships and passed right through – the body setting fire – to the hydrogen gas. The airship reached the ground about one-and-a-half minutes afterwards – falling probably with relatively small trim down by the tail, and burnt for several hours.

It is apparent from photos taken on the morning after the disaster that a great deal of information as to the arrangement and general construction of the ship could have been obtained from an inspection of the wreck, but unfortunately, the French authorities lost no time in breaking up all the larger pieces of structure and in removing pieces of machinery, &c. from the places at which they fell – thereby destroying much of the evidence.

The information obtained was considerable, and will be of great value, but if it had been possible to make a careful examination of the remains as they existed immediately after the fire was extinguished, the information obtained would have been, very much, more complete. It would, therefore, appear desirable to arrange that in the event of another ship being brought down under similar circumstances, the air department representative in Paris should apply at once to the French authorities to allow the ship to remain untouched for as long as possible, and that it should be arranged that officers sent out from England should arrive there at the earliest possible moment.

General design and construction

The diameter of the parallel body has been estimated, from somewhat inadequate data, to be about 10 metres – or about the same as the British no. 23 class. The number of sides of the polygon is supposed to have been 17. No exact information as to the length could be obtained, but from the load of machinery, &c. carries, and from the fine stern, it is inferred that the length was not far short of 10 diameters, or 160 metres.

No definite indication of the number of gas bags was obtained, but a guide plate was found with 14 small wires passing through it – apparently for gas-bag valve control.

It is nearly certain that the tail fins stopped at least seven metres from the tail, and that the rudders and elevators – the total number of which was four – were hinged to the after edges of the four fins.

The cars were probably two in number: the after one carrying three engines – one of which drove a propeller at the end of the car and the other two drove two wing propellers placed well up the sides of the ship, while the forward one carried the main controls, and one engine driving a propeller at its after end.

The cars were fitted with buffer bags for landing purposes.

The engines were all of nearly equal power – and the total bhp was about 880.

The armament consisted of six machine-guns – the location of which in the ship is not known. The workmanship throughout was very good, and in the hull construction, the manner in which the details of construction were varied to suit the needs of each part was evidence of large experience. The machinery and fittings generally were of substantial construction and followed generally the line of progress existing before the war.

Structure

The length of a side of the polygonal section amidships was measured from one rather battered girder, which appeared to have been part of the parallel body structure, and found to be 296 cm. The distance between transverse sections could not be directly ascertained, but measurements of distance between certain wire attachments suggested that the distance might be 8.8 metres. An attempt has been made to determine the number of sides by measuring the angles of two or three main points – and the results vary from 17 sides to 19 sides. The best specimen measured would give 17 sides – and if this is taken to be correct, the diameter would be 16 metres.

As regards the structure, no traces were found of the bow structure. In the structure amidships, the longitudinals appear to have consisted almost entirely of triangular girders 20½ × 14 cm with channels outwards. A few longitudinal girders of 'W' section are reported to have been found. The transverse girders appear to have been composed in about equal proportions of 'W' section 19½ cm deep and 14½ cm wide outside and 25½ cm wide on inner side – and of triangular girders 20 × 14 cm having channels inwards.

The continuous members of the girders were made of an aluminium alloy of the duralumin type. Channels 1" × 7" × .7" × .043", angles .7" × .7" × .05" edges of both channels and angles turned slightly inwards to stiffen them.

The corresponding sections for no.23 class are channels .9" × .9" × .9" × .05", angles .9" × .9" × .05". Portions of rectangular section girders 20 × 18.5 cm were also found – having corner angles .8" × .8" × .07" evidently suited for use as a pure compression member. The girder bracing pieces are probably hard-rolled aluminium of the sectional form usual in Zeppelin practice. The weight of the bracing pieces per foot run of girder is proportionately greater than in Vickers designs, but the strength of the girders is not known. Experiments on this point will shortly be proposed.

The main joints were of an exceedingly rigid and substantial construction, and of novel design. It is clear that the Germans have found it necessary to give special attention to these parts.

The wiring in the transverse frames appears to have been very elaborate – some of the main joints having as many as seven wires attached to them. The wires varied from 2½ to 3 mm in diameter, and were of hard steel – probably galvanised throughout. In the panels between transverse and longitudinal girders, an elaborate system of wires appears to have existed, but the system, on which they were arranged, could not be ascertained. None of the wires throughout the structure had means of adjustment, as far as could be seen – the ends of the wires being passed through eyes in the structure and either twisted several times round the wire, or bound to it with fine wire seizing over about four inches in length and soldered. Representative specimens of the girders and main joints were brought back to the Admiralty – and drawings of them will be made and circulated.

The stern was nearly intact for a length of over 20 feet from the after end. It was very finely tapered and of very light construction. It had 16 sides – and only four of the main longitudinals extended to the stern. These were placed at the ends of the horizontal and vertical diameters. The other girders, and also the transverse frames at this part, were replaced by single channels as used in the construction of the ordinary girders – the frames passing inside the long channel frames. The extreme end was formed by a small cap of duralumin, into which the ends of the longitudinals were riveted.

Fins

No trace of any distinctive structure which could be attributed to the fins was found – and it is to be inferred that they were composed of members similar to in the main structure. It is clear from the very light construction of the stern that the after end of the fins was at least seven metres from the after end of the ship, and it is understood that this is in accordance with recent Zeppelin practice.

Rudders and elevators

One rudder was found nearly intact – and the remains of three apparently similar rudders, or elevator planes, were all found. Each of these four planes had a separate opening sector, and it is supposed that they were hinged to the after ends of the four fins; two forming elevators and two steering rudders. It is understood that such an arrangement accords with recent Zeppelin practice. The area of the rudder found nearly complete was about 150 square feet and its maximum thickness was about four inches. Its construction was exceedingly good (see fig. 1).

Keel and cars

The remains of at least two cars were found. The cars had open tops and corrugated duralumin sides and platforms and duralumin framing. They were fitted with fabric buffer bags. The cars were connected to the hull by wire ropes and by light wooden struts. The engines rested on cast aluminium pads on built-up duralumin seats.

It was probable that only two cars were carried, as previously stated, and that one of these – possibly the after one – was fitted with three engines, all on the centre line, and that the forward one carried the main controls in addition to an engine.

No traces were found of any external keel girder – and it is probable that none was fitted in view of the large diameter of two propellers at the after ends of the cars.

A small length was seen of an internal walkway, 30 cm wide of 5-ply wood, with a layer of fabric glued to the underside and round the wood – secured to the top of a triangular longitudinal girder (from which the bracings on the upper face had obtained).

It appears almost certain that the main communication passage and the keel girder, if any, was internal. No traces could be recognised of cabin accommodation. None of the pieces of structure found showed traces of varnish.

Portions of a girder, a hull casting, bracing wires and a piece of sheet duralumin alloy have been handed to the N.P.L. for analysis and tests.

Propellers

The propellers were four in number – all two blades pushers and slightly over 18 feet in diameter. Two of them were wing propellers placed well up the sides of the body and driven through reduction and reversing gears from two engines – both placed fore and aft in one of the cars (probably the after one). The other two propellers were placed at the ends of two cars. They were each driven through reduction gearing from an engine placed on the centre line in the after end of the car.

The speed of rotation of the propellers was relatively low – about 500 rpm – assuming the speed of the engines to be 1,200 rpm.

The propellers were of walnut; the surface was veneered to two directions for the outer two-thirds of the blade area. The blade area is shown in fig.2. The edges were bound with brass strip approximately as in fig.3. The maximum width of blade was 16 inches – depth of boss being 8¾ inches.

Machinery

Number of engines found in wreck = 4.
Type of engines: three in number of improved Maybach design – believed to be of 210 hp each. One engine of either Mercedes or new Maybach design (probably the latter) – believed to be of 250 hp.
Total power of installation: 880 hp

Main points notice in the two types of engines:

Improved Maybach:

(1) Carburettor
This is of slightly different design from the carburettors fitted in the Maybach engines in this country, the differences being:
(a) The fitting of three small holes before the main jet. These are apparently pilot jets.
(b) An adjustment of the jet needle. This was worked by a lever fitted on the engine, which also operated the advancing and retarding gear.
(c) No vent cock was fitted to the petrol chamber.
(d) The remaining parts of the carburettor were apparently identical to those fitted to existing Maybach engines in this country.
Note: a complete carburettor was obtained from the wreck.

(2) Cam shafts
These were driven by wheels at each end.

(3) Magnetos
(a) No automatic advance gear was fitted.
(b) The range of advance was 30 degrees.
(c) Porcelain Bosch plugs were tilted to the engines – two being fitted to each cylinder head.

(4) Starting arrangements
These were approximately the same as the Maybach – six cylinders being fitted.

New Maybach or Mercedes engine:

(1) Overall dimensions
These were approximately the same as the Maybach – six cylinders fitted.

(2) Cylinder valves
These were in the cylinder head; two induction and three exhaust valves were fitted to each cylinder.

(3) Cam shafts
Same as for Maybach, the valves being operated by bell cranks carried on the cylinder heads.

(4) Sparking plugs
Two plugs are fitted to each cylinder in the sides of the combustion space – each plug going to a separate magneto.

(5) Carburettor
These were of different design from the Maybach, but of the same principle – two being reconstructed.

(6) There was no restriction in the induction pipe between nos. 3 and 4 cylinders.

(7) Usual pipe, for breaking locks, was fitted to the tops of the cylinders.

Note: A cylinder was brought back and will be further examined.

General:

(1) Silencers
Two air-cooled silencers of the usual type were seen – and two silencers 9 feet, 6 inches long of larger and quite different type, which may have been adapted for water recovery (see figs. 4 and 5).
The use of silencers for water recovery appears improbable, as there was no orifice from which the water could have been collected. It is not, however, clear for what reason these two special silencers were fitted, but it is possible that they were intended for cooling the exhaust gas before passing the ring space.

(2) Radiators
These were of the usual honeycomb type – 2 feet, 9 inches by 3 feet, 7 inches by 6 inches – with tubes ⅜ inch diameter. They were fitted with a fabric screen, after the style of a telescopic blind, which could cover the whole of one side of the radiator (see fig. 6).

(3) One telegraph was found (see fig.7). This was of very light design and about eight inches in diameter.

(4) Three petrol tanks only were seen – each holding about one ton of petrol.
The petrol tanks were of cylindrical aluminium construction made with welded joints. A special form of filler cap and safety strainer were used – and a bursting disc secured by cylinder was also fitted in the filler cap. The tanks appear to have rested in built-up duralumin girders. A section through the tanks is shown in the attached sketch (see fig. 8).

(5) The design of the reduction gear grating &c. was of a very heavy type.

(6) Shafting
The length of shaft connecting each of the wing propellers with the car was approximately 40 feet, with two supporting bearings and no universal joints. The shaft struts were tubular, as seen in photographs taken on the 22nd, but no traces of them were seen by us. The maximum unsupported length was 16 feet.
The shafts for the midship propellers were 2½ inches external diameter, 1½ inches inside diameter.
The maximum unsupported length was 16 feet.
Couplings were forged solid ⅜ inch thick, ¼ inch bolts on 3¾ pitch circle.
The bolts were not evenly pitched.
The bearings for shaft were as indicated in sketch (see fig. 9).
The forward engine was driven by shaft – four inches external diameter; about 12 feet in length. The gear wheels reducing speed of propeller shaft to 500 revolutions per minute were secured roughly as indicated in fig.10. The large diameter of this shaft is interesting; no reason could be seen for this – especially as shaft for aft propeller was about 2½ inches external diameter.

General arrangement of machinery:
From a partial reconstruction of the wreck, it is considered that the arrangements of the engines was as follows (see fig. 11):

(1) Two short lengths of pipe were found passing through a circular guard, which may have formed the means of heating the cars (see fig. 13).

(2) A valve which appeared to be from a fabric ballast tank was obtained. This valve was about five inches diameter and worked by means of a wire-operated lever.

(3) A fair number of tubes (apparently of duralumin) of about four inches diameter and one millimetre thick – with connection at right angles – were seen. A few tubes of about six inches diameter were also seen.

(4) Great care was exercised in carrying electrical leads. A set of leads was enclosed in a flexible metallic hose of aluminium.

(5) One gun mounting was found. This was alongside the walkway, and consisted of a very light three-leg tripod with a centre supporting tube.

(6) No split pins or spring washers were fitted anywhere except on the engines – although castellated nuts were fitted and the bolts drilled ready for pins.

(7) Small portions of what is believed to be gas-bag fabric and outer-cover fabric were found. These have since been tested with the following results:

Report of samples of fabric and cordage:

No. *Z 1*: Fragments of outer cover (?) These pieces were a good deal charred. They are composed of a single-ply fabric painted blue on the outside and dope. The dope consists apparently of cellulose acetate and is not exceptional either in flexibility or in its adherence to the fabric. The stuff was not very inflammable, but it has apparently not been so treated as to be absolutely non-inflammable.

Strips were sewn on at intervals – and at one place, a two-inch strip was stuck on diagonally. The nature of the adhesive was not determined, but probably dope.

The weight of the fabric complete is 172 grams per square metre.
It is noted that Mr Reinberg states that the fabric is either flax or ramie.

No. *Z 2*: This is apparently rudder fabric and consists of stout canvas – to which is stuck pieces of fabric similar to the preceding. The adhesive is probably dope. It is noted that the edges of strips stuck on are frayed out.

No. *Z 3*: Shock-absorbing bag; this consists of the following layers: heavy canvas, rubber, light cotton, thick layer of rubber, light cotton dope. The dope is similar to that used on the outer cover, and the rubber is very little vulcanised, if at all. Possibly some mineral grease has been mixed with the rubber.

No. *Z 4*: This is a sample very much burnt. Adhering to it was a much damaged piece of animal matter, which is, in all probability, goldbeater's skin. So far as can be seen, there is no evidence of this having been two-ply fabric; it is at present single-ply only.

No. *Z 5*: A two-ply fabric rubbered between pliers and on one face. The weight is 295 grams per square metre. On one face, the rubber has a peculiar appearance – which may possibly be due to the attachment of goldbeater's skin, subsequently removed, but nothing certain can be said on this point. The fabric is composed of vegetable fibres whose nature was not further investigated. It contains approximately 160 threads per inch and 13 in the other direction. Warp and weft were not distinguishable. The count of the yarn used in this was decidedly lower than in the subsequent sample.

No. *Z 5a*: Unrubbered single-ply cotton – alleged to be imported into Switzerland. Ends per inch approximately 126 lying in pairs. Picks per inch about 160 – the warp being of lower count than the weft.
This fabric does not appear to be of particularly good quality for aircraft purposes.

Sample of window in one of the cars: This consists of non-inflammable celluloid substitute, principally cellulose acetate.

Cordage sample: The strength of four pieces of this is 111, 128, 140 and 115 lbs – mean 123 lbs = 56 kilos.
Weight – 4.35 grams per square metre.
Breaking length – 12,800 metres.
This does not appear particularly good, but it is noted that the sample was a trifle burnt in places; care, however, was taken so far as possible not to include any burnt piece in the test pieces.

(8) The outer cover appears to have been laced together by lacing hooks as used for aeroplane fairing and secured to the framework by cord.

(9) A gas valve was seen in an almost undamaged condition; its points are of great advantage over the type at present in use in our own airships. A valve obtained and working drawings are being made (fig.14).

(10) A framework which appears to have been a pressure-controlled diaphragm was found, but its condition was so bad that it was difficult to obtain accurate details. It appears probably that this diaphragm was fixed in the lower part of the gas bag and connected to the gas valve at the top of the bag. The area of this diaphragm would be sufficient to open the top valve as soon as the pressure became appreciable.

(11) A length of control wire was obtained; its flexibility is very much greater than that of a wire used in our own air service. It appears that only part of the whole length of the control wire is made use of the flexible material – the remainder being piano wires.
Diameter – 0.197 inch. Nineteen wires to strand, 11 strands coiled around core 0.125 inch diameter.
Diameter wire – 0.008 inch. 10 feet, 2 inches, weight 8 oz. One foot weighs 0.79 oz. 20.3 feet per 1 lb.
(1) End used with original splice about 3½ inches long. Thimble in to take pin ½ inch diameter. Other end looped, bound and soldered.
Wire broken at end of splice – 1,770 lbs – apparently damaged by fire.
(2) End with original splice. No thimble, so tested on pin ⅝ inch diameter. Other end doubled, bound and soldered.
Wire broken at 2,450 lbs. Original splice held.
Reference – 20 feet of Craddock's C.D. wire (25 cwt) weighs 11¼ oz. 28.5 feet per lb. This is not nearly so flexible as the Zeppelin cable.

(12) A drum was found that would appear to be wireless aerial coiled on it. The condition was not, however, such as to give any useful information.

(13) A length of trail rope was obtained and is found to be length 3 feet, weight 12 oz. 4 feet = 1 lb (under slight pull), circumference 3.75 inches (under slight pull, about 3.62 inches)
Broken tension at (1) 4,000 lbs
(2) 3,850 lbs
The rope was rather worn.
The extensibility of the rope is, by reason of its construction, very great – and this should form a very elastic method of securing the ship.

(14) The armament is said to have consisted of six machine-guns – probably of the German Maxim type. A bomb release gear was obtained and had been given to 'G' section for examination. It was apparently operated both electrically and mechanically.
It is understood that a complete electrical switchboard with provisions for releasing 24 bombs was found.

(15) The number of crew found is said to have been 15.

(16) The remains were found of what appears to have been a calcium container. It is understood that these are dropped from the ship to make smoke and light – from which the speed over the ground can be calculated.

(17) The following information as regards date when ship was built is submitted with a view to indicate whether a ship was one of the latest types. One of the radiators was stamped 23/6/15. One of the engines was numbered 189 and modified motor was numbered 422. It would appear that latter motor would have replaced one of the earlier types. Further, records in office show that Maybach motor no. 86 was tested 15th January 1914; several earlier numbers – 70 to 86 – were tested just previous to this date. It is, therefore, not unlikely that ship was completed in 1915.

T R Cave-Brown-Cave, Squadron Commander.
G Villar, Engineer Lieutenant
H L Woodcock, Commander
A E Hyne, Commander
C I R Campbell, D.N.C. (Representative)
Air Department, April 1916.

The National Archives (TNA) Air 1/2103/207/30/11.

Appendix VIII

Summary of operations by aeroplane or seaplane carried out over England between 1914 and 1916

1	21 December 1914	Dover
2	24 December 1914	Dover
3	25 December 1914	Sheerness, Gravesend, Chatham, Thanet
4	21 February 1915	Braintree, Coggeshall, Colchester
5	23 February 1915	Off Essex Coast
6	26 February 1915	Off Essex Coast
7	20 March 1915	The Downs
8	16 April 1915	Sittingbourne, Kingsferry, Bridge, Faversham, Deal
9	23 May 1915	Westgate, Dover
10	3 July 1915	Off Essex Coast
11	13 September 1915	Margate, Cliftonville
12	14 September 1915	Off Westgate
13	9 January 1916	Dover
14	22-23 January 1916	Dover
15	23 January 1916	Dover, Capel
16	24 January 1916	Capel, Dover
17	9 February 1916	Broadstairs, Ramsgate
18	20 February 1916	(i) Lowestoft (ii) Walmer
19	1 March 1916	Cliftonville, Kingsgate
20	19 March 1916	Dover, Deal, Ramsgate, Margate
21	23 April 1916	Dover
22	24 April 1916	Dover, Ringwold
23	3 May 1916	Deal
24	20 May 1916	St Peters, Dover, Sholden, Ringwold

25	9 July 1916	(i) Manstone, Westgate (ii) Dover
26	12 August 1916	Dover
27	22 September 1916	Dover, Deal
28	22 October 1916	(i) Sheerness (ii) Off the Thames Estuary
29	23 October 1916	Margate
30	28 November 1916	London

The aeroplane raids carried out over Great Britain from occupied Belgian aerodromes during 1914 to 1916 formed only a small fraction of the aerial activity over the North Sea. German seaplanes constantly patrolled the southern portion – and on occasions, actively interfered with shipping. The object of the raiders that crossed the coastline appeared to have been that of:

a) Reconnaissance of naval bases, such as those at Dover or Sheerness. In most cases, the enemy aeroplanes were seen flying from Mariakerke (Ostend).
b) Reconnaissance of an aerodrome, such as Manston or Westgate. In addition to taking photographs, the raided often attempted to bomb the hangars or other targets of opportunity.
c) Bombing or torpedo attacks by seaplanes or aeroplanes directed against freight steamers or warships. These attacks were frequent – and their occurrence had not necessarily been logged on shore.
d) Bombing attacks on fortified bases and East Coast towns such as Colchester, Lowestoft, Ramsgate and Dover.
e) Attack on London.

Very few of these attacks were carried out by night – and those that were, were carried out when there was a moon and clear skies (although the raid against London was carried out during a hazy day as the raiding pilot's chief objective was to elude observation).

The majority of the raids directed against East Kent were of a 'tip and run' nature – and the raiders rarely ventured more than one or two miles inland.

The results of anti-aircraft fire was relatively ineffective – although on occasions had driven away the raiders before they could reach their intended target. The quantity of ammunition expended in each case was considerable, but the same was true of anti-aircraft fire on the Western Front, where a great volume of ammunition was necessary to prevent the enemy's observers from obtaining their desired information by crossing over the lines.

Appendix IX

The problems of finding, intercepting and bringing down Zeppelins at night – reports regarding events of 31 March 1916

The problems of finding, intercepting and bringing down Zeppelins at night are graphically illustrated by this series of reports regarding events of 31 March 1916:

Reports on Zeppelin raid for the night of 31 March 1916 by Major F V Holt; Officer Commanding 18 Wing, Royal Flying Corps, 15, Albermarle Street, London:

The gradient wind was about 20 miles per hour from the west.

1. An uncertain number of Zeppelins were reported over or off the Eastern Counties – and it was necessary to keep a reserve of aeroplanes to deal with late arrivals.
2. Information was rather uncertain owing to telephone and telegraph wires having been brought down by a storm on the previous evening.
3. All Zeppelins which might have been making for London struck the Norfolk Coast and then turned southwards.

The night was clear and calm from 8pm to 11pm. There were some light clouds at about 5,000 feet, but it was clear above that. After 11pm mist started to rise on several grounds, and at 2am the position at the various grounds was:

Hounslow	Slight mist
Hendon	ditto
Hainault's Farm	Mist (too thick for flying)
Sutton's Farm	Mist (too thick for flying)
Joyce Green	Slight mist
Farningham	Slight mist
Croydon	Quite clear
Wimbledon	Slight mist
Northolt	Slight mist in places

Aircraft (BE2cs) RFC available for operations:

Hounslow	2
Hendon	2
Hainault's Farm	4
Sutton's Farm	2
Joyce Green	2
Farningham	1
Croydon	2
Wimbledon	2
Northolt	2

Every machine carried Ranken Darts or 16 lb HE bombs and incendiary bombs.

At 9.50pm – when it was quite certain that one airship which had come down the coast was making for London from the NE and was under 30 miles away – the following aeroplanes were sent up:

Joyce Green	1
Sutton's Farm	1
Hainault's Farm	2
Hendon	1
Northolt	1

With instructions to patrol at 6,000 feet from their own grounds – outwards from London in order to engage the Zeppelin before it dropped its bombs – at the same time, one machine was told to patrol at 10,000 feet over the centre of London and act after bombs had been dropped.

Machines were sent up afterwards on low patrol (6,000 feet) during the danger period and to fly outside their landing grounds on the east-north-east and north of

London (and a high patrol at 10,000 feet of the two machines over the east-centre of London).

As the attack came from the east, the high patrols were found from stations on the west and south-west and low patrols from the stations on the north-east, east and south-east.

I was in direct telephonic communication with all stations from Room 242, War Office. Thirteen machines went up. One pilot was killed getting off the ground; no other pilot was injured. Three machines were completely wrecked and two partially wrecked.

A conference of all pilots was held at this office the next day – and the following conclusions were arrived at:

a) **Lighting aerodromes**: Some of the lighting arrangements were too complicated and confused pilots trying to land upon them.
b) **Visibility of airships**: Three pilots saw the airship from below when the searchlights were upon it. Two of them followed it without the searchlights, but found it difficult to follow. No pilot on high patrol saw the Zeppelin, though Captain Dunn must have been 2-3,000 feet above and within a few miles when the searchlights were on it. There was, therefore, no evidence yet that a Zeppelin can be picked up from above. The height of the Zeppelin was about 8,000 feet – and it does not appear to have got any higher.
c) **Armament**: Lieutenant Brandon was heavily fired at with machine-guns, but was not certain if the fire came from above or below the Zeppelin. Several shots hit his machine.
d) **Anti-aircraft guns**: All pilots said that the shells were bursting no higher than 6,000 feet and the three pilots who saw the Zeppelin said that it was at least 2,000 feet above the shells. Many pilots were under anti-aircraft fire.
e) The BE 2cs were faster and apparently out-climbed the Zeppelin.
f) The Rankin Darts did not ignite the gas, but they were not expected to as they only contain a violent explosive, which was expected to blow in the balloons.
g) The pilot is fully employed flying his machine – and an observer would have a much better chance of following the Zeppelin.

All pilots showed great keenness, but I should like especially to your notice:

2nd Lieutenant A de B Brandon, Royal Flying Corps (SR): a young pilot who showed great determination in his successful attack upon the Zeppelin. He is the first pilot to succeed in dropping bombs on a Zeppelin at night – and his success will inspire others with renewed enthusiasm.

2nd Lieutenant C Ridley, Royal Flying Corps (SR) for great keenness and good work during this and former raids.

F V Holt, Major, Commanding 18th Wing, Royal Flying Corps.

Report from 2nd Lieutenant G H Birlay regarding the events of the night of 31 March 1916:

Sir, I have the honour to report that last night at 9.45pm on the receipt of orders to attack a Zeppelin over London, I left the ground on a BE2c. I climbed to 5,000 feet over Hounslow Aerodrome when I made straight for the NE corner of London. I was climbing all the time, and from the time I left the aerodrome at 5,000 feet for at least 20 minutes, I did not see any flares owing to clouds just below 5,000 feet. I climbed to 9,000 feet – circling over London – and remaining at that height looking for the Zeppelin. Seeing flashes on the ground of anti-aircraft guns about the NNE corner of London, I made in that direction, but at no time saw the Zeppelin; during this time, I had lost sight and direction of Hounslow, but saw other landing grounds from time to time. At 11.45pm – having seen no signs of the Zeppelin – I decided to come down. I saw landing grounds between the clouds and made for one. Below 4,000 feet there was a mist which made the distance from the ground difficult to judge. I sent down a parachute flare about 2,000 feet to attract attention – and perhaps a rocket. I sent down another from 1,200 feet which failed to ignite. I made rather a fast landing – overshooting the mark and running through some hurdles into a pond, breaking the propeller and the leading edge of the left-hand bottom plane. I beg to state that if there had been a searchlight in front (from 100 to 250 yards) and at right angles to the long arm of the landing flares, the landing would have been made much more easy. I landed at Sutton's Farm.

I have the honour to be, Sir,
Your obedient servant,
G H Birley. 2nd Lieut RFC.

Report from C G Ridley 2nd Lt., RFC, Joyce Green, of events of 31 March 1916:

Sir, I have the honour to report that on 31st March I received orders from War Office to patrol for Zeppelins 6,000 feet. I left the ground at 9.30pm. Ten minutes after leaving the ground, I saw a Zeppelin in the beam of searchlights high above and in front of me. I fired about 20 rounds and gave chase, but it got out of range of searchlights and I lost it. I landed safely at 11.40pm having reached a height of 9,000 feet.

I have the honour to be, Sir,
Your obedient servant,
C G Ridley.

Report of the events of the night of 31 March 1916 by 2nd Lt A de B Brandon RFC, SR:

I left Hainault Farm at 9.25pm and circled round the aerodrome until I got to a height of 6,000 feet at about 9.40pm. I then saw the Zeppelin high up on my right in the light of the searchlights. She appeared to be heading in my direction. After about five minutes, the searchlights lost the Zeppelin and I continued in its direction until it was 5-600 feet over my head. I circled round in front, and climbed, and passed over the Zeppelin – I think at about 3-400 feet – and dropped no.1 lot of darts. I

heard three reports and thought that I had made a hit. Shortly after this, I heard more reports, which were probably from a machine-gun, and this made me uncertain whether I had made a hit or not. I continued and circled in front of the Zeppelin, and turned round to get in its rear – and ongoing there was a tremendous amount of machine-gun-firing going on. At this point, I switched off my lights and continued in my direction for 2-300 hundred yards – and then turned and got in a direct line with the Zeppelin. I was then about 500 feet above it; I closed the throttle and volplaned towards the Zeppelin; the nose of my machine was pointing about quarter way from the rear. I then got out an incendiary bomb, and in trying to get it into the tube, I had to take my eyes off the Zeppelin – and on looking up again, I was astonished to find that in a very few seconds I would have passed the Zeppelin, so I quickly placed the incendiary bomb in my lap and let off no.2 and 3 lots of darts. I did not hear any report from this. I concluded that the Zeppelin was, in reality, coming towards me, so I opened up the engine again and turned completely round and following a southerly course – continuing for some considerable time, as I thought the Zeppelin had got a good start. In the meantime, I turned my lights on again and I was at 8,000 feet. I cruised round at 8,000 feet for some time and saw nothing, and then dropped to 6,000 feet and cruised around for some considerable time without also seeing any sign of the Zeppelin. At this height I saw one lot of flares, which subsequently turned out to be Farningham. An examination of the machine shows that one Holt landing flare and wing skid were broken in landing, and there were three bullet-holes in the right aileron, the left tail and the right elevator respectively. I arrived down at 11.10pm. When I first saw the Zeppelin, I was flying at 6,000 feet; the flashes from our shells appeared to me to be about 6,500 feet – and I should say the Zeppelin was 8-9,000 feet up. I first saw the Zeppelin at 9.40pm and lost sight of it at 10.05pm. The searchlights were on it for four to five minutes; one flashed across it twice, but did not seem to pick it up.
Signed A De B Brandon,
2nd Lieut, RFC, SR.

Report of events by Clifford Ross, 2nd Lieutenant, Joyce Green:
Sir, I have the honour to report that on 31st March I received orders from the War Office to patrol for hostile aircraft and left the ground at 9.50pm. After being in the air about an hour, I noticed a number of shells bursting on a point a few miles north of Sutton's Farm, where several searchlights were concentrated. I immediately flew in this direction, but on reaching the place, the searchlights had been subdued and the guns ceased firing. I landed safely at 1.10am – having patrolled at between 8,000 feet and 11,000 feet.
I have the honour to be, Sir,
Your obedient servant,
Clifford Ross, 2nd Lieut. Joyce Green.

Report by Captain F G Dunn, RFC, Croydon:
Sir, I beg to make the following report on flight made by me on the night of 31st March. I left the ground at 9.55pm on BE2c, 2584 carrying four 20 lb HE bombs; three HL incendiary bombs and two parachute flares. I made two large circuits of aerodrome – climbing to 5,000 feet. I could then see flares at Wimbledon. Went in this direction for a while, still climbing; when nearing Wimbledon, I turned and went towards east where I saw lots of flares (Farningham and Joyce Green). I was then at 7,000 feet. After continuing east for about 10 minutes, I turned north and could see lights at Hendon. Going in this direction, I crossed the Thames at 9,000 feet. At this point I noticed two searchlights; one flashed for a moment on the planes. I then turned south and still climbing, arrived near our aerodrome (Croydon) at a height of 11,000 feet. I again turned north and crossed the Thames at 11,700 feet. At this point I could get no petrol to service tank, so decided to land. So I turned – and gliding down, landed safely in our aerodrome at 10.56pm. During whole flight, I noticed no aeroplane or airship.
I am, Sir,
Your obedient servant,
F G Dunn, Capt, RFC.

Report by P Rader, 2nd Lieutenant RFC of Home Defence Detachment, Croydon:
Sir, I beg to hand you the following report on flight made by me on the night of the 31st March 1916.

I ascended from Croydon Aerodrome at 11.55pm on BE2C, 2574 carrying with me four HE 20 lb bombs and five HL incendiary bombs, two parachute flares, a Veries pistol and four cartridges. After two circuits of the aerodrome, I headed due east from Croydon in the direction of Joyce Green – climbing all the time. In 12 minutes, I was almost directly over another aerodrome, which I am sure was Farningham. At the end of 20 minutes, I had reached an altitude of 5,500 feet and could see Joyce Green. I crossed the river, which was easily discernible, and here passed within 200 feet of another aeroplane travelling in a westerly direction. I patrolled this section in large circles for 35 minutes, and saw nothing – and as the ground appeared to be getting developed in mist in spots, I headed west again towards Croydon. About half-way, I was being followed by a searchlight, which was evidently attracted by the noise of my engine. I also observed two bright blue lights in a very black patch – one of which was blinking intermittently. As Croydon Aerodrome was now plainly visible – and fearing a sudden ground fog – I descended at 1am. My maximum altitude was 9,500 feet.
I am, Sir,
Your obedient servant (sd),
P Rader, 2nd Lieut, RFC.

Report by 2nd Lieutenant H S Powell RC on the night's activities:
Sir, I have the honour to submit following report:
On night of March 31st, at 9.15pm I left the ground at Sutton's Farm for the first patrol. Having received orders to patrol at 6,000 feet, I flew in large circles at that height and at 10pm saw a Zeppelin at about 8,500 feet. At that time, I was about a mile away. Heavy fire was being maintained by anti-aircraft guns, but all the shells were bursting around me – and practically at the same height that I was – and about 2,000 feet beneath the Zeppelin. I distinctly saw something fall on the Zeppelin from above, but I was too far away to make any definite statement what it was.
I have the honour to be, Sir,
Your obedient servant,
H S Powell, 2nd Lieut, RFC.

Letter from Major W G S Mitchell, RFC, Northolt:
Reference accident to Lieutenant Bailey:
On receiving W.O. instructions, I sent off Lt Bailey. The night was dark and with a slight haze near the ground, but I did not consider it too bad to fly. It was quite clear up above. The aerodrome was very heavy, but night flying had already been practised successfully. I watched Lt Bailey start and saw him leave the ground, as far as I could judge, about opposite the last flare. The engine appeared to be going well. He disappeared, and some three minutes afterwards, I heard a dull thud and saw a green Veries light go off on the ground. On going to the spot, we found the machine wrecked and Lt Bailey dead. From the evidence of an officer, Lt Turner, and the mechanics on duty with the flares, Lt Bailey was about 20 feet off the ground at the end flare. The machine was wrecked about 200 yards beyond the flares. It appears to have side-slipped and struck the ground nose first. There was a slight ground mist, and it is possible that Lieut Bailey ran into a patch of it – losing control of the machine.
Signed,
W G S Mitchell, Major, RFC.

The National Archives (TNA) Air 1/1799/204/156/7.

Appendix X

Names adopted by the Royal Flying Corps for aerodromes in Great Britain as of 29 December 1916

Much confusion was being caused by the fact that stations of the Royal Flying Corps in Great Britain were not called by their proper names (e.g. Filton was frequently called Bristol, Rendcombe called Cirencester, Bramham Moor called Tadcaster). In order to obviate this in future, it was decided to adopt the names of the actual locality in which the unit was situated as the official station name.

The list reproduced below was drawn up along the above mentioned lines and was to be adhered to on all occasions:

Directorate of Air Operations	Adastral House, Victoria Embankment, London, EC
Directorate of Aircraft Equipment	ditto
Military Aeronautical Contracts	ditto
Aeronautical Inspection Department	ditto
Ordnance Aircraft Department	ditto
Training Brigade, RFC	ditto
Home Defence Wing, RFC	ditto
18th Wing Headquarters	ditto
Administrative Wing:	
Headquarters	South Farnborough
Recruits' Depot	ditto
Recruits' Training Centre	Halton Camp West, Bucks
School for Wireless Operators	South Farnborough
Special Recruiting Office	ditto
Southern Aircraft Depot:	
Headquarters	South Farnborough

Aircraft Park, Farnborough:	
Headquarters	ditto
Aeroplane Dispatch Section	Hawkinge Aerodrome, Folkestone
ditto	Marden
Engine Repair Park	South Farnborough
Aeroplane Repair Park	ditto
Central Aircraft Depot:	
Headquarters	Ascot
Aeroplane Stores Department	King Street, Hammersmith
ditto	Brook Street Skating Ring, Hammersmith
ditto	Austin Stores, Northfield, Birmingham
ditto	Dudley Skating Rink, Dudley
ditto	The Zoo, Glasgow
Aircraft Park, Chelsea:	
Headquarters	Chelsea, London, SW
Aircraft Park, Hurst Park:	
Headquarters	Hurst Park
Northern Aircraft Depot	Bradford
Balloon Training Wing:	
Headquarters	Polo Pavilion, Roehampton Club, Roehampton, SW
No. 1 Balloon School	Rollestone Camp (Larkhill)
No. 2 Balloon School	Lydd
School of Military Aeronautics	Reading
School of Military Aeronautics	Oxford
Cadet Wing, RFC	Denham
School of Aerial Gunnery	Hythe
Central Flying School and Netheravon	Upavon
Wireless and Observers' School	Brooklands
Scottish School of Fitters	Edinburgh
Civilian Flying School:	
The Grahame White School	Hendon
The London and Provincial Aviation Co	ditto
The Ruffy-Baumann School of Flying	ditto
The Beatty School of Flying	ditto

The Cheltenham and West of England Aviation Co	Cheltenham
Experimental Station, RFC	Orfordness
Experimental Works, RFC	Feltham
Wireless Testing Park	Joyce Green, Dartford, SE
Testing Station, RFC	Upavon
Royal Aircraft Factory	South Farnborough
Training Brigade, RFC:	
Brigade Headquarters	Adastral House, Victoria Embankment, EC
6th Wing Headquarters	Barming Place, Maidstone
No. 10 Reserve Squadron	Joyce Green
No. 13 Reserve Squadron	Dover
No. 17. Reserve Squadron	Croydon
No. 20 Reserve Squadron	Wye, Kent
No. 49 Squadron	Dover
7th Wing Headquarters	Norwich
No. 9 Reserve Squadron	Norwich
No. 12 Reserve Squadron	Thetford
No. 25 Reserve Squadron	Thetford
No. 50 Reserve Squadron	Narborough
No. 35 Squadron	Narborough
No. 59 Squadron	Narborough
No. 64 Squadron	Sedgeford
8th Wing Headquarters	York
No. 6 Reserve Squadron	Catterick
No. 14 Reserve Squadron	Catterick
No. 15 Reserve Squadron	Doncaster
No. 36 Reserve Squadron	Beverley
No. 46 Reserve Squadron	Bramham Moor
No. 53 Squadron	Catterick
17th Wing Headquarters	Gosport
No. 1 Reserve Squadron	Gosport
No. 16 Reserve Squadron	Beaulieu
No. 27 Reserve Squadron	Gosport
No. 28 Squadron	Gosport
18th Wing Headquarters	Adastral House, Victoria Embankment, London, EC

No. 2 Reserve Squadron	Brooklands
No. 3 Reserve Squadron	Shoreham
No. 4 Reserve Squadron	Northolt
No. 18 Reserve Squadron	Hounslow
No. 42 Reserve Squadron	Hounslow
No. 43 Squadron	Northolt
No. 56 Squadron	London Colney
Wireless and Observers' School	Brooklands
School of Instruction	Hendon
19th Wing Headquarters	Newcastle-upon-Tyne
No. 18 Reserve Squadron	Montrose
No. 26 Reserve Squadron	Turnhouse
No. 39 Reserve Squadron	Montrose
No. 58 Squadron	Cramlington
No. 63 Squadron	Cramlington
Scottish School of Fitters	Edinburgh
21st Wing Headquarters	Cirencester
No. 38 Reserve Squadron	Rendcombe
No. 40 Reserve Squadron	Port Meadow (Oxford)
No. 51 Reserve Squadron	Filton (Bristol) – to Wye on 7 January 1917
No. 55 Reserve Squadron	Yatesbury
No. 48 Squadron	Rendcombe
No. 62 Squadron	Filton (Bristol)
No. 66 Squadron	Filton (Bristol)
23rd Wing Headquarters	South Carlton (near Lincoln)
No. 37 Reserve Squadron	Scampton
No. 41 Reserve Squadron	Waddington
No. 45 Reserve Squadron	South Carlton (near Lincoln)
No. 47 Reserve Squadron	Waddington
No. 48 Reserve Squadron	Waddington
No. 69 Squadron	South Carlton
24th Wing Headquarters	Spittlegate
No. 31 Reserve Squadron	Wyton
No. 44 Reserve Squadron	Harlaxton
No. 49 Reserve Squadron	Spittlegate
No. 65 Squadron	Wyton
25th Wing Headquarters	Castle Bromwich

No. 5 Reserve Squadron	Castle Bromwich
No. 28 Reserve Squadron	Castle Bromwich
No. 34 Reserve Squadron	Tern Hill
No. 43 Reserve Squadron	Tern Hill
No. 54 Squadron	Castle Bromwich
No. 55 Squadron	Lilbourne
Central Flying School and Netheravon, Headquarters	Upavon
No. 7 Reserve Squadron	Netheravon
No. 8 Reserve Squadron	Netheravon
No. 24 Reserve Squadron	Netheravon
"A" Squadron, CFS	Upavon
"B" Squadron CFS	Upavon
"C" Squadron CFS	Upavon
"D" Squadron CFS	Upavon
Northern Aircraft Depot Headquarters	Bradford
NAD Detachment.	Coal Aston, Dronfield Station, Sheffield
School of Aerial Gunnery	Hythe
Home Defence Wing, RFC:	
Wing Headquarters	Adastral House, Victoria Embankment, London, EC
No. 33 (HD) Squadron	Gainsborough (The Lawns)
"A" Flight	Brattleby (Scampton)
"B" Flight	Kirton Lindsey
"C" Flight	Elsham
Landing Ground	Carlton
"	Hedon
"	East Retford
"	Brampton
"	Thorne
"	Broomhill (Wombwell)
"	Bellasize
"	Winterton
"	New Holland
"	North Coates Fitties
"	Bylborough
"	Coakthorns (Market Rasen)

“	Cuxwold (Caister)
“	Kelstern (Louth)
“	Bucknall (Horncastle)
“	Wigsley (Lincoln)
“	Redmires (Sheffield)
“	Greenland Top (Stallingborough)
“	Brancroft (Finningley)
“	Gainsborough
No. 36 (HD) Squadron	Newcastle-upon-Tyne, Monaise, Fernwood Road, Jesmond
“A” Flight	Seaton Carew
“B” Flight	Hylton
“C” Flight	Ashington
Landing Ground	Penteland
“	Cleadon (South Shields)
“	Currock Hill (Chopwell)
“	Spennymoor
“	Thornaby
“	Southfields (Acklington)
“	Bishopton
“	Beacon Hill (Morpeth)
“	Catley Hill (Trimdon)
“	Rennington (Alnwick)
“	Easington (Seaham Harbour)
“	Tynemouth
“	Stamford (Alnwick)
No. 37 (HD) Squadron	Woodham Mortimer, The Grange, Woodham Mortimer (near Maldon)
“A” Flight	Rochford.
“B” Flight	Stow Maries
“C” Flight	Goldhanger
Landing Ground	North Benfleet
“	Burnham-on-Crouch
“	Easthorpe
“	Plough Corner (Little Clacton)
“	Broomfield (Chelmsford)
“	Martlesham
“	Sible Hedingham

"	Wormingford (Bures)
No. 38 (HD) Squadron	Melton Mowbray, Scalford Road
"A" Flight	Stamford
"B" Flight	Buckminster
"C" Flight	Leadenham
Landing Ground	Kingswinford (Dudley)
"	Papplewick (Nottingham)
"	Thurgarton (Nottingham)
"	Swinstead (Bourne)
"	Moorby (Horncastle)
"	Ruddington (Nottingham)
"	Stretton-under-Posse (Rugby)
"	Meriden (Coventry)
"	Perton (Wolverhampton)
"	Kings Heath (Birmingham)
"	Anwick (Sleaford)
"	Braceby (Grantham)
"	Plungar
"	Castle Donnington (Derby)
"	Lullington (Burton-on-Trent)
"	Queniborough (Leicester)
"	Stanton-by-Dale
"	Chasetown (Lichfield)
"	Roston (Ashbourne)
"	Peckleton (Leicester)
"	Burton-on-Wolds (Loughborough)
"	Willoughby Hills (Boston)
"	Gosberton (Spalding)
"	Scalford (Melton Mowbray)
"	Blaston (Uppingham)
No. 39 (HD) Squadron	Woodford, Selway Lodge, Woodford Green
"A" Flight	North Weald Bassett
"B" Flight	Sutton's Farm (Hornchurch)
"C" Flight	Hainault Farm (Ilford)
Landing Ground	Sawbridgeworth
"	Hackney Marshes
"	Palmer's Green (Shenfield)

"	Wimbledon Common
"	Orsett
"	Chessington (Kingston-on-Thames)
"	Fyfield (Ongar)
"	Plumstead Marshes
"	Hertford
No. 50 (HD) Squadron	Harrietsham, Stede Court
"A" Flight	Dover
"B" Flight	Bekesbourne (Canterbury)
"C" Flight	Throwley (Faversham)
Landing Ground	Biggin Hill (Westerham)
"	South Ash (Wrotham)
"	Marden
"	Hunton (Maidstone)
"	Broad Salts (Sandwich)
"	Broomfield (Herne Bay)
"	Allhallows (Sheerness)
"	Leigh Green (Tenderten)
"	Rye
"	Pett (Hastings)
No. 51 (HD) Squadron	Hingham, The Old Grammar School
"A" Flight	Harling Road (Roundham)
"B" Flight	Mattishall
"C" Flight	Marham
Landing Ground	Freethorpe
"	Earsham (Bungay)
"	Hadleigh
"	Bedfield
"	Newmarket
"	Tibenham
"	Taverham
"	Frettenham
"	Gooderstone Warren
"	Saxthorpe (Aylsham)
"	West Rudham (Fakenham)
"	Ashfield (Elmswell)
"	Tydd St Mary

No. 75 (HD) Squadron	Bedford, The Grange, Goldington
"A" Flight	Yelling (St Neots)
"B" Flight	Old Weston (Thrapston)
"C" Flight	Therfield (Baldock)
Landing Ground	Little Staughton (Bedford)
"	Thrapston
"	Litchborough
"	Horseheath
"	Little Downham
"	Fowlmere (Royston)
"	Biggleswade
"	Willian (Hitchin)
"	Coldham (Wisbeach)
"	Kingscliff (Peterborough)
"	Hanslope (Newport Pagnell)
"	Orton (Peterborough)
"	Clipston (Market Harborough)
"	Flitwick (Ampthill)
"	Cottenham (Cambridge)
"	Moulton (Northampton)
No. 76 (HD) Squadron	Ripon, Racecourse Buildings
"A" Flight	Copmanthorpe
"B" Flight	Helperby
"C" Flight	Catterick
Landing Ground	Dunkeswick
"	Winn Moor (Seacroft)
"	Manywells Heights (Cullingworth)
"	Farsley (Bradford)
"	Middleton (Leeds)
"	Barmby (Pocklington)
"	Atwick
"	South Cave
"	Pontefract
"	South Otterington
"	Gilling (New Malton)
"	Binsoe (West Tanfield)
No. 77 (HD) Squadron	Edinburgh, Old Dick Veterinary College, Clyde Street

"A" Flight	Turnhouse (Edinburgh)
"B" Flight	Whiteburn (Grant's House), New Haggerston (Berwick-on-Tweed)
"C" Flight	Cairnsross (Reston)
Landing Ground	Kincairn (Gargunnock)
"	South Kilduff (Kinross)
"	Hoprig Mains (Tranent)
"	South Belton (Dunbar)
"	Horndean (Berwick-on-Tweed)
"	Gilmerton (Edinburgh)
"	Penston (Tranent)
No. 78 (HD) Squadron	Brighton, Brocker Hill, New Church, Hove
"A" Flight	Telscombe Cliffs (Newhaven)
"B" Flight	Gosport
"C" Flight	Chiddingstone Causeway (Tonbridge)
Landing Ground	Stonegate (Ticehurst)
"	Hooe (Bexhill)
"	Arlington (Hailsham)
"	New Chapel (East Grinstead)
"	Blackboys (Uckfield)
No. 11 Reserve (HD) Squadron	Northolt
Ordnance Aircraft Department:	
Assistant Director of Ordnance Stores	Adastral House, Victoria Embankment, EC
Chief Ordnance Officer, OAD. Engines	Barlby Road, Ladbroke Grove, North Kensington, W
Chief Ordnance Officer, OAD. Wireless, Photography, Mt Spares etc.	Blackheath Road, Greenwich
Chief Ordnance Officer, OAD. Aeroplanes, Spares and Misc	Hilton, Steventon, Berkshire
Aeronautical Inspection Department, Chief Inspector AID	Adastral House, Victoria Embankment, EC
Aerodromes:	
Officer i/c, AID, Farnborough Branch	South Farnborough
Officer i/c AID. Aerodrome	Coventry
Officer i/c AID. Aerodrome	Patchway, Bristol

Officer i/c AID. Aerodrome	c/o Messrs Sir V G Armstrong, Whitworth & Co, Newcastle-upon-Tyne
Officer i/c AID. Aerodrome	Hendon, London NW
Chief Aeroplane Examiner i/c ADI. Aerodrome	Norwich
Chief Aeroplane Examiner i/c ADI. Aerodrome	Lincoln
Chief Aeroplane Examiner i/c ADI. Aerodrome	Portholme, Huntingdon
Chief Aeroplane Examiner i/c ADI. Aerodrome	Crossens, Southport, Lancs
Local Headquarters:	
Officer i/c Engines, London District	Adastral House, Victoria Embankment, EC
Officer i/c Engines, Coventry District	Aerodrome, Coventry
Officer i/c Engines, Birmingham District	78, Bristol Road, Edgbaston, Birmingham
Officer i/c Engines, Scottish District	c/o Messrs Arrol-Johnston Ltd, Dumfries
Chief Examiner i/c Engines, Bedford District	c/o Messrs W H Allen, Son & Co Ltd, Bedford
Chief Examiner i/c Engines, Lincoln District	c/o Messrs Ruston Proctor & Co Ltd, Lincoln
Officer i/c Western Aeroplane District	63, Above Bar, Southampton
Officer i/c Southern Aeroplane District	Adastral House, Victoria Embankment, EC
Officer i/c Eastern Aeroplane District	Adastral House, Victoria Embankment, EC
Officer i/c Midland Aeroplane District	Aerodrome, Coventry
Officer i/c Northern Aeroplane District	27, Bridgewater Chambers, Brown Street, Manchester
Officer i/c Scottish Aeroplane District	31, St Vincent Place, Glasgow
Officer i/c Sheffield District (Materials)	28, Blonk Street, Sheffield
Officer i/c AID. at OAD (Aeroplanes)	Milton, Steventon, Berkshire
Officer i/c AID. at OAD (Aeroplanes)	Greenwich
Chief Examiner i/c AID at OAD (Engines)	Barlby Road, North Kensington, London, W

The National Archives (TNA): Air 1/823/204/5/44.

Appendix XI

The performance of British anti-aircraft guns of 1914–1918

	Muzzle velocity	Rate of fire	Effective ceiling	Weight of shell
	feet / second	rpm	feet	lbs
1 pdr Pom-Pom	1,310	250	3,000	1
12 pr	2,200	15	19,500	12
13 pr, 9 cwt	2,100	20	18,000	13
13 pr. mk 4	1,600	20	16,000	12.5
3", 5 cwt	1,600	20	16,000	12.5
3", 20 cwt	2,500	15	20,000	12.5
18 pr	1,600	15	18,000	18.5
3.6"	2,000	20	26,000	25
4", mk 5	2,400	10	29,000	31
5.5", mk 1	2,600	5	35,000	82

Data compiled from:
Hogg, Ian V. *Anti-Aircraft; a history of air defence.* Macdonald & Jane's Publishers Ltd (London) 1978 and various sites on worldwide web.

Appendix XII

Details and numbering of German airships used during the Great War

Military no.	Werke nr.	Type	Details of final fate
Manufactured by Zeppelin:			
Z II	*LZ 9*	f	Scrapped; 1 August 1914
Viktoria Luise	*LZ 11*	g	Destroyed while entering shed at Liegnitz; 8 August 1915
Z III	*LZ 12*	f	Scrapped; 1 August 1914
Hansa	*LZ 13*	g	Scrapped; 1 August 1914
Z IV	*LZ 16*	h	Scrapped; Jüterbog, autumn 1916
Sachsen	*LZ 17*	h	Scrapped; Düren, autumn 1916
Z V	*LZ 20*	h	Shot down by AA fire; 28 August 1914
Z VI	*LZ 21*	k	Scrapped near Bonn, Germany following combat damage over Liège, Belgium; 6 August 1914
Z VII	*LZ 22*	l	Hit by AA fire and forced down near St Quirin, France; 21August 1914
Z VIII	*LZ 23*	l	Shot down by AA fire near Bavonville, France; 21 August 1914
L 3	*LZ 24*	m	Stranded near Fanö, Denmark following a reconnaissance operation; 17 February 1915
Z IX	*LZ 25*	m	Bombed in hangar at Düsseldorf and burnt out; 8 October 1914
Z XII	*LZ 26*	n	Decommissioned; 8 August 1917
L 4	*LZ 27*	m	Destroyed in a forced landing on the Danish Coast on return from operations; 17 February 1915

Military no.	Werke nr.	Type	Details of final fate
L 5	*LZ 28*	m	Force landed at Plungiany, Mitau, Lithuania having been damaged by ground fire; 6 August 1915
Z X	*LZ 29*	m	Force landed near St Quirin, Lothringen, Germany following a raid on Paris; 21 March 1915
Z XI	*LZ 30*	m	Damaged while leaving hangar at Posen, Germany and burnt out; 20 May 1915
L 6	*LZ 31*	m	Caught fire and burnt out while being inflated at Fuhlsbüttel, Hamburg, Germany; 16 September 1916
L 7	*LZ 32*	m	Crashed near Horns Ref, Denmark after being hit by fire from British warships; 4 May 1916
L 8	*LZ 33*	m	Force landed at Tirlemont, France following damage due to enemy action; 5 March 1915
LZ 34	*LZ 34*	m	Caught fire on landing due to damaged sustained in action Insterburg, Germany; 21 May 1915
LZ 35	*LZ 35*	m	Destroyed during a storm at Aeltre, Belgium; 14 April 1915
L 9	*LZ 36*	o	Caught fire while being inflated at Fuhsbüttel, Hamburg, Germany; 16 September 1916
LZ 37	*LZ 37*	m	Shot down over Ghent, Belgium; 7 June 1916
LZ 38	*LZ 38*	p	Destroyed in air raid at Brussels-Evère, Belgium; 7 June 1915
LZ 39	*LZ 39*	o	Force landed at Luck, Ukraine due to enemy action; 18 December 1915
L 10	*LZ 40*	p	Struck by lightning and burnt out near Cuxhaven, Germany; 3 September 1915
L 11	*LZ 41*	p	Decommissioned at Hage, Germany; 25 April 1917
LZ 72	*LZ 42*	p	Decommissioned at Jüterborg, Germany; 16 February 1917
L 12	*LZ 43*	p	Crashed into sea near Ostend, Belgium due to enemy action; 10 August 1915

Military no.	Werke nr.	Type	Details of final fate
LZ 74	*LZ 44*	p	Struck a mountain near Orthe, Schnee Eifel, Germany and stranded; 8 October 1915
L 13	*LZ 45*	p	Decommissioned at Hage, Germany; 25 April 1917
L 14	*LZ 46*	p	Decommissioned in September 1918 and destroyed 23 June 1919
LZ 77	*LZ 47*	p	Shot down by AA fire and crashed near Révigny, France; 22 February 1916
L 15	*LZ 48*	p	Crashed into North Sea off Knock Deep, England due to enemy action; 1 April 1916
LZ 79	*LZ 49*	p	Force landed at Ath, Belgium having been damaged by AA fire; 30 January 1916
L 16	*LZ 50*	p	Damaged while landing at Nordholz, Germany and decommissioned; 19 October 1917
LZ 81	*LZ 51*	p	Stranded at Turnovo, Bulgaria during a raid on Bucharest; 27 September 1916
L 18	*LZ 52*	p	Caught fire and destroyed while gassing up at Tondern, Germany; 17 November 1915
L 17	*LZ 53*	p	Caught fire after colliding with hangar door, Tondern, Germany; 28 December 1916
L 19	*LZ 54*	p	Crashed and sank in the North Sea near Ameland, Holland; 2 February 1916
LZ 85	*LZ 55*	p	Crashed in Vardar Marshes, Salonika, Greece; 5 May 1916
LZ 86	*LZ 56*	p	Crashed at Temesvar, Romania; 4 September 1916
LZ 87	*LZ 57*	p	Decommissioned; 20 August 1917
LZ 88 / L 25	*LZ 58*	p	Decommissioned at Jüterborg, Germany; 15 September 1917
L 20	*LZ 59*	p	Forced landed near Stavanger, Norway and wrecked; 3 May 1916
LZ 90	*LZ 60*	p	Broke away from mooring at Wittmundhafen, Germany in a storm and lost over the North Sea; 7 November 1916

Military no.	Werke nr.	Type	Details of final fate
L 21	*LZ 61*	q	Shot down over the North Sea off Norfolk, England; 28 November 1916
L 30	*LZ 62*	r	Decommissioned 17 November 1917; given to Belgium as war reparations in 1920
LZ 93	*LZ 63*	q	Decommissioned Trier, Germany; summer 1917
L22	*LZ 64*	q	Shot down over the North Sea near Terschelling, Holland; 14 May 1917
LZ 95	*LZ 65*	q	Damaged during operations and force landed near Vitry-le-François, France; 21 February 1916
L23	*LZ 66*	q	Shot down over North Sea near Jutland, Denmark; 21 August 1917
LZ 97	*LZ 67*	q	Decommissioned at Jüterborg, Germany; 5 July 1917
LZ 98	*LZ 68*	q	Decommissioned at Schneidenmühl, Germany; August 1917
L 24	*LZ 69*	q	Caught fire at Tondern, Germany; 28 December 1916
LZ 101	*LZ 71*	q	Decommissioned at Schneidenmühl, Germany; August 1917
L 31	*LZ 72*	r	Shot down over Great Britain; 2 October 1916
LZ 103	*LZ 73*	q	Decommissioned at Königsberg, Germany; August 1917
L 32	*LZ 74*	r	Shot down over Great Britain; 24 September 1916
LZ 37	*LZ 75*	r	Decommissioned 24 December 1917; given to Japan as war reparations in 1920
L 33	*LZ 76*	r	Shot down over Great Britain; 24 September 1916
LZ 107	*LZ 77*	q	Decommissioned at Darmstadt, Germany; 7 July 1917
L 34	*LZ 78*	r	Shot down over the North Sea off Hartlepool, England; 28 November 1916
L 41	*LZ 79*	r	Decommissioned at Nordholz, Germany; 29 May 1918 (destroyed on 23 September 1919)

Military no.	Werke nr.	Type	Details of final fate
L 35	*LZ 80*	r	Decommissioned at Jüterborg, Germany; September 1918.
LZ 111	*LZ 81*	q	Decommissioned Seddin, Germany; 10 August 1917
L 36	*LZ 82*	r	Crashed on the frozen River Aller, near Rethen, Germany (scrapped); 7 February 1917
LZ 113	*LZ 83*	r	Withdrawn from service at Seddin; 8 October 1918 (given to France as war reparations 8 October 1920)
L 38	*LZ 84*	r	Stranded at Seerappen, Kurland, Germany; 29 December 1916
L 45	*LZ 85*	r	Stranded following low on fuel and destroyed, Sisteron, France; 20 October 1917
L 39	*LZ 86*	r	Shot down by AA fire and crashed at Compiègne, France; 7 March 1917
LZ 47	*LZ 87*	r	Caught fire and burnt out at Ahlhorn, Germany; 5 January 1918
L 40	*LZ 88*	r	Damaged on landing and decommissioned. Nordholz, Germany; 16 June 1917
L 50	*LZ 89*	r	Collided with a mountain near Dammartin-les-Templiers, France where two gondolas broke off (rest of airship lost over the Mediterranean Sea); 20 July 1917
LZ 120	*LZ 90*	r	Decommissioned at Seerappen, Germany; 8 October 1917. Given to Italy as war reparations (destroyed 24 December 1920)
L 42	*LZ 91*	s	Decommissioned Nordholz; 9 November 1918 (destroyed 23 June 1919)
L 43	*LZ 92*	s	Shot down over North Sea; 14 June 1917
L 44	*LZ 93*	t	Shot down over St Clément, Lunevill, France; 20 October 1917
L 46	*LZ 94*	t	Burnt out at Ahlhorn, Germany; 5 May 1918
L 48	*LZ 95*	u	Shot down over Great Britain; 17 June 1917
L 49	*LZ 96*	u	Force landed at Bourbonne-les-Bains, France on return from operations; 20 July 1917

Military no.	Werke nr.	Type	Details of final fate
L 51	*LZ 97*	u	Burnt out at Ahlhorn, Germany; 5 January 1918
L 52	*LZ 98*	u	Decommissioned Nordholz, Germany; November 1918 (destroyed 23 June 1919)
L 54	*LZ 99*	u	Destroyed in air raid at Tondern, Germany; 19 July 1918
L 53	*LZ 100*	v	Shot down over the North Sea near Terschelling, Holland; 11 August 1918
L 55	*LZ 101*	v	Damaged by enemy action and force landed at Tiefenort, Germany; 1 September 1917
L 57	*LZ 102*	w	Hit hangar at Jüterbog, Germany and burnt out; 8 October 1917
L 56	*LZ 103*	v	Destroyed at Wittmundhafen, Germany; 23 June 1919
L 59	*LZ 104*	w	Crashed in flames into the Mediterranean Sea off Corsica; 7 April 1918
L 58	*LZ 105*	v	Caught fire and destroyed at Ahldhorn; 5 January 1918
L 61	*LZ 106*	v	Given to Italy as war reparations; August 1920
L 62	*LZ 107*	v	Shot down over the North Sea off Heligoland, Germany; 10 May 1918
L 60	*LZ 108*	v	Destroyed in air raid at Tondern, Germany; 19 July 1918
L 64	*LZ 109*	v	Given to Great Britain as war reparations (destroyed Fulham, London in a storm; 21 July 1920)
L 63	*LZ 110*	v	Destroyed at Nordholz, Germany; 23 June 1919
L 65	*LZ 111*	v	Decommissioned 15 August 1918 (destroyed Nordholz, Germany; 23 June 1919)
L 70	*LZ 112*	x	Shot down over the North Sea off Hartlepool, England; 5 August 1918
L 71	*LZ 113*	x	Flown to Fulham, London as war reparations; 1 July 1920

Military no.	Werke nr.	Type	Details of final fate
Manufactured by Luftschiffbau Schütte-Lanz:			
SL 2		B1	Stranded at Luckenwalde, Germany due to lack of fuel and decommissioned; 12 January 1916
SL 3		C1	Structure degraded and stranded near Riga, Latvia; 1 May 1916
SL 4		C2	Crushed by collapsing hangar due to weight of snow at Seddin, Germany; 14 December 1915
SL 5		C3	Stranded at Giessen, Germany; 5 July 1917
SL 6		D1	Exploded over Seddin, Germany; 10 November 1915
SL 7		D2	Decommissioned Jüterborg, Germany; 6 March 1917
SL 8		E1	Decommissioned Seddin, Germany; 20 November 1917
SL 9		E2	Crashed into the Baltic Sea; 30 March 1917
SL 10		E3	Lost over the Black Sea off Sevastapol, Russia; 28 July 1916
SL 11		E4	Shot down over Great Britain; 12 August 1916
SL 12		E5	Decommissioned after accident, Ahlhorn, Germany; 28 December 1916
SL 13		E6	Wrecked by collapsing hangar due to weight of snow at Leipzig, Germany; 8 February 1917
SL 14		E7	Damaged at Wainoden, Latvia 9 May 1917 and decommissioned at Seerappen, Germany; 18 May 1917
SL 15		E8	Decommissioned at Sandhofen, Mannheim, Germany; August 1917
SL 16		E9	Scrapped near Cologne, Germany; August 1917
SL 17		E10	Scrapped Allenstein, Germany; August 1917
SL 18		E11	Destroyed when roof of hangar collapsed due to weight of snow at Leipzig; 8 February 1917

Military no.	Werke nr.	Type	Details of final fate
SL 20		F1	Caught fire at Ahlhorn, Germany; 5 January 1918
SL 21		F2	Decommissioned at Zeesen, Germany; February 1918
Manufactured by Luft-Fahrzeug-Gesellschaft / Parseval:			
PL 16	P.14		Used by the German Army and decommissioned; 24 March 1916
PL 17			Used by the Italian Army until 1915
PL 18	No.4		Used by the Royal Navy (decommissioned July 1917)
PL 19			Used by the German Navy. Damaged by enemy fire on operations and crashed into the sea off Liepaja, Latvia; 21 May 1915
PL 25			Used by the German Navy (decommissioned in 1916)
PL 26			Caught fire on landing during maiden flight; 26 October 1916

Appendix XIII

Transcript of a hand-written letter regarding *Zeppelin LZ 5*

The transcript of a hand-written letter – that came with a few pieces of *Zeppelin LZ 5* – that crashed into a tree during a flight from Friedrichshafen to Berlin in May 1909 and gives a charming insight into the character of Count von Zeppelin and early operations of airships.

How I happened to have such delightful world travels at so young an age – and how rudeness paid off for once:

When I was seven years old, I was taken from [illegible] to New York City by my grandfather, Charles Henry Jones – affectionately called 'Bompa' all his life – the name I gave him at a very early age trying to say 'Bon Perè' in French. This trip was to have my tonsils taken out. It seems at that time, New York had the only doctors who knew how to do a tonsillectomy which, as the years passed, proved to be nothing more than a passing job. This, according to my vivid recollection, was done in what strangely resembled a dentist's chair under local anaesthetic. The only preparation I had for that was a lecture from 'Bompa' as to my [illegible] in the doctor's office. If I was a good little girl and behaved like a lady and did not cry – should it hurt a little – I would be allowed to go to an 'ice-cream parlour' and eat all the ice-cream I wanted. 'Simple!' I thought… and eating all the ice-cream I wanted was a reward [illegible] in heaven. The doctor took one look at my throat, turned to his assistant and asked for several of the most gruesome and [illegible] instruments imaginable in French. Little did he know I already spoke three languages: Spanish with my father, French with my nurse and English with mother. This frightened me so – thinking it must be something horribly painful, as apparently he did not want me to know what he was getting – though I am sure that in French they sounded much more brutal. Anyway, I let out a yell – and as I remember, that yell did not subside until I heard the words: "That is all Miss Martyn; now that wasn't so bad, was it?" All during that seemingly endless operation, one thought ran through my mind: 'Now I won't get any ice-cream' – for 'Bompa' was certainly a man of his word. I will never forget how shocked I was when we headed straight for an ice-cream parlour – and it seemed that I had already eaten a gallon, while with every spoonful my trust and faith in 'Bompa' returned until he explained that the doctor recommended me to eat a lot of ice-cream to keep my throat frozen for a while and check the bleeding.

'Bompa''s doctor advised his going to Europe every winter – which he had been doing for a number of years – and that year neither my mother, nor I, nor he, were very well so his doctor suggested he stay in Europe for two years. 'Bompa' asked mother to let me go with him as 'part of my education' – an expression I heard thousands of times from him. We in April of 1904; I had my eighth birthday on the steamer, with a wonderful party given by the captain. 'Bompa' always has a seat of honour at the captain's table – being such a prominent man – and I, being his granddaughter, was treated royally. 'Bompa''s health failed steadily; through each year he thought we would be able to come back to America – he never did – alive. Mother came over and got me after eight years – and 'Bompa' died the following year in an American hospital in Italy.

My [illegible] had been in the southern part of Germany in Ravensburg, Wurtenburg – near the Bodensee on Lake Constance – and near Friedrichshafen, where Count Zeppelin kept his first dirigible balloon. I stayed with a German family – very devout Catholics and delightful people – but travelled with 'Bompa' whenever possible. My aunt, Sophie Bierta; her sister, Antoinette; their adorable old mother and I lived on the second floor of a lovely, typically German home. Their brother, Paul, and his wife occupied the first floor – having a florist's shop in the front of their home. Uncle Paul owned some 30 greenhouses and grew every kind of flower and shrub; worked from 20 to 30 men at all times and they had their own living quarters on the premises. I had to do jobs for uncle Paul, who was my idol, and being able to do anything for him was a great joy. I picked violets, which he usually sold in bunches of 100, and strawberries and gooseberries by the quart. I think I always ate more than I put in the baskets.

On occasions, my [illegible] would take their niece, Hilde Hoch, who was two years younger than I, with us on an all-day excursion to the 'Weingarten' near Friedrichshafen. One of these occasions was when I had only been in Germany about two months and I hadn't learned to speak German well yet. The British family was asked never to speak to me in English, if possible, in order that I might learn German quicker – and as a result, I was enrolled at an all-German school after being there five months. Hilde and I were playing tag around the building, while aunt Sophie sat it out at a table under the shade of trees – waiting for our lunch to be served – and always keeping a watchful eye on us two girls. As I was making my way around the building at full speed, I found myself encountering an old man, whom I nearly knocked off-balance. Now being polite and courteous and respectful to my elders was one of the main lessons in life I had been taught, and so I must have said 'I'm sorry' and 'excuse me' as I hastened on. The eagle-eye of aunt Sophie caught this – and she called me to her table and told me to follow the man and apologise as best I could. Goodness knows what I said, but he laughed as he recognised a 'foreigner' – and seemed to be quite interested. I don't think I understood a word he said, but pointed towards aunt Sophie and marched over to her with him. It wasn't until then that she recognised him as Graf Zeppelin. Hilde joined their little chit-chat, while I held my head low in embarrassment. All this ended with making a date for aunt Sophie, Hilde and I to meet him on a certain date for a ride in his dirigible. I remember the feeling of floating in space and looking down on favourite landmarks – although I don't think we were much higher than the Eiffel Tower in Paris.

When this dirigible crashed some few years later in a wooded area, one of uncle Paul's gardeners went there (at uncle Paul's request, I am sure) to get some souvenirs for me. He brought back a pretty, colourful handkerchief with a picture of the balloon in flight; and a picture of Graf Zeppelin; and a piece of bark from one of the trees where the balloon wrecked; a piece of the aluminium frame; a piece of canvas covering; and a piece of cord. I kept these in a box for years – and as soon as my children were old enough to study about Graf Zeppelin in school, they wanted take these souvenirs to school, so my husband mounted them in this glass-covered display case so they would not get lost.

This I am giving to my grandson, Carl William, who is fluent in German and German history – and I am sure he will treasure them as much as I do.

Dorothy M Freeman, June 1974.

Bibliography

Unpublished sources

The National Archives (TNA):

ADM137/4125	German airship bases: notes and photographs, 1918-19.
ADM 195/79	Portsmouth: photographs of bomb damage caused by Zeppelin raid in 1915.
Air 1/6B/4/56/3	German Gotha aircraft: notes and photographs.
Air 1/7/6/98/1-8-16	RNAS: photographs of crashed Zeppelins.
Air 1/15/15/1/64	*Zeppelin L 62* attacked and brought down into sea off Heligoland by large American flying boat.
Air 1/22/15/1/113	Reparation for destroyed Zeppelin airship.
Air 1/34/15/1/210	German map taken from Zeppelin brought down in France, 20 October 1917.
Air 1/94/15/9/252	German aircraft reports, 1918.
Air 1/146/15/59	Scheme for repelling Zeppelins over England, April 1916.
Air 1/148/15/89	Proposed operations to deter Zeppelins, February 1916.
Air 1/296/15/226/143	Hostile air raids on England, December 1914 to December 1917.
Air 1/296/15/226/146	Enemy airship movements in the North Sea.
Air 1/296/15/226/147	Photographic copies of letters, photos etc. found in *LZ 77*.
Air 1/343/15/226/283	Zeppelin destroyed on 11 August 1918 by Lt S D Culley, RAF.
Air 1/344/ 15/226/287	Report of attack on Zeppelin sheds at Tondern by aeroplanes from HMS *Furious*.
Air 1/495/15/312/316	French report: bombardment of Calais by Zeppelin.
Air 1/495/15/312/318	French report: destruction of Zeppelins.
Air 1/495/15/312/319	Histories of the German airships: ' L', 'SL', 'LZ' and 'Z' types.
Air 1/495/15/312/320	French report on Zeppelin *L 49*.
Air 1/495/15/312/321	German airship tactics, 24/10/16 – 1/2/17.
Air 1/495/15/312/323	Airships of the Rhine Valley.

Air 1/537/16/13/1	Information obtained from prisoners after Zeppelin raid on England 19-20 October 1917; four Zeppelins destroyed.
Air 1/545/16/15/15	Report on construction, movements, damage and losses of German Zeppelins.
Air 1/547/16/15/18	Air raids on England: operational files, 28 April 1917 to 17 June 1917.
Air 1/550/16/15/25	Notes on various types of German Zeppelins and aeroplanes.
Air 1/564/16/15/72	Air raid on Newcastle-upon-Tyne during the night of 15-16 June 1915.
Air 1/564/16/15/73	Summary of airship and seaplane raids on England 23 December 1914 to 1 March 1917.
Air 1/564/16/15/74	Air raids on England: manuscript reports re: hostile aeroplane raids on England, 21 December 1914 to 23 October 1916.
Air 1/564/16/15/77	Air raids on England: report of engagement between a Zeppelin and BE6 no.8612 off the Norfolk Coast, 31 July 1916.
Air 1/564/16/15/78	Air raids on England: Zeppelin raid on Goole and neighbourhood, 9-10 August 1915.
Air 1/564/16/15/79	Air raids on England: Zeppelin raid on Hull during the night of 6-7 June 1915.
Air 1/564/16/15/80	Air raid on Newcastle.
Air 1/564/16/15/81	Zeppelin raid on north of England during the night of 15-16 April 1915.
Air 1/564/16/15/83	Reports and courses re: hostile naval raids and bombardments of the English Coast with list of casualties, 3 November 1914 to 15 May 1918.
Air 1/567/16/15/119	Zeppelin papers dealing with the visibility and audibility, August 1918.
Air 1/567/16/15/120	Airship attacks on England. List of those carried out before and not later than 9.30pm, 19 January 1915 to 28 November 1916.
Air 1/567/16/15/122	Zeppelin movements from 1 September 1916 to 31 March 1917.
Air 1/567/16/15/123	Zeppelin Book IV, 1 April 1917 to 21 August 1917.
Air 1/567/16/15/124	Zeppelin Book V, 22 August 1917 to 31 May 1918.
Air 1/567/16/15/125	Zeppelin Book IV, 1 June 1918 to 4 November 1918.
Air 1/586/16/15/186	Aeroplane raid: 22 October 1916 (Sheerness).

Air 1/586/16/15/187	Aeroplane raid: 23 October 1916 (Margate).
Air 1/586/16/15/188	Air raid: 27-28 November 1916.
Air 1/589/16/15/200	Air raid: 16-17 June 1917 and destruction of *L 48*.
Air 1/604/16/15/238	Unfortified places attacked by German Zeppelins.
Air 1/604/16/15/239	German crews of *L 49*, *L 50* and *L 51*.
Air 1/604/16/15/242	Air raids on England.
Air 1/605/16/15/245	Reports on the courses of three Zeppelins: *L 33*, *L 21* and *L 15*.
Air 1/605/16/15/247	Reports on air raids in 1915.
Air 1/605/16/15/248	Miscellaneous air raids.
Air 1/605/16/15/249	Air raids on England.
Air 1/608/16/15/264	Court of Inquiry: loss of articles from wrecked German Zeppelin *L 33*.
Air 1/609/16/15/272	Lists of Zeppelin crews (PoWs) in England.
Air 1/609/16/15/274	Zeppelin crews who are PoWs in Fulham Military Hospital.
Air 1/609/16/15/320	*L 48* salvage details.
Air 1/609/16/15/321	Enemy aircraft intelligence.
Air 1/613/16/15/303	Method of attacking Zeppelins by decoy lights.
Air 1/613/16/15/307	Examination of prisoners of *L 33*, 25 September 1916 to 18 January 1918.
Air 1/613/16/15/308	Court of Inquiry: charges of pilfering from bodies of crew of destroyed Zeppelin.
Air/614/16/15/315	*L 34* (salvaging of) at West Hartlepool, 7 December 1916 to 29 January 1917.
Air 1/615/16/15/319	Papers concerning Zeppelin and crews destroyed by hostile aircraft.
Air 1/615/16/15/320	Salvage operations and crew details of destroyed Zeppelin *L 48*.
Air 1/615/16/15/321	Enemy aircraft intelligence after interrogation of captured Zeppelin and aeroplane crews.
Air 1/619/16/15/355	Report on Zeppelin raid on Hull, 5-6 August 1918.
Air 1/626/17/33	Lecture by Count Zeppelin on German airships.
Air 1/629/17/122/15	Reports of 2 Wing RNAS: operations against Zeppelins and sheds.
Air 1/630/17/122/26	Salvage operations on Zeppelin brought down off Hartlepool, 28 November 1916.

Air 1/630/17/122/33	RNAS Dover: remarks on recent enemy air attacks in the vicinity of Dover, 22 February 1916 to 9 November 1916.
Air 1/632/17/122/58	Report of Zeppelin raid on RNAS Station, Redcar and subsequent pursuit of Zeppelin by BE2 aeroplane.
Air 1/632/17/122/76	Report of seaplane attack on Zeppelin off Spurn Head.
Air 1/633/17/122/89	Report of Zeppelin raid on London.
Air 1/634/17/122/100	Destruction of Zeppelin off Lowestoft, 28 November 1916.
Air 1/634/17/122/101	Examination of Zeppelin brought down at Hartlepool, 27 November 1916.
Air 1/634/17/122/111	Report of air raid by Zeppelin on Goole.
Air 1/634/17/122/112	Report of air raid by Zeppelin on Lowestoft.
Air 1/634/17/122/113	Report of attack by hostile aircraft on Dover, 9-10 August 1915.
Air 1/635/17/122/114	Report of air raid by Zeppelin on Tyne.
Air 1/637/17/122/148	Report of attack on Zeppelin by flying boat no.8666.
Air 1/637/17/122/153	Enemy air attacks: report of destruction of Zeppelin *L 22* on 14 May 1917 RN Air Station, Yarmouth; 14 May 1917 to 12 June 1917.
Air 1/637/17/122/156	Enemy air attacks: report of destruction of Zeppelin *L 43* on 14 June 1917 RN (Seaplane) Station, Felixstowe; 14 June 1917 to 24 June 1917.
Air 1/638/17/122/162	Report of attack on Zeppelins.
Air 1/638/17/122/163	Report on raid by German aircraft on Ramsgate area, 22 August 1917.
Air 1/638/17/122/166	Report of attack on Zeppelin *L 45*.
Air 1/638/17/122/167	Report of attack on Zeppelin, 14 June 1917.
Air 1/638/17/122/173	Report of attack on Zeppelin, 12 June 1917.
Air 1/640/17/122/207	Report of air raid on Ramsgate, 17 June 1917.
Air 1/645/17/122/235	Salvage of destroyed Zeppelin *L 15*, June to July 1916.
Air 1/45/17/122/335	Report of aircraft attack on Zeppelins, 23-24 September 1916.
Air 1/651/17/122/444	Confirmation of Zeppelin *L 15* destroyed off Kent Coast, April 1916.
Air 1/657/17/122/558	Violation of Dutch neutrality by German Zeppelins, August 1915 to May 1916.
Air 1/657/17/122/563	Memorandum on Zeppelin in time of war.

Air 1/657/17/122/564 Attack by Lt Freeman RN on Zeppelin and subsequent rescue by Dutch ship, 2 August 1916.

Air 1/660/17/122/625 Report on the destruction of *L 22*, 14 May 1917.

Air 1/661/17/122/646 Rough notes taken from log book of Zeppelin *L 45* and details of Zeppelin *L 57*, November 1917.

Air 1/661/17/122/649 Extracts from war log of Zeppelin *L 49*, December 1917.

Air 1/672/17/134/21 East Coast of England and London: airship attack, 7-8 September 1915.

Air 1/672/17/134/34 Report on attack against Zeppelins, 15 May 1915.

Air 1/672/17/134/36 Report on destruction of two Zeppelins, 7 June 1915.

Air 1/673/17/138 Report on destruction of Zeppelin *L 7*, 4 May 1916.

Air 1/679/21/13/2193 Photo from Canadian newspaper of Zeppelin over Hendon, February 1916.

Air 1/705/27/8/37 Confidential memo: German Gotha twin-engine aeroplanes.

Air 1/721/59/12/1 Destruction of Zeppelin on 21 and 28 November 1916 by F/Sub Lt E L Pulling RNAS.

Air 1/776/204/4/397 Trials of Holt flares and fire bombs against Zeppelins, July 1913 to March 1915.

Air 1/823/204/5/61 Report from 1 Naval Squadron of attack on Zeppelin, 17 May 1915.

Air 1/863/204/5/491 Firing grapnels for attack on Zeppelins, April to May 1916.

Air 1/910/204/5/827 HQ; RFC; BEF; Zeppelin *L 15*: intelligence obtained from the crew captured, April 1916.

Air 1/918/204/5/828 Intelligence: German Air Force reports of crew of Zeppelin *LZ 85*, May 1916.

Air 1/1214/204/51/2632 German type of hangars: sheds on aerodromes, 1918.

Air 1/1259/204/9/1 Home defence: action against Zeppelin raids, October 1915 to April 1916.

Air 1/1259/204/9/1a Home defence: reports on Zeppelin raids, October 1915.

Air 1/1259/204/9/3 Home defence: reports of attack on Zeppelins, June 1915.

Air 1/1283/204/11/6 Report of information from crew of destroyed Zeppelin *L 15*, April 1916.

Air 1/1363/204/22/16 Zeppelin attack reports, 10 Squadron RFC, May to June 1915.

Air 1/1799/204/156/7 Reports of pilots on Zeppelin raid: 18 Wing RFC, 31 March 1916.

Air 1/1882/204/221/28	Reports and photographs of giant aeroplanes and PoW interrogation, 1915 – 1918.
Air 1/1977/204/273/53	Report on German aircraft: Gotha.
Air 1/2099/207/20/2	Reports of reconnaissance and operations and attacks of Zeppelin airship factory at Friedrichshaven, November to December 1914.
Air 1/2103/207/30/11	RNAS report on the remains of German airship *LZ 77*, April 1916.
Air 1/2123/207/73/1 to /33	Air raids on Great Britain: intelligence summaries.
Air 1/2251/209/54/24	Action on warning of Zeppelin attack, February to March 1916.
Air 1/2255/209/58/2	Air photo taken by German airman over London, July 1917.
Air 1/2290/209/75/64	Trail bomb against Zeppelins, August 1914 to February 1915.
Air 1/2327/223/79/1	Extracts from ships logs of HMS *Agamemon* and *TB 18* on destruction of German Zeppelin *LZ 85*, May 1916.
Air 1/2397/267/1	Articles by *Kapitänleutnant* A D J Brietharpt commanding Zeppelins *VI* and *XV* during the war, 1919.
Air 1/2397/267/6	Personal account by commander of Zeppelin *L 65* of air raid, August 1918.
Air 1/2397/267/9	Account of Zeppelin cruises during the war: *Oberleutnant* R Frey, 1914 – 1918.
Air 1/2398/267/12	An account by *Oberleutnant* zur See *Leutnant* Dr Hans Gabauer of Zeppelin raid over London, 1919.
Air 1/2398/267/17	Chart showing standard patrol tracks followed by Zeppelins, 1919.
Air 1/2398/267/27	The development of Zeppelin airships,1926.
Air 1/2413/303/14/1	HQ Home Forces Intelligence circular on the new type of Zeppelin airship, August 1917.
Air 1/2494	Report on the remains of German airship *LZ 77*.
Air 1/ 2566	Rigid airship committee: report on Zeppelin *L 15*.
Air 1/2579	Further report on *L 15*.
Air 1/2584	Report on Zeppelin *L 31*, which fell at Potters Bar.
Air 1/ 2598	Information obtained from the crew of *L 7*.
Air 1/2599	Information obtained from the crew of *L 15*.
Air 1/2646	Communiqué on Zeppelin raid.

Air 10/864	German rigid airships Zeppelin *L 33*, 1917.
DSIR 23/643	Zeppelin airship: report on lattice girder, 1916.
DSIR 23/708	Zeppelin airship *LZ 77*: examination of pieces submitted by Air Department, Admiralty and Department of Naval Construction, 1916.
DSIR 23/769	Zeppelin airship *L 15*: material taken from various parts of structure, 1916.
DSIR23/848	Zeppelin bombsight, 1916.
DSIR 23/1222	Zeiss bombsight from Zeppelin airship *L 49*, 1918.
DSIR 23/1257	Zeiss bombsight from Zeppelin *L 70*, 1918.
MEPO 2/1652	Details of raid and destruction of Zeppelin at Potters Bar, 1 October 1916.
MEPO 2/1654	Details of raid and destruction of Zeppelin at Cuffley, 4 September 1916.

Published sources

Anon. *Zeppelin uber England.* Werlag Whilheim & Co (Berlin). 1916.

Anon. *The War Zone in England. Thanet 1914 – 1918.* Tomson & Wotton Ltd (Ramsgate, Kent). 1919.

Anon. *Unsere Luftstreitkräfte 1914 – 1918.* Vaterländischer Verlag, C A Weller (Berlin). 1930.

Anon. *Zeppelin – Weltfahrten*; Volume I and II (Germany). No date.

Bauer, Manfred. *Airship sheds in Friedrichshafen.* Zeppelin Museum, Friedrichshafen (Germany). 2001.

Bavington Jones, O.G. *Dover in the European War 1914-18.* Dover Express (Snargate Street, Dover). 1919.

Bendale, Eugen. *The story of a Zeppelin mechanic. My flights 1931 – 1938.* Zeppelin Museum, Friedrichshafen (Germany). 1992.

Bills, L Wm. *A Medal for Life; Biography of Capt Wm.Leefe Robinson VC.* Spellmont Ltd (Kent). 1990.

von Buttlar Brandenfels, T. *Zeppelins over England.* George G Harrap & Co Ltd (London). 1931.

Castle, H G. *Fire over England; The German Air Raids of World War 1.* Leo Cooper (London). 1982.

Castle, Ian. *London 1914 – 17. The Zeppelin Menace.* Osprey Publishing Ltd (Oxford). 2008.

Castle, Ian. *London 1917 – 18. The Bomber Blitz.* Osprey Publishing Ltd (Oxford). 2010.

Castle, Ian. *The Zeppelin base raids, Germany 1914.* Osprey Publishing Ltd (Oxford). 2011.

Chant, Christopher. *The Zeppelin. The history of German airships from 1900 – 1937.* Amber Books Ltd (London). 2000.

Charlton, L. *War over England.* Longmans, Green & Co Ltd (London). 1936.

Cole, Christopher & Cheeseman, E F. *The Air Defence of Britain 1914 – 1918.* Putnam (London). 1984.

Cooksley, Peter G. *The Air VC's of the First World War.* Sutton Publishing Ltd (Stroud, Gloucestershire). 1996.

Cross, W. *Zeppelins of World War 1. The dramatic story of Germany's lethal airships.* I B Tarius (London). 1991.

Deeson, A F L. *An illustrated history of airships.* Spurbooks Ltd (Bucks). 1973.

Deighton, Len & Schwartzman, Arnold. *Airshipwreck.* Jonathan Cape Ltd (London). 1978.

Dudley, E. *Monsters of the Purple Twilight; Life and Death of the Zeppelins. First menace from the skies.* George G Harrap & Co Ltd (London). 1960.

Easdown, Martin with Genth, Thomas. *A Glint in the Sky; German First World War Air Attacks on Folkestone,Dover, Ramsgate, Margate and other Kentish Towns.* Pen and Sword Books Limited (South Yorkshire). 2004.

Faulkner, Dr Neil & Durrani, Dr Nadia. *In search of the Zeppelin War. The archaeology of the first blitz.* Tempus Publishing (Stroud, Gloucestershire). 2008.

Fegan, Thomas. *The Baby Killers; German Air Raids on Britain in the First World War.* Leo Cooper (Barnsley, South Yorkshire). 2002.

Fleischer, Wolfgang. *German air-dropped weapons to 1945.* Midland Publishing. (Leicester). 2004.

Franks, Norman, Bailey, Frank & Duiven, Rick. *Casualties of the German Air Service. 1914 – 1920.* Grub Street (London). 1999.

Fredette, Major Raymond H, USAF. *The First Battle of Britain 1917 – 1918 & the birth of the Royal Air Force.* Cassell (London). 1966.

Gibson, Mary. *Warneford VC. The first naval airman to be awarded the VC.* The Fleet Air Arm Museum (Yeovilton, Somerset). 1979.

Griehl, M & Dressel, J. *Zeppelin, the German Airship Story.* Arms and Armour. (London). 1990.

Guttery, Wing Commander T E. *An illustrated life of Count Ferdinand von Zeppelin 1838 – 1917.* Shire Publications (Aylesbury, Bucks). 1973.

Haddow, G & Gross, P. *The German Giants; The German R-Planes 1914 – 1918.* Putnam & Co Ltd (London). 1962.

Hammerton, Sir J A. (ed.) *The Great War, I was there. Undying memories of 1914 – 1918.* Various chapters. The Amalgamated Press (London). No date.

Ch. 84, vol 1, p. 448. *I was London's first Zepp raider.* By Major Erich Linnarz.

Ch. 85, vol 1, p. 452. *Grizly death over the Gaiety.* By James Wickham.

Ch. 157, vol 2, p. 866. *I saw the doom of L 32; The thrill of watching falling Zepps.* By Michael Macdonogh from "In London during the Great War".

Ch. 158, vol 2, p. 870. *How I shot down L 31. Breathtaking description of the Potters Bar triumph.* By Major W J Tempest.

Ch. 245, vol 2, p. 1,334. *I saw London's worst daylight raid. When the Gothas flew away unharmed.* By Francis Perrot.

Hanson, Neil. *First Blitz. The secret German plan to raze London to the ground in 1918.* Corgi Books (London). 2009.

Hobson Chris. *Airmen Died in the Great War 1914 – 1918; The Roll of Honour of the British and Commonwealth Air Services of the First World War.* J B Hayward & Son (Suffolk). 1995.

Hogg, Ian V. *Anti-Aircraft; a history of air defence.* Macdonald & Jane's Publishers Ltd (London). 1978.

Hyde, Andrew P. *The First Blitz. The German Campaign against Britain 1917 – 1918.* Leo Cooper (Barnsley, S. Yorkshire). 2002.

Imrie Alex. *Pictorial History of the German Air Service; 1914 – 1918.* Ian Allan Ltd (Surrey). 1971.

Imrie, Alex. *German bombers of World War One.* Arms & Armour Press (London). No date.

Jones, H A. *The War in the Air. Being the Story of the Part Played in the Great War by the Royal Air Force.* Volume II. 1928.

Jones, H A. *The War in the Air. Being the Story of the Part Played in the Great War by the Royal Air Force.* Volume III, including separate map box. 1931.

Jones, H A. *The War in the Air. Being the Story of the Part Played in the Great War by the Royal Air Force.* Volume IV. 1934.

Jones, H A. *The War in the Air. Being the Story of the Part Played in the Great War by the Royal Air Force.* Volume V, including separate map box. 1935.

Jones, H A. *The War in the Air. Being the Story of the Part Played in the Great War by the Royal Air Force.* Volume VI. 1937.

Jones, H A. *The War in the Air. Being the Story of the Part Played in the Great War by the Royal Air Force.* Appendices. 1937.

Jones, James Hartington. *The German attack on Scarborough, December 16, 1914.* Quoin Publishing (Huddersfield, Yorkshire). 1989.

Malben Rolf. *Zeppelin Adventures.* John Hamilton Ltd (London). No date.

Mason, Francis K. *Battle over Britain.* McWhirter Twins Ltd (London). 1969.

Meighörner-Schardt Wolfgang. *Pioneer of Intercontinental aviation by chance. The history of Zeppelin airship type "W".* Zeppelin Museum, Friedrichshafen (Germany). 1992.

Morris, Captain Joseph RA, AFRAeS. *The German Air Raids on Great Britain.* Sampson Low, Marston & Co Ltd (London). 1920.

Mower, Mark. *Zeppelins over Suffolk. The final raid of the L 48.* Pen & Sword Military (Barnsley, South Yorkshire). 2008.

Poolman, Kenneth. *Zeppelins over England.* Evans Brothers Ltd (London). 1960.

Rawlinson, A. *The Defence of London 1915 – 1918.* Andrew Melrose Ltd (London & New York). 1923.

Rayleigh, Walter. *The War in the Air; being the story of the part played in the Great War by the Royal Air Force.* Volume I. Oxford University Press (London). 1922.

Rimmell, Raymond L. *Air war over Great Britain 1914 – 1918.* Arms & Armour Press (Poole, Dorset). 1987.

Rimmell, Raymond Laurence. *World War One in the air.* Arms and Armour Press (London). 1998.

Robinson. Douglas H. *The Zeppelin in combat. A history of the German Naval Airship Division 1912 – 1918.* Schiffer Publishing Ltd (Atglen, PA,USA). No date.

Smith, Peter J C. *Zeppelins over Lancashire. The story of the air raids on the county of Lancashire in 1916 and 1918.* Neil Richardson. 1991.

Stephenson, Charles. *Zeppelins: German Airships 1900 – 40.* Osprey Publishing Ltd (Oxford). No date.

Swinton, Major-General Sir Ernest KBE, CB. (ed.) *Twenty Years After. Supplementary volume, chapter XI, Zeppelins over Britain.* George Newnes Ltd (London). No date.

White, C M. *The Gotha Summer; the German Daytime Air Raids on England, May – August 1917.* Robert Hale Ltd (London). 1986.

Whitehouse, Arch. *The Zeppelin Fighters.* Robert Hale Ltd (London). 1968.

Williams, Captain T B AFC. *Airship Pilot No.28.* William Kimber & Co Ltd (London). 1974.

Wyatt, R J. *Death from the skies. The Zeppelin raids over Norfolk 19 January 1915.* Gilddon Books (Norwich, Norfolk). 1990.

Index

INDEX OF PLACES

INDEX OF PEOPLE

INDEX OF AEROPLANES

INDEX OF AIRSHIPS

INDEX OF SHIPS

INDEX OF MILITARY UNITS